CCNA Wireless Study Guide

Exam IUWNE 640-721 Objectives

OBJECTIVE	CHAPTER
Describe WLAN fundamentals	
Describe basics of spread spectrum technology (modulation, DSS, OFDM, MIMO, Channels reuse and overlap, Rate-shifting, CSMA/CA)	3, 4
Describe the impact of various wireless technologies (Bluetooth, WiMAX, ZigBee, cordless phone)	4
Describe wireless regulatory bodies, standards and certifications (FCC, ETSI, 802.11a/b/g/n, WiFi Alliance)	4
Describe WLAN RF principles (antenna types, RF gain/loss, EIRP, refraction, reflection, etc.)	2
Describe networking technologies used in wireless (SSID → WLAN_ID → Interface → VLAN, 802.1q trunking)	1
Describe wireless topologies (IBSS, BSS, ESS, Point-to-Point, Point-to-Multipoint, basic Mesh, bridging)	1
Describe 802.11 authentication and encryption methods (Open, Shared, 802.1X, EAP, TKIP, AES)	5
Describe frame types (associated/unassociated, management, control, data)	4
Install a basic Cisco wireless LAN	
Describe the basics of the Cisco Unified Wireless Network architecture (Split MAC, LWAPP, stand-alone AP versus controller-based AP, specific hardware examples)	7
Describe the Cisco Mobility Express Wireless architecture (Smart Business Communication System—SBCS, Cisco Config Agent—CCA, 526WLC, 521AP—stand-alone and controller-based)	8
Describe the modes of controller-based AP deployment (local, monitor, HREAP, sniffer, rogue detector, bridge)	7
Describe controller-based AP discovery and association (OTAP, DHCP, DNS, Master-Controller, Primary-Secondary-Tertiary, n+1 redundancy)	7
Describe roaming (Layer 2 and Layer 3, intra-controller and inter-controller, mobility groups)	7
Configure a WLAN controller and access points WLC: ports, interfaces, WLANs, NTP, CLI and Web UI, CLI wizard, LAG AP: Channel, Power	9
Configure the basics of a stand-alone access point (no lab) (Express setup, basic security)	9
Describe RRM	7

W0010414

nt of
iLEY

OBJECTIVE	CHAPTER

Sybex®
An Imprint of
 WILEY

CCNA®
Wireless
Study Guide

CCNA®
Wireless
Study Guide

Todd Lammle

WILEY
Wiley Publishing, Inc.

Acquisitions Editor: Jeff Kellum
Development Editor: Amy Breguet
Technical Editors: Keith Parsons, Benjamin Miller, Patrick Conlan, and George Stefanick
Production Editor: Christine O'Connor
Copy Editor: Elizabeth Welch
Editorial Manager: Pete Gaughan
Production Manager: Tim Tate
Vice President and Executive Group Publisher: Richard Swadley
Vice President and Publisher: Neil Edde
Media Project Manager 1: Laura Moss-Hollister
Media Associate Producer: Marilyn Hummel
Media Quality Assurance: Josh Frank
Book Designer: Judy Fung, Bill Gibson
Compositor: Craig Johnson, Happenstance Type-O-Rama
Proofreader: Beth Prouty, Word One New York
Indexer: Robert Swanson
Project Coordinator, Cover: Lynsey Stanford
Cover Designer: Ryan Sneed

Library of Congress Cataloging-in-Publication Data

Lammle, Todd.
  CCNA wireless study guide (IUWNE 640-721) / Todd Lammle.—1st ed.
    p. cm.
Summary: "A complete guide to the CCNA Wireless exam by leading networking authority Todd Lammle. The CCNA Wireless certification is the most respected entry-level certification in this rapidly growing field. Todd Lammle is the undisputed authority on networking, and this book focuses exclusively on the skills covered in this Cisco certification exam. The CCNA Wireless Study Guide joins the popular Sybex study guide family and helps network administrators advance their careers with a highly desirable certification. The CCNA Wireless certification is the most respected entry-level wireless certification for system administrators looking to advance their careers. Written by Todd Lammle, the leading networking guru and author of numerous bestselling certification guides. Provides in-depth coverage of every exam objective and the technology developed by Cisco for wireless networking. Covers WLAN fundamentals, installing a basic Cisco wireless LAN and wireless clients, and implementing WLAN security. Explains the operation of basic WCS, basic WLAN maintenance, and troubleshooting. Companion CD includes the Sybex Test Engine, flashcards, and entire book in PDF format. Includes hands-on labs, end-of-chapter review questions, Exam Essentials overview, Real World Scenarios, and a tear-out objective map showing where each exam objective is covered. The CCNA Wireless Study Guide prepares any network administrator for exam success."—Provided by publisher.

  ISBN-13: 978-0-470-52765-8 (pbk.)
  ISBN-10: 0-470-52765-X (pbk.)
  ISBN: 978-0-470-90169-4 (ebk)
  ISBN: 978-0-470-90171-7 (ebk)
  ISBN: 978-0-470-90170-0 (ebk)

  1. Wireless LANs—Examinations—Study guides. 2. Telecommunications engineers—Certification—Study guides. I. Cisco Networking Academy Program. II. Title.
  TK5105.78.L36 2010
  004.6'8—dc22
                    2010015495

10 9 8 7 6 5 4 3 2 1

Dear Reader,

Thank you for choosing *CCNA Wireless Study Guide*. This book is part of a family of premium-quality Sybex books, all of which are written by outstanding authors who combine practical experience with a gift for teaching.

Sybex was founded in 1976. More than 30 years later, we're still committed to producing consistently exceptional books. With each of our titles, we're working hard to set a new standard for the industry. From the paper we print on, to the authors we work with, our goal is to bring you the best books available.

I hope you see all that reflected in these pages. I'd be very interested to hear your comments and get your feedback on how we're doing. Feel free to let me know what you think about this or any other Sybex book by sending me an email at nedde@wiley.com. If you think you've found a technical error in this book, please visit http://sybex.custhelp.com. Customer feedback is critical to our efforts at Sybex.

Best regards,

Neil Edde
Vice President and Publisher
Sybex, an Imprint of Wiley

Acknowledgments

I'd like to thank the entire team Sybex assembled for their hard work and dedication in putting this book together, but especially my acquisitions editor Jeff Kellum as well as Christine O'Connor, my production editor, for hanging with me, yet once again, during this sometimes daunting project. I can't thank you both enough for continuing to work with me, book after book—and yet I still can't figure out why you both don't go screaming from the room when you see my name pop up on the radar of each new book!

Monica Lammle's writing style, encouragement, and dedication to ensuring that this book is concise yet highly readable has been invaluable to my success of this and many other projects.

Also, a big thank you to Troy Mcmillan, who helped me personally lay out almost every chapter in this book from end to end. He was indispensable when it came to writing this book, and I can't say enough how much his help and support kept me sane during the writing of this book. Troy was dependable and was very timely with his work. I look forward to hopefully working with him again in the future.

Big thanks to my development editor, Amy Breguet. Amy's tireless effort helped to shape the book into a much more readable format, although I am sure I've aged her some in the last few months! But she was a real trouper throughout this project.

I'd also like to thank my technical editors, Keith Parsons, Ben Miller, Patrick Conlan, and George Stefanick, who found all the little but all-so-important issues that needed to be clarified—their importance to this project can't be overstated. Also, thanks to Liz Welch, my copy editor, who kept me in my favorite coffee shop way more than I wanted to be, but who worked and reworked every sentence in this book. Last, but absolutely not least, my best friend Patrick Conlan was instrumental in helping me at all hours of the day and night understanding the smallest of details that I struggled with as I was trying to finish this book. Thanks once again, Pat, for your continued support, amazing technical advice, and encouragement.

About the Author

Todd Lammle CCSI, CCNA/CCNA Wireless/CCNP/CCSP/CCVP, MCSE, CEH/CHFI, FCC RF Licensed, is the authority on Cisco certification Wireless and Internetworking. He is a world renowned author, speaker, trainer, and consultant. Todd has over 29 years of experience working with LANs, WANs, and large licensed and unlicensed wireless networks, and has published over 50 books, including the very popular *CCNA: Cisco Certified Network Associate Study Guide*, and this book, *CCNA Wireless Study Guide (640-721)*. He runs an international training and consulting company based in Colorado and Texas. You can reach Todd through his forum and blog at www.lammle.com.

Contents at a Glance

Contents

Introduction

Welcome to CCNA Wireless Study Guide, a comprehensive guide that covers everything you need for Cisco's new exam 640-721. For readers who are new to Cisco certifications, there is a well-defined structure to the different levels that network administrators can achieve.

Cisco's current certification structure has the following five levels of certification:

- Entry level
- Associate
- Professional
- Expert
- Architect

This book is written for the associate level of certification. Cisco considers this level to be the "apprentice or foundation level" for network administrators.

Cisco has recently broadened its associate-level certifications to include not only a certification for routing and switching (CCNA) and design (CCDA) but also more targeted associate-level certifications for security (CCNA Security), wireless (CCNA Wireless), and voice (CCNA Voice). These new certifications target specific areas of Cisco technology and are to be used as stepping-stones for the professional and expert levels of certification that Cisco offers.

Cisco's Wireless Certifications

Cisco offers three distinct levels of Wireless certifications. The following diagram shows that the CCNA Wireless certification is a building block to the professional- and expert-level wireless certifications:

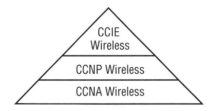

This book covers the CCNA Wireless certification exam 640-721. As of the writing of this book, the exam costs $250 USD. The exam tests your knowledge a great deal in areas both theoretical and technically specific to Cisco hardware and software.

Once you achieve your CCNA Wireless certification, you can choose to continue on the wireless path and achieve higher certifications, such as the CCNP Wireless or the ultimate CCIE Wireless Expert. But even if you stop after achieving your CCNA Wireless certification, you will have demonstrated to your current or prospective employers that you have a sound knowledge of the interoperations of wireless and Cisco wireless technologies. This assurance to employers will make it easier for you to land that dream job you've always wanted!

What Skills Do You Need to Become a CCNA Wireless?

Cisco Certified Network Associate Wireless (CCNA® Wireless) validates associate-level knowledge and skills to configure, implement, and support wireless LANs, specifically those networks using Cisco equipment. With a CCNA Wireless certification, network professionals can support a basic wireless network on a Cisco WLAN in a small to medium-sized business (SMB) to enterprise network. This CCNA Wireless study guide includes written and hands-on labs to prepare you for configuring, monitoring, and troubleshooting basic tasks of a Cisco WLAN in SMB and enterprise networks.

The 640-721 exam tests your knowledge of installing, configuring, operating, and troubleshooting small to medium-sized WLANs utilizing skills that enable you to:

- Describe WLAN fundamentals
- Install a basic Cisco wireless LAN
- Install wireless clients
- Implement basic WLAN security
- Operate basic WCS
- Conduct basic WLAN maintenance and troubleshooting

 Be sure to check my and/or Cisco's website for the latest Cisco CCNA objectives and other Cisco exams, objectives, and certifications—they can change at a moment's notice.

How Do You Become a CCNA Wireless?

The way to become a CCNA Wireless is to pass two tests, the CCNA 640-802 and then the CCNA Wireless 640-721, each at $250 a pop, although the path may vary depending on your experience.

I can't stress this enough: it's critical that you have some hands-on experience with Cisco devices. If you can get a hold of some Cisco wireless gear, you're set. But if you can't, I've worked hard to provide hundreds of configuration examples throughout this book to help network administrators (or people who want to become network wireless administrators) learn what they need to know to pass the CCNA Wireless exam (although I can't think of anyone who's passed the CCNA or the CCNA Wireless exams without some type of hands-on experience).

For Cisco Authorized hands-on training, please see www.1ammle.com. Each student will get hands-on experience by configuring their own controller and lightweight access points, as well as experience with WCS software, a wireless analyzer, and other tools.

What Does This Book Cover?

This book covers everything you need to know in order to pass the CCNA Wireless (640-721) exam. However, taking the time to study and practice with Cisco's new Cisco new wireless gear is the real key to success.

You will learn the following information in this book:

- Chapter 1, "Wireless Networks and Topologies," introduces you to wireless networking and topologies. You will learn the basics of wireless the way Cisco wants you to learn them. A review of switching, VLANs, and native VLANs is presented as well. There are written labs and plenty of review questions to help you focus on the exam objectives for this chapter.

- Chapter 2, "WLAN RF Fundamentals," provides you with the background necessary for discussing the real-world WLAN radio frequency fundamentals. This in-depth chapter picks up where Chapter 1 left off and starts discussing the pros and cons of radio frequencies and the basic principles of RF. Both written and practice exam questions are included at the end of the chapter.

- Chapter 3, "Spread Spectrum Technologies and Modulations," introduces you to modulating the RF signal you learned in Chapter 2. Although this is a technical chapter, Spread Spectrum is important information to understand for the CCNA Wireless objectives. Plenty of help is found in this chapter if you do not skip the written lab and review questions.

- Chapter 4, "Wireless Regulation Bodies, Standards, and Certifications," introduces you to the wireless standards and certifications that are in use today. Nonstandard wireless products are also covered in this chapter. Be sure to complete the written lab and review questions.

- Chapter 5, "Introduction to Wireless Security," provides you with the advanced wireless security that you must fully understand for the CCNA Wireless objectives. This is not the easiest chapter in the book, but it is imperative for your wireless career that you grasp the concepts provided in this chapter. Cisco's objectives cover mostly nonproprietary security standards. Complete the written lab and review questions to help you focus on the chapter and reread as many times as necessary.

- Chapter 6, "Wireless Clients and the Cisco Extension (CCX)," teaches you about the wireless clients that are used in today's networks. Some of the objectives were already out of date when I wrote the book, so I tried to update the chapter as much as possible without going too far outside the objectives. The written lab, hands-on labs, and review questions will help you master the understanding you need to meet the objectives.

- Chapter 7, "Introduction to the Cisco Unified Wireless Network (CUWN)," is where we can finally get out of the WLAN fundamentals and start talking Cisco-specific wireless with an introduction to the Cisco Unified Wireless Network (CUWN). This is a great chapter to start your understanding of the Cisco wireless solutions. The written lab and review questions will provide the direction you need to understand this portion of the exam.

- Chapter 8, "Introduction to the Cisco Mobility Express Wireless Architecture," provides an introduction to the less expensive alternative to the CUWN enterprise controllers and APs and discusses the Cisco Mobility Express, specifically the Cisco 500 series CUWN products. Go through the written lab and review questions as well as the hands-on labs to learn how to start configuring a small CUWN.

- Chapter 9, "Installing the Cisco Unified Wireless Network (CUWN)," is where we start getting into the enterprise model of the CUWN and learn about the controller and configuration of a larger network. The written lab and review questions reinforce the material, but the hands-on labs are critical to your success on the exam objectives.

- Chapter 10, "Configuring Wireless Security on the CUWN," covers the security options in the enterprise products for the CUWN and how to configure the networks. Written and hands-on labs, along with review questions, will help you study for the security configuration portion of the CCNA written exam.

- Chapter 11, "Wireless Control System (WCS)," is not a small chapter, but the WCS objectives are not as large as the chapter. I added much more information in this chapter than is necessary for the CCNA Wireless exam, but I wanted to provide you with information that is hard to find but necessary when designing and implementing an enterprise CUWN. The hands-on labs, written lab, and review questions will help you grasp the CCNA Wireless objectives in full.

- Chapter 12, "WLAN Maintenance and Troubleshooting," is another large chapter, but all the information I added in this chapter is fair game in the objectives. WLAN maintenance and troubleshooting is one of the main jobs of a CCNA Wireless certified administrator. The hands-on lab, written lab, and review questions focus on the exam objectives.

How to Use This Book

If you want a solid foundation for the serious effort of preparing for the Cisco Certified Network Associate Wireless (640-721) exam, then look no further. I have spent hundreds of hours putting together this book with the sole intention of helping you to pass the CCNA Wireless exam and learn how to configure Cisco controllers and lightweight access points (among hundreds of other things!).

This book is loaded with valuable information, and you will get the most out of your studying time if you understand how I put the book together.

To best benefit from this book, I recommend the following study method:

1. Take the assessment test immediately following this introduction. (The answers are at the end of the test.) It's okay if you don't know any of the answers; that's why you bought this book! Carefully read over the explanations for any question you get wrong. This information should help you plan your study strategy. My recommendation is to just start reading from Chapter 1 and don't stop until you're all the way through Chapter 12.

2. Study each chapter carefully, making sure that you fully understand the information and the test objectives listed at the beginning of each one. Pay extra-close attention to any chapter that includes material covered in questions you missed in the assessment test.

3. Complete each written lab at the end of each chapter. Do not skip these written exercises because they directly relate to the CCNA Wireless objectives and what you must glean from the chapters in which they appear. Do not just skim these labs! Make sure you understand completely the reason for each answer.

4. Complete all hands-on labs in the chapter (not all chapters have hands-on labs), referring to the text of the chapter so that you understand the reason for each step you take. If you do not have Cisco equipment available, either buy some from eBay or your local Cisco reseller, or rent some Cisco Wireless pods from a Cisco Authorized training center.

5. Answer all the review questions related to each chapter. (The answers appear at the end of the chapters.) Note the questions that confuse you and study those sections of the book again. Do not just skim these questions! Make sure you understand completely the reason for each answer. Remember that these will not be the exact questions you find on the exam; they are written to help you understand the chapter material.

6. Try your hand at the two bonus exams that are included on the companion CD. The questions in these exams appear only on the CD. Check out `www.lammle.com` for more Cisco exam prep questions. The questions found at my website will be updated at least monthly, if not weekly or even daily! Before you take your test, be sure and visit my website for questions, videos, audios, and other useful information that might be available.

7. Test yourself using all the flashcards on the CD. This is a brand-new updated flashcard program to help you prepare for the CCNA Wireless exam. It is a great study tool!

To learn every bit of the material covered in this book, you'll have to apply yourself regularly, and with discipline. Try to set aside the same time period every day to study, and select a comfortable and quiet place to do so. If you work hard, you will be surprised at how quickly you learn this material.

If you follow the steps listed here and study and practice the review questions, bonus exams, and the electronic flashcards, as well as all the written and hands-on labs, it would be hard to fail the CCNA Wireless exam. However, studying for the CCNA Wireless exam is like trying to get in shape—if you do not go to the gym every day, you won't get in shape.

Recommended Home Lab Setup

It is critical to get some hands-on experience with both Cisco controllers and lightweight access points. The following is a list of equipment I recommend you try to acquire (at a minimum) for your home lab studies. If you are concerned about the high cost of purchasing the equipment, keep in mind that Cisco hardware can be easily resold on used markets such as Craigslist or eBay. Combine that fact with adding an extremely hot certification to your resume, and it's an investment well worth the initial cost.

Qty	Item
1	Cisco 1140 or 1242 Access Point
1	Cisco 2100 Series Controller
1	Wireless laptop
1	Switch and Ethernet cables
1	Bonus: Wireless Analyzer software on wireless laptop
1	Bonus: Fast PC with WCS Software

This equipment should give you the ability to practice configuring Cisco Unified Wireless Networks (CUWNs) using the command line, web GUI, and CCA methods detailed in this book. There are various combinations of controllers and lightweight APs that you can use that will get the same results as the products I listed here. Keep in mind that the CUWN 500 series devices can also be used, but I don't recommend them because of their limited upgrade path, and they do not cover all the exam objectives.

Todd Lammle Videos and Audios

I have created a full CCNA series of videos and audios that can be purchased in either DVD or iPod downloadable format. These can be found at www.lammlepress.com. While you're there, be sure and check out my forum and blog, which is updated weekly at www.lammle.com.

What's on the CD?

We worked hard to provide some great tools to help you with your certification process. All of the following tools should be loaded on your workstation when you're studying for the test.

The Sybex Test Preparation Software

The test preparation software prepares you to pass the CCNA Wireless exam. In this test engine, you will find all the review and assessment questions from the book, plus two additional bonus exams that appear exclusively on the CD.

Electronic Flashcards for the PC

To prepare for the exam, you can read this book, study the review questions at the end of each chapter, and work through the practice exams included in the book and on the companion CD. But wait, there's more! You can also test yourself with the flashcards included on the CD. If you can get through these difficult questions and understand the answers, you'll know you're ready for the CCNA exam.

The flashcards include over 100 questions specifically written to hit you hard and make sure you are ready for the exam. Between the review questions, bonus exams, and flashcards on the CD, you'll be more than prepared for the exam.

CCNA Wireless Study Guide (640-721) in PDF

Sybex offers the CCNA Wireless Study Guide (640-721) in PDF on the CD so you can read the book on your PC or laptop. (Acrobat Reader is also included on the CD.)

Where Do You Take the Exams?

You may take the CCNA Wireless exam at any of the Pearson VUE authorized centers (www.vue.com) or call (877) 404-EXAM (3926).

To register for a Cisco Certified Network Associate exam:

1. Determine the number of the exam you want to take. (The CCNA Wireless exam number is 640-721.)

2. Register with the nearest Pearson VUE testing center. At this point, you will be asked to pay in advance for the exam. As of this writing, the exam is $250 and must be taken within one year of payment. You can schedule exams up to six weeks in advance or as late as the same day you want to take it—but if you fail a Cisco exam, you must wait

five days before you will be allowed to retake it. If something comes up and you need to cancel or reschedule your exam appointment, contact Pearson VUE at least 24 hours in advance.

3. When you schedule the exam, you'll get instructions regarding all appointment and cancellation procedures, the ID requirements, and information about the testing center location.

Tips for Taking Your CCNA Wireless Exam

The CCNA Wireless exam contains about 75–85 questions and must be completed in 90 minutes or less. This information can change per exam. You must get a score of about 85 percent to pass this exam, but again, each exam can be different.

Many questions on the exam have answer choices that at first glance look identical—especially the syntax questions! Remember to read through the choices carefully because close doesn't cut it. If you get commands in the wrong order or forget one measly character, you'll get the question wrong. So, to practice, do the hands-on exercises at the end of this book's chapters over and over again until they feel natural to you.

Also, never forget that the right answer is the Cisco answer. In many cases, more than one appropriate answer is presented, but the correct answer is the one that Cisco recommends. On the exam, you're always instructed to pick one, two, or three, never "choose all that apply." The CCNA Wireless 640-721 exam may include the following test formats:

- Multiple-choice single answer
- Multiple-choice multiple answer
- Drag-and-drop
- Fill-in-the-blank
- Simulations

In addition to multiple choice and fill-in response questions, Cisco Career Certification exams may include performance simulation exam items, which makes hands-on experience even more important before taking the exam.

Here are some general tips for exam success:

- Arrive early at the exam center so you can relax and review your study materials.

- Read the questions carefully. Don't jump to conclusions. Make sure you're clear about exactly what each question asks.

- When answering multiple-choice questions that you're not sure about, use the process of elimination to get rid of the obviously incorrect answers first. Doing this greatly improves your odds if you need to make an educated guess.

- You can no longer move forward and backward through the Cisco exams, so double-check your answer before clicking Next since you can't change your mind.

After you complete an exam, you'll get immediate, online notification of your pass or fail status, a printed Examination Score Report that indicates your pass or fail status, and your exam results by section. (The test administrator will give you the printed score report.) Test scores are automatically forwarded to Cisco within five working days after you take the test, so you don't need to send your score to them. If you pass the exam, you'll receive confirmation from Cisco, typically within two to four weeks, sometimes longer.

How to Contact the Author

You can reach Todd Lammle through his forum at `www.lammle.com`.

Assessment Test

1. You need to change the native VLAN on a switched trunk link. Which IOS command and prompt is correct?

   A. `switch(config)#switchport trunk native vlan 500`

   B. `switch(config-if)#switchport native vlan 400`

   C. `switch(config-if)#switchport trunk native vlan 300`

   D. `switch(config)#switchport trunk-access native vlan 200`

2. When a station is roaming through an ESS network, how is the station informed that it has roamed?

   A. The station will not know it has roamed because the SSID is the same on all APs.

   B. The MAC address of each station is stored in the MAC Address Table on the AP.

   C. The AP assigns a derived MAC address for each SSID on the AP.

   D. The Trunk link connected to the AP uses frame tagging to identify each frame using only 802.1q.

3. If you have an AP with an output of 20dB, connected to a 21dBi antenna and a 50-foot cable, what is your EIRP?

   A. 200mW

   B. 500mw

   C. 2.5W

   D. 5W

   E. 10W

4. You have connected an antenna that radiates perfectly in all directions. What is the name of the value used for reference?

   A. dBi

   B. dBm

   C. dBd

   D. dB

5. What is the encoding used to achieve 1 and 2Mbps when DSSS with DBPSK and DQPSK is used to encode data in the RF signal?

   A. CCK

   B. DSSS

   C. QAM

   D. Barker 11

6. Which of the following techniques helps reduce multipath issues by using subcarriers to carry data, which in turn increases bandwidth?

    A. QAM

    B. DSSS

    C. QPSK

    D. OFDM

7. An AP, when using the RTS/CTS CSMA/CA timing in a DSSS CCK wireless network, uses what protocol to provide high priority to an ACK?

    A. DCF

    B. PCF

    C. SIFS

    D. DIFS

8. Which 5GHz band allows an EIRP of up to 36dBm?

    A. UNII-1

    B. UNII-2

    C. UNII-2 Extended

    D. UNII-3

9. You are a consultant at a large company and an entry-level wireless technician asks you in which protocol PACs are used. Which answer do you give this person?

    A. EAP-MD5

    B. EAP-TLS

    C. EAP-Fast

    D. PEAP

10. WPA authentication establishes the PTK during what process?

    A. The four-way handshake

    B. The exchange of nonces

    C. The distribution of the group transient key

    D. The exchange of the broadcast keys

11. In the CSSC, which two of the following security types allow choosing AES or TKIP?

    A. WPA Personal

    B. WPA Enterprise

    C. 802.1X

    D. Shared WEP

12. Linux has built-in tools. Which of the wireless tools allows scripting or automating actions when the computer boots up or when a particular SSID is encountered?

    A. NetworkManager

    B. NetworkManagerDispatcher

    C. iwconfig

    D. AirPort Extreme

13. An AP cycles through many states before it can work with a WLC and it is important that the states are remembered in order. Which would be the last state that an AP cycles through to locate the WLC and to become fully functional?

    A. Join

    B. Config

    C. Image Data

    D. Run

14. When a single WLAN is operating in symmetric roaming mode while the others are in asymmetric roaming mode, those clients will use what as their WLC regardless of where they roam?

    A. Anchor

    B. Master controller

    C. Mobility anchor

    D. Secondary controller

15. You boot a Cisco 521 AP and need to know the IP address set by default. What did Cisco set the address to when configured at the factory?

    A. No configuration; it is set as a DHCP client.

    B. 192.168.1.100

    C. 192.168.1.1

    D. You must statically configure the AP IP address each time.

16. If you are using the CCA and your APs are in standalone mode, how many APs are supported in the Cisco Mobility Express solution?

    A. Two

    B. Three

    C. Four

    D. Five

17. You need to provide 802.1X authentication. How many TACACS+ servers can be defined for override on the WLAN?

   A. Two

   B. Three

   C. Four

   D. Five

18. You have two physical ports, and you can see in the WLC that logical interfaces are available as well. Which of the followings statements are true about the ports and interfaces on the WLC?

   A. Multiple ports can be mapped to an interface.

   B. Multiple interfaces can be mapped to a port.

   C. An interface is a physical connection.

   D. A port is a logical connection.

19. When configuring Local EAP-Fast on the controller, four parameters must be set. Which four of the following are the parameters?

   A. Authority ID

   B. Server Key

   C. Time To Live For The PAC

   D. Certificate Authority

   E. Authority ID Information

20. You have an older WLAN that still uses static WEP for some reason. This older WLAN has security configured to use static WEP as well as 802.1X. How does the system know which process to invoke when a client is attempting to connect on this WLAN?

   A. If the client starts with an EAPoL hello, the 802.1X process starts.

   B. If the client starts with an EAPoW hello, the 802.1X process starts.

   C. If the client fails the WEP process, the 802.1X process begins.

   D. If the client fails the 802.1 process, the static WEP process begins.

21. You need to maintain consistency between the WLC configuration and the configuration in the WCS database. Which three of the following functions are not used?

   A. Audit

   B. Replicate

   C. Synchronize

   D. Transfer

22. You want to gather information on your WCS system from your 12 distributed Cisco Spectrum Experts; however, you cannot get information from all the devices. What could the problem be?

    A. You don't have enough licenses to support 12 instances of Cisco Spectrum Experts.

    B. WCS cannot import data from Cisco Spectrum Experts—only from AirMagnet.

    C. WCS can only gather information from 10 Cisco Spectrum Experts at a time.

    D. You don't have a clue as to how to do any of this.

23. You want to achieve the best fidelity for your clients from your APs. What is the best distance that is recommended?

    A. 30 to 50 feet

    B. 50 to 70 feet

    C. 75 to 125 feet

    D. 900 to 1100 feet

24. The Sales AP cannot associate to the WLC. What approach should you take when troubleshooting? (Choose two.)

    A. Reset and reload the AP.

    B. Telnet to the AP.

    C. SSH to the WLC.

    D. Execute debug lwapp events enable on the WLC.

    E. Execute debug lwapp events enable on the AP.

    F. Reboot the AP and the controller.

Answers to Assessment Test

1. C. To change the native VLAN on a switch trunk link, from the switch interface configured as a trunk, use the `switchport trunk native vlan vlan#`, in this example, vlan 300. For more information, please see Chapter 1.

2. C. Stations are associated to an AP using a MAC address that the APs derive from their base MAC address. The stations, when handed off to another AP, see the new address they are receiving from the new AP they roamed to. For more information, please see Chapter 1.

3. D. To begin, 20dB is 100mW. We'll start by adding a tenfold increase in power twice for the 21dB passive antenna, which first is 1000mW, or 30dB and then tenfold again to 10,000mW (10W). But wait, we still need to take the loss of the 50 feet of cable, which is a 3.5dB loss. This cuts the power in half, so our answer is 5W—which is illegal in most, if not all, places. For more information, please see Chapter 2.

4. A. An isotropic radiator is a perfect antenna that radiates in all directions. The value that references an antenna's gain against this antenna is dBi. For more information, please see Chapter 2.

5. D. DBPSK and DQPSK use barker 11 to achieve only 1 and 2Mbps throughput. To get the 5.5 and 11Mbps speeds of DSSS, CCK is used to encode the data in the RF signal. For more information, please see Chapter 3.

6. D. OFDM uses 52 subcarriers that are used to help reduce and resist multiple issues. For more information, please see Chapter 3.

7. C. DIFS is normal priority whereas SIFS is high priority. For more information, please see Chapter 4.

8. D. The UNII-3 band was intended for outdoor bridge products and permitted the use of external antennas. Output power should not exceed 1W (30dBm), with no more than 36dBm EIRP. For more information, please see Chapter 4.

9. C. EAP-Fast is the only method that creates and uses PACs. For more information, please see Chapter 5.

10. A. The purpose of the four-way handshake is to establish the pairwise transient key (PTK). For more information, please see Chapter 5.

11. A, B. Shared WEP and WEP options do not allow for choosing AES or TKIP, but both versions of WPA do. For more information, please see Chapter 6.

12. B. NetworkManagerDispatcher allows scripting or automating actions when the computer boots up or when a particular SSID is encountered. For more information, please see Chapter 6.

13. D. The order of states is Discovery, Join, Image Data, Config, and Run. For more information, please see Chapter 7.

14. C. When a single WLAN is operating in symmetric roaming mode while the others are in asymmetric roaming mode, those clients will use a mobility anchor WLC regardless of where they roam. For more information, please see Chapter 7.

15. A. The 521 is set as a DHCP client as the default. For more information, please see Chapter 8.

16. B. In standalone mode only three APs are supported by the CCA. For more information, please see Chapter 8.

17. B. Three TACACS+ servers can be defined in the WLC. For more information, please see Chapter 9.

18. B. Ports are physical interfaces. Interfaces are logical, and multiple interfaces can be mapped to a port. For more information, please see Chapter 9.

19. A, B, C, E. The four parameters to be set are Authority ID, Authority ID Information, Server Key, and Time To Live For The PAC. For more information, please see Chapter 10.

20. B. If the client starts with an EAPoW hello (EAP over wireless), the 802.1X process starts. An EAPoL (EAP over LAN) frame would not originate from the wireless network. For more information, please see Chapter 10.

21. B, C, D. The Audit function is used to maintain consistency between the WLC configuration and the configuration in the WCS database. For more information, please see Chapter 11.

22. C. Up to 10 Cisco Spectrum Experts can send information to the WCS. For more information, please see Chapter 11.

23. B. For good location fidelity, the APs should be within 50 to 70 feet of one another, but each situation will vary. For more information, please see Chapter 12.

24. C, D. To troubleshoot an AP that cannot associate with the WLC, you could either SSH to the WLC and use the GUI to observe the message logs or you could execute `debug lwapp events enable` on the WLC. For more information, please see Chapter 12.

Chapter

1

Wireless Networks and Topologies

THE CCNA WIRELESS EXAM TOPICS COVERED IN THIS CHAPTER ARE:

✓ **Describe WLAN fundamentals**

- Describe networking technologies used in wireless (SSID → WLAN_ID → Interface → VLAN, 802.1Q trunking)

- Describe wireless topologies (IBSS, BSS, ESS, Point-to-Point, Point-to-Multipoint, basic Mesh, bridging)

Sipping coffee at a café or hanging out in an airport until they finally fix the plane you're waiting to board no longer requires reading papers and magazines to avoid mind-numbing boredom. Now, you can just connect to the local wireless network and catch up on your email, blog, do a little gaming—maybe even get some work done! It's come to the point that many of us wouldn't even think of checking into a hotel that doesn't offer this important amenity. So clearly, those of us already in or wishing to enter the IT field better have our chops down regarding wireless network components and their associated installation factors, right? (Answer: a resounding YES!)

With that established, we've come to a great starting point: if you want to understand the basic wireless LANs (WLANs) most commonly used today, just think 10BaseT Ethernet with hubs—except the wireless devices we connect to are called access points (APs). This means that our WLANs run half-duplex communication—everyone is sharing the same bandwidth, and only one device is communicating at a time per channel.

This isn't necessarily bad; it's just not good enough. Because so many people rely on wireless networks today, it's critical that they evolve faster than greased lightning to keep up with our rapidly escalating needs. The good news is that this is actually happening—and it even works securely!

In this chapter, I am going talk about the various types of wireless networks, and then discuss the minimum devices needed to create a simple wireless network. I'll then show you some basic wireless topologies, and finish with a review on switching and VLANs. Why am I going to talk about switching and VLANs? Because if you think about it for a minute, you come to the important realization that APs have to connect to something. If not, how else would all those hosts hanging around in a wireless network area be able to connect to your wired resources, or to the Internet? This is why you absolutely must have a basic understanding of switching.

    To find dynamic updates to this chapter, please see www.lammle.com.

Wireless Networks

Wireless networks come in many forms, cover various distances, and provide a range of low to high bandwidth depending on the type installed. The typical wireless network today is an extension of an Ethernet LAN, and wireless hosts use Media Access Control (MAC) addresses, IP addresses, and so forth, just like any host would on a wired LAN. Figure 1.1 shows how the simple, typical wireless LAN looks today.

FIGURE 1.1   Wireless LANs are an extension of our existing LANs.

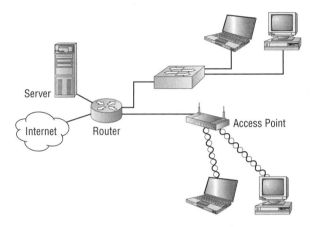

But wireless networks are more than just run-of-the-mill LANs because—you guessed it—they're wireless. And as I mentioned, they cover a range of distances from short-range personal area networks, all the way to wide area networks (WANs) that really go the distance. Figure 1.2 illustrates how different types of wireless networks look and the related distances they'll provide coverage for in today's world.

FIGURE 1.2   Today's Wireless Networks

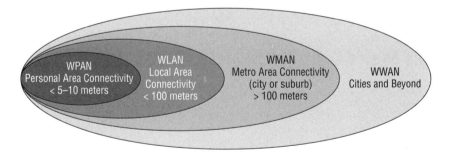

Okay, now that you've got the picture, we'll explore each of these networks in more detail.

Wireless Personal Area Network (WPAN)

A wireless personal area network (PAN) works in a very small area and connects devices like mice, keyboards, PDAs, headsets, and cell phones to our computers. This conveniently eliminates the cabling clutter of the past. If you're thinking Bluetooth, you've hit it, because it's by far the most popular type of PAN around! I'll discuss everything you need to know about this standard in Chapter 3, "Wireless Regulation Bodies, Standards, and Certifications."

PANs are low power, they cover short distances, and they're pretty small. The distance you'll get out of one of these is about 30 feet max, but most devices on a PAN have a short reach, making them popular for small and/or home offices. Bigger isn't always better—you don't want your PAN's devices stretching out so far that they interfere with your other wireless networks, or someone else's, and make a mess. Plus you've got the usual security concerns to manage. So, basically PANs are the perfect solution for small devices that you want to connect to your PC.

The standard use for PANs is unlicensed, meaning that the users involved don't have to pay to use the type of devices in the network. As you can imagine, this attribute promotes the development of devices that can use PAN frequencies.

Wireless LAN (WLAN)

Wireless LANs (WLANs) were created to have longer distance and higher bandwidth than PANs and are the most popular type of wireless networks in use today.

The first WLAN had a data rate up to 2Mbps, could go about 200–300 feet depending on the area, and was called simply 802.11. The typical rates in use today are higher and are 11Mbps and 54Mbps; these are called IEEE 802.11b and 802.11g/a, respectively. You'll learn more about these IEEE standards in Chapter 3.

The idea of a WLAN is to have many users connect to the network at the same time, but this can cause interference and collisions as users are competing for the same bandwidth.

Like PANs, WLANs use an unlicensed frequency band, which means you do not have to pay for the frequency band in order to transmit. This fact encourages development of devices for use in this type of network, and we've seen an explosion of new development in the WLAN area.

Wireless Metro Area Network (WMAN)

Wireless metro area networks (WMANs) are essentially a network that covers a fairly large geographic area like a city or small suburb. They're becoming increasingly common as more and more products are introduced into the WLAN arena and their price tags continue to drop.

You can think of WMANs as low-budget, bridging networks—something I talk about more in a bit. They offer a frugal alternative to the much more costly T1 or T3 point-to-point leased lines, but there's a catch: to get your discount long-distance wireless network to work, you've got to have a line of sight between each hub or building.

If you can get fiber connections in your metropolitan area, they're what you want because they'll provide you with an ultra-solid backbone for your network. This is why more and more fiber networks are being installed these days. But if your ISP doesn't offer the fiber option, or you lack the cash to pony up for it, a WMAN is a perfectly fine, economical alternative design to cover a campus or some other large area as long as you've got that vital line of sight factor in check!

Wireless Wide Area Network (WWAN)

So far, it's seriously rare to come across a wireless wide area network (WWAN) that can provide you with WLAN speeds, but there sure is a lot of chatter about them. A good example of a WWAN would be the latest cellular networks that can transmit data at a pretty good clip. Even so, they're still not speedy enough to replace our ubiquitous WLANs. But WWANs can certainly cover plenty of area!

Some people—especially those in TV commercials—claim to adore their infallible, turbo-charged cellular networks. These terminally happy, ceaselessly smiling people are usually watching high-speed video on their shiny new smart phones, but I don't know anyone who lives outside the TV (including me) who actually gets that kind of speed. And that "coverage anywhere" thing—sorry! Off the set and into reality, dead zones and frozen phones are things we must all deal with for now.

Hopefully we'll see more efficiency and growth in WWANs soon. But to be real, because WWANs are used to provide connectivity over a really large geographic area, it follows that implementing one will separate your cell service provider from a large quantity of cash. Therefore, as more and more people want this type of service and are willing to pay for it, cellular companies will gain the resources to expand and improve upon these exciting networks.

Here are another couple of positives in favor of WWAN growth and development: they meet a lot of business requirements, and technology is growing in a direction that the need for this type of long-distance wireless network is only getting stronger. So it's a fairly good bet that development will continue to grow in this industry. Connectivity between a WLAN and a WWAN will be critical to many things in our future—for instance, when we have more IPv6 networks, the "pass-off" between these two types of networks may be seamless.

Basic Wireless Devices

Though it might not seem this way to you right now, *simple* wireless networks (WLANs) are less complex than their wired cousins because they require fewer components. To make a basic wireless network work properly, all you need are two main devices: a wireless AP and a wireless network interface card (NIC). This also makes it a lot easier to install a wireless network, because basically, you just need an understanding of these two components in order to do so.

Wireless Access Points

You'll find a central component like a hub or switch in the vast majority of wired networks that's there to connect hosts together and allow them to communicate with each other. It's the same thing regarding wireless networks; they also have a component that connects all wireless devices together, only that device is known as a wireless *access point* (AP). Wireless APs have at least one antenna. Usually there's two for better reception (referred to as diversity), and a port to connect them to a wired network. Figure 1.3 gives you an example of a Cisco wireless AP. It happens to be one of my personal favorites—an 871W that I use in my home office.

FIGURE 1.3   A wireless access point

APs have the following characteristics:

- APs function as a central junction point for the wireless stations much like a switch or hub does within a wired network. Due to the half-duplex nature of wireless networking, the hub comparison is more accurate, even though hubs are rarely found in the wired world anymore.

- APs have at least one antenna—most likely two.

- APs function as a bridge to the wired network, giving the wireless station access to the wired network and/or the Internet.

- SoHo APs come in two flavors—the stand-alone AP and the wireless router. They can and usually do include functions like network address translation (NAT) and Dynamic Host Configuration Protocol (DHCP).

Even though it's not a perfect analogy, you can compare an AP to a hub because it doesn't create collision domains for each port like a switch does, but APs are definitely smarter than hubs. An AP is a portal device that can either direct network traffic to the wired backbone or back out into the wireless realm. If you look at Figure 1.1 again, you can see that the connection back to the wired network is called the distribution system (DS), and it also maintains MAC address information within the 802.11 frames. What's more, these frames are capable of holding as many as four MAC addresses, but this would only be the case when a wireless DS is in use—something I'll discuss in detail in Chapter 4, "Introduction to Wireless Security." For now, just know that this capability allows the AP to track where everything is going.

An AP also maintains an association table and you can view that from the web-based software that's used to manage the AP. So what's an association table? It's essentially a list of all workstations currently connected to or associated with the AP that are listed by their MAC addresses. Another cool AP feature is that wireless routers can function as NAT routers, and they can perform DHCP addressing for workstations as well.

In the all-important Cisco world, there are two types of APs: autonomous and lightweight. An autonomous AP is one that is configured, managed, and maintained in isolation with regard to all the other APs that exist in the network. A lightweight AP gets its configuration from a central device called a wireless controller. In this scenario, the APs are functioning as antennas and all information is sent back to the wireless LAN controller (WLC). There are a bunch of advantages to this, like the capacity for centralized management and more seamless roaming. You'll learn all about using WLC and lightweight APs throughout this book.

You can think of an AP as a bridge between the wireless clients and the wired network. Additionally, you can use an AP as a wireless bridge (depending on the settings) to bridge two wired network segments together.

In addition to the stand-alone AP, there's another type of AP that includes a built-in router (the type shown in Figure 1.3), which you can use to connect both wired and wireless clients to the Internet. These devices are usually employed as NAT routers.

Wireless Network Interface Card (NIC)

Every host you want to connect to a wireless network needs a wireless *network interface card* (NIC) to do so. Basically, a wireless NIC does the same job as a traditional NIC, only instead of having a socket/port to plug a cable into, the wireless NIC has a radio antenna. Figure 1.4 shows an example of a wireless NIC.

FIGURE 1.4   Wireless NIC

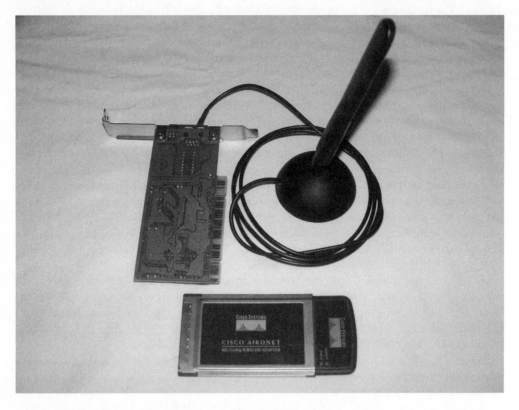

The wireless card shown in Figure 1.4 is used in a desktop computer, and most late model laptops have wireless cards plugged into or built into the motherboard.

These days, it's pretty rare to use an external wireless client card because all laptops come with them built in, and desktops can be ordered with them too. But it's good to know that you can still buy the client card shown in Figure 1.4. Typically, you would use cards like the ones shown in the figure for areas of poor reception, or for use with a network analyzer because they can have better range—depending on the antenna you use.

Wireless Antennas

Wireless antennas work with both transmitters and receivers. There are two broad classes of antennas on the market today: *omni-directional* (or point-to-multipoint) and *directional* (or point-to-point). An example of omni antennas is shown back in Figure 1.3. (They're connected to my 871W.)

Yagi antennas usually provide greater range than omni antennas of equivalent gain. Why? Because yagis focus all their power in a single direction. Omnis must disperse the same amount of power in all directions at the same time, like a large donut.

A downside to using a directional antenna is that you've got to be much more precise when aligning communication points. It's also why most APs use omnis, because often, clients and other APs can be located in any direction at any given moment.

To get a picture of this, think of the antenna on your car. Yes, it's a non-networking example, but it's still a good one because it clarifies the fact that your car's particular orientation doesn't affect the signal reception of whatever radio station you happen to be listening to. Well, most of the time, anyway. If you're in the boonies, you're out of range—something that also applies to the networking version of omnis.

Wireless antennas will be discussed in more detail in Chapter 2.

Wireless Topologies

Now that I've discussed the very basics of wireless devices used in today's simple networks, I want to describe the different types of networks you'll run across or design and implement as your wireless networks grow.

These include the following:

- IBSS
- BSS
- ESS
- Workgroup bridges
- Repeater APs
- Bridging (point-to-point and point-to-multipoint)
- Mesh

Let's take a look at these networks in detail.

Independent Basic Service Set (Ad Hoc)

This is the easiest way to install wireless 802.11 devices. In this mode, the wireless NICs (or other devices) can communicate directly without the need for an AP. A good example of this is two laptops with wireless NICs installed. If both cards were set up to operate in ad hoc mode, they could connect and transfer files as long as the other network settings, like protocols, were set up to enable this as well. We'll also call this an *independent basic service set (IBSS)*, which is created as soon as two wireless devices communicate.

To create an ad hoc network, all you need is two or more wireless-capable devices. Once you've placed them within a range of 20–40 meters of each other, they'll "see" each other and be able to connect—assuming they share some basic configuration parameters. One computer may be able to share the Internet connection with the rest of them in your group. Figure 1.5 shows an example of an ad hoc wireless network. Notice that there's no access point!

FIGURE 1.5   A wireless network in ad hoc mode

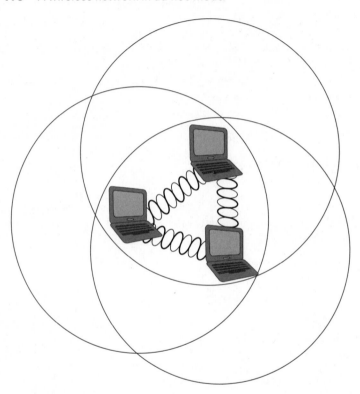

An ad hoc network, also referred to as peer to peer, doesn't scale well and I wouldn't recommend it due to collision and organization issues in today's corporate networks. With the low cost of APs, you don't need this kind of network anymore, except for maybe in your home, but maybe not even there.

Additionally, ad hoc networks are a fairly insecure method, and care should be taken to have the AdHoc setting turned off prior to connecting to your wired network.

Basic Service Set (BSS)

A basic service set (BSS) is the area, or cell, defined by the wireless signal served by the AP. It can also be called a basic service area (BSA) and the two terms, BSS and BSA, can be interchangeable. Even so, BSS is the most common term that's used to define the cell area. Figure 1.6 shows an AP providing a BSS for hosts in the area and the basic service area (cell) that's covered by the AP.

FIGURE 1.6   Basic service set/basic service area

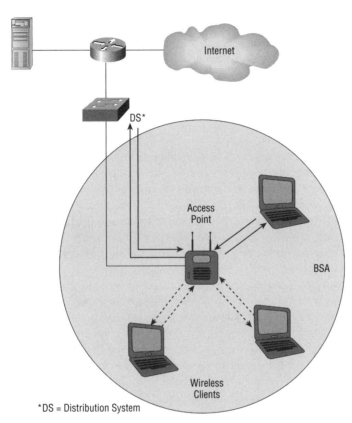

*DS = Distribution System

The AP is not connected to a wired network in this example, but the AP provides management of wireless frames so the hosts can communicate. Unlike the ad hoc network, this network will scale better and more hosts can communicate in this network because the AP manages all network connections.

Infrastructure Basic Service Set

In infrastructure mode, wireless NICs only communicate with an access point instead of directly with each other as they do when they're in ad hoc mode. All communication between hosts, as well as any wired portion of the network, must go through the access point. An important fact to remember is that in this mode, wireless clients appear to the rest of the network as though they were standard, wired hosts.

Figure 1.6 shows a typical infrastructure mode wireless network. Pay special attention to the access point and the fact that it's also connected to the wired network. This connection from the access point to the wired network is called the *distribution system (DS)* and this is how the APs communicate to each other about hosts in the BSA. Basic standalone APs do not communicate with each other via the wireless network, only through the DS.

When you configure a client to operate in wireless infrastructure mode, you need to understand what is called the SSID. The *service set identifier (SSID)* refers to the unique 32-character identifier that represents a particular wireless network and defines the BSS. (By the way, a lot of people use the terms SSID and BSS interchangeably, so don't let that confuse you!) All devices involved in a particular wireless network may be configured with the same SSID. Sometimes access points may even have multiple SSIDs. Let's talk about that in a little more detail.

Service Set ID

SSID is a basic name that defines the BSA transmitted from the AP. A good example of this is "Linksys." You've probably seen that name pop up on our host when looking for a wireless network. This is the name the AP transmits out to identify which WLAN the client station can associate with. The SSID can be up to 32 characters long. It normally consists of human-readable ASCII characters, but the standard doesn't require this. The SSID is defined as a sequence of 1–32 octets, each of which may take any value.

The SSID is configured on the AP and can be either broadcasted to the outside world or hidden. If the SSID is broadcasted, when wireless stations use their client software to scan for wireless networks the network will appear in a list identified by its SSID. But if it's hidden, it either won't appear in the list at all or it will show up as an "unknown network" depending on the client's operating system.

Either way, a hidden SSID will require that the client station be configured with a wireless profile, including the SSID, in order to connect. This requirement is above and beyond any other normal authentication steps or security essentials.

The AP associates a MAC address to this SSID. It can be the MAC address for the radio interface itself (called the basic service set identifier [BSSID]), or it can be derived from the MAC address of the radio interface if multiple SSIDs are used (sometimes called a virtual MAC address). In the latter case, you would call it a multiple basic service set identifier (MBSSID), as shown in Figure 1.7.

There are two things you really want to make note of in this figure: first, there's a "Contractor BSSID" and a "Sales BSSID"; second, each of these SSID names is associated with a separate virtual MAC address, which was assigned by the AP.

These SSIDs are virtual, and implementing things this way won't improve your wireless network or AP performance—you just have more hosts sharing the same half-duplex radio. By doing this, you're not breaking up collision domains or broadcast domains by creating more SSIDs on your AP. The reason for creating multiple SSIDs on your AP is so that you can set different levels of security for each client that's connecting to your AP(s).

Extended Service Set

A good to thing to know is that if you set all your access points to the same SSID, mobile wireless clients can roam around freely within the same network. This is the most common wireless network design you'll find in today's corporate settings.

Doing this creates something called an *extended service set (ESS)*, which provides more coverage than a single access point and allows users to roam from one AP to another without having their host disconnected from the network. This design creates the ability to move more or less seamlessly from one AP to another. Figure 1.8 shows two APs configured with the same SSIDs in an office, thereby creating the ESS network.

FIGURE 1.7   A network with MBSSIDs configured on an AP

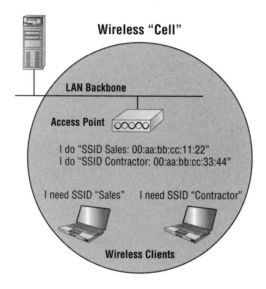

FIGURE 1.8   Extended service set (ESS)

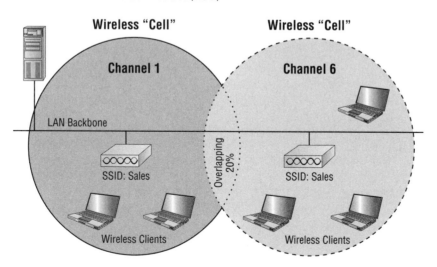

For users to be able to roam throughout the wireless network—from AP to AP without losing their connection to the network—all APs must overlap by at least 10 percent of their signal or more to their neighbor's cells. To make this happen, be sure the channels (frequency) on each AP are set differently. No worries—we'll go over this important detail in greater depth later, in Chapter 3.

Workgroup Bridge

If you have a bunch of hosts that need to connect to the wireless network but they don't have wireless cards or wireless capability, it's time to go with implementing a wireless workgroup bridge (WGB). A WGB is used in a typical network where it's just not feasible to install an Ethernet or fiber run. Usually, this is because it's just not in the budget, or because you're dealing with a particular environment, like a historic building where cable runs are forbidden. Figure 1.9 shows an example of such a network.

FIGURE 1.9   Basic WGB wireless network

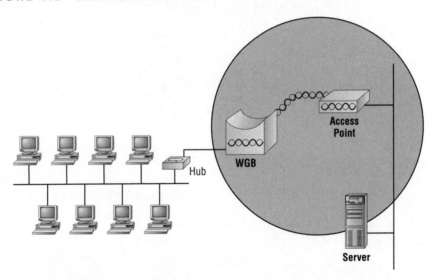

Cisco supports two types of WGBs: autonomous, which is the type shown in Figure 1.9 (sometimes called aWGB), and the universal WGB (uWGB). The uWGB will establish a single wireless connection for multiple Ethernet clients to an AP and appear as a nonstandard client on the AP (This is a proprietary solution provided by Cisco.). Good to know is that the uWBG is a nonproprietary version that supports an Ethernet client by enabling it to connect through an uWGB to an AP from another vendor and still appear as a single, normal client to the AP.

You need to remember the two types of WGBs and the definitions included here.

Repeaters

If you need to extend the coverage of an AP, you can either increase the gain of a directional antenna or add another AP in the area. If neither of those options solves your problem, try adding a repeater AP to the network and extending the range without having to pull an Ethernet cable for the new AP.

Figure 1.10 gives you a picture of what this network design looks like.

FIGURE 1.10   An AP repeater network

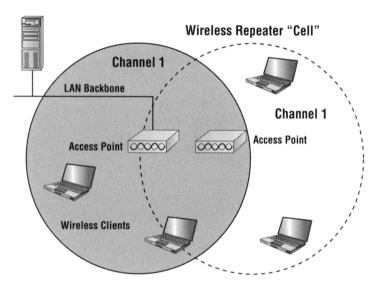

A wireless repeater AP isn't connected to the wired backbone. It uses its antenna to receive the signal from an AP that's directly connected to the network, and repeats the signal for clients located too far away from it.

To make this work, you need appropriate overlap between APs, as shown in Figure 1.10. Another way to get this to happen is to place a repeater AP with two radios in use, with one receiving and the other one transmitting. This works somewhat like a dual half-duplex repeater.

But there is a rather nasty downside to this design—for every repeater installed you lose about half of your throughput, so the hosts off Repeater 2, shown in Figure 1.10, would only get about 5.5Mbps throughput at best when running in an 11Mbps wireless network.

Since no one likes less bandwidth, a repeater network should only be used for low-bandwidth devices, like a barcode reader in a warehouse.

Bridging

Bridges are used to connect two or more wired LANs, usually located within separate buildings, to create one big LAN. Bridges operate at the MAC address layer (Data Link layer), which means they have no routing capabilities. So you've got to put a router in place if you want to be able to do any IP subnetting within your network. Basically, you would use bridges to enlarge the broadcast domains on your network. Armed with a firm understanding of how bridging works, you can definitely improve your network's capacity.

To build wireless networks correctly, it's important to have a working knowledge of root and nonroot bridges (sometimes referred to as parent and child bridges). Some bridges allow clients to connect directly to them, but others don't, so make sure you understand exactly your business requirements before just randomly buying a wireless bridge. Figure 1.11 shows the typical bridge scenarios used in today's networks.

FIGURE 1.11   Typical bridge scenarios

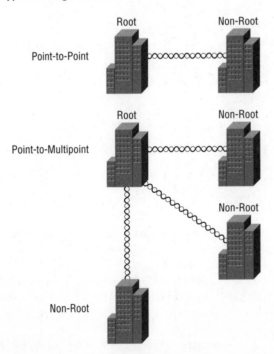

A point-to-point wireless network is a popular design that's often used outdoors to connect two buildings or LANs together.

A point-to-multipoint design works well in a campus environment where you have a main building with a collection of ancillary buildings that you want to be able to connect back to the main one, as well as to each other, through it. Wireless bridges are commonly used to make these connections, and they just happen to be pricier than a traditional AP. The thing you want to remember about point-to-multipoint wireless networks is that each remote building won't be able to communicate directly with each other. To do that, they must first connect to the central, main point (main building) and then to one of the other ones (multipoint buildings).

Okay—now let's get back to that root/nonroot issue I brought up a minute ago. I've got to tell you more about this because it becomes important to understand, especially when you're designing outdoor networks!

So look back to Figure 1.11 and find the terms root and nonroot. This figure shows a traditional point-to-point and point-to-multipoint network when one bridge, the root, accepts communications only from nonroot devices.

Root devices are connected to the wired network, which allows nonroot devices, like clients, to access the wired resources through the root device. Here are some important guidelines to help you design your wireless networks:

- Nonroot devices can only communicate to root devices. Nonroot devices include nonroot bridges, workgroup bridges, repeater access points, and wireless clients.

- Root devices cannot communicate to other root devices. Examples of devices that can be roots are APs and bridges.

- Nonroot devices cannot communicate to other nonroot devices.

But wait, there's one exception to that last bullet point. If you have a nonroot bridge set up as a repeater AP with two radios, the device must be configured as a nonroot device. It will then repeat and extend the distance of your outdoor, bridged network, as shown in Figure 1.12.

FIGURE 1.12   A repeater AP bridge configured as a nonroot bridge

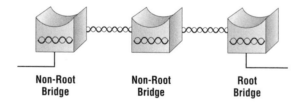

Non-Root   Non-Root   Root
Bridge   Bridge   Bridge

Figure 1.12 demonstrates that a nonroot bridge will communicate to another nonroot bridge only if one of the nonroot bridges has a root bridge in its uplink.

Mesh Networks

As more vendors migrate to a mesh hierarchical design, and as larger networks are built using lightweight access points that are managed by a controller, you can see that we need a standardized protocol that governs how lightweight access points communicate with

WLAN systems. This is exactly the role filled by one of the Internet Engineering Task Force's (IETF's) latest draft specifications, Lightweight Access Point Protocol (LWAPP).

Mesh networking infrastructure is decentralized and comparably inexpensive for all the nice amenities it provides because each host only needs to transmit as far as the next host. Hosts act as repeaters to transmit data from nearby hosts to peers that are too far away for a manageable cabled connection. The result is a network that can span a large area, especially over rough or difficult terrain.

Remember that mesh is a network topology in which devices are connected with many redundant connections between host nodes, and we can use this topology to our advantage in large wireless installations. Figure 1.13 shows a large meshed environment using Cisco outdoor managed APs to "umbrella" an outdoor area with wireless connectivity.

FIGURE 1.13   Typical large mesh outdoor environment

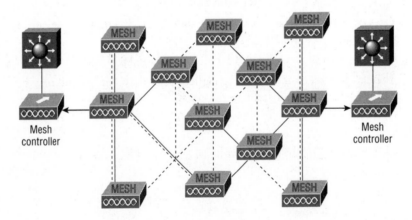

Oh, and did I mention that mesh networks also happen to be extremely reliable? Because each host can potentially be connected to several other hosts, if one of them drops out of the network because of hardware failure or something, its neighbors simply find another route. So you get extra capacity and fault tolerance automatically just by adding more hosts!

Wireless mesh connections between AP hosts are formed with a radio, providing many possible paths from a single host to other hosts. Paths through the mesh network can change in response to traffic loads, radio conditions, or traffic prioritization.

At this time, mesh networks just aren't a good solution for home use or small companies on a budget. As the saying goes, "If you have to ask…" As with most things in life, the more bells and whistles, the more it costs, and mesh networks are certainly no exception.

Switching

Yes, I know this book is a wireless book, but just trust me on this one—it's very important for you to understand some vital switching terms and configurations. Can you guess why? Well, if you thought of something along the lines of "Because all those wireless devices such as access points must connect into something, and that something is a Cisco switch," you nailed it!

Having these switching basics down will come in super handy when we get to managed wireless networks later in this book. That's when you'll find out about controllers, how they need to be configured so that they'll connect to a switch, and vice versa. So as you can see, a basic knowledge of switches, related terminology, and how to configure them will be helpful to you.

> Please see my *CCNA: Cisco Certified Network Associate Study Guide: Exam 640-802* (Sybex, 2007) for a complete discussion and configuration examples on switching.

As shown in Figure 1.14, Layer 2 switched networks are typically designed as flat networks. Every broadcast packet transmitted is seen by every device on the network, regardless of whether or not the device needs to receive that data.

By default, routers only permit broadcasts to circulate within the originating network segment, but switches forward broadcasts to all segments. The reason for this is also the reason this type of network is called a *flat network*. The name means that it's only one *broadcast domain*, not that its actual design is physically flat.

In Figure 1.14, you can see Host A sending out a broadcast, and all ports on all switches forwarding the broadcast—except for the port that originally received it.

FIGURE 1.14   Flat network structure

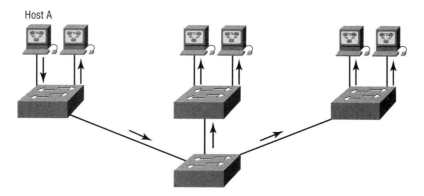

Now look at Figure 1.15, which pictures a switched network. It shows Host A sending a frame with Host D as its destination, and as you can see, that frame is only forwarded out the port where Host D is located. This is a huge improvement over the old hub networks, unless having only one *collision domain* by default is what you want.

FIGURE 1.15   The benefit of a switched network

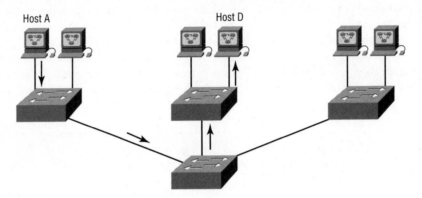

You already know that the main benefit gained by having a Layer 2 switched network is that it allows you to create individual collision domain segments for each device plugged into each port on the switch. This scenario frees us from the original Ethernet distance constraints, so now larger networks can be built. But with each new advance, we often encounter new issues—the larger the number of users and devices, the more broadcasts and packets each switch must handle.

And here's another big advantage—security! This one's a real problem because within the typical Layer 2 switched internetwork, all users can see all devices by default. Worse, you can't stop devices from broadcasting or users from trying to respond to broadcasts. Your security options are dismally limited to placing passwords on the servers and other critical devices.

But they're not if you create a *virtual LAN (VLAN)*. You can solve many of the problems associated with Layer 2 switching with VLANs—as you'll soon see.

Here are some ways that VLANs simplify network management:

- Network additions, moves, and changes are achieved by configuring a port into the appropriate VLAN.

- A group of users who require high security can be put into their own VLAN so that no users outside their specific VLAN can communicate with them.

- As a logical grouping of users by function instead of a physical one, VLANs are by nature independent of their physical or geographic locations.

- VLANs can help strengthen network security.

- VLANs increase the number of broadcast domains while decreasing their size.

Next, I'm going to cover some cool switching features and show you how switches provide better network services than hubs can within a network. You'll also learn how to configure switches with VLAN and trunk links.

VLAN Memberships

VLANs are most often created by an administrator who then assigns switch ports to each of them afterward. This kind of VLAN is called a *static VLAN*. If the administrator wants to do a little more work up front and assign all the host devices' hardware addresses into a database, the switches can be configured to assign VLANs dynamically whenever a given host is plugged into a switch. This variety is predictably called a *dynamic VLAN*. Let's check out the static type first.

Static VLANs

Static VLANs aren't just the most common way to create VLANs; they're also the most secure. This is because the switch port that you assign a VLAN association to will always maintain that particular association until you manually change the port assignment.

This type of VLAN configuration also happens to be kind of the "easy button" version because it's relatively painless to set up and monitor. Dynamic VLANs can make certain things easier too.

Basically, static VLANs work well in a network where the movement of users is tightly controlled. Plus, even though it can be helpful to use network management software to configure the ports, it's not required.

This is how it works—you configure each switch port with a VLAN membership based on the specific VLAN that the host needs to be a member of. (Remember, the device's physical location doesn't matter.) The broadcast domain the hosts will become a member of is an administrative choice. Don't forget that each host must also have the correct IP address information configured or things won't work so well.

It is also important to remember that if you plug a host into a switch, you've got to verify the VLAN membership of the precise port you're plugging into. If the membership doesn't match the specific host, it won't be able to access or provide the network services it's intended to. For instance, a host machine that you want to act as a workgroup server won't be able to function in that capacity.

Dynamic VLANs

A dynamic VLAN determines a node's VLAN assignment automatically. Using intelligent management software, you can base VLAN assignments on hardware (MAC) addresses, protocols, or even applications when you create dynamic VLANs.

Choosing between static or dynamic VLANs for your network comes down to your personal preferences and needs. For example, let's say you've got all MAC addresses entered into a centralized VLAN management application. If a host is then attached to an unassigned switch port, the VLAN management database can look up the host's hardware address and assign and configure the switch port to match the right VLAN. This is very cool—it makes management and configuration easier because if a user moves, the switch will simply assign them to the correct VLAN automatically. But as usual, there's a catch…

Just know that there's a lot more up-front work you have to do when initially setting up that database!

Cisco administrators can use the VLAN Management Policy Server (VMPS) service to set up a database of MAC addresses that can then be used for the dynamic addressing of VLANs. A VMPS database essentially maps MAC addresses to VLANs.

A dynamic-access port can belong to one VLAN, (VLAN ID 1 to 4094), which is dynamically assigned by the VMPS. You can have dynamic-access ports and trunk ports on the same switch, but you've got to connect the dynamic-access port to an end station or hub and not to another switch.

Types of Switch Ports

Okay—so we all know that switch ports are Layer 2–only interfaces associated with a physical port. Switch ports can belong to one or more VLANs, and they can be an access port or a trunk port. You can manually configure a given port as an access port or trunk port, or you can just let the Dynamic Trunking Protocol (DTP) operate on a per-port basis to set the switch port mode by negotiating with the port on the other end of the link.

As frames are switched throughout the network, switches must be able to keep track of all the different types, as well as understand what to do with them depending on their hardware addresses. And remember, frames are handled differently according to the type of link they are traversing. Figure 1.16 depicts the difference between an access link and a trunk link.

Let's talk about the various types of switch ports—starting with access ports.

FIGURE 1.16   Access and trunk links in a switched network

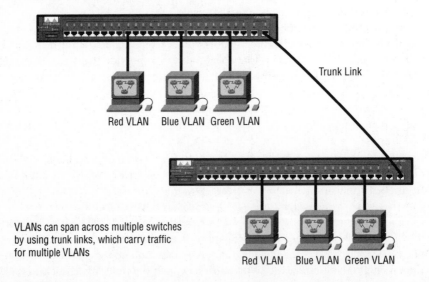

Trunk Link

Red VLAN   Blue VLAN   Green VLAN

VLANs can span across multiple switches
by using trunk links, which carry traffic
for multiple VLANs

Red VLAN   Blue VLAN   Green VLAN

Access Ports

An access port belongs to one specific VLAN and only carries its traffic that's received and sent in native formats with no VLAN tagging at all. Another thing to remember is that all traffic that arrives on an access port is assumed to belong to the VLAN that's assigned to that port, and if an access port happens to receive, say, an IEEE 802.1Q tagged packet, it will be promptly dropped. Because tagged traffic can only be processed on trunk ports, the source address of the dumped packed will remain a mystery.

This type of link is known as the *native VLAN* of the port, and a device attached to an *access link* is unaware of a VLAN membership. The device just assumes that it's part of a broadcast domain, but it doesn't have an understanding of the physical network.

Switches remove any VLAN information from the frame before it's forwarded out to an access link device. Access link devices can't communicate with devices outside their VLAN unless the packet is routed. And you have to be decisive—you have to designate a switch port as an access port or a trunk port. Remember, if you choose the access port option, that port can almost always be assigned to a single VLAN only.

Voice Access Ports

Here's what I meant when I said, "almost always"... although an access port can only be assigned to one VLAN, most late-model switches will allow you to add a second VLAN to the access port to be designated as your voice VLAN. This is technically considered to be a different type of link, but it's still just an access port that can be configured for both data and voice VLANs. It is pretty cool, though, because it allows you to connect a phone and PC device to one switch port, and yet still have each device in a separate VLAN.

Trunk Ports

Trunks can carry multiple VLANs and got their name because of the telephone system trunks that can carry multiple telephone conversations.

A *trunk link* is a 100 or 1000Mbps point-to-point link between two switches, between a switch and router, or between a switch and server. These carry the traffic of multiple VLANs—from 1 to 4094 at a time—but it's only up to 1005 unless you're using extended VLANs.

A very nice feature of trunking is that it allows you to make a single port out of multiple VLANs at the same time. This can be a major advantage because it makes it possible for you to set things up in a way that a server can be in two broadcast domains simultaneously. This means that your users won't have to cross a Layer 3 device (a router) to log in and access it. Another benefit to trunking is when you're connecting switches. Trunk links can carry some or all VLAN information across the link, but if the links between your switches aren't trunked, only VLAN 1 information will be switched across the link by default.

All VLANs send information on a trunked link unless cleared manually by an administrator, and I'll show you how to clear individual VLANs from a trunk in the configuration section later in this chapter.

Okay—next up is frame tagging and the VLAN identification methods used with it.

Frame Tagging

So you know that you can create your VLANs to span more than one connected switch. This flexible, power-packed capability is probably the main advantage to implementing VLANs.

But it can get kind of complicated—even for a switch—so there needs to be a way for each one to keep track of all the users and frames as they travel the switch fabric and VLANs. (Remember, a switch fabric is basically a group of switches sharing the same VLAN information.) This is where *frame tagging* comes in. This frame identification method uniquely assigns a user-defined ID to each frame. Sometimes people refer to it as a "VLAN ID" or "color."

And here's how it works: each switch that the frame reaches must first identify the VLAN ID from the frame tag, and then it finds out what to do with the frame by looking at the information in the filter table. If the frame reaches a switch that has another trunked link, the frame will be forwarded out the trunk-link port.

Once the frame reaches an exit (determined by the forward/filter table) to an access link matching the frame's VLAN ID, the switch removes the VLAN identifier. This is so the destination device can receive the frames without having to understand their VLAN identification.

A trunk port will support simultaneous tagged and untagged traffic and is assigned a default port VLAN ID (PVID). All untagged traffic travels on the port default PVID (also called the native VLAN), which is by default VLAN 1.

All untagged traffic and tagged traffic with a NULL (unassigned) VLAN ID is assumed to belong to the port default PVID—VLAN 1 by default. A packet with a VLAN ID equal to the outgoing port default PVID will be sent untagged and will only be allowed to communicate to hosts or devices in VLAN 1. All other VLAN traffic has to be sent with a VLAN tag in order to communicate in another particular VLAN.

VLAN Trunking Protocols

So VLAN identification is what switches use to keep track of all those frames as they're traversing a switch fabric. It's how switches identify which frames belong to which VLANs, and there's more than one trunking method, as you'll see in this section.

Inter-Switch Link (ISL)

Inter-switch link (ISL) is a way of explicitly tagging VLAN information onto an Ethernet frame. This tagging information allows VLANs to be multiplexed over a trunk link through an external encapsulation method (ISL) and allows the switch to identify the VLAN membership of a frame over the trunked link.

By running ISL, you can interconnect multiple switches and still maintain VLAN information as traffic travels between switches on trunk links. ISL functions at Layer 2 by encapsulating a data frame with a new header and cyclic redundancy check (CRC).

Of note, this is proprietary to Cisco switches, and it's used for Fast Ethernet and Gigabit Ethernet links only. *ISL routing* can be used on a switch port, router interfaces, and server interface cards to trunk a server.

There are some important differences between ISL and 802.1q: ISL does not support untagged packets on the trunk links, all frames will be encapsulated. Another limitation of ISL is that only 1024 VLANs can ever be carried across the link. These limitations are some of the main reasons ISL isn't being used as much anymore

IEEE 802.1Q

Created by the IEEE as a standard method of frame tagging, 802.1Q inserts a field into the frame to identify the VLAN. If you're trunking between a Cisco switched link and a different brand of switch, you have to use 802.1Q for the trunk to work.

It works like this: you must designate each 802.1Q port to be associated with a specific VLAN ID. The ports that populate the same trunk create a group that's known as a native VLAN, and each port gets tagged with an identification number that reflects its native VLAN (the default is VLAN 1).

 The basic purpose of ISL and 802.1Q frame-tagging methods is to provide inter-switch VLAN communication. Also, remember that any ISL or 802.1Q frame tagging is removed if a frame is forwarded out an access link— tagging is used across trunk links only.

Configuring VLANs

Configuring VLANs is pretty easy. Figuring out which users you want in each VLAN is not. It's super time-consuming, but once you've decided on the number of VLANs you want to create and establish the users you want to belong to each one, it's time to bring your first VLAN into existence.

To configure VLANs on a Cisco Catalyst switch, you use the global config vlan command. In the following example, I'm going to demonstrate how to configure VLANs on the S1 switch by creating three VLANs for three different departments (VLAN 1 is the native and administrative VLAN):

```
S1#config t
S1(config)#vlan ?
  WORD      ISL VLAN IDs 1-4094
  internal  internal VLAN
S1(config)#vlan 2
S1(config-vlan)#name Sales
```

```
S1(config-vlan)#vlan 3
S1(config-vlan)#name Marketing
S1(config-vlan)#vlan 4
S1(config-vlan)#name Accounting
S1(config-vlan)#^Z
S1#
```

From this output, you can see that you can create VLAN from 2–4094, but as I mentioned, this is only mostly true. VLANs can only be created up to the limit of 1001, and you can't use, change, rename, or delete VLANs 1 and 1002 through 1005 because they are reserved. Any VLAN numbers above that are called extended VLANs and won't be saved in the database unless your switch is set to VTP Transparent mode. You won't see these VLAN numbers used too often in production. Here's a demonstration of setting my S1 switch to VLAN 4000 when my switch is set to VTP Server mode (the default VTP mode):

```
S1#config t
S1(config)#vlan 4000
S1(config-vlan)#^Z
% Failed to create VLANs 4000
Extended VLAN(s) not allowed in current VTP mode.
%Failed to commit extended VLAN(s) changes.
```

Find more information on switching and VTP in my *CCNA Study Guide*.

After you create the VLANs that you want, you can use the show vlan command to see them. But notice that by default, all ports on the switch are in VLAN 1. To change the VLAN associated with a port, you need to go to each interface and tell it which VLAN to be a part of.

```
S1#sh vlan
```

VLAN	Name	Status	Ports
1	default	active	Fa0/3, Fa0/4, Fa0/5, Fa0/6
			Fa0/7, Fa0/8, Gi0/1
2	Sales	active	
3	Marketing	active	
4	Accounting	active	

[output cut]

Remember that a created VLAN is unused until it is assigned to a switch port or ports, and that all ports are always assigned in VLAN 1 unless set otherwise.

You can't change, delete, or rename VLAN 1, because it's the default VLAN and you just can't change that—period. It's the native VLAN of all switches by default, and Cisco recommends that you use this as your administrative VLAN. Native VLAN basically means that any packets that aren't specifically assigned to a different VLAN will be sent down the native VLAN. The frames sent down the trunk are therefore "untagged."

In the previous S1 output, you can see that ports Fa0/3–8 and the Gi0/1 uplink are all in VLAN 1, but where are ports 1 and 2? Any port that's designated as a trunk port will not show up in the `show vlan` output. Use the `show interface trunk` command instead if you want to check out all your trunked ports.

Okay—now that we can see the VLANs that have been created, we can assign switch ports to specific ones. Each port can be part of only one VLAN.

Assigning Switch Ports to VLANs

You configure a port to belong to a VLAN by assigning a membership mode that specifies the kind of traffic that port will carry, as well as the number of VLANs that it can belong to. You configure each port on a switch to be in a specific VLAN (access port) by using the interface command `switchport`. You can also configure a bunch of ports at the same time with the `interface range` command.

Don't forget that you can configure either static memberships or dynamic memberships on a port. I'm going to configure interface Fa0/3 to VLAN 3. Check it out:

```
S1#config t
S1(config)#int fa0/3
S1(config-if)#switchport ?
    access        Set access mode characteristics of the interface
    backup        Set backup for the interface
    block         Disable forwarding of unknown uni/multi cast addresses
    host          Set port host
    mode          Set trunking mode of the interface
    nonegotiate   Device will not engage in negotiation protocol on this
                  interface
    port-security Security related command
    priority      Set appliance 802.1p priority
    protected     Configure an interface to be a protected port
    trunk         Set trunking characteristics of the interface
    voice         Voice appliance attributes
```

Looking at this output, you can see some commands that I've already shown you, but I'm also going to cover the access, mode, nonegotiate, trunk, and voice commands in this section. Let's start with setting an access port on S1s that's probably the most widely used type of port on production switches that has VLANs configured:

```
S1(config-if)#switchport mode ?
  access   Set trunking mode to ACCESS unconditionally
  dynamic  Set trunking mode to dynamically negotiate access or
trunk mode
  trunk    Set trunking mode to TRUNK unconditionally

S1(config-if)#switchport mode access
S1(config-if)#switchport access vlan 3
```

By starting with the `switchport mode access` command, you're essentially telling the switch that this is a Layer 2 port. Then you can move on and assign a VLAN to the port with the `switchport access` command. Remember, you can choose boatloads of ports to configure at the same time if you use the `interface range` command. The `dynamic` and `trunk` commands are used for trunk ports exclusively.

That's it. Well, sort of. If you plugged devices into each VLAN port, they can only talk to other devices in the same VLAN. We want to enable inter-VLAN communication by using a router or a Layer 3 switch—something that's just not necessary to cover in this book. But let's take a look at how to create trunk ports...

Configuring Trunk Ports

Good to know is that some Cisco switches only run the IEEE 802.1Q encapsulation method. To configure trunking on a Fast Ethernet port, you use the interface command trunk [*parameter*]. It's a tad different on a switch that can run both ISL and the 802.1Q switch, and I'll show you that in a minute.

This switch output shows the trunk configuration on interface Fa0/8 as set to trunk on:

```
S1#config t
S1(config)#int fa0/8
S1(config-if)#switchport mode trunk
```

This list describes the options available to you when configuring a switch interface:

switchport mode access   This option puts the interface (access port) into permanent nontrunking mode and negotiates to convert the link into a nontrunk link. The interface becomes a nontrunk interface regardless of whether the neighboring interface is a trunk interface, and this port would become a dedicated Layer 2 port.

switchport mode dynamic auto   This option allows the interface to convert the link to a trunk link. The interface becomes a trunk interface if the neighboring interface is set to trunk or desirable mode. This is now the default switchport mode for all Ethernet interfaces on all new Cisco switches.

switchport mode dynamic desirable   This option makes the interface actively attempt to convert the link to a trunk link. The interface becomes a trunk interface if the neighboring interface is set to trunk, desirable, or auto mode. I used to see this as the default on some older switches but not anymore. The default is dynamic auto now.

switchport mode trunk   This option puts the interface into permanent trunking mode and negotiates to convert the neighboring link into a trunk link. The interface becomes a trunk interface even if the neighboring interface isn't one.

switchport nonegotiate   This option prevents the interface from generating DTP frames. You can use this command only when the interface switchport mode is access or trunk. You must manually configure the neighboring interface as a trunk interface to establish a trunk link.

Dynamic Trunking Protocol (DTP) is used for negotiating trunking on a link between two devices, as well as the encapsulation type of either 802.1Q or ISL. I use this nonegotiate command when I want dedicated trunk ports and want no questions asked!

To disable trunking on an interface, use the `switchport mode access` command, which sets the port back to a dedicated Layer 2 switch port.

Trunking with Switches That Support ISL and 802.1Q

For this type of 3750 switch, you have the `encapsulation` command available—a feature that the 2960 switch doesn't offer:

```
Core(config-if)#switchport trunk encapsulation ?
  dot1q     Interface uses only 802.1Q trunking encapsulation
 when trunking
  isl       Interface uses only ISL trunking encapsulation
 when trunking
  negotiate Device will negotiate trunking encapsulation with peer on
            interface
Core(config-if)#switchport trunk encapsulation dot1q
Core(config-if)#switchport mode trunk
```

As you can see, you can add either the IEEE 802.1Q (dot1q) encapsulation or the ISL encapsulation to this switch. After you set the encapsulation, you've still got to set the interface mode to trunk. Honestly, it's pretty rare that you'd continue to use the ISL encapsulation method because Cisco is moving away from ISL.

Defining the Allowed VLANs on a Trunk

As I said, trunk ports send and receive information from all VLANs by default, and if a frame is untagged, it will be sent straight to the management VLAN. By the way, this includes any extended range VLANs as well.

But I haven't told you that you can remove VLANs from the allowed list. Doing so can prevent traffic from certain VLANs from traversing a trunked link. Here's how to make that happen:

```
S1#config t
S1(config)#int f0/1
S1(config-if)#switchport trunk allowed vlan ?
   WORD    VLAN IDs of the allowed VLANs when this port is in
trunking mode
   add     add VLANs to the current list
   all     all VLANs
   except  all VLANs except the following
   none    no VLANs
   remove  remove VLANs from the current list
S1(config-if)#switchport trunk allowed vlan remove ?
   WORD  VLAN IDs of disallowed VLANS when this port is in trunking mode
S1(config-if)#switchport trunk allowed vlan remove 4
```

The above command stopped the trunk link configured on S1 port F0/1 to drop all traffic sent and received for VLAN 4. You can try to remove VLAN 1 on a trunk link, but it will still send and receive management like CDP, PAgP, LACP, DTP, and VTP, so what's the point? Well, doing this can be a great way to mess with other people's heads since they would then be unable to telnet or ping to another switch in the VLAN 1 management VLAN. So if you're feeling a bit mischievous…

To remove a range of VLANs, just use the hyphen:

```
S1(config-if)#switchport trunk allowed vlan remove 4-8
```

If by chance someone has removed some VLANs from a trunk link and you want to set the trunk back to default, just use this command:

```
S1(config-if)#switchport trunk allowed vlan all
```

Or this one, which accomplishes the same thing:

```
S1(config-if)#no switchport trunk allowed vlan
```

Now is a great time to show you how to configure pruning for VLANs before we start routing between VLANs.

Changing or Modifying the Trunk Native VLAN

Believe it or not, you can change the trunk port native VLAN from VLAN 1, and some people do this for security reasons, so pay attention. To change the native VLAN, use the following command:

```
S1#config t
S1(config)#int f0/1
```

```
S1(config-if)#switchport trunk ?
  allowed  Set allowed VLAN characteristics when interface is
in trunking mode
  native   Set trunking native characteristics when interface
is in trunking mode
  pruning  Set pruning VLAN characteristics when interface is
in trunking mode
S1(config-if)#switchport trunk native ?
  vlan  Set native VLAN when interface is in trunking mode
S1(config-if)#switchport trunk native vlan ?
  <1-4094>  VLAN ID of the native VLAN when this port is in
  trunking mode
S1(config-if)#switchport trunk native vlan 40
S1(config-if)#^Z
```

Sweet—we successfully changed our native VLAN on our trunk link to 40! And now, by using the show running-config command, we'll get to see the configuration under the trunk link:

```
!
interface FastEthernet0/1
 switchport trunk native vlan 40
 switchport trunk allowed vlan 1–3,9–4094
 switchport trunk pruning vlan 3,4
!
```

Sounds, looks, and seems simple, right? Uh huh, in a perfect world... You really didn't think that it was this easy, did you? Of course not! So here's the rub: if all switches do not have the same native VLAN configured on the trunk links, you will start to receive this error:

```
19:23:29: %CDP-4-NATIVE_VLAN_MISMATCH: Native VLAN mismatch discovered on
FastEthernet0/1 (40), with Core FastEthernet0/7(1)
19:24:29: %CDP-4-NATIVE_VLAN_MISMATCH: Native VLAN mismatch discovered on
FastEthernet0/1 (40), with Core FastEthernet0/7(1)
```

Actually, this a good, noncryptic error, so either you go to the other end of your trunk link(s) and change the native VLAN, or set the native VLAN back to the default. Here's how you'd do that:

```
S1(config-if)#no switchport trunk native vlan
```

Now, everything is coming up roses and our trunk link is using the default VLAN 1 as the native VLAN. Just remember that all switches must use the same native VLAN or you'll experience some serious grief!

Summary

This chapter was a great way to begin your journey through the wonderful world of wireless networking. You got a lot of information on wireless technologies in this chapter, plus some critical terms and basics to ensure that you're well prepared for things to come.

I started off by telling you about various wireless technologies and then described the differences between a PAN, WLAN, WMAN, and WWAN. After talking about the basic wireless networks you'll run into today, I described in detail the various wireless topologies like BSS, IBSS, ESS, and SSID.

You learned about antennas, repeaters, and some really important fundamentals regarding bridging. You then gained the crucial information on switches and how they work that you'll need for this rest of this book.

I wrapped up this chapter by delving into the necessary basics of switching and VLANs, as well as how access links, trunk links, and native VLANs all work within switched networks.

Exam Essentials

Remember what an IBSS is.   An IBSS is actually two things: an independent basic service set and an infrastructure basic service set. An independent BSS is an ad hoc or peer-to-peer network, and an infrastructure is a wireless network with an AP managing traffic between wireless clients.

Know what an aWBG is.   The autonomous workgroup bridge (aWGB) will establish a single wireless connection for multiple Ethernet clients to an upstream AP to appear as a nonstandard client.

Know what a uWGB is.   The universal workgroup bridge (uWGB) is used to support one Ethernet client connected through a WGB to an AP from another vendor to appear as a single normal client.

Understand when you would use a repeater.   A repeater is an AP that extends the cell of the root AP. The repeater AP must be set in the same frequency (channel) and must overlap by 50 percent.

Understand how to trunk and change the native VLAN on a switch port.   When configuring controllers, you must be able to configure a switch with access and trunk ports, set the encapsulation, and change the native VLAN. An example would look something like this:

```
Interface f0/1
switchport trunk encapsulation dot1q
switchport mode trunk
switchport trunk native vlan 50
```

Written Lab

1. True/False: A uWGB is used to connect a single Ethernet client through a WGB to a root AP from a non-Cisco device.

2. True/False: A aWGB is used to connect a single Ethernet client through a WGB to a root AP from a non-Cisco device.

3. If you have multiple APs connected in the same distribution system and they use the same SSID, what is this type of network called?

4. What is an ad hoc wireless network called?

5. True/False: Root bridges can communicate to other root devices.

6. What type of wireless network only goes 10m?

7. What is an MBSSID?

8. SSIDs can have how many characters configured?

9. True/False: The distribution system (DS) is used to trunk between switches so that MBSSIDs can be used.

10. The native VLAN on switches is VLAN 10 by default and cannot be changed.

Review Questions

1. Which of the following is true regarding uWGBs?

  A. The uWGB will establish a single wireless connection for multiple Ethernet clients to an upstream AP to appear as a nonstandard client.

  B. The uWGB is used to support one Ethernet client connected through a WGB to an AP from another vendor to appear as a single normal client.

  C. The aWGB is used to support a single wireless connection connected through a WGB to an AP from another vendor to appear as a single normal client.

  D. The aWGB is used to support one Ethernet client connected through a WGB to an AP from another vendor to appear as a single normal client.

2. Which of the following is true regarding aWGBs?

  A. The uWGB will establish a single wireless connection for multiple Ethernet clients to an upstream AP to appear as a nonstandard client.

  B. The uWGB is used to support one Ethernet client connected through a WGB to an AP from another vendor to appear as a single normal client.

  C. The aWGB is used to support a single wireless connection connected through a WGB to an AP from another vendor to appear as a single normal client

  D. The aWGB is used to support one Ethernet client connected through a WGB to an AP from another vendor to appear as a single normal client

3. Which best describes an ad hoc network?

  A. Basic service set

  B. Extended service set

  C. Independent basic service set

  D. Mesh network

  E. WiMAX network

4. How long can an SSID name be?

  A. 10 characters

  B. 32 characters

  C. 64 characters

  D. 128 characters

5. If you have a small wireless network that connects devices such as your PDA and wireless headset to your PC, what is this network called?

  A. WPAN

  B. WLAN

  C. WMAN

  D. WWAN

6. If you have a wireless network that connects buildings for very long distances and covers a large geographic area, what is this network called?

   A. WPAN

   B. WLAN

   C. WMAN

   D. WWAN

7. If you have a wireless network that connects users in your office together at high speeds, what is this network called?

   A. WPAN

   B. WLAN

   C. WMAN

   D. WWAN

8. If you have a wireless network that connects buildings in your campus area that are line of sight, what is this network called?

   A. WPAN

   B. WLAN

   C. WMAN

   D. WWAN

9. Which of the following is true of independent basic service sets (IBSSs)?

   A. They only provide high-speed wireless across a campus environment.

   B. They only provide high-speed wireless in a small area, are limited in scope, and are not scalable.

   C. The can only send wireless signals about 10m.

   D. You must have multiple APs in order to make this function.

10. What of the following is true of a basic service set (BSS)?

   A. They only provide high-speed wireless across a campus environment.

   B. They only provide high-speed wireless in a small area, are limited in scope, and are not scalable.

   C. The can only send wireless signals about 10m.

   D. They can use multiple APs to extend the WLAN.

11. The wired section of the network that is reachable through the AP is called what?

   A. IBSS

   B. Distribution system (DS)

   C. Ad hoc

   D. ESS

12. If you have an extended service set (ESS), how much do the cells need to overlap in order for users not to lose their connection when roaming from one AP to another?

    A. 5–7 percent

    B. 10–15 percent

    C. 20–25 percent

    D. 35–50 percent

13. If you have a repeater network with two APs, how much do the cells need to overlap in order for users not to lose their connection when on the repeating AP?

    A. 5 percent

    B. 10 percent

    C. 25 percent

    D. 50 percent

14. In order to create an ESS, what must you do to each AP?

    A. If you have two or more APs, they must be set to the same frequency channel.

    B. If you have more than one AP, they must be in separate VLANs.

    C. If you have two or more APs, they must have the same SSID name.

    D. One of the APs in the ESS must be in repeater mode.

15. If you have an ESS network, how does the client understand that it is communicating to different APs when it roams?

    A. It doesn't since the SSID is the same on all APs.

    B. The AP assigns a derived MAC address for each SSID on the AP.

    C. The MAC address of the hosts is stored in a MAC address table on the AP.

    D. The trunk link connected to the AP uses frame tagging to identify each frame.

16. If you have an AP with multiple SSID configured, what is this called?

    A. BSS

    B. ESS

    C. BSSID

    D. MBSSID

17. Which of the following networks have the best redundancy for wireless networks?

    A. IBSS

    C. MBSISS

    C. MESH

    D. ESS

18. Which of the following is true regarding bridged networks?

    A. Root bridges can only communicate to other root bridges.

    B. Nonroot bridges can only communicate to root bridges.

    C. Root bridges can only communicate to APs.

    D. Nonroot bridges can only communicate to nonroot bridges.

19. What are the two types of links on a switch? (Choose two.)

    A. Full-duplex

    B. Half-duplex

    C. Access

    D. Trunk

20. Which command will change the native VLAN on a switch to VLAN 50?

    A. `switch(config-if)#switchport trunk native vlan 50`

    B. `switch(config-if)#switchport native vlan 40`

    C. `switch(config)#switchport trunk native vlan 50`

    D. `switch(config-if)#switchport access native vlan 50`

Answers to Review Questions

1. A. This can be a tricky question. You need to pay attention if the question is asking about universal or autonomous WGBs. This question is about universal, which is nonproprietary and appears to a Cisco AP as a nonstandard client.

2. B. You need to pay attention if the question is asking about universal or autonomous WGBs. This question is about autonomous, which is proprietary and appears to a Cisco AP as a single normal client.

3. C. The ad hoc network, or peer to peer, is also called an independent basic service set (IBSS).

4. B. The service set identifier (SSID) is used to define the basic service area (BSA) and can be up to 32 characters long. You can have multiple SSIDs configured on an AP.

5. A. Wireless personal area networks are used to connect your devices in a small office area. The maximum distance for a WPAN is about 10m (30 feet) and the most common type of WPAN is Bluetooth.

6. D. Wireless wide area networks are typically cellular networks that cover a large geographic area but do not have the speeds of a WLAN.

7. B. Wireless local area networks are the most common type of wireless networks in use in our homes and offices today. They provide high speeds and can cover as much area as you need depending on how many APs you install.

8. C. Wireless metropolitan area networks are used in a campus environment to connect buildings together using bridges. In this type of network, all connections must be line of sight.

9. B. Independent basic service sets, or ad hoc networks, are typically not used in today's networks because they are no longer needed, but you can use them. Take two PCs with wireless capability and they can communicate, just like taking a crossover cable between two hosts with Ethernet.

10. D. Basic service sets, or WLANs, are the most popular LANs and can be very easy to set up. Just buy an AP and connect to your ISP and they typically just work. However, the commercial-grade APs, such as Cisco's, do not work out of the box. You must configure at least the SSID on them to make them work.

11. B. The wired section of the network that is reachable through the AP is called distribution system (DS). If you want to have an extended service set (ESS), all APs must be set to the same SSID and connect to the same DS.

12. B. The cells must overlap by at least 10 percent; 15 percent would be better, but the minimum must be at least 10 percent.

13. D. The cells in a repeater number must overlap by at least 50 percent.

14. C. To create an ESS, you must set the SSID the same on all APs. Also, the APs must all connect to the same distribution system (DS).

15. B. The APs all associate clients using a MAC address that they derive from the AP's MAC address. The clients, when handed off to another AP, see that they are communicating to another AP based on the new AP address they are receiving from the new AP they connected to.

16. D. An AP can have more than one SSID configured. If you have an AP with more than one SSID configured, this is called a multiple basic service set identifier, and it is a MAC address that the AP basically just makes up.

17. C. Bridges networks have a downside: if the central point gets disconnected, the whole network may go down. A mesh network has fully redundancy. If one AP drops out of the network, the neighbor APs simply find another route.

18. B. Nonroot devices, such as bridges, APs in nonroot mode, clients, and WGBs, can only communicate to root devices.

19. C, D. Switch ports are basically configured to be access links, which means they are a member of only one VLAN, or trunk links, which pass information about all, or many, VLANs.

20. A. To change the native VLAN on a switch trunk link, from the switch interface configured as a trunk, use the command `switchport trunk native vlan` *vlan#* (in this example, vlan 50).

Answers to Written Lab

1. False

2. True

3. Extended Service Set (ESS)

4. Independent basic service set (IBSS)

5. False

6. Personal area networks (PANs)

7. A multiple basic service set identifier is an AP configured with multiple SSIDs.

8. 32

9. False

10. False

Chapter

2

WLAN RF Fundamentals

THE CCNA WIRELESS EXAM TOPICS COVERED IN THIS CHAPTER ARE:

✓ **Describe WLAN fundamentals**

  ▪ Describe WLAN RF principles (antenna types, RF gain/loss, EIRP, refraction, reflection, etc.)

Chapter 1 got you off to a great start by equipping you with some important fundamentals about wireless networks and by providing you with some critical refresher information on LAN switching. With the basics covered, you're now ready to move on to more in-depth technical discussions about radio frequencies (RF) that wireless LANs (WLANs) use, which are radiated into the air from an antenna that creates radio waves. As I guide you through RF technology, I'll tell you about these antennas because understanding them is integral in order for you to gain a solid grasp of wireless technology.

RF waves can be absorbed, refracted, or reflected by walls, water, and metal surfaces, all of which can cause interference and result in low signal strength. Because of this innate vulnerability to surrounding environmental factors, wireless just can't offer us the same robustness as a wired network can, but clearly that doesn't mean people are going to opt out of wireless and run wired only. Wireless networking will become even more popular in the future! This is why it's so important for you to understand the various behaviors of radio frequency, and to also be aware of the factors that typically present challenges to making our wireless networks work well. To successfully mitigate the obstacles that can, and commonly do, give anyone designing and implementing a wireless network grief, you just have to really know about this technology!

But that's not all—I'm also going cover the operational requirements for successful wireless networking and show you how to use RF Math. And in addition to reading all about antennas, you're also going to learn about many types of wireless devices and other accessories.

With a working knowledge of these vital wireless fundamentals, you'll be nicely prepared for Chapter 3, where I'll cover something called spread spectrum: the way that our data is modulated into the air and sent through an antenna. I'll also discuss the various wireless standards and the different spread spectrum technologies that each use in that chapter, but for now, let's get started with a bit of background.

To find dynamic updates to this chapter, please go to www.lammle.com.

Introducing Radio Frequency (RF)

Wireless communication is definitely not a new technology, but employing it as a means to transmit the data that travels around our LANs is a relatively new implementation. Transmitting analog information in the way that radio stations do is a technology that's existed since 1900 or earlier—not exactly fresh, but the first official IEEE standard for wireless 802.11 LANS wasn't adopted until about 100 years later in 1997. Subsequent amendments to the 802.11 standard have followed over the years since and will certainly continue into the future.

Widespread adoption and application of the technology in the enterprise environment was slowed down by well-founded security concerns. These worries centered on unsecured data transmissions and the nasty potential hazard wireless networks posed of providing an easy way for bad guys to access the wireless network's Mother Ship—the related wired network and its resources through them. So it follows that it wasn't until specifically designed encryption mechanisms and security processes were developed to mitigate these vulnerabilities that the widespread use of wireless began to take off.

Even so, the performance of WLANs continues to trail that of wired networks, but the gap is becoming ever smaller with time and ingenious innovations like 802.11n, which uses a process called Multiple In, Multiple Out (MIMO). Via 802.11n, a WLAN's performance may reach 600Mbps —a far cry from the original 802.11 standard transmission rate of a meager, dribbling 1Mbps!

RF Basics

It all starts when an electrical signal like one that represents data from a LAN needs to be transmitted via radio waves. First, the signal is sent to an antenna where it is then radiated in a pattern that's determined by the particular type of antenna. The pattern radiated from an antenna is an electrical signal called an alternating current, and the direction of the signal's current changes cyclically. This cycle creates a pattern known as a waveform. The waveform has peaks and valleys that repeat in a pattern, and the distance between one peak or valley and the next is known as the wavelength. The wavelength determines certain properties of the signal—for example, the impact of obstacles in the environment.

Some AM radio stations use wavelengths that stretch well over a thousand feet, or 400–500 meters, but our wireless networks use a wavelength that's smaller than your outstretched hand. Believe it or not, satellites use tiny waves that only measure about one millimeter!

Because cable, fiber, and other physical media impose various limitations upon data transmission, the ultimate goal is for us to use radio waves to send information instead. A radio wave can be defined as an electromagnetic field that radiates from a sender, which hopefully gets to the intended receiver of the energy that's been sent. A good example of this concept is the electromagnetic energy we call light that our eyes can interpret and send to our brains, which then transform it into impressions of colors. Figure 2.1 shows the RF spectrum that we use today to send our wireless data.

FIGURE 2.1   RF spectrum

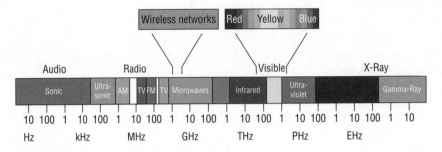

It is good that our eyes can't see these kinds of waves, because if we could, we would be so bombarded with them that we wouldn't be able to see much else!

When traveling through the air, certain wave groups are more efficient than others depending on the type of information being sent because they have different properties. So it follows that different terms are used to define different signals generated in the transmitter when they're sent to the antenna to create the movements of the electrons generated within an electric field. This process creates an electromagnetic wave, and we use the terms frequency and wavelength to define them.

The frequency determines how often a signal is "seen," with one frequency cycle called 1 hertz (Hz). The size or distance of the cycle pattern is called the wavelength. The shorter the wavelength, the more often the signal repeats itself, and the more often it repeats, the higher its frequency is considered to be when compared with a wavelength that repeats itself less often in the same amount of time. To get a picture of this, check out Figure 2.2.

FIGURE 2.2   Frequency

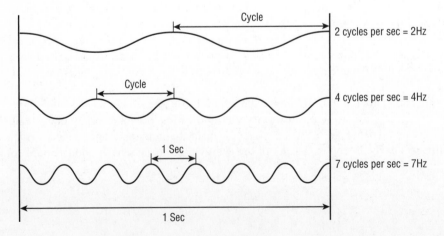

Here are some important RF terms to remember:

- 1Hz = The RF signal cycle occurs once a second
- 1MHz = The signal cycle occurs one million times a second
- 1GHz = The signal cycle occurs one billion times a second

Also good to know is that lower frequencies can travel farther, but provide less bandwidth. Higher frequencies have a wavelength with fast repeat times, which means that although they can't travel long distances, they can carry higher bandwidth. Another important term to get cozy with before we move on and talk about how RF is affected by many factors, is amplitude. Amplitude refers to the strength of the signal, and is commonly represented by the Greek symbol α.

It has a profound effect on signal strength because it represents the level of energy injected into one cycle. The more energy injected in a cycle, the higher the amplitude. The term *gain* is used to describe an increase in the RF signal.

In Figure 2.3, the top signal has the least amplitude or signal strength and the bottom example has the greatest amplitude or signal strength. By the way, that's the only difference among each of these signals—all three have the same frequency because the distance between the peaks and valleys in them are the same.

FIGURE 2.3　Amp

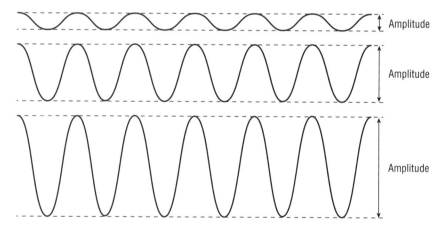

Okay, let's say you're playing an electric guitar that you've plugged into your amp. If you turn up the amp's volume knob, the increased or amplified signal would look like the one on the bottom. Of note, attenuation also happens naturally the further the signal moves from the transmitter—another reason for the use of amplifiers. We can even use certain antennas to give us more gain, which in combination with the transmitter power can determine our signal's ability to go the distance.

A downside to amps is that they can distort the signal and/or overload and damage the receiver if too much power is pushed into it. So finding the right balance takes experience, and yes, sometimes parting with some good ol' cash, to score better equipment.

Radio Frequency Behaviors

When you're armed with a solid understanding of RF signals, the challenges inherent to wireless networking and the things you can do to mitigate factors that negatively affect transmissions become oh-so-much-easier to deal with! So coming up next, I'm going to cover vital RF characteristics.

Free Space Path Loss

Attenuation is defined as the effect of a signal over the time, or length of a cable or other medium. The signal is weakened the further it travels from the transmitting device. Free space path loss is similar because it's a limiting factor with regard to the distance that RF signals can successfully travel and be received properly. We call it "Free Space Path Loss" because it isn't caused by environmental obstacles. Instead, it's simply a result of the normal attenuation that happens as the signal gradually weakens over the distance it travels. Figure 2.4 shows an example of free space path loss.

FIGURE 2.4   Free space path loss

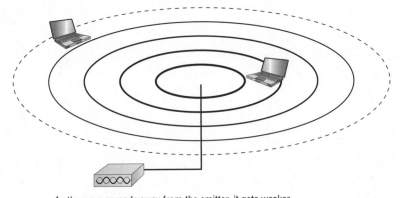

As the wave spreads away from the emitter, it gets weaker.

There are two major factors on both ends of a transmission that determine the effects of free space path loss; the strength of the signal delivered to the antenna and the type of antenna it's delivered to. The AP can amplify the signal to a certain extent because with most APs and many client devices, signal strength can be controlled. This type of signal gain is called *active* gain.

As I pointed out back in Chapter 1, a directional antenna focuses the same amount of energy in one direction that an omnidirectional antenna sends horizontally in all directions. This results in a signal of the same strength being able to travel farther. In this scenario, the antenna provides what we call *passive* gain, which means that it comes from the particular shape of the antenna pattern itself.

On the receiving end, the same factors come into play. First, the receiver has a certain listening strength, called received sensitivity, and second, the shape of the receiving antenna has the same kind of effect on a signal that the shape of a sending antenna does. This means that two highly directional antennas that happen to be aimed perfectly at each other can carry a signal of the same strength much farther than two omnidirectional antennas.

Absorption

Since our world isn't flat and has lots of objects on it, as a signal radiates away from the antenna, it will invariably encounter obstacles like walls, ceilings, trees, people, buildings, cars—you get the idea. Even though the signal can pass through most of these obstacles, a price is paid when it does so in the form of decreased amplitude. Earlier, you learned that amplitude is the height and depth of each wave in the pattern that represents the signal strength. So when the signal manages to pass through the object—which, surprisingly, in most cases it will—however, it always emerges on the other side weaker. This is what's referred to as *absorption*, because the people and things the signal passes through actually absorb some of its energy as heat.

To get a picture of the absorption phenomenon, check out Figure 2.5.

FIGURE 2.5   Absorption

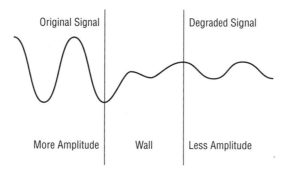

Important to note is that the amount of signal degradation depends on the nature of what it has passed through. Clearly, drywall is not going to cause the same amount of signal degradation that concrete will, and yes, there are some materials that will block the signal completely. This is why we perform site surveys—to define where the problem areas are and figure out how to get around them by strategically placing AP(s) where they will be able to function with the least amount of obstruction.

Reflection

Now you know that absorption occurs when a signal travels through an obstacle and loses some of its energy, right? Well, *reflection* occurs when a signal strikes an object at an angle instead of directly. When this happens, some of the energy will be absorbed, but some will reflect off at an angle equal to the angle at which it struck the object. Figure 2.6 illustrates reflection.

FIGURE 2.6   Reflection.

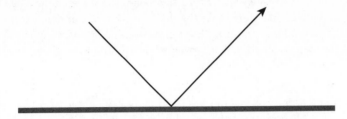

Reflection occurs when RF waves bounce off an object and are
reflected into a new direction.

The exact ratio of the amount absorbed to the amount reflected depends on how porous
the material is that the signal ran into and the angle at which it hit the material. The more
porous the material, the more of the signal's energy will be absorbed by it.

Another thing that influences how much of the signal is reflected and how much is
absorbed is the signal's frequency. Signals in the 2.4GHz range can behave differently than
those in the 5GHz range. So just remember that these three factors influence absorption/
reflection ratio:

- Angle of the signal

- Frequency of the signal

- Nature of the surface

One of the main problems reflection causes is a phenomenon called multipath.

Multipath

Multipath occurs when reflection is occurring. Remember, there's lots of stuff around that
reflected signals can bounce off before they finally arrive at the receiver, and since these
bounced signals took a longer path to get to the receiver than the ones that took a direct
path, it makes sense that they typically arrive later. This is illustrated in Figure 2.7.

This is definitely not a good thing—because they arrive later, they'll be out of phase with
the main signal, as shown in Figure 2.7. Remember how the signal wavelength has a recur-
ring pattern? Well, if the pattern of the main signal doesn't line up with that of the reflected
signal, they're out of phase—and how much they're out of phase varies in degrees.

This is ugly because out-of-phase signals are degraded signals, and if those signals are
120–170 degrees out, multipath can weaken them. This concept is known as *downfade*. It
gets worse too—if they arrive 180 degrees out, they cancel each other entirely, a nasty effect
suitably called *nulling the signal*. If it's your lucky day and they go full circle, the rogue
signals arrive 360 degrees out and blam—they're right back in phase and arrive at the same
time. This boosts the amplitude or signal, and is known as *upfade*.

Clearly, being able to deal with multipath events well is an important skill, but no worries. I'll cover strategies for multipath mitigation a little later in this chapter, but for now

just one last thought: although I just said how bad multipath can be (and it can be!), IEEE 802.11n can take advantage of this to get higher speeds, as you'll learn in Chapter 3.

FIGURE 2.7 Multipath

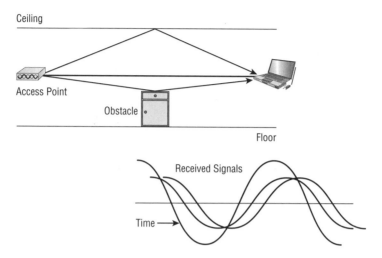

Refraction

Refraction refers to a change in the direction of a signal as a result of it passing through different mediums. Since this mostly happens when a signal passes from dry air to wet, or vice versa, it's more of a concern with long-range outdoor wireless links. Figure 2.8 shows how refraction might look.

FIGURE 2.8 Refraction

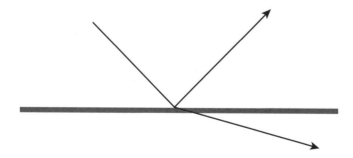

As the figure shows, refraction occurs when waves pass through a heterogeneous medium and some of the waves are reflected and others are bent. Drier air tends to bend the signal away from the earth, whereas humid air tends to bend the signal toward earth.

Diffraction

Diffraction happens when a signal bends around an object. Think about what happens when you throw a rock into a quiet pool of water. As soon as your rock plunks in, it sends perfect rings of waves radiating outward from where it sank in all directions. If these waves slam into an object in the pool, you can see the wave bend around the object and change direction. RF signals do this too, and when they do, we experience this in the form of dead spots in places behind, say, a building.

Figure 2.9 shows a simple example of what diffraction may look like with an RF signal. Diffraction is commonly confused with refraction, but the two are vastly dissimilar because diffraction bends the RF, whereas in refraction the RF bounces.

FIGURE 2.9   Diffraction

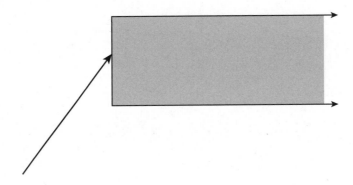

Scattering

Scattering is a lot like refraction, but the difference is that when signals strike an object, or objects, their scattered reflections bound off in many unpredictable directions instead of just bouncing back off at an angle pretty much equal to the angle at which it hit the object. This phenomenon is caused by the attributes of the object or objects. Here are some objects and conditions that can cause scattering:

- Dust, humidity, and micro-droplets of water in the atmosphere and rain
- Density fluctuations within a given object and its surface irregularities
- Uneven surfaces like moving water and tree leaves

Figure 2.10 shows what scatter might look like to an RF signal.

The worst thing about scattering is—you guessed it—its unpredictable nature, which makes mitigation efforts more than just a little difficult!

All this brings me back to that all-important site survey. I'm repeating this because nothing is more important than performing a thorough one before and after you design a WLAN! There's just nothing else that can help you to accurately identify, predict, and mitigate RF behaviors; determine proper AP placement; select the right type of antenna(s); or even make adjustments to the physical environment itself if possible (like trimming some trees).

FIGURE 2.10   Scattering

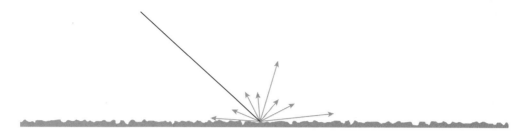

RF Operational Requirements

Even in WLAN environments that exist mostly in fantasy where most or none of the afore-mentioned potential problems are present, there are still certain operational requirements if you want your WLAN to work well—or even at all. Those absolute necessities that affect the performance of WLANs, and in some cases, directly affect whether or not they'll function at all, are what I'm going to cover next.

Line of Sight

Okay—so while it's true that in an indoor scenario where there are usually not as many things signals can bounce off of, they still exist there too. So again, do that site survey! Whether your WLAN will only cover a small outside or inside area, signals can usually travel through and even bounce off a few objects and still reach the receiver in fine shape. But when you're dealing with a larger coverage area using omnidirectional and semidirectional antennas, like in an outdoor area—especially when creating a point-to-point wireless bridge between, say, two buildings—something known as *line of sight* becomes critical for success. And if you're faced with creating a long-distance wireless connection using highly directional and/or dish antennas, line of sight becomes even more critical.

I want you to understand that line of sight is not as simple as having the center of the two antennas properly lined up. That's visual line of sight, and RF line of sight and visual line of sight are two different things. Regarding WLANs, RF line of sight is what you need, and to help you understand that, first let's review how spread spectrum technology works.

In narrowband RF, the signal is set to a single frequency and stays there. In spread spectrum, although people talk about channels and the like, the signal is actually being spread across a range of frequencies (which is discussed in Chapter 3). What I mean by this is that when we say that a device is using "Channel 6," that channel is actually 22MHz wide and the signal is spread across the entire 22MHz range. Furthermore, if a signal is spread out like this, it means that all of it, or at least a certain percentage of it, must be received in order for it to be interpreted well.

The following obstructions might obscure a line-of-sight link:

- Topographic features, such as mountains
- Curvature of the earth
- Buildings and other man-made objects
- Trees

Even if the visual line of sight is perfect, the RF line of sight can still be lacking if the distance is so far that the curvature of the earth gets in the way. Check out Figure 2.11.

FIGURE 2.11   Line of sight.

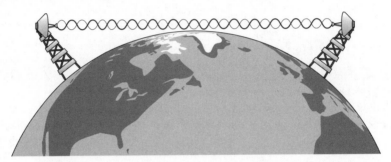

Line of sight disappears at 6 miles (9.7 km) because of the curvature of the earth.

Look at Figure 2.12. See that tree? Okay, I know it's not actual size, but what it signifies is that objects can block even a small part of what we call the *Fresnel zone*, which is closely related to RF line of sight, and what you're going to learn about next.

Fresnel Zone

The Fresnel zone (see Figure 2.12) is an elliptical-shaped area between the transmitter and receiver that must be at least 60 percent clear for the signal to be received properly. In Figure 2.12, even though visual line of sight looks just great, there's major blockage of the football-shaped area around the center line of the signal. This is very bad. You've personally experienced RF line-of-sight blocking if you've ever had a tree branch grow a lot over the summer and interfere with your satellite dish or TV antenna.

FIGURE 2.12   Fresnel zone

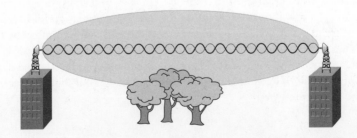

Interestingly, these zones are in alternating bands, with the inner band being in phase, the next being out of phase, and then the next one in phase again. So if one of us could figure out how to block only the out-of-phase band while leaving the in-phase bands alone, it just might be a technological breakthrough. (Hasn't happened yet!)

RSSI and SNR

We've logged a lot of ink discussing signals and signal strength, but so far, I haven't told you how these are measured. There are two terms used to discuss signal strength: received signal strength indicator (RSSI) and signal-to-noise ratio (SNR). RSSI is designed to describe the strength of the signal received, and SNR refers to the ratio of the signal to the surrounding RF noise that is always present in the environment.

First, let's talk about RSSI, which is a measure of the amount of signal strength that actually arrives at the receiving device. It's a grade value ranging from 0 to 255. For each grade value, an equivalent dBm (decibels relative to a milliwatt) value is displayed. For example, 0 in the scale may equal –95dBm and 100 might be –15dBm. So 0 would equal a much greater loss of signal than 100 would.

I'll get into dBm in more detail soon, but for now understand that dBm is not an absolute measure; it's a relative one. What I mean by *relative* is that it's a value referenced against another value—in this case, milliwatts. Decibels are used to measure an increase or decrease in power as opposed to an absolute value, meaning that decibel values come through as positive (gain) and negative (loss). RSSI values are negative and represent the level of signal loss that can be experienced en route with the card still able to receive the signal correctly. Most manufacturers will have a table listing the RSSI that's required at each frequency.

RSSI values can't be compared from one card vendor to another because each company typically uses a different scale. For example, Company A might be using a scale of 0 to 100, while Company B is using a scale from 0 to 60. Since the scales are different, the resulting RSSI values can't be compared, right?

Figure 2.13 depicts the relationship between these values.

FIGURE 2.13   SNR

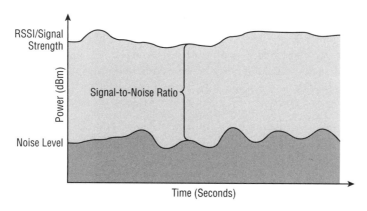

SNR is a critical comparison of the amount of signal as compared to the surrounding noise. If the level of noise is too close to the level of signal, the signal can't be picked out from the noise and understood. Think of this as someone whispering in a really loud room. A higher value is good for SNR.

Now, let's have some fun doing RF math! Let me show you how easy this can be.

RF Math

Radio frequency math is a method used to determine various values used in your wireless network radios. Here are a few examples:

- The amount of power delivered by a transmitter
- The amount of passive gain introduced by an antenna
- The amount of loss introduced by connectors

To understand how to use RF math, you first have to understand two types of measurement values and their relation to each other. So let's get started!

RF Values

Two types of measurement values can be used to describe signal strength: relative and absolute. An absolute value is a static measurement taken at a point in time, whereas a relative measurement attempts to describe a change in a value from one point to another. You can use both in RF math, but as you'll see, it's usually a whole lot easier to use relative measurements—it's these values that you'll most often see used in the industry when describing signal power. Even so, I'll tell you about both.

Absolute Measurements

The types of absolute measurements are:

Watt   A watt (W) refers to the measure of energy spent, emitted, or consumed per second, and is named after James Watt. One watt represents 1 joule (J) of energy per second. A joule is the amount of energy generated by a force of 1 newton (N) moving one meter (m) in one direction. A newton is the force required to accelerate 1 kilogram (kg) at a rate of 1 meter per second squared (m/s2). So there you have it—and I know, it's a mouthful! To put it as simply as possible, a watt is 1 volt with 1 ampere of power.

mW   A milliwatt (mW) is fraction of a watt. You will encounter the use of this term in describing the output of transmitters. It takes 1000 milliwatts to equal 1 watt of power.

Relative Measurements

Using absolute measurements is all well and good, but we should focus on changes in power, either gain or loss, that are easier to understand using relative measurements. That's because once you've settled on a single point of reference, you're stuck with it and forced to describe the change from that reference point only. So with that, let's get into the relative values commonly used in RF math and for describing component behavior:

dB   A decibel (dB) is a general term that describes either positive or negative change. The difference in the types I'll go over next relate to the dB as the value that's being referenced against. Basically, think of this concept as the starting point.

dBi   A dBi is referenced against an isotropic antenna—a theoretical antenna that radiates in all directions equally that doesn't really exist. This theoretical antenna is important because it allows us to compare one antenna to another, since the antenna will be labeled in reference to the same point of comparison.

Check out Figure 2.14, which displays this theoretical radiation pattern.

FIGURE 2.14   dBi

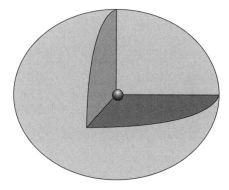

What do we see here? This is a sort of cross-section where the antenna is the little gradient-gray round ball in the center and the larger blue ball represents the area of waves radiating out from it equally in all directions. So, what dBi measures is essentially the effective gain of an antenna compared to an isotropic antenna, and it tells us that the greater the dBi value, the higher the gain, and the higher the gain, the more acute the angle of coverage.

dBd   Okay—here's something real and not theoretical—a dBd is referenced against a dipole antenna, which does actually exist. The radiation patterns of a dipole antenna are shown in Figure 2.15; the shape is probably familiar to you.

FIGURE 2.15   Dipole

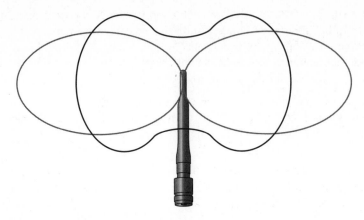

So how does dBi compare to dBd? Converting one to the other is simply a matter of adding or taking away 2.14:

- dBi = dBd + 2.14

- dBd = dBi – 2.14

Therefore, the dBd measures the effective gain of an antenna as compared to a dipole antenna.

dBm   A dBm is referenced against a milliwatt. The arbitrator reference point is 1 milliwatt, so 1 milliwatt equals 0dbm, or no change from the reference point.

Gain and Antennas

It's important to understand how gain is used with antennas. Here are some final goodies about gain and antennas:

- Remember that intuitively, gain will always be measured as a positive number and loss as a negative number.

- Antennas will never introduce loss into the equation, but some accessories, such as connectors, will.

- The signal will also suffer loss, as we have discussed, from free space path loss and other behaviors.

All right—now that you've got the terms nailed, it's time to put everything all together and learn how to use relative measurements when working with wireless. Always keep in mind that the goal is to ensure that enough signal strength reaches the receiver in order for the data to have integrity.

As I said earlier, 1mw = 0dBm. Milliwatt is the point of reference, so 0dBm reflects no change from the reference point. We could use a log calculator to determine the exact value for each degree of decibel referenced against a milliwatt if we wanted to be perfectly accurate. This is exactly what I did in Table 2.1, and I also rounded to simplify things.

TABLE 2.1   dBm to mW (0dBm = 1mW)

dBm	mW	dBm	mW	dBm	mW
0	1	11	12.5	21	128
1	1.25	12	16	22	160
2	1.56	13	20	23	200
3	2	14	25	24	256
4	2.5	15	32	25	320
5	3.12	16	40	26	400
6	4	17	50	27	512
7	5	18	64	28	640
8	6.25	19	80	29	800
9	8	20	100	30	1 watt
10	10			36	4 watts

Nice, huh? But just so you know, this level of accuracy isn't necessary unless you're dealing with long-distance point-to-point bridging scenarios. No worries, though—I'll go over a cool, shorthand method for working with decibels for you next.

Rule of 3s and 10s

Examine the graph closely for a minute—you know, like you would those illusory dot matrix pictures you stare at and, suddenly, you see the picture? If you checked it out, you probably discerned the following relationships:

- Increase of 3dB = double transmit (Tx) power
- Decrease of 3dB = half the power
- Increase of 10dB = 10× power
- Decrease of 10dB = 1/10 power

You can use this "rule of 3s and 10s" to perform RF math calculations. Here's what I mean—if a radio transmitter emits a signal at 100mW and an amplifier introduces a 3dB gain into the signal, the resulting signal will be double to 200mW. Taking that another step, if the antenna introduces 10dB of gain, then the signal leaving the antenna will now be 2000mW. And then there's negative dB as well to consider. If the free space path loss reduces the signal by 10dB, then the receiving antenna will get the signal back down to 200mW. Let's look at this in more detail and go through some examples calculating something called EIRP.

EIRP

With a bit of work, you can nail the output power of effective isotropic radiated power (EIRP), which is the amount of signal, or power, leaving the antenna. According to the Federal Communications Commission (FCC), do not measure the output at the radio; you must take everything into consideration to be in compliance—connectors, cables, antenna, and so forth. Also, you need to measure the output from the antenna. Figuring out your EIRP is not an exact science, nor does the calculation have to be exact. But by using a simple formula, you can get close enough to follow the FCC rules and be in compliance. The formula for EIRP looks like this:

EIRP = Tx power (dBm) + Antenna Gain (dBi) – Cable Loss (dB)

The pieces of your wireless network that you take into consideration when calculating EIRP are shown in Figure 2.16.

FIGURE 2.16   EIRP

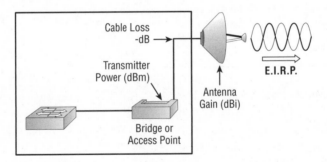

As you can see, this formula factors in cable loss, which occurs at variable rates per feet depending on the grade and type of the cable, but typically you can consider that a 50-foot cable is 3.35dB loss. A 100-foot cable would have 6.7dB loss, as a rule of thumb. Other things, like attenuators and connectors, can also create loss, and amps can add more power. I'll talk about them in the Antenna and Accessory section later in this chapter.

Here's an example of this calculation, including all possible influences:

- Your transmitter emits a 100mW signal: +20dB
- The antenna introduces 6dB of gain: +6 dB
- 50 feet of cable introduces 3.35dB of loss: –3.35dB
- An attenuator introduces 3 more dB of loss: –3dB
- An active amp provides 10dB of gain: +10dB

First, you've got to nail down the net gain:

Start with the transmitter power	+20dB	Equals 100mW
Add the antenna gain	+6dB	Each 3dB doubles
Total power with antenna gain	+26dB	100mW × 2 × 2 = 400mW
Add the power from the amp	+10dB	10dB equals 10× power
Total power with amp	+36dB	400mW × 10 = 4000mW
The same as 4W	+36dB	4000mW = 4W

Now let's take a look at our loss:

Start with the total power gain	+36dB	Equals 4W
Subtract loss from 50 feet of cable	-3.35dB	Round to −3dB, which divides by 2
Total power minus cable	+33dB	4W/2 = 2W
Subtract loss from attenuator	-3dB	Again divides by 2
Total power minus attenuator	+30dB	2W/2 = 1W

That first table shows +20dB + 6dB + 10dB = +36dB, which is 4W, right? Because 20dB is 100mW, and we double it twice (3dB + 3dB) to go from 100mW, to 200mW, and finally to 400mW. Nice...we've got a net gain of 26dB, but now we need to increase it tenfold (+10dB), which is how we get our 4 watts (36dB). So now, let's take out our loss, laid out in the second table—36dB, minus 6.35dB (we'll just subtract 3dB twice because it is close enough)—which takes us to about 30dB, or back to about 1W transmit power.

Here is another example. You have a 20dBm (100mW) transmitter using a 50-foot cable (3.35dB loss) and a 21dBi dish antenna. What is the EIRP? 20dB is 100mW. We need to add 21dB, or increase the power tenfold twice. We start at 100mW, increase it tenfold to 1W, then increase it tenfold again, and get 10W. That a lot of power! But we still need to take out our loss, which is 3.35dB, or we just cut the power in half . Starting at 10W, we'll cut it in half to 5W.

Laid out as a table equation, it looks like this:

Start with the transmitter power	+20dBm	Equals 100mW
Add the antenna gain	+21dBi	Increase power tenfold twice
Total power with antenna gain	41dbm	10 Watts
Subtract loss from 50 feet of cable	-3.35dB	Cut the power in half
Total power minus cable	37.65dB	5 Watts

Let's do one more. Suppose you have an AP with an output of 100mW (20dB), connected to a 10dBi antenna, with a 100-foot cable. What is your EIRP?

Pretty simple: 100Mw times 10 is 1W, or 30dB. With a 100-foot cable, we need to cut the power in half twice. So starting at 1W, we'll get 500mW, and cut it in half one more time to get our answer of about 250mW.

Laid out as a table equation, it looks like this:

Start with the transmitter power	+20dBm	Equals 100mW
Add the antenna gain	+10dBi	Increase power tenfold
Total power with antenna gain	30dbm	1 Watts
Subtract loss from 100 feet of cable	-6.7dB	Cut the power in half twice
Total power minus cable	23.3dB	250mW

WLAN Antennas

Transmitting antennas convert electrical energy into RF waves, and receiving ones turn RF waves into electrical energy. The physical dimensions of an antenna, such as its length, are directly related to the frequency at which the antenna can create and receive waves. An RF antenna is used to convert high-frequency RF signals on a transmission line—either a cable or waveguide—and propagate waves into the air. The electrical fields emitted from antennas are called beams or lobes.

Antenna Principles

It makes sense that the radiation pattern a given antenna creates is determined by the specific physical characteristics of that antenna. Things like the material the antenna's made of, as well as its thickness and shape, are all attributes that will affect its radiation pattern.

Clearly, this pattern is actually three-dimensional, but most vendors only publish a two-dimensional view. The pattern could be circular or narrow and focused in one direction.

There are two views of the radiation pattern. The H-plane depicts how it would be seen if you were looking down on it from the top and demonstrates how the signal radiates ahead, behind, left and right, but not up or down. That's up to the E-plane, or elevation chart, which shows you the pattern you would see if you were standing beside the antenna. The E-plane demonstrates the way that the signal radiates ahead, behind, up and down, but not left and right. So if you want a three-dimensional picture, all you've got to do is combine them to get a picture of how the pattern radiates in the real world. Some vendors refer to the E-plane as the "vertical" plane.

Figure 2.17 illustrates both views and how they relate to each other.

FIGURE 2.17   Radiation

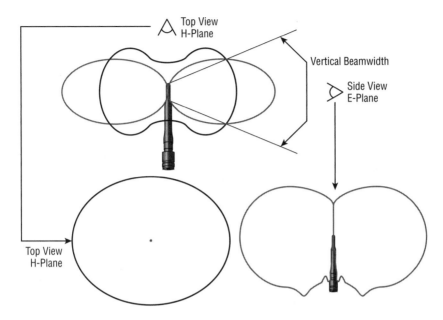

The strength of the pattern is expressed in dBi. Vendors pick a reference point wherever the signal is strongest (which is usually in front of the antenna) and assign that point a value of 0dB. The other points are labeled –xdB to represent how much the signal is decreased in that particular direction. If you want, you can set up the antenna and verify this by measuring the RSSI at various points.

Polarization

Polarization describes the orientation of the electrical field emitted from the antenna. This wave can move in three ways:

Vertical Polarization   The waves move up and down in a linear fashion.

Horizontal Polarization   The waves move left and right in a linear fashion.

Circular Polarization   The wave circles as it moves forward. The polarization is determined by the antenna positioning.

In Figure 2.18, each of these patterns is displayed so you can compare them.

FIGURE 2.18 Polarization

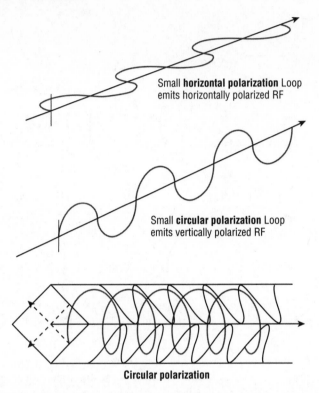

Small **horizontal polarization** Loop
emits horizontally polarized RF

Small **circular polarization** Loop
emits vertically polarized RF

Circular polarization

Antennas can use any type of polarization, but it should be the same on both ends. That's because if one antenna is positioned straight up but the other one is positioned at an angle, signal reception will be degraded since the antenna polarity is mismatched. This is a seriously more important factor when you are dealing with outdoor links rather than indoor ones.

 NOTE   Most antennas are vertically polarized.

Diversity

Remember multipath, where the main signal and reflected signals arrive at the receiver out of phase? Good! Then you'll also recall that this causes degradation and even possible nulling of the signal. Because of the diversity of available antennas today, this snag is not nearly so common anymore.

Check out diversity in Figure 2.19.

FIGURE 2.19   Diversity

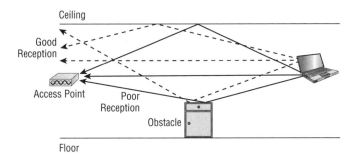

   The AP manufacturer typically implements antenna diversity by placing two antennas on the device about a wavelength away from each other. When the AP receives a frame from a wireless station, it uses the preamble of the frame to test both antennas and automatically switches the rest of the frame to the antenna with the best signal. Multipath rarely affects both antennas equally, so if it happens to be degrading the signal on one antenna, the other one will either be just fine or not affected as badly, which is why this is a way to solve the multipath problem.

Antenna Types

Antennas fall into three major categories, differing mainly in their radiation patterns. Here's where that site survey is again imperative, because different types of antennas will be better suited for different implementations. The same amount of energy is radiated by the transmitter, regardless of which antenna type you use. The difference is how the antenna focuses the energy, which is demonstrated in Figure 2.20.

FIGURE 2.20   Antennas

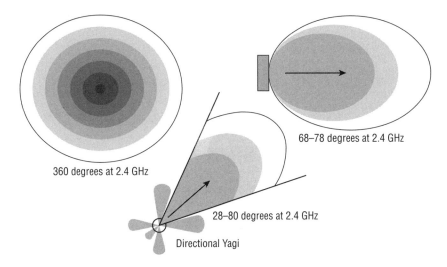

Think of an old garden hose with no fancy attachments added to it. Sure, if you turn the water on, it will certainly flow out, just not very impressively. But what if you crimp the end? Well, just like sticking your thumb into the stream coming from the hose, the flow will be focused and it will shoot the water a much greater distance. This is pretty much how a directional antenna focuses the same amount of power to achieve a much greater range in the specific direction it's pointed. An omnidirectional antenna will radiate in all directions but for a much shorter distance because the force of the flow is dispersed in all directions simultaneously. The two antennas produce the same amount of power; they just apply it differently.

Omnidirectional

An omnidirectional antenna sends a signal of the same strength in all directions, but not completely—it's usually only omnidirectional in the azimuth plane. You can see this general pattern by looking back to Figure 2.20 at the 360-degree antenna in the upper-left corner. But if you were to draw it out on paper, it would like something Figure 2.21.

FIGURE 2.21   Omnidirectional

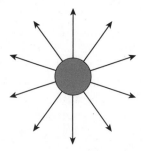

We can also get high-gain omnidirectional antennas. A good example would be if we were to continue to push in on the ends of the balloon; we can get a pancake effect with very narrow vertical beamwidth but very large horizontal coverage. This type of antenna design can deliver very long communications distances, but has one drawback when mounted high above your client devices: poor coverage directly below the antenna, as shown in Figure 2.22.

FIGURE 2.22   High-gain omnidirectional

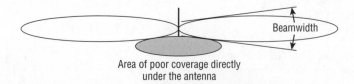

With high-gain omnidirectional antennas, this problem can be partially solved by designing in something called *downtilt*. An antenna that uses downtilt is designed to radiate at a slight angle rather that at 90 degrees from the vertical element. This does help for local coverage, but reduces effectiveness of the long-range ability.

Dipole

The *dipole* radiation pattern is shown in Figure 2.23, which in this case, depicts a 2.14dBi dipole that also happens to be called a rubber duck because of its shape. Don't worry—kind of an ink blot thing—it doesn't really look much like a rubber duck to me either! Anyway, just remember that it's not all that powerful and is designed for indoor use.

FIGURE 2.23   The basic omnidirectional: dipole

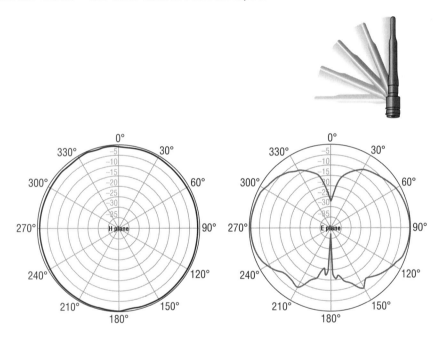

The dipole will radiate everywhere within the H-plane, but the E-plane (up and down) will be restricted to a doughnut-shaped radiation pattern; it has a hole in the middle.

Ceiling Mount

If you're still indoors but want better and more coverage than a dipole installation will give you, use a ceiling mount instead, which will increase coverage by 5.2dBi. Remember, this is passive gain created by the physical characteristics of the antenna that isn't achieved through amplification. The gain is gained by reducing the E-plane to make it flatter, which results in the H-plane's greatly enhanced range. The radiation pattern is shown in Figure 2.24.

FIGURE 2.24   Ceiling mount

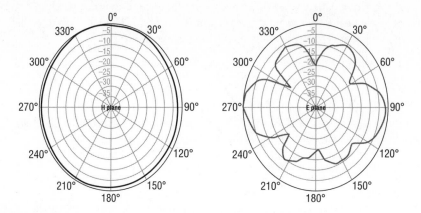

Mast Mount

Just as it sounds, this installation is secured onto a mast or pole or column. Antennas used in these situations require a different pattern than ceiling mounts, and are installed head up instead of head down as you would install a ceiling mount. By increasing the gain, as a result of the physical structure of the antenna, you can increase the range at the cost of flattening the pattern. Two possible radiation patterns are depicted in Figure 2.25.

FIGURE 2.25   Mast

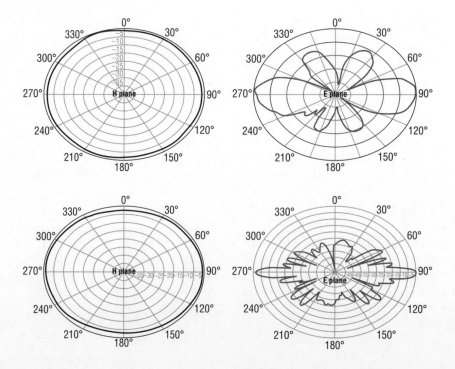

Dual Patch

A dual patch antenna consists of two patch or wall antennas placed back to back. This is so you can radiate in two directions with gain in both directions. A good place for this type of configuration would be in the middle of a long hallway like an aisle in a retail environment. Focus the signal strongly down the hall in both directions at the cost of narrowing the beam. A dual patch and its radiation pattern are pictured in Figure 2.26.

FIGURE 2.26　Dual patch

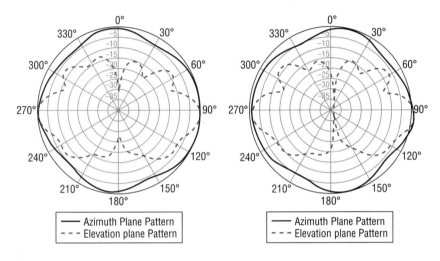

Semidirectional

A semidirectional antenna operates just as the name implies. It focuses the signal, just not as extremely as it would via a highly directional antenna. These antennas can be used in situations where you want to cover a somewhat broad area, but you don't need coverage in all directions.

Patch

Single-patch antennas operate exactly like you think they would—like half of a dual patch. They focus the beam in one direction at the expense of other directions, but as a result, you get some great gain in the direction you've pointed it. The pattern of an 8.5dBi patch antenna is shown in Figure 2.27.

FIGURE 2.27   Patch

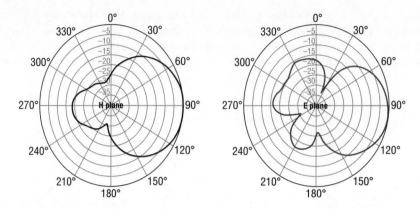

Yagi

The last semidirectional antenna became known as the antenna that one can make out of a Pringles can. This refers to the enclosure used to protect the actual elements in the antenna, as shown in Figure 2.28. It has quite a distinctive radiation pattern—Rorschach Test, anyone? As you can see, it will give you some coverage behind the main lobe, as well as various side lobes that come out.

FIGURE 2.28   Yagi

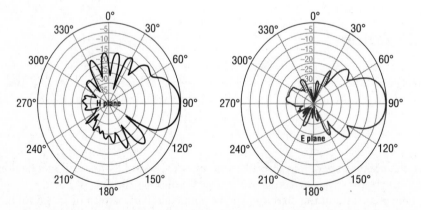

Highly Directional

Highly directional antennas take beam focusing to its extreme. The beam is very tightly focused, so it gives you some great range. Let's take a look at a Cisco highly directional antenna, the parabolic dish.

Parabolic Dish

The radiation pattern of the parabolic dish is similar to that of a yagi. The antenna element is mounted in a dish structure that helps to achieve greater focus. These are usually used in outdoor wireless bridging applications where the alignment of the two antennas is extremely important. This is because the beam is so narrow, even a really small mistake on one antenna can cause the beam to miss the receiver by hundreds of yards! Figure 2.29 show a parabolic dish and its radiation pattern.

FIGURE 2.29   Parabolic highly directional

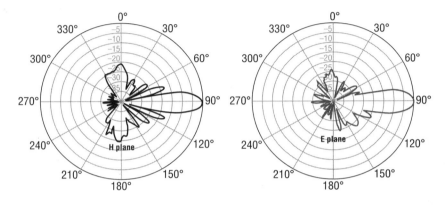

Antenna Accessories

There are lots of other pieces and parts involved in transmitting besides just the antenna and the transmitter. Each of them can have an impact on the EIRP created by the system.

Attenuators

In some cases you actually want to decrease the EIRP. Why? Because the FCC regulates the amount of signal that can come out of an antenna in various situations, so sometimes you've got to trim the signal back to comply with regulations. This task is what you use an attenuator for—because it's designed to introduce a certain amount of loss, just buy the one that introduces the dB loss you need. You simply place this device on the cable between the radio and the antenna.

Amplifiers

Remember—amplifiers are used to boost the signal, but unlike antenna gain that's known as passive gain, amplification is active gain. Just place the amp on the cable running from the radio to the antenna and it boosts the signal before it reaches the antenna. Keep in mind that you should place it as close to the antenna as possible for maximum gain.

Figure 2.30 shows an amp that was created for use outside of the United States. Why can't we use this amp here in the U.S.? The reason is that it has Cisco connectors on it and the FCC mandates that all connectors manufactured in the U.S. have proprietary connectors. That way, only the manufacturer of the radio can create antennas and amps. No one can add a high gain amp (such as the one shown in Figure 2.30) and send out more power than is legally regulated by the FCC. (FCC rules and regulations are covered in Chapter 4.)

FIGURE 2.30   High-gain amp

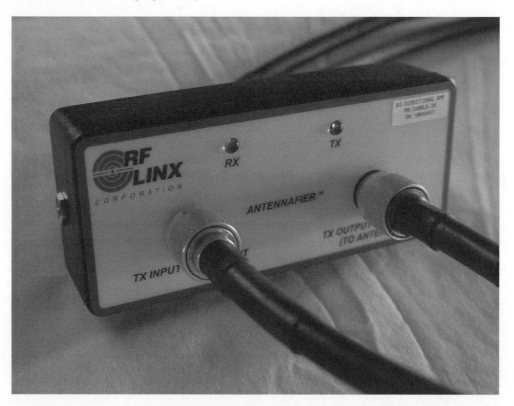

A friend gave me the amp shown in Figure 2.30, but I won't use this amp because it would be illegal for me to connect to my network and I would never do anything that would break the FCC rules and regulations by transmitting too much power.

Real World Scenario

AMP Your Wireless!

One of my friends had an active amp, just like the one shown in Figure 2.30, that provided 33dB of power (2W of gain!). By connecting this amp to his Cisco wireless AP, he was able to see the AP in downtown Boulder, Colorado, even though he lives a couple miles above the city, in the mountains. By using this active amp—with very short cables producing virtually no loss and using a high-gain semidirectional antenna attached to his AP—he was able to see his network in Boulder without any problem. With this amp and the high-gain antenna connected, he has a wireless network of 1,000 watts. To begin, we have 20dB output from the AP, plus 33dB from the amp, and a 10dBi passive antenna; 30dB is 1W; and adding 20dB from the AP, we increase the power tenfold a total of four times. Starting at 100mW, we go to 1W, 10W, 100W, and 1,000W. With no loss, he could see the network down in Denver, or so he said! It's all fun until someone goes to jail.

However, my friend called me and told me that he could see the network but could not connect to the wireless network and he really wanted to connect from his favorite pub in downtown Boulder using his WLAN. Do you know why he was not able to connect to his high-gain network, which had more power than even the local radio station could dish out? I'll discuss this in more detail in Chapter 4, but the wireless frames cannot travel that far before timing out. Not only that, unless he had a high-gain antenna on his laptop, he might be able to receive the frames but he cannot transmit that far. So, other than causing a lot of interference in Boulder (and maybe all the way to Denver International Airport) for a day or two—plus having fun in the pub watching people trying to connect to this new, free wireless network that popped up—there was no value in my friend amping his wireless network to this amount of power. Glad he didn't get caught!

Lightning Arrestors

These are not what you might think. Lightning arrestors are used to protect the system components and connection back to the wired network from a nearby lightning strike, because the system just can't protect itself against a direct hit on the antenna. But a lightning arrester will offer protection when there is a strike nearby that causes a surge of powerful electricity in the line. It shunts that power to the ground and saves the equipment behind it in the system.

Another approach to this little problem is to use a run of fiber cable somewhere in the line. Since it won't conduct electricity, it can also serve as a sort of firewall to stop a surge. See Figure 2.31.

FIGURE 2.31   Adding a fiber connection

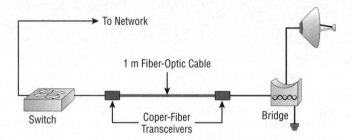

Please understand that adding a lightning arrestor won't help with a direct strike. If you have a direct strike on your wireless dish, your network will be fried, which is why we buy business insurance. Adding a fiber connection will help you if you do receive a direct strike, but nothing will protect you completely. Make sure the fiber connection is at least one meter long (3.38 feet).

Splitters

Splitters are used to send the signal out to more than one antenna, or to take a signal from an antenna pointed in one direction and send it to another antenna pointed in a different direction. A splitter and its use are shown in Figure 2.32.

FIGURE 2.32   Splitter

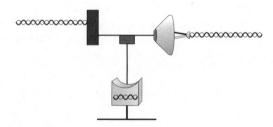

Splitters have a couple of downsides:

- Loss of gain—they will introduce up to 4dB of loss.
- Throughput will be cut in half.

Because of this, splitters are normally something to avoid using if possible.

Cables and Connectors

The final components in the system are the cables and the connectors, and both of them introduce loss. The good news is that when you buy either one, the documentation included usually indicates the amount of loss per connector, or per foot of cable. Another good thing to consider with each of these components is something known as *impedance*, or resistance of the cable and connectors causing a loss in signal strength. If there's an impedance mismatch in the cables and connectors, it will introduce a possible large loss. But again, this topic should be covered in the documentation and is something you should remember to stop and read.

A variety of connector types can be used with WLAN implementations. Most Cisco APs use RP-TNC (reverse-polarity threaded Neil-Concelman) connectors. Other types used are:

SMA   Subminiature version A

RP-SMA   Reverse-polarity SMA

SMA-RS   SMA Reverse Sex

MC   Multipoint controller

MMC   The connectors you will find on a client PC card

SMA   Subminiature version A

RP-SMA   reverse-polarity SMA

SMA-RS   SMA Reverse Sex

MC   multipoint controller

MMC   these the connectors you will find on a client PC card

Okay, nice, now let's stop and have a short discussion on what I covered in this chapter.

Summary

Wow! I'll bet you're glad you got this chapter out of the way right? After all, we covered a lot of ground in this chapter, and most of the hike wasn't through terrain abounding with glorious scenery. No—pretty desolate and dry, I know! But you made it through it; you learned all about RF behaviors, such as absorption, free space path loss, reflection, refraction, diffraction, multipath, and scattering.

You also learned about operational requirements, including the application of RF math. We covered types of decibels and the difference between relative and absolute measurement.

Finally, you discovered the many types of antennas, their radiation patterns, and other important components like amplifiers and attenuators.

This chapter leads nicely into Chapter 3, where you'll learn how data is modulated, transmitted, and received on an antenna.

Exam Essentials

Understand how multipath occurs.   Multipath occurs when a signal arrives at the receiver via multiple paths out of phase with one another, resulting in a signal loss, also called fading.

Be able to describe the Fresnel zone.   In an outdoor point-to-point application, the Fresnel zone must be at 60 percent clear for proper transmission.

Know that decibel measurements are relative rather than absolute.   The dBi measures the change in the gain introduced by an antenna as referenced against an isotropic radiator.

Remember your 3's and 10's when calculating dB.   A 3dB increase in power is a doubling of the power, and a 10dB increase is a tenfold increase in the power.

Define EIRP.   EIRP is a measurement of the power leaving an antenna after factoring in the radio gain, connector and cable loss, and then adding antenna gain.

Understand antenna polarization.   Antennas can be polarized either vertically or horizontally. Omnidirectional antennas are usually polarized vertically.

Understand antenna performance.   Antenna performance can be measured with respect to its beamwidth (narrowly focused or widely focused) and its gain (range). The more gain, the tighter the beamwidth.

Written Lab

1. What is the term to describe when multiple signals arrive out of phase on an antenna?

2. To make a tight beamwidth between a point-to-point link, what do you need to add more of?

3. The area that must be clear between two antennas is called the _____ zone.

4. 0dBm is equal to how many milliwatts?

5. True/False: Adding 6dB doubles your power.

6. True/False: Adding 10dB doubles your power twice.

7. Why would you use two antennas on an AP?

8. If you measure your power output at the antenna, what is this called?

9. _____ refers to a change in direction of the signal as a result of it passing through different mediums.

10. _____ happens when a signal bends around an object.

Review Questions

1.   What is the term used to describe the RF behavior that occurs when reflected signals arrive at the receiver out of phase with the main signal?

     A.   Absorption

     B.   Refraction

     C.   Multipath

     D.   Diffraction

2.   Which type of antenna produces the least amount of passive gain?

     A.   Omnidirectional

     B.   Yagi

     C.   Semidirectional

     D.   Parabolic dish

3.   Which antenna type is sometimes called a rubber duck because of its shape and appearance?

     A.   Dipole

     B.   Yagi

     C.   Parabolic dish

     D.   Patch

4.   Which of the following behaviors occurs when an RF signal changes direction as a result of passing from dry air to wet air?

     A.   Multipath

     B.   Refraction

     C.   Scattering

     D.   Absorption

5.   What percentage of the Fresnel zone must be clear of obstructions for a clean signal?

     A.   20 percent

     B.   40 percent

     C.   60 percent

     D.   70 percent

6.   Which of the following is used to measure the signal strength compared to the surrounding RF noise?

     A.   RSSI

     B.   VSWR

     C.   SNR

     D.   EIRP

7. Which of the following represents the strongest signal as measured in RSSI?

   A. −15dBm

   B. −60dBm

   C. −75dBm

   D. −90dBm

8. Which of the following is an absolute measurement?

   A. dBm

   B. dBi

   C. dBd

   D. mW

9. Which of the following is referenced against an antenna that radiates perfectly in all directions?

   A. dBm

   B. dBi

   C. dBd

   D. dB

10. Which of these values is equal to 0dBm?

    A. 10mW

    B. 100mW

    C. 1mW

    D. 1W

11. Which of the following is not true?

    A. +3dB = doubling of power

    B. +10dB = 10× the power

    C. −10dB = doubling of power

    D. −3dB = cutting the power in half

12. If a radio transmitter produces 3dB of gain, the cable introduces 3dB of loss, and the antenna creates 5dB of passive gain, what is the EIRP?

    A. +3dB

    B. +5dB

    C. −11dB

    D. +11dB

13. If it is determined that the EIRP is +10dB, what is the answer when converted to absolute values?

   A. 1W

   B. 200mW

   C. 10mW

   D. 2mW

14. EIRP is signal measured:

   A. After the radio transmitter

   B. After the radio transmitter and the cable loss

   C. After the radio transmitter, cable loss, and antenna gain

   D. As received at the receiver

15. Which RF behavior is antenna diversity designed to mitigate?

   A. Refraction

   B. Free space path loss

   C. Multipath

   D. Absorption

16. At 1Hz, how often does the signal occur?

   A. One million times a second

   B. Once a second

   C. One thousand times a second

   D. One billion times a second

17. What does amplitude measure?

   A. The number of cycles per second

   B. The level of energy injected into each cycle

   C. The distance between each cycle

   D. The speed of the cycles

18. If you have a 20dB AP, with a 16dBi antenna, with a 50-foot cable connecting the AP to the antenna, what is your EIRP?

   A. 500mW

   B. 1W

   C. 2W

   D. 4W

19. If you have a 20dB AP, with a 10dBi antenna and a 50-foot cable connecting the AP to the antenna, what is your EIRP?

   A. 200mW

   B. 500mW

   C. 1000mW

   D. 2000mW

20. If you have an AP with an output of 20dB, connected to a 21dBi antenna and a 100-foot cable connecting the AP to the antenna, what is your EIRP?

   A. 200mW

   B. 500mW

   C. 2.5W

   D. 5W

   E. 10W

Answers to Review Questions

1. C. Multipath, also called fading, occurs when reflected signals arrive at the receiver out of phase with the main signal. This causes degradation of the main signal, possibly even canceling or nulling the signal.

2. A. Passive gain is introduced through the physical characteristics of the antenna. It is a result of the amount of focus applied to the signal. The more tightly the beam is focused, the more gain that is created. Since omnidirectional antennas apply the least focus and send in all directions, they introduce the least passive gain. All the other choices are types of semi- or highly directional antennas.

3. A. The dipole antenna is also called a rubber duck because it looks like a duck beak and can be tilted to change polarity.

4. B. Refraction occurs when an RF signal changes direction as a result of passing from dry air to wet air. Drier air bends the signal away from Earth and wet air bends it toward Earth.

5. C. The Fresnel zone must be 60 percent clear of obstructions for a clean signal.

6. C. The signal-to-noise ratio (SNR) is used to measure the signal strength compared to the surrounding RF noise.

7. A. SNR is always a negative value measuring signal loss; therefore –15dBm is the strongest signal represented.

8. D. Any measurement that is given in decibels is a relative measurement. Therefore, only milliwatt (mW) is an absolute measurement.

9. B. An isotropic radiator is a perfect antenna that radiates in all directions. The value that references an antenna's gain against this antenna is dBi.

10. C. The point of reference for 0dBm, representing no change, is 1 milliwatt.

11. C. Gain is measured with positive dBm and loss with negative dBm. +3dBm is a doubling of power and 10dBm is 10× the power. Therefore, C is incorrect because –10dBm would be cutting the power by a power of 10.

12. B. When calculating EIRP, gains and losses introduced by the various components can be added and subtracted to arrive at the EIRP, which is the amount of signal leaving the antenna. In this case, it is (+3dB) + (–3dB) + (5dB) = +5dB.

13. C. Since 0dB = 1mW, then +0dB increases the signal by a power of 10, arriving at 10mW.

14. C. EIRP is the signal measured at the antenna, after the radio transmitter, cable loss, and antenna gain.

15. C. Antenna diversity is designed to mitigate multipath. It does this by sampling both antennas and selecting the antenna suffering the least (if at all) from multipath.

16. B. At 1Hz, the signal occurs once a second.

17. B. Amplitude measures the strength of the signal or the power injected into each cycle.

18. C. 20dB is 100mW. We need to add 16dBi; we'll start by adding a tenfold increase in power, which is 1000mW, or 30dB, and then add 6dB by doubling the power twice. Starting at 1W, add 3dB, which gives us 2W; then add 3dB, which takes us to 4W. We still need to take into account the loss of the 50 feet of cable, which is 3.35dB. This cuts the power in half, so our answer is about 2W, or 33dB.

19. B. 20dB is 100mW. We'll start by adding a tenfold increase in power, which is 1000mW, or 30dB. But we still need to take into account the loss of the 50 feet of cable, which is 3.35dB. This cuts the power in half, so our answer is about 500mW, or 27dB.

20. C. 20dB is 100mW. We'll start by adding a tenfold increase in power twice for the 21dB passive antenna, which first is 1000mW, or 30dB, and then another tenfold increase, to 10000mW (10W). But we still need to take into account the loss of the 100 feet of cable, which is about a 7dB loss. This cuts the power in half twice, so our answer is just above 2.5W.

Answers to Written Lab

1. Multipath or fading

2. Gain. You can do this by installing a high-gain antenna to get a tighter beamwidth.

3. Fresnel

4. 1mW

5. False. Adding 6dB doubles your power twice.

6. False. Adding 10dB increased the power by tenfold.

7. To resolve multipath issues.

8. EIRP

9. Refraction

10. Diffraction

Chapter

3

Spread Spectrum Technologies and Modulations

THE CCNA WIRELESS TOPICS COVERED IN THIS CHAPTER ARE:

✓ **Describe WLAN fundamentals**

- Describe basics of spread spectrum technology (modulation, DSSS, OFDM, MIMO, Channels reuse and overlap, Rate-shifting, CSMA/CA)

Equipped with what you've learned in Chapter 2, you're now prepared to discover some important ways used for transforming the electrical or optical signals traveling around the wired portion of the network into radio waves, which can then be subsequently converted back to their original form on the other end.

A great place to begin is by exploring two general categories of transmission methods commonly used today.

To find dynamic updates to this chapter, please see www.lammle.com.

Transmission Methods: An Overview

As you've probably guessed, you can create RF transmissions a number of different ways. Even though WLANs don't use narrowband transmission, it's still a good thing to go over because it's great to understand for the sake of comparison.

Two important ways that narrowband transmission and transmission methods used by WLANs differ are:

- The amount of power used to transmit
- The way interference is dealt with

In narrowband transmission, the signal is sent on a single frequency; a good example of this transmission type is a radio station. In narrowband, very little bandwidth is used. Check out Figure 3.1.

In order to get around that interference issue, the signal is broadcasted at a much higher power level than a spread spectrum transmission would be. The amount of power is regulated by the FCC and has to be licensed so that the frequencies and controls used by each frequency in a given area won't interfere with one another. See Figure 3.2.

The developers of spread spectrum took a different approach to handling interference and also developed a method of dealing with the unlicensed nature of the frequency band used by WLANs.

FIGURE 3.1   Narrowband RF

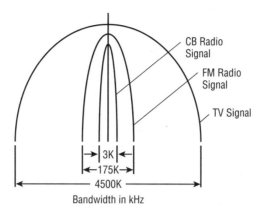

FIGURE 3.2   Narrowband transmission

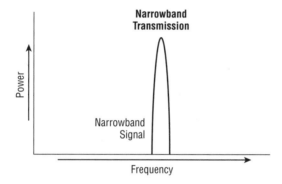

Spread Spectrum

The people who worked on the 802.11 specifications designing wireless networks and protocols clearly had to consider that other devices would cause interference, and also needed to find a way to mitigate the impact of that interference occurring on the RF signal that's used by WLANs. A key issue they confronted is the fact that wireless networks use an unlicensed frequency band, meaning that unlike with licensed bands, you don't have the FCC to arbitrate the use of the band. In answer to this dilemma, they decided to use something that's been around since the 1940s, called spread spectrum technology.

As the name suggests, in spread spectrum the signal is "spread" across a whole band of frequencies instead of being broadcasted on a single frequency as in narrowband. The receiver on the other end is set to listen to the same range of frequencies, as shown in Figure 3.3.

FIGURE 3.3   Spread spectrum

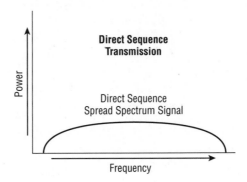

There are two great benefits to this:

- The signal doesn't have to use as much power to overcome narrowband interference.
- The signal can be degraded by interference and still be received in fairly good condition.

So how does spread spectrum achieve this? Well, the answer depends on the specific type of spread spectrum technology you're using. Each type employs a different method to use the minimum amount of power and still avoid interference.

There are two types of spread spectrum:

- Frequency hopping spread spectrum (FHSS)
- Direct sequence spread spectrum (DSSS)

Even though there are two main types of spread spectrum, all current WLANs today only use DSSS or methods derived from it. I'll talk about these methods in more detail soon, but for now, understand that the FHSS that's used by some cordless phones and Bluetooth devices might cause interference on WLANs. Another reason that both technologies are referred to as spread spectrum is because both FHSS and DSSS use more than just a single peak frequency, thereby spreading the signal over a larger part of the spectrum.

Let's take a look at both of these technologies next.

Frequency Hopping Spread Spectrum

Frequency hopping spread spectrum isn't the technique of choice for either vendors or the IEEE 802.11 committee, which is one of the reasons why you won't find FHSS used by today's WLANs. As I said, FHSS is what cordless phones and Bluetooth employ, so it's already getting pretty crowded.

FHSS modulates the data signal with a carrier signal that changes in a random pre-defined hop sequence of frequencies over time. These changes also occur over a wide frequency band, with a spreading, or hopping, code establishing which transmission frequencies are used. The receiver is set to the same code, again allowing it to listen to the incoming signal at the right time and frequency so it can receive the signal properly.

So you get that FHSS uses a radio that "hops" from frequency to frequency at predetermined times on predetermined channels, right? What you probably didn't know is that manufacturers use 75 or more frequencies per transmission channel with the maximum *dwell time*—time spent during a specific hop at a particular frequency—that's established by the FCC at 400ms. Figure 3.4 shows an example of what an FHSS system can look like when transmitting onto the RF.

FIGURE 3.4   FHSS

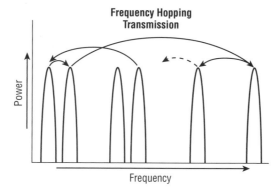

Any 1 or 2Mbps FHSS system must utilize at least 75 channels, and it must use every channel before reusing any of them. But since the duration of time spent at that frequency is typically only 300 to 400 milliseconds before hopping along to another one, the interference source impacts only a small amount of data at any given time. But as I'm pretty certain you've experienced, there will still be interference since the whole 2.4GHz band is used from end to end.

Encoding and Modulation

The rates possible to obtain from FHSS, DSSS, or a few other methods that I'll talk about in a bit are a function of the modulation and encoding method that's employed by the technology. FHSS uses Gaussian frequency shift keying (GFSK) to encode the data. Two-level GFSK (2-GFSK) uses two frequencies, to represent 0 and 1. Four-level GFSK (4-GFSK) uses four frequencies with each frequency representing 2 bits (00, 01, 10, and 11).

So to sum this up, FHSS requires little power and is usually used in short-distance situations like personal area networks. It mitigates interference by simply "dancing" around it. Unfortunately, FHSS only achieves 1 and 2Mbps while utilizing the 2.4GHz frequency range.

Direct Sequence Spread Spectrum

If you judge DSSS solely by its ability to deal with interference, it's not much better than FHSS. Where it shines lies in its superior capacity for speed.

Let me start with two important facts. *Encoding* is the process of transforming a single digit that's to be sent into a longer sequence of symbols in a way that part of the sequence can be lost but still understood on the receiving end. *Modulation* is the way in which the symbols are represented through the radio wave itself.

Now back to combat with those ubiquitous interference issues: DSSS creates a redundant bit pattern or sequence for each bit that's transmitted. A nice benefit of this is that if any bits in the bit pattern are damaged in transmission, we've got a good chance at recovering the original data from the redundant bits. The cost of this advantage is that you end up with a high amount of overhead.

Still, think of it like this: 11 symbols are sent in parallel, not one at a time. So at a rate of 1 per use, or 1Mbps, the DSSS 22MHz wide channel can contain 11 parallel symbols and get you 1Mbps of actual throughput. I know this sounds better, but it's still not good enough for today's networks.

This redundant information, called chips or pseudorandom noise (PN) codes, are encoded into the RF signal. Every data bit is expanded into a string of chips called a chipping sequence, also known as the Barker sequence.

A narrow band of data is "spread" over 22MHz wide channels, and the chips allow the receiving end to reconstruct the data back to its original, narrowband form. This graphic shows how a DSSS signal looks on a frequency analyzer:

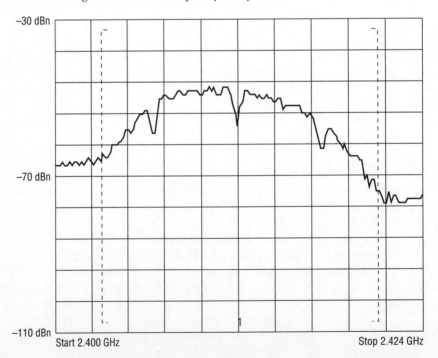

As you can see here, the more chips we send, the more redundant the data, which provides better data, but at the cost of lower throughput. The DSSS output is somewhat rounded, with the most important bits located in the middle, and the redundant chips on the sides. This means that the bit you're trying to send has a better chance of getting through—even through interference and/or distortion.

I'll get to the FCC rules regarding this in more detail in Chapter 4. For now, remember this chipping rate mandated by the FCC:

▪ 1 and 2Mbps: 11 chips per bit of data

It looks something like this. If the data bit was 0110, the chipping code would be:

      0=10110111000   1=01001000111

and the transmitted data would be:

10110111000   01001000111   01001000111   10110111000

0   1   1   0

I know it seems pretty crazy that this much information is sent just to get a few bits of data, but the designers assumed the worst and designed accordingly. It's a good thing they did, too, because by doing this, the same information is sent over multiple frequencies simultaneously. So if there's any interference, it's still possible that data will be picked up by the receiving device in a readable form.

DSSS Modulation

DSSS uses a type of modulation called differential binary phase shift keying (DBPSK) for 1Mbps DSSS, and differential quadrature phase shift keying (DQPSK) for 2Mbps DSSS.

DBPSK makes use of changes in the radio wave to represent the 1s and 0s. There are only two possibilities in shifts. When a value to be sent is a 0, no change is made at all to the wave. When a value of 1 is to be sent, the direction of the wave will be changed 180 degrees.

Check out Figure 3.5 and notice that the two times that the wave changes 180 degrees are when the next symbol to be sent is a 1.

FIGURE 3.5 DSSS

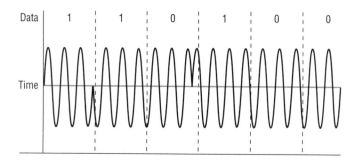

The receiver can interpret these shifts as 1s and 0s.

DQPSK groups the symbols into sets of two wherein the alteration of the wave is meant to represent two symbols at a time rather than one as in DBPSK. Since there are four possible combinations of 1s and 0s when grouped as two (00, 01, 10, 11), there need to be four actions that can be taken on the wave to represent each of the four possibilities:

00   Take no action on the wave at all.

01   Rotate the wave 90 degrees.

10   Rotate the wave 270 degrees.

11   Rotate the wave 180 degrees.

The possibilities are shown in Figure 3.6.

FIGURE 3.6   DQPSK

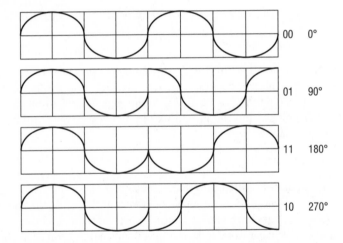

The end result is that twice as many chips can be sent in the same amount of time by bundling them into groups of two while still using the same Barker code method.

So this is great in that it helps make sure we get 1 and 2Mbps throughput, even with interference, but we need something better to help us even touch 5.5Mbps and 11Mbps data rates. To attain rates like those, we need a different modulating technique called complementary code keying (CCK). Instead of using 11 bits like Barker, CCK uses groups of 4 bits, and encodes them in chips of 8 bits each. CCK works by using a combination of phase changes and employing DQPSK (four "rotations" of 90 degrees). Doing things this way achieves the loftier 5.5Mbps rate. And we can really go big using 8 bits per symbol to achieve 11Mbps.

The cool thing here is that all three modulation schemes are compatible and can coexist by using standardized rate-switching procedures—nice! In the year 2000 this was awesome, but as you have probably guessed, it's almost sadly unusable by today's standards. Why?

Well, as I mentioned, 1, 2, 5.5, and 11Mbps just won't cut it today, so we can't use Barker with its 11 chips and CCK and related rotation methods to get the higher speeds we so need today. For this little snag, it's orthogonal frequency-division multiplexing (OFDM) to the rescue! But before we get into OFDM, let's tie together some of this information you just learned to make sure you've really got it.

IEEE Standards and DSSS

I'll cover the IEEE standards extensively in Chapter 4, but let's look at how all this information relates to the IEEE standards that use DSSS. The original IEEE standard for WLAN was 802.11 created in 1997, and included both FHSS and DSSS in it. 802.11, with no amendments or letters, is sometimes called 802.11 prime. The modulation and encoding it uses at various speeds is shown here:

Modulation	Encoding	Total Data Rate (Mbps)
DBPSK	Barker 11	1
DQPSK	Barker 11	2

802.11b

The first amendment to the 802.11 standard was 802.11b. This amendment didn't include FHSS, and was concerned with increasing the data rate by charging the modulation and encoding while maintaining backward compatibility with 802.11. The modulation and encoding that 802.11b uses at various speeds is shown here:

Modulation	Encoding	Total Data Rate (Mbps)
DQPSK	CCK 16 Codes	5.5
DQPSK	CCK 128 Codes	11

Orthogonal Frequency Division Multiplexing

Okay—on to orthogonal frequency division multiplexing. To get higher speeds, we need to use something other than DSSS to encode our data. The higher rate standards use a type of OFDM, which happens to be the modulation technique used by 802.11a and 802.11g.

Subchannels

The 802.11a and 802.11g standards use OFDM with a system of 52 carriers (sometimes referred to as subcarriers) that are modulated by by BPSK, QPSK, 16-QAM and 64-QAM. OFDM can resist multipath problems (by carrying data within these subcarriers that make it more resistant to RF interference) and presents lower multipath distortion—big reasons why we use it in our higher-speed wireless networks today!

The OFDM encoding scheme works by splitting the 20MHz radio channel into 52 smaller subcarriers. To get a picture of this, check out Figure 3.7.

FIGURE 3.7   OFDM

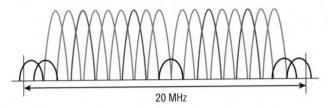

Forty-eight of the 52 subcarriers are used to transmit data, with the remaining 4 sub-carriers used as pilot carriers for monitoring path shifts and intercarrier interference (ICI). These subcarriers, depicted in Figure 3.7, are then transmitted simultaneously at different frequencies to the receiver. In OFDM, the carrier is 20MHz, not 22MHz, and can be any size—the bigger, the better, because bigger means higher throughput. Notice in the next graphic that the OFDM output shown on my trusty analyzer is not rounded as it is with DSSS. It's shaped more like a mesa than a peak or mound.

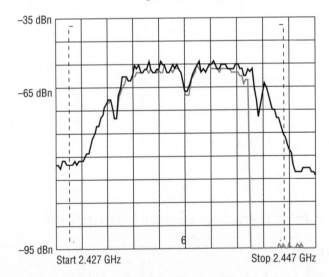

In OFDM, multiple carriers (or tones) are used to divide the data across the available spectrum, similar to frequency division multiplexing (FDM). But in an OFDM system, each tone is considered to be orthogonal, which means the tone is independent or unrelated to adjacent tones, so it doesn't require a guard band. Since OFDM only requires guard bands around a set of tones, it's a whole lot more efficient spectrally than FDM. Also, because OFDM is made up of many narrowband tones, narrowband interference will degrade only a small portion of the signal, which has little to no effect on the remainder of the frequency components. And this allows us to use less redundant chips.

OFDM's spread spectrum technique distributes the data over these 52 carriers, which are spaced apart at precise frequencies. This spacing approach helps prevent demodulators from seeing frequencies other than their own.

OFDM works by breaking one high-speed data carrier into several lower-speed sub-carriers, which are then transmitted in parallel. Each high-speed carrier is 20MHz wide and is broken up into 52 subchannels, and each is approximately 300KHz wide. OFDM uses 48 of these subchannels for data, whereas the remaining four are used for error correction. Coded orthogonal frequency division multiplexing (COFDM) delivers higher data rates and a high degree of multipath reflection recovery thanks to its encoding scheme and error correction—sweet!

Encoding and Modulation with OFDM

With OFDM, we use the following encoding and modulation techniques:

BPSK   Each subchannel in the OFDM implementation is about 300KHz wide. At the low end of the speed gradient, binary phase shift keying (BPSK) is used to encode 125Kbps of data per channel, resulting in a 6,000Kbps, or 6Mbps, data rate.

The rule that BPSK uses for alerting the waves to represent 1s and 0s is similar to the DSSS rule but slightly different. Remember, in DSSS, the rule is "when the next value is 0, do nothing, and when the next value is 1, change direction 180 degrees." In BPSK the rule is when the next value is the same as the last, do nothing to the wave, but if it's different, change direction 180 degrees.

We can also increase the density of information per subcarrier to 187.5Kbps per subcarrier and achieve 9Mbps via BPSK.

QPSK   To go higher than 9Mbps and do better than DSSS using CCK, OFDM uses something called quadrature phase shift keying (QPSK). Interestingly, QPSK appears to be the same as DQPSK, but note the D is missing. Anyway, QPSK uses a rule similar to DQPSK that's also used in DSSS, but again, it's slightly different. QPSK is more like a reversed version of DQPSK, and it's definitely more robust. Alternatively, OFDM is inherently more robust when it comes to handling interference and multipath, and it uses a more complex coding scheme so it doesn't need to use the differentiated technique.

To compare the rules for DQPSK and QPSK, check out Table 3.1.

TABLE 3.1   DQPSK and QPSK

Bit Pattern	DQPSK	QPSK
00	Take no action on the wave at all.	Rotate the wave 270 degrees.
01	Rotate the wave 90 degrees.	Rotate the wave 180 degrees.
10	Rotate the wave 270 degrees.	Rotate the wave 90 degrees.
11	Rotate the wave 180 degrees.	Take no action on the wave at all.

Using quadrature phase shift keying (QPSK), you can double the amount of data encoded to 250Kbps per channel, yielding an improved 12Mbps data rate.

QAM   With quadrature amplitude moderation (QAM), another possible alteration is made to the wave in the form of amplification. We now have four different amplitudes being used, creating 16 possibilities and resulting in what's called 16-level quadrature amplitude modulation (16-QAM). Figure 3.8 shows the original 90-degree directions used in DSSS with the added capacity that having four different amplitudes offers.

FIGURE 3.8   QAM

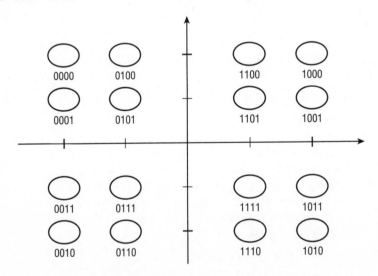

QAM's four different amplitudes are good because by using 16-QAM, encoding 4 bits per hertz, we can achieve a data rate of an even more enhanced 24Mbps. The 802.11a standard specifies that all 802.11a-compliant products must support these basic data rates, but it also lets the vendor extend the modulation scheme beyond 24Mbps.

Data rates of up to 54Mbps are achieved via 64-level quadrature amplitude modulation (64-QAM), which yields 8 bits per cycle, or 10 bits per cycle, instead of a measly 4. This get us a total of up to 1.125Mbps per 300KHz channel, and combined with 48 available channels, results in a 54Mbps data rate because we're reducing the amount of redundant bits. 128-QAM is theoretically possible, but not one network vendor supports it because there aren't any redundant bits. Remember, the more bits per cycle (hertz) that are encoded, the more susceptible the signal will be to interference. The signal will also be limited to a shorter range unless the power output is increased, and if you do that, distortion becomes a factor, which is why power output is limited at higher frequencies.

Applications

The next two amendments to the 802.11 standard, 802.11a and 802.11g, achieved higher speeds through the use of the modulation and coding techniques. To see how these are utilized, check out Table 3.2.

TABLE 3.2 OFDM Modulation Data Rates

Modulation with Subchannels	Data Rate per Subchannel (Kbps)	Total Data Rate (Mbps)
BPSK	125	6
BPSK	187.5	9
QPSK	250	12
QPSK	375	18
16-QAM	500	24
16-QAM	750	36
64-QAM	1000	48
64-QAM	1125	54

There are a few more vital things we need to cover before moving on to Chapter 4, such as how to manage channels in each frequency range, as well as how to deal with an ugly thing known as channel overlap.

Channel Management and Overlap

In both the 2.4GHz and the 5GHz frequency band, channels are defined by the standards. 802.11, 802.11b, and 802.11g use the 2.4GHz band also known as the industrial, scientific, and medical (ISM) band. 802.11a uses the 5GHz band. When two access points are operating in same area on the same channel or even an adjacent channel, they will interfere with each other. Interference lowers the throughput. Therefore, channel management to avoid interference is critical to ensure reliable operation. In this section, we will examine issues that impact channel management.

2.4GHz Band

Within the 2.4GHz (ISM) band are 11 channels approved for use in the United States, 13 in Europe, and 14 in Japan. Each channel is defined by its center frequency, but remember, that signal is spread across 22MHz. There's 11MHz on one side of the center frequency and 11MHz on the other side, so each channel encroaches on the channel next to it—even others further from it to a lesser extent. Take a look at Figure 3.9.

FIGURE 3.9   2.4GHz band 22MHz wide channels

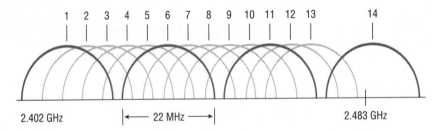

This means that consequently, within the United States, only channels 1, 6, and 11 are considered nonoverlapping. So when you have two APs in the same area that are operating on overlapping channels, the effect depends on whether they're on the same channel or on adjacent channels. Let's examine each scenario.

When APs are on the same channel, they will hear each other and defer to one another when transmitting. This is due to information sent in the header of each wireless packet that instructs all stations in the area (including any APs) to refrain from transmitting until the current transmission is received. The APs perform this duty based partially on the duration field—more on that is coming in Chapter 4 when we cover frame types in WLANs. Anyway, the end result is that both networks will be slower because they'll be dividing their transmission into windows of opportunity to transmit between them.

When the APs are only one or two channels apart, things get a little tricky, because in this case, they may not be able to hear each clearly enough to read the duration field. The ugly result of this is that they'll transmit at the same time, causing collisions that cause retransmissions and can seriously slow down your throughput—ugh! Therefore, although the two behaviors are different within these two scenarios, the end result is the same: greatly lowered throughput.

5GHz Band

802.11a uses the 5GHz frequency that's divided into three unlicensed bands called the Unlicensed National Information Infrastructure (UNII) bands. Two are adjacent to each other, but there is a frequency gap between the second and third. These bands are known as UNII-1, UNII-2, and UNII-3—the lower, middle, and upper UNII bands. Each of these bands hosts discrete channels, as in the ISM.

The 802.11a amendment specifies the location of the center point of each frequency, as well as the distance that must exist between the center point frequencies, but it failed to specify the exact width of each frequency. The good news is that the channels only overlap with the next adjacent channel so it's easier to find nonoverlapping channels in 802.11a. In the lower UNII band the center points are 10MHz apart, and in the other two the center frequencies are 20MHz apart. Figure 3.10 illustrates the overlap of the UNII bands (top and bottom), compared to the 2.4GHz band (middle).

FIGURE 3.10   5GHz band 20MHz wide channels

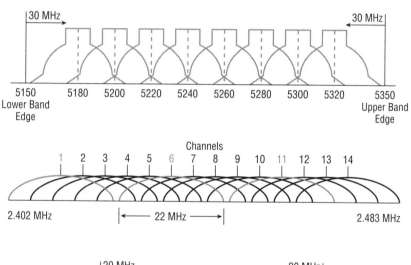

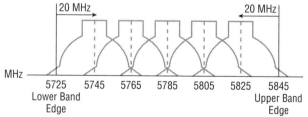

The channel numbers in the lower UNII are 36, 40, 44, and 48. In the middle UNII, the channels are 52, 56, 60, and 64. The channels in UNII-3 are 149, 153, 157, and 161.

Channel Overlap Techniques

Sometimes it becomes necessary to deploy multiple APs, and here are two scenarios that certainly scream for doing this:

- You have a large number of users in a relatively small area. Considering the nature of the contention method used by WLANs (CSMA/CA, which we'll discuss in Chapter 4), the more users associated with a particular access point, the slower the performance. By placing multiple access points in the same area on different channels, the station-to-AP ratio improves and performance improves accordingly.

- The area to be covered exceeds the range of a single AP and you would like to enable seamless roaming between the APs when users move around in the area.

Considering the channel overlap characteristics of both the 2.4GHz and the 5GHz bands, you must implement proper channel reuse when necessary to deploy multiple APs in the same area. It's also important if you want to deploy multiple APs within a large area to provide maximum coverage.

Multiple APs, Same Area

When deploying multiple APs in the same area, you need to choose channels that don't overlap. With the 2.4GHz band, the channels must have at least four channels' space between them, and remember—only 1, 6, and 11 are nonoverlapping.

When deploying APs in the 5GHz band (802.11a), the space between the channels can be two channels, given that there's no overlap.

Also vital to remember is that when choosing channels in a wide area, they can be reused if there's enough space between each channel's usage area or cell. For example, in Figure 3.11 Channel 6 is used eight times, but no two areas using Channel 6 overlap.

FIGURE 3.11 Channel overlap in the 2.4GHz range

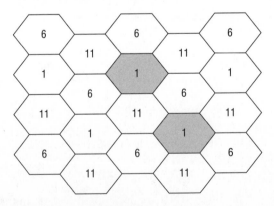

In the 5GHz band, there are two cells between cells that use the same channel, as shown in Figure 3.12.

FIGURE 3.12   Channel overlap in the 5GHz band

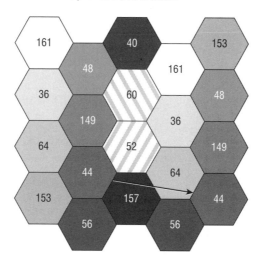

The default number of 5GHz, 802.11a nonoverlapping channels is 12, but with 802.11h options, we have up to 23 nonoverlapping channels. You'll learn more about this topic in the next chapter.

Summary

So now you know all the CCNA Wireless objectives that cover narrowband and spread spectrum transmission methods, and you learned that spread spectrum is the method used in WLANs.

You also now know that there are two types of spread spectrum: frequency hopping (FSSS) and direct sequence (DSSS). 802.11 and 802.11b use DSSS, and 802.11g and 802.11a use OFDM.

Finally, you learned about the specific channels used in the 2.4GHz and 5GHz frequency bands and the importance of proper channel management when placing multiple APs within a given area.

With all of this knowledge in mind, next you'll learn about the various organizations that create standards, enforce regulations, and issue certifications within the industry. I'll also cover these standards and their related amendments in great detail. You'll learn about the frame types involved in managing access to your wireless network. You'll also be introduced to wireless technologies other than 802.11, which I'll be focusing on in detail.

So keep up the good work—I'll be building on all the knowledge gained through each chapter until, by the end of this book, you'll have a solid grasp of wireless technologies and know how to implement them really well!

Exam Essentials

Know the modulation and encoding techniques used in DSSS.   DSSS uses DBPSK and DQPSK with Barker 11 encoding to get 1 and 2Mbps. DSS also uses DQPSK and DQPSK with CCK encoding to achieve data rates of 5.5 and 11Mbps.

Understand the modulation and encoding techniques used with OFDM.   OFDM uses BPSK, QPSK, and QAM to modulate and encode data within a RF signal.

Remember the nonoverlapping channels in the 2.4GHz band.   The 2.4 frequency band has 14 channels, 11 of which are configurable in the United States. Of those 11, only three are considered nonoverlapping: 1, 6, and 11.

Written Lab

1. True/False: Fading is defined as when the desired signal reaches the receiving antenna via multiple paths, each of which has different propagation delay and path loss.

2. True/False: DSSS reduces multipath problems by carrying data in subcarriers.

3. Which frequency range is considered in the UNII bands?

4. _____ modulates the data signal with a carrier signal that changes (hops) in a random, yet over time predictable, sequence of frequencies.

5. What are the three encoding and modulation techniques used with OFDM?

6. How wide is a 2.4GHz channel?

7. How wide is a 5GHz channel?

8. Which OFDM modulation technique provides 54Mbps?

9. DSSS uses how many chips to achieve 11Mbps?

10. OFDM uses a system of _____ carriers, sometimes referred to as subcarriers that are modulated by BPSK or QPSK.

Review Questions

1. What is the number of nonoverlapping channels with the 2.4GHz frequency range?
   A. 1
   B. 3
   C. 6
   D. 11

2. Which of the following is the modulation technique used to provide 54Mbps with OFDM?
   A. BPSK
   B. DSSS
   C. QPSK
   D. QAM

3. What increases bandwidth and resists multipath problems by carrying data in subcarriers?
   A. QAM
   B. DSSS
   C. OFDM
   D. QPSK

4. Which of the following describes fading?
   A. Another signal source producing energy on the channel in which you are trying to operate
   B. The desired signal reaching the receiving antenna via multiple paths, each of which has different propagation delay and path loss
   C. A time-varying change in the path loss of a link, with the time variance governed by the movement of objects in the environment, including the transmitter and the receiver themselves
   D. A function of the frequency that should be provided in the cable specification by the vendor
   E. The minimum signal level for the receiver to be able to acceptably decode the information
   F. The time delay from the reception of the first instance of the signal until the last instance

5. What is the maximum data rate possible with the OFDM modulation technique BPSK?
   A. 1
   B. 2
   C. 6
   D. 9
   E. 11

6. What is the maximum data rate possible with the OFDM modulation technique QPSK?

   A. 6

   B. 9

   C. 11

   D. 18

   E. 54

7. How wide are the channels in the 2.4GHz frequency?

   A. 11MHz

   B. 20MHz

   C. 22MHz

   D. 54MHz

8. How wide are the channels in the 5GHz frequency?

   A. 11MHz

   B. 20MHz

   C. 22MHz

   D. 54MHz

9. When would you deploy multiple APs in an area?

   A. When the area to be covered limits the range of a single AP and you would like to disable seamless roaming between the APs when users move around in the area

   B. When the area to be covered exceeds the range of a single AP and you would like to enable seamless roaming between the APs when users move around in the area

   C. When you are running a point-to-point wireless network and the bandwidth is saturated

   D. When you have an unlimited budget and you don't want any holes in your coverage, so it is best to place as many APs as possible if you have the budget

10. DSSS uses DBPSK and DQPSK with what encoding to achieve 1 and 2Mbps?

   A. CCK

   B. Barker 11

   C. QAM

   D. DQPSK

Answers to Review Questions

1. B. The 2.4GHz range uses a 22MHz wide channel, and three are considered nonoverlapping: 1, 6, and 11.

2. D. QAM-64 is used to modulate data up to 54Mbps using OFDM.

3. C. OFDM uses 52 subcarriers that are used to help reduce and resist multiple issues.

4. B. Fading occurs when a signal arrives at the receiver via multiple paths out of phase with one another resulting in a signal loss, also called multipath.

5. D. BPSK has a data total data rate per subchannel of 187.5Kbps, for a total of 9Mbps.

6. D. QPSK has a data total data rate per subchannel of 375Kbps, for a total of 18Mbps.

7. C. The 2.4GHz frequency uses 22MHz wide channels.

8. B. The 5GHz frequency uses 20MHz wide channels.

9. B. If you have a large office, or a large area that needs coverage, it is best to use multiple APs to provide wireless access where needed. Be careful to use nonoverlapping channels to limit interference issues.

10. B. DBPSK and DQPSK use Barker 11 to achieve 1 and 2Mbps. To get the 5.5 and 11Mbps speeds of DSSS, CCK is used to encode the data in the RF signal.

Answers to Written Lab

1. True

2. False

3. 5GHz

4. FHSS

5. BPSK, QPSK, and QAM

6. 22MHz

7. 20MHz

8. QAM-64

9. 8

10. 52

Chapter 4

Wireless Regulation Bodies, Standards, and Certifications

THE CCNA WIRELESS EXAM TOPICS COVERED IN THIS CHAPTER ARE:

✓ **Describe WLAN fundamentals**

- Describe wireless regulatory bodies, standards and certifications (FCC, ETSI, 802.11a/b/g/n, WiFi Alliance)

- Describe frame types (associated/unassociated, management, control, data)

- Describe the impact of various wireless technologies (Bluetooth, WiMAX, ZigBee, cordless phone)

We're going to pick right up where we left off in Chapter 3 and get straight into the various regulations and standards that are used in most wireless networks today—with a major focus on the IEEE standards.

The act of sending information through wireless devices implies the required use of the RF spectrum. Although countries have their own rules about which transmit power they allow within specific frequencies, it follows that vendors must use a common set of protocols that ensure interoperability in order to send information. So clearly you need to be familiar with the specific bodies that regulate use of the wireless spectrum as well as the organization that creates the protocols used in wireless networks. It's also imperative to be savvy about the organization that ensures those protocols are implemented the same way among all vendors for the sake of interoperability.

Later on in this chapter, I'll cover the data, management, and control frames used within IEEE wireless networks, and we'll conclude by exploring the various non-IEEE standards and their effect on our IEEE wireless networks you'll see presently installed all over the world.

To find dynamic updates to this chapter, please go to www.lammle.com or www.sybex.com/go/ccnawireless.

Wireless Regulations

Most wireless networks use the industrial, scientific, and medical (ISM) band. But being able to use a band, or "range of frequencies," doesn't mean you get to use it in any way that you want. To get wireless devices to communicate, these hosts need to understand the various modulation techniques to use, how a frame should be coded, what type of headers need to be in that frame, what the physical transmission mechanism should be, and similar information. In addition, they all have to be accurately defined or machines just won't be capable of communicating with one another effectively. All these elements just happen to be specified by the Institute of Electrical & Electronics Engineers, Inc. (IEEE), a nonprofit organization composed of more than 370,000 researchers and engineers worldwide whose aim is to develop communication standards in electrical and computer sciences, engineering, and related fields. As of this writing, the IEEE has published over 900 standards and has over 400 more in process.

The IEEE's communication committee defined several network communication areas, which were then further divided into working groups. This is why most network protocols today start with 802—*80* stands for the year 1980 and 2 represents February. The lion's share of all vendors follow the IEEE 802.11 family of protocol specifications when building wireless devices. So today, whenever a wireless device is used, its Layer 1 and Layer 2 functions are defined by an IEEE 802.11 series protocol.

IEEE 802.11 Transmission

Transmitting a signal using the typical 802.11 specifications works a lot like it does with a basic Ethernet hub: they're both two-way forms of communication, and they both use the same frequency to transmit and receive, but they can only transmit or receive at one time. (This is often referred to as half-duplex, as I mentioned in Chapter 1.)

We can also increase the transmitting power to gain a greater transmitting distance, but since doing this can create some pretty ugly distortion, you've got to do it carefully. You can use the higher frequencies to attain higher data rates, but unfortunately, it will cost you because going this way will result in decreased transmitting distances. Opt for the lower frequency approach, and you'll get to transmit further but at lower data rates. This is just one factor that should give you a clue as to just how important it is to be highly knowledgeable about all the various types of WLANs you can implement. Coming up with the best LAN solution—the one that most effectively meets the specific requirements of the unique situation you're faced with—can be real challenge.

Also important to note is the fact that the 802.11 specifications were developed to avoid licensing requirements in most countries, so you get to enjoy the freedom to install and operate without being socked with any licensing or operating fee-oriented surprises, which is nice. It also means that any manufacturer can create wireless networking products and sell them at a local computer store or pretty much wherever, and that all our computers should be able to communicate wirelessly without configuring much or anything at all.

Several agencies have been around for a surprisingly long time to help govern the use of wireless devices, frequencies, standards, and how the frequency spectrums are used. Table 4.1 lists the current agencies involved in this endeavor to help create, maintain, and even enforce wireless standards worldwide.

TABLE 4.1   Wireless Agencies and Standards

Agency	Purpose	Website
Institute of Electrical and Electronics Engineers (IEEE)	Creates and maintains operational standards	www.ieee.org
Federal Communications Commission (FCC)	Regulates the use of wireless devices in the U.S.	www.fcc.gov
European Telecommunications Standards Institute (ETSI)	Chartered to produce common standards in Europe	www.etsi.org
Wi-Fi Alliance	Promotes and tests for WLAN interoperability	www.wi-fi.com

Because WLANs transmit over radio frequencies, they're regulated by the same laws used to govern devices like AM/FM radios, and in the United States the FCC regulates the use of wireless LAN devices. The IEEE takes it from there and creates standards based on the frequencies the FCC releases for public use.

Unlicensed Bands

To date, the FCC has released three unlicensed bands for public use: 900MHz, 2.4GHz, and 5GHz (and there is talk about releasing a few more bands in the near future). The 900MHz and 2.4GHz bands are referred to as the ISM bands, and the 5GHz band is known as the Unlicensed National Information Infrastructure (UNII) band. Figure 4.1 shows where the unlicensed bands sit within the RF spectrum.

FIGURE 4.1   Unlicensed frequencies

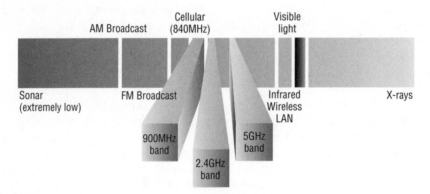

This is all good, but what if you want to deploy wireless in a range outside of the three public bands shown in Figure 4.1? For that, you need to get permission in the form of a specific license from the FCC. Predictably, as soon as the FCC opened the three frequency ranges to the public, manufacturers began offering a full menu of products that flooded the market, with 802.11b/g leading the way as the most widely used wireless network found today.

The 2.4GHz ISM band ranges from 2.4 to 2.4835GHz; (2.4970GHz in Japan), a range that offers 11 channels in the United States, 13 in Europe, and 14 in Japan. The 5GHz has an ISM band ranging from 5.725 to 5.875GHz and overlaps with the UNII bands:

- UNII-1 ranges from 5.15 to 5.25GHz (4 channels).

- UNII-2 ranges from 5.25 to 5.35GHz (4 channels).

- UNII-2 extended ranges from 5.470 to 5.725GHz (up to 11 channels).

- UNII-3 ranges from 5.725 to 5.825GHz (4 channels).

The 5GHz range gives us a lot more configurable channels in the United States, and I'll be mentioning both the 2.4GHz ISM and 5GHz bands a lot throughout this chapter.

The FCC added rules about spread spectrum technologies in 1994, which mandates that any antenna sold with a product must be tested and approved with that specific product. And to keep users from installing any antenna they want to, the FCC also implemented a rule stating that any removable antenna must use a unique, nonstandard connector that's not available through general distribution channels.

Cisco uses a reverse-polarity threaded Neill-Concelman (RP-TNC) connector that complies with FCC requirements, which looks like a standard threaded Neill-Concelman (TNC) except that the center contacts have been reversed. Cisco came up with this design because it prevents any old standard off-the-shelf antenna from being attached to a Cisco Aironet RF product.

I thought this would be a good place to jump in and bring up the slice of WLAN history that's important for you to know about. Although wireless transmissions date way back, we want to focus on wireless transmissions as related to WLANs that only date back to the 1990s. This is because the ISM band began being used commercially in the late '90s and it's now deployed in a whole slew of environments, like outdoor links, mesh networks, office buildings, health care, warehousing, and homes. Check out Figure 4.2 to get a picture of this.

FIGURE 4.2   Wireless LAN history

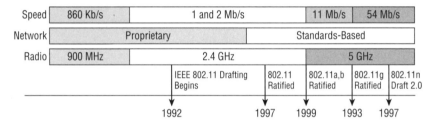

The Wi-Fi Alliance grants certification for interoperability among 802.11 products offered by various vendors, which creates a sort of comfort zone for users who find themselves purchasing the legions of stuff out there on the market. Still, I have to say that from personal experience, life is just much better if you buy all your access points (APs) from the same manufacturer.

In the present U.S. WLAN market, there are several accepted operational standards and drafts created and maintained by the IEEE, and we've come to the point for me to tell you more about them, as well as about how the most commonly used standards work.

So What Is Wi-Fi?

You may have seen products that are 802.11 compliant with a small sticker on them that says "Wi-Fi." It's a plausible guess that this quirky little acronym stands for wireless fidelity, but understanding what wireless fidelity actually *is,* and knowing what its implications are, is a different story. So I'll brief you: that little sticker means that the product in question has passed certification testing for 802.11 interoperability by the Wi-Fi Alliance. This vendor association was formed to ensure that all 802.11a/b/g/n wireless devices could communicate seamlessly. Basically, just know that it's good if the gizmo you're scoring has "Wi-Fi" stuck on it somewhere.

IEEE Wireless

You know that wireless networking has its own 802 standards group and that Ethernet's committee is 802.3. The wireless group starts with 802.11, and there are some other up-and-coming standards groups as well, including 802.16 and 802.20. And if you use a cell phone and/or watch TV, you know that even cellular networks are becoming huge players in our wireless experience. For now, though, we're going to concentrate on the 802.11 standards committee and subcommittees.

IEEE 802.11 was the first, original standardized WLAN at 1 and 2Mbps and it runs in the 2.4GHz radio frequency range. It was ratified in 1997, although we didn't see a whole lot of products pop up until around 1999, when 802.11b was formally introduced. All the committees listed in Table 4.2 made amendments to the original 802.11 standard, except for 802.11F and 802.11T, which produced stand-alone documents. Table 4.2 is a great table to refer to—maybe even commit to memory.

TABLE 4.2   802.11 Committees and Subcommittees

Committee	Purpose
IEEE 802.11a	54Mbps, 5GHz standard.
IEEE 802.11b	Enhancements to 802.11 to support 5.5 and 11Mbps.
IEEE 802.11c	Bridge operation procedures; included in the IEEE 802.1d standard.
IEEE 802.11d	International roaming extensions.
IEEE 802.11e	Quality of service and packet bursting.
IEEE 802.11F	Inter-Access Point Protocol; group is no longer active.
IEEE 802.11g	54Mbps, 2.4GHz standard (backward compatible with 802.11b).
IEEE 802.11h	Dynamic Frequency Selection (DFS) and Transmit Power Control (TPC) at 5GHz. Avoids radar interference.
IEEE 802.11i	Enhanced security.
IEEE 802.11j	Extensions for Japan and U.S. public safety.
IEEE 802.11k	Radio resource measurement enhancements.
IEEE 802.11m	Maintenance of the standard; odds and ends.

TABLE 4.2   802.11 Committees and Subcommittees *(continued)*

Committee	Purpose
IEEE 802.11n	Higher throughput improvements using multiple input, multiple output (MIMO) antennas.
IEEE 802.11p	Wireless Access in Vehicular Environments (WAVE).
IEEE 802.11r	Fast roaming.
IEEE 802.11s	ESS Extended Service Set Mesh Networking.
IEEE 802.11T	Wireless Performance Prediction (WPP).
IEEE 802.11u	Internetworking with non-802 networks (cellular, for example).
IEEE 802.11v	Wireless network management.
IEEE 802.11w	Protected management frames.
IEEE 802.11y	3650–3700 operation in the U.S.

There's one type of wireless networking that doesn't get much attention: infrared wireless. Infrared wireless uses the same basic transmission method as your everyday TV remote control. The same infrared technology that makes you the god of your TV is primarily used for short-distance, point-to-point communications, like those between a peripheral and a PC, and the Infrared Data Association (IrDA) standard is the most widely used for these kinds of peripherals.

Next let's delve into some important specifics regarding the most popular 802.11 WLANs.

2.4GHz (802.11b)

In early 1999, the IEEE released the 802.11 specifications and some manufacturers developed products in the 1 and 2Mbps speeds. However, these weren't very popular because of their slow speeds. Not until late 1999 did manufacturers start producing products that had speeds up to 11Mbps. Now this was catching people's attention! This IEEE specification was called 802.11b. First on the menu to be deployed in home and corporate environments was the 802.11b standard. It used to be the most widely deployed wireless standard, and it operates in the 2.4GHz unlicensed radio band that delivers a maximum data rate of 11Mbps. The 802.11b standard has been widely adopted by both vendors and customers who've found that its 11Mbps data rate works pretty well for most applications. But now that we've got 802.11b's big brother, 802.11g, people rarely go out to get an 802.11b card or AP anymore. Why would you buy a 10Mbps Ethernet card when you can score a 10/100 Ethernet card for the same price?

An interesting thing about all Cisco 802.11 WLAN products is that they have the ability to "data-rate-shift" while in operation. This ability is cool because it allows someone operating at 11Mbps to shift to 5.5Mbps, then 2Mbps, even 1Mbps—the farthest communication rate from the AP—and do it all without losing connection and with no interaction from the user. Rate shifting also occurs on a transmission-by-transmission basis, which means that the AP can support multiple clients running at varying speeds depending on the location of each. Figure 4.3 shows all four 802.11b rate speeds.

FIGURE 4.3   802.11b speed rate coverage

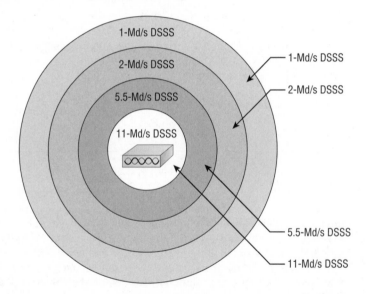

The problem with 802.11b is how it handles things at the Data Link layer. To solve problems in the RF spectrum, a type of Ethernet collision detection called *Carrier Sense Multiple Access with Collision Avoidance (CSMA/CA)* was created (we'll will discuss this in complete detail later in this chapter in the section "Wireless Frames"). However, for now, to clarify this concept, check out Figure 4.4.

CSMA/CA is also called a *Request to Send, Clear to Send (RTS/CTS)* because of the way it requires hosts to communicate to the AP. For every packet sent, an RTS/CTS *and* acknowledgment must be received, which doesn't exactly meet present-day networking demands efficiently!

As I said, 11 channels are available that we can configure in the United States within the 2.4GHz range. However, only three of these channels are considered nonoverlapping: 1, 6, and 11.

FIGURE 4.4   802.11b CSMA/CA

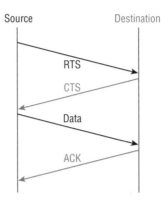

Figure 4.5 shows the 14 different channels (each 22MHz wide) that the FCC released within the 2.4GHz range.

FIGURE 4.5   ISM 2.4GHz channels

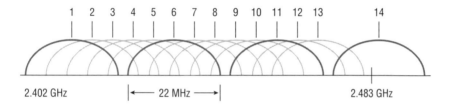

In the ETSI domains, 13 channels are available. Having 13 channels makes having four mostly nonoverlapping channels possible (1, 5, 9, and 13), but the noise level on each channel is higher than it is on the three U.S. nonoverlapping channels. This is because the U.S. channels don't overlap. Japan is the winner in the channel game because it has an additional usable channel located at the top end of the band for a total of four nonoverlapping channels: 1, 6, 11, and 14. Note the fact that the fourth channel is far apart from the first three—the reason it's considered nonoverlapping. Sure would be nice to have that fourth channel here in the United States, right?

Okay—back to the U.S. Since we've got three channels (1, 6, and 11) that don't overlap, we get to have three APs in the same area without experiencing interference.

Table 4.3 shows each channel's center frequency from within the 2.4GHz frequency band.

TABLE 4.3   2.4GHz Center Frequencies

Channel	1	2	3	4	5	6	7	8	9	10	11	12	13	14
Frequency (MHz)	2412	2417	2422	2427	2432	2437	2442	2447	2452	2457	2462	2467	2472	2484

The channels and center frequencies in Table 4.3 happen to be the exact same channels and center frequencies that are used with 802.11g.

2.4GHz (802.11g)

The 802.11g standard was ratified in June 2003 and is backward compatible with 802.11b. The 802.11g standard delivers the same 54Mbps maximum data rate that you'll find in the 802.11a range, but runs in the 2.4GHz range—the same as 802.11b.

Because 802.11b/g operates in the same 2.4GHz unlicensed band, migrating to 802.11g is a nice, affordable option for anyone with existing 802.11b wireless infrastructures. The catch is that 802.11b products can't be "software upgraded" to 802.11g because 802.11g radios use a completely different chipset that makes them capable of delivering that higher data rate.

Still, just as with Ethernet and Fast Ethernet, 802.11g products can be commingled with 802.11b products within the same network. The problem is that 802.11b devices can't understand orthogonal frequency-division multiplexing (OFDM). This means they can't detect that an 802.11g client is sending unless direct sequence spread spectrum (DSSS) modulation is used. If it's not, the 802.11b devices will just perceive noise and mistakenly believe that the carrier is free, which can cause collisions.

The 802.11g protocol has a way to prevent these collisions built straight into it—as soon as an 802.11g AP signals the presence of an 802.11b device within the cell, the AP informs the clients of the cell by sending out this information in the beacons that APs use to send out routine RF broadcasts:

- Non-ERP present: yes
- Use protection: yes

"Non-ERP present" refers to 802.11b clients; the Extended Rate Physical (ERP) means that the 802.11g hosts have a higher rate capacity. The "protection" it refers to is a simple warning mechanism, which basically says, "Hey, everyone, pay attention—we have a really slow dinosaur of a client in our network now!"

When an 802.11g client is about to send a frame, it first sends a "request to send" (RTS) message at 802.11b speed so all the 802.11b clients can hear the message. The RTS basically says, "I intend to transmit for X period of time." So, to optimize performance, I highly recommend that you disable the 802.11b-only modes on all your APs.

This is essentially a unicast message sent to the recipient (the AP in this case) of the frame that will respond with a "clear to send" (CTS) answer at 802.11b speed. After this exchange, all clients in range of the AP will hear this message and will know that the exchange is about to occur.

802.11g clients using OFDM perform much better at the same ranges as 802.11b clients do, but—and remember this—when 802.11g clients are operating at the 802.11b rates (11, 5.5, 2, and 1Mbps), they're actually using the same modulation 802.11b does (DSSS).

Figure 4.6 shows the 802.11b/g cell speeds. Notice there are 12 speeds for 802.11g and that 802.11b only has 4.

🌐 Real World Scenario

You Won't Use 802.11b in My Network!

By now you should get the idea that we really shouldn't be using IEEE 802.11b clients or APs in our wireless networks, and since most laptops and other wireless devices all run a/b/g, we should be able to disable the 802.11b capabilities on our APs. One time when I was installing some APs at a client, I disabled all the 802.11b capabilities on all access points. The next day a woman working in sales came up to me and said her wireless laptop stopped working. She had an older laptop with an external PCMIA wireless card, so I pretty much figured out the problem right away. Once I pulled the card out, I showed her that it was old and defective and that she needed to get a new wireless card (it really wasn't defective, but it was defective in my network!). The next day she came back with a new wireless card in hand. Since it is impossible these days to buy an 802.11b card, except maybe a used one from eBay, I wasn't worried that the card was a "b only" card; however, after looking at the card, sure enough, it was a brand-new 802.11b card. I was stunned! Where would she get a brand-new 802.11b card? She said that CompUSA was going out of business and she found this new card for only four bucks in a clearance bin! Perfect.

FIGURE 4.6   802.11b/g cell speeds

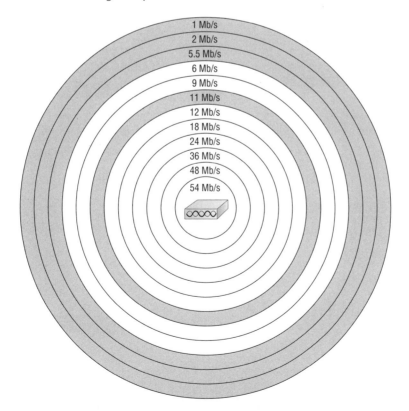

Because of the sideband noise generated by OFDM modulation, the power has to be backed off for OFDM (802.11g) so it's able to handle the peaks of the modulation and still meet regulations. The overall maximum power settings vary from country to country.

For example, in the United States, DSSS and OFDM have the limitations shown in Table 4.4.

TABLE 4.4 Maximum Power Output Limitations in the 2.4 GHz Range

DSSS (CCK)	OFDM
100 milliwatt (mW) (100 mW – 20dBm)	N/A
50mW (17dBm)	N/A
30mW (15dBm)	30mW (15dBm)
20mW (13dBm)	20mW (13dBm)
10mW (10dBm)	10mW (10dBm)
5mW (7dBm)	5mW (7dBm)
1mW (0dBm)	1mW (0dBm)

The FCC is all about rules and regulations and takes them really seriously—even its obscure ones. In fact, the FCC takes them so seriously, it can slap you with some pretty heavy fines for repeat offenders. Of course, they have to find you first, but I'm just saying that the FCC's rules and regs are definitely not just mere suggestions and that you must follow them, period!

Figure 4.7 shows you the effective isotropic radiated power (EIRP) output rules in the 2.4GHz range that are governed by the FCC.

FIGURE 4.7 EIRP output rules for the 2.4GHz range

Point-to-Multipoint

	Transmitter Power - dBm	Maximum Gain	EIRP
FCC Maximum	30 dBm	6 dBm	36 dBm
Cisco Maximum	20 dBm	16 dBm	36 dBm

The above values reflect the 1:1 rule.

Point-to-Point

	Transmitter Power - dBm	Maximum Gain	EIRP
FCC Maximum	30 dBm	6 dBm	36 dBm
Cisco Maximum	20 dBm	36 dBm	56 dBm

The above values reflect the 3:1 rule.

Figure 4.7 depicts the transmitter allowed by the FCC, as well as the transmitter power that Cisco uses for both point-to-point and point-to-multipoint. Figure 4.8 shows you the ETSI's EIRP output rules.

FIGURE 4.8   ETSI's EIRP output rules

Point-to-Multipoint and Point-to-Point

	Transmitter Power - dBm	Maximum Gain	EIRP
Gov. Body Maximum	17 dBm	3 dBm	20 dBm
Cisco dipole Antennae	17 dBm	2.2 dBm	19.2 dBm
Reduced Tx Power	15 dBm	5 dBm	20 dBm
Reduced Tx Power	13 dBm	7 dBm	20 dBm
Reduced Tx Power	7 dBm	13 dBm	20 dBm
Reduced Tx Power	0 dBm	20 dBm	20 dBm

The above values reflect the 1:1 rule.

Figure 4.8 delimits the transmitter power, maximum gain, and EIRP used in Europe, France, Singapore, Israel, and Mexico.

5GHz (802.11a)

The IEEE ratified the 802.11a standard in 1999, but the first 802.11a products didn't begin appearing on the market until late 2001. And boy, could these hot new commodities seriously set you back! The 802.11a standard delivers a maximum data rate of 54Mbps with up to 28 nonoverlapping frequency channels—a whopping 23 of them available in the United States.

Another 802.11a benefit is that when operating in the 5GHz radio band, the frequency is immune to interference from devices that operate in the 2.4GHz band, like microwave ovens, cordless phones, and Bluetooth devices. As you probably guessed, 802.11a isn't backward compatible with 802.11b because they're different frequencies, so you don't get to just "upgrade" pieces and parts of your network and expect everything to sing in perfect harmony. But no worries—there are plenty of dual-radio devices that will work in both types of networks. Oh, and another definite plus for 802.11a is that it can work in the same physical environment without having to take measures to avoid interference from 802.11b users.

Like 802.11b radios, all 802.11a products also have the ability to data-rate-shift while moving. The difference is that 802.11a products allow someone moving at 54Mbps to shift to 48Mbps, 36Mbps, 24Mbps, 18Mbps, 12Mbps, and 9Mbps, and finally still communicate farthest from the AP way down at 6Mbps.

There are three different sections called the UNII bands within the 5GHz band, making it a little more complicated than our 2.4GHz radios. Figure 4.9 shows the frequency ranges used within the 5GHz range. The lower bands have 30MHz wide channels and the upper ones are 20MHz wide.

FIGURE 4.9   802.11a frequency spectrum and the UNII bands

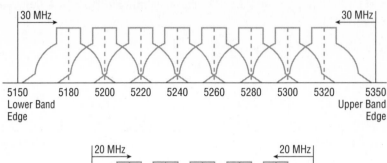

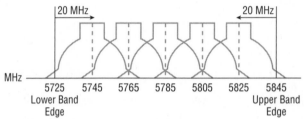

These UNII bands have different limitations and restrictions that vary between those designated for transmitting power, for antenna gain, and for those pertaining to antenna styles and usage.

- The UNII-1 band was designated for indoor operations and initially had a restriction requiring the antenna to be permanently attached. Output power should not exceed 50mW (17dBm), with 22dBm EIRP maximum.

- The UNII-2 band was designated for indoor or outdoor operations and allowed for the use of external antennas. Output power should not exceed 250mW (24dBm), with 29dBm EIRP.

- The UNII-3 band was intended for outdoor bridge products and permitted the use of external antennas. Output power should not exceed 1W (30dBm), with 36dBm EIRP.

UNII-2 has 11 extended channels (output power of the extended channels should not exceed 1W [30dBm], with 36dBm EIRP) that can be used indoors or out, and has two features that are part of the 802.11h specification:

- Transmit power control (TPC)
- Dynamic frequency selection (DFS)

I'll talk more about 802.11h in a minute, but first, understand that in the ETSI domain, the regulation offers these channels:

UNII-1 and 2 indoor (5150–5350MHz)   Devices must be part of a "mobile/nomadic network" and compatible with TPC and DFS. The maximum EIRP is 200mW (23dBm), versus 50mW in the United States.

UNII-2 Extended (5470–5725MHz)   Devices must be part of a "mobile/nomadic network" and compatible with TPC and DFS. The maximum EIRP is 1W (30dBm), versus 250mW in the United States.

UNII-3   The UNII-3 can be used outdoors, but only in a licensed mode—it's not a free spectrum like it is in the United States. But the maximum EIRP is 4W, which is the same as it is in the United States.

So basically, in both the U.S. and the ETSI domains, the same eight channels (36, 40, 44, 48, 52, 56, 60, and 64) are allowed within the UNII-1 and the UNII-2 spectrums. In the UNII-2 extended, the same 11 channels are allowed in both the U.S. and ETSI domains: 100, 104, 108, 112, 116, 120, 124, 128, 132, 136, and 140. The U.S. domain also allows four channels: 149, 153, 157, and 161 in the UNII-3 band, but in the ETSI region, these channels aren't freely available. The 11 channels in UNII-2 are an extension to the 802.11a specifications called 802.11h, which is what we'll focus on next.

5GHz (802.11h)

The FCC added 11 new channels in February 2004, and in 2008, we finally began using these channels when manufacturers released more 802.11a 5GHz products. We can now gain access to up to 23 nonoverlapping channels. In addition, there are two new cool features to the 5GHz radio that are part of the 802.11h specification:

Dynamic Frequency Selection (DFS)   This beauty continuously monitors a device's operating range for any radar signals that are allowed to operate in portions of the 5GHz band as well as 802.11a before transmitting. If DFS discovers any radar signals, it'll either abandon the occupied channel or mark it as unavailable to prevent interference from occurring on the WLAN—sweet!

Transmit Power Control (TPC)   Even though it's been employed by the mobile phone industry for a long time, this technology has some handy new uses. You can set the client machine's adapter and the AP's transmit power to cover various size ranges—a feature that's useful for many reasons. For one, setting the AP's transmit power to 5mW reduces cell range, which works great if you've got a compact area with high-density usage.

More benefits include the fact that TPC enables the client and the AP to actually communicate, meaning the client machine can fine-tune its transmit power dynamically. This ability enables the client to use the minimum amount of energy required to preserve its connection to the AP, conserve its battery power, and reduce interference on the neighboring WLAN cells.

Now take a look at Figure 4.10, which delimits the range comparisons of each 802.11 standard and shows these various ranges using an indoor open-office environment as a factor. (I'm using default power settings.)

FIGURE 4.10   Range comparisons of 802.11a/b/g standards

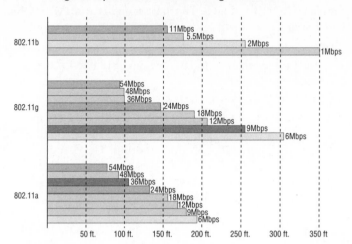

You can see that to get the full 54Mbps benefit of both 802.11a and 802.11g, you need to be somewhere between 50 feet and 100 feet (at the farthest) away. Keep in mind that the 100 foot maximum will most likely be reduced if there happen to be any obstructions between the client and the AP.

Before we move on to IEEE 802.11n, take at peek at Figure 4.11, which lists the years each standard was ratified, the frequency of each, the number of nonoverlapping channels, the physical layer transmission technique, and the data rates for each of the IEEE standards in use today.

FIGURE 4.11   Standards for spectrums and speeds

	802.11	802.11b	802.11a	802.11g		802.11n
Ratified	1997	1999	1999	2003		Not Ratified
Frequency Band	2.4GHz	2.4GHz	5GHz	2.4GHz		2.4GHz, 5GHz
No. of Channels	3	3	Up to 23	3		Varies
Transmission	IR, FHSS, DSSS	DSSS	OFDM	DSSS	OFDM	DSSS, CCK, OFDM
Data Rates (Mbps)	1, 2	1, 2, 5.5, 11	6, 9, 12, 18, 24, 36, 48, 54	1, 2, 5.5, 11	6, 9, 12, 18, 24, 36, 48, 54	100+

802.11n is included in this figure because 802.11n is basically just an extension of the 2.4GHz and 5GHz frequencies with new options and fixes to make the wireless networks run faster. But the channels, nonoverlapping channels, and frequencies are the same as you'll see in the next section. Back in Chapter 2, I mentioned that 802.11b runs DSSS, whereas 802.11g and 802.11a both run the OFDM modulation technique. Now let me show you what 802.11n has in store.

2.4GHz/5GHz (802.11n)

802.11n builds on previous 802.11 standards by adding *Multiple In, Multiple Out (MIMO)*, which uses multiple transmitters and receiver antennas to increase data throughput. 802.11n can allow up to eight antennas, but most of today's APs only use three. This setup permits considerably higher data rates than 802.11a/b/g does. In fact, some marketing people claim it will provide up to 600Mbps, but in reality, the actual throughput is a lot less.

The following three vital items are combined in 802.11n to enhance performance. I'll talk about each factor in more detail throughout this section:

- At the physical layer, the way a signal is sent is changed, enabling reflections and interferences to become an advantage instead of a source of degradation.

- Two channels are combined to increase throughput.

- At the Media Access Control (MAC) layer, a different way of managing packet transmission is used.

You should know that 802.11n isn't truly compatible with 802.11b, 802.11g, or even 802.11a, but it is designed to be backward compatible with them. How 802.11n achieves backward compatibility is by changing the way frames are sent so that they can be understood by 802.11a/b/g.

802.11n uses a protection mechanism that is closer in design to the 802.11g than the 802.11b system. 802.11n employs something called CTS-to-self that works like this: A station that wants to send a message using the 802.11n specs would send a message containing "Clear to send for this duration" at a lower speed—802.11a, b, or g, depending on the cell. The other machines would then stay quiet for the specified time window while the station is sending, even though they can't actually read the signal.

Since 802.11n adds superior physical enhancements to the specification, RTS/CTS isn't needed because the 802.11n station signal has far more chances to reach all the devices in the cell and tell the hosts that it's going to transmit onto the network medium.

Here's a list of some of the primary components of 802.11n that together sum up why people claim 802.11n is more reliable and predictable:

40MHz Channels   802.11g and 802.11a use 20MHz channels and employ tones on the sides of each channel that are not used to protect the main carrier. This means that 11Mbps go unused and are basically wasted. 802.11n aggregates two carriers to double the speed from 54Mbps to more than 108Mbps. Add in those wasted 11Mbps rescued from those the side tones, and you get a grand total of 119Mbps!

MAC Efficiency   802.11 protocols require acknowledgment of each and every frame. 802.11n can pass many packets before an acknowledgment is required, which saves you a huge amount of overhead. This is called *block acknowledgment.*

Multiple-In, Multiple-Out (MIMO)   Several frames are sent by several antennas over several paths and are then recombined by another set of antennas to optimize throughput and multipath resistance. This is called *spatial multiplexing*. Figure 4.12 illustrates how spatial multiplexing would look if we had two transmit and two receive antennas in place on our 802.11n network.

FIGURE 4.12   Spatial multiplexing

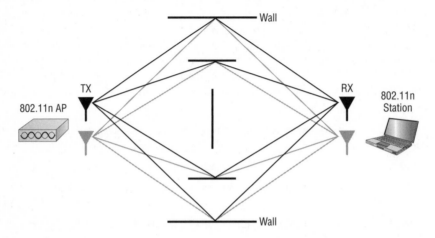

The following describes how MIMO can work to concentrate the beam and thereby improve data reception through the use of transmit beamforming and maximal ratio combining. Let me explain a bit and give you some figures to clarify what I'm saying.

Transmit Beamforming   Transmit beamforming is a technique that's used when there's more than one transmit antenna, yet the receiver has only a single antenna. Check out Figure 4.13 for a visual.

FIGURE 4.13   Transmit beamforming

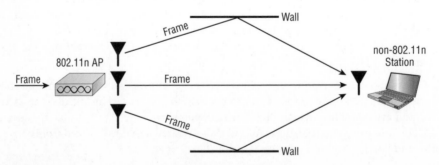

For this to work, the reflection sources need to be stable in an indoor environment. It cannot be done at the transmitter without information from the receiver about the signal—a capacity that's only available in the 802.11n specifications. Keep in mind that any physical movement by the transmitter, receiver, or other elements quickly negate the benefits of transmit beamforming.

Maximal-Ratio Combining   Spatial multiplexing and transmit beamforming are only used with devices that have multiple transmitters. Maximal-ratio combining (MRC) is where you have one transmitter (a host) running 802.11n connecting to multiple receivers—an AP, in this example.

The MRC receiver analyzes the signals received from all its antennas and sends the signals into the radio to be decoded so that they're in phase, and can add the strength of each signal to all the other signals. This very cool feature is shown in Figure 4.14.

FIGURE 4.14   Maximal ratio combining

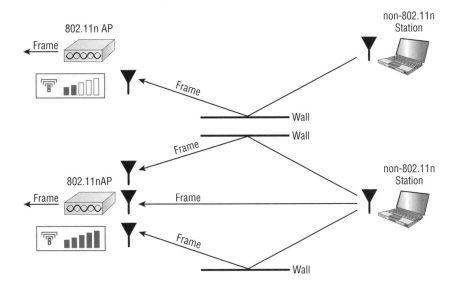

It's important for you to understand that MRC doesn't resolve or use multipath in any way. Multipath refers to multiple signals being received *out of phase* on a single antenna, but MRC can only be used when multiple signals are received *in phase* on each antenna. It then combines all the in-phase signals to enhance total signal quality on the radio. Multipath issues can still cause a problem for each antenna receiving multiple signals out of phase, but when you get MRC working to combine all the signals together, the multipath on each antenna becomes much less of an issue.

To bring this home to you, the overall performance gain is a result of MIMO smart antenna technology, which allows wireless APs to receive signals more reliably over greater distances. It also allows clients to operate at higher data rates than they can with standard diversity antennas—up to 30 percent higher compared to conventional 802.11a, b, and g networks. For example, at the distance from the AP where an 802.11a or g client that's communicating with a conventional AP might drop from 54Mbps to 48Mbps or 36Mbps, that same client that's communicating with a MIMO-enabled AP instead has a good chance at being able to continue humming along at 54Mbps.

So when considering MIMO, remember these three critical advantages:

- MIMO provides better receive sensitivity for a stationary client by using beamforming.
- MIMO provides better receive sensitivity for the AP through the use of MRC.
- Better receive sensitivity translates into a higher data rate at a given distance from the AP.

Now that you've nailed down the understanding of our 802.11a/b/g/n networks, it's time to move on and get into some detail about the way wireless frames are sent, frame shapes and speeds, and the management frame used to discover and connect to the wireless network.

Wireless Frames

You know by now that wireless network devices are half-duplex devices, just like hosts connected to an Ethernet hub, right? This means that if two hosts transmit at the same time a collision will occur and both frames will be discarded, just as they would be in a half-duplex Ethernet environment.

It also means that the transmission of frames must be controlled, and Distributed Coordination Function (DCF), a common media access method that's used at the Data Link layer, is a tool devised to do exactly that. It's called "distributed" because each device typically handles this job, but an AP can perform it as well. If the AP only performs this function, it's called something else—Point Coordination Function (PCF), although no vendors actually use PCF.

If a host wants to transmit onto the frequency spectrum being used, that host must wait until there's a silence on the frequency to make sure that any multipath issues are avoided. The time the host must wait can vary and depends on the priority of the frame.

Frames can be sent in high priority, and if they are, the host uses something called Short Interframe Space (SIFS) to count down the period of time to wait through before transmitting. Typically, all our frames are sent out using low priority, and this is what DCF networks use. With DCF in the mix, the length of time a station has to wait before transmitting is determined by Distributed Interframe Space (DIFS).

CSMA/CA

Ethernet half-duplex hubs use Carrier Sense Multiple Access with Collision Detection (CSMA/CD), but 802.11 half-duplex networks use the similar yet different Carrier Sense Multiple Access with Collision Avoidance (CSMA/CA) to get the job done instead. Wireless networks using CSMA/CA work like this: When a host needs to send a frame, it picks a random number between 0 and 31 and then starts counting down. Each type of 802.11 network has a different countdown speed, or slot time. For instance, 802.11b counts down in 20-microsecond intervals, 802.11g and 802.11a can count down in 9-microsecond intervals, and just like in Ethernet half-duplex, you call this the backoff timer.

Okay, again, using Ethernet half-duplex as our fairly analogous example, the wireless host must listen to make sure that no other host is transmitting on the frequency before it does in order to prevent an ugly collision from happening. So, while another host is busy transmitting away, our host has to stop counting down until it's pretty sure the other host has stopped sending before it can begin counting down again. Then it can jump in and finally begin transmitting onto the frequency itself. The total time our host had to wait before transmitting—the countdown, plus the time it waited for other hosts to stop transmitting—is called the contention window.

So did you catch the fact I said our host was *pretty sure* the other one was done? If you did, good catch, because interestingly, once it hears another host transmitting, our host didn't actually keep listening for the other host to stop transmitting before continuing to count down—it guessed! That's right—our little host basically just guesses how long it will take for the other host to transmit, based on a mathematical algorithm, and then continues its own countdown. This "time-guessing" behavior is known as the Network Allocation Vector (NAV). What really went down is that the host that was waiting to send a frame onto the network medium simply added this NAV value to its predetermined countdown value before continuing to count down, reached zero, and finally sent away.

If this process sounds a bit iffy, well, it kind of is. After all, our host only assumed the media was free; it didn't really know for sure, right? And that's definitely the case if our wireless host is using NAV to make guesstimates based on slot time to determine when to begin transmitting. It's just hoping for the best and keeping its fingers and toes crossed that it receives that oh-so-needed ACK back from the AP! So as you probably guessed, with this approach our host just might run into trouble in the form of a failed transmission. But there's hope—there's a second method our host can use that's a physical method, unlike NAV (which is a logical one). This physical method is called Clear Channel Assessment (CCA), and it's used to make sure our host doesn't hear a signal before transmitting. So, after our wireless host does all that counting down, waiting patiently to transmit, it's got to do yet one more check on the frequency before transmitting. And it does all this for *one* measly frame! After reading this, you probably find it pretty hard to believe that wireless networks even work at all!

The Frame Transmission Fails

So what if, after our little host buddy waits all that time counting down, adding NAV and/or CCA, and then transmits—holding its breath, hoping for the best—and the frame doesn't get fragmented because of a collision but the transmission fails anyway? If you thought, "Oh, no—our little wireless host buddy will have to start all over!" you're right. But it gets worse... our host will be faced with having to pick new random numbers, with longer microsecond intervals between 0 and 127 the second time it tries to send, 0 and 255 for the third attempt, and 0 and 1023 for all the other attempts until it becomes exhausted and just gives up. Do you blame the poor little guy? I think we've all seen this when we are in a busy wireless environment and we just can't get our host to connect to the AP. It's frustrating for users too!

The Frame Transmission Is Successful—What's Next?

But let's pretend we live in a perfect, recession-less world and have the perfect wireless network with endless resources, that our little host buddy got to transmit without a hitch, and the AP actually did receive the one frame that it's been so valiantly trying to send. Whew, nice—but wait... things aren't exactly perfect yet. Our host still needs to get an acknowledgment back from the AP confirming that the AP received it, or it will still have to resend its frame. The AP will use SIFS to ensure that ACKs are sent with a higher priority than any other frame. So we're on the right track. But if the AP didn't get a chance to send one because another host that also wanted to communicate had its timer reach zero and transmitted before the ACK was sent, our little host buddy would think that the frame wasn't received. Depressing, yes... and after all that work too! This is an illusion, though, because in reality, the frame really was received; it was just delayed because some other bandwidth hog took our host buddy's time slot. This is why we use SIFS and not DIFS for the ACK—to get that frame back to the sending host ASAP! You see, using SIFS, when our host sent the frame, it reserved the network medium for the duration of the frame, the SIFS time, and the possible period of time it could take for the ACK to be received. So, when the AP received the frame, it essentially waited for an SIFS, and sent the ACK back before any other station wishing to send whose timer reaches zero will wait for a full DIFS to be able to transmit. It's kind of like a policy that ensures that your spot in line is protected from anyone taking cuts.

I know my little analogy of what wireless hosts go through just to get a single frame sent to an AP would only work if you believe that a host can be a buddy, take a breath, has fingers and toes, and can even get depressed. Sounds a bit like Windows Vista to me, but hey, at least you don't need to believe in the Tooth Fairy to understand how wireless networks work, now do you?

With all that nailed, let's dive even deeper into the fray and take a look inside this frame our little host buddy has been endeavoring to send. You'll also learn about the management and control frames used to manage data in our wireless network.

Three Frames Types

Regardless of the type of 802.11 frame that's being sent, all 802.11 frames have a similar structure. Their headers are longer and have more control information than an 802.3 Ethernet frame does. This is because 802.11 has to assume that there's going to be interference, plus more collisions than an 802.3 network has to worry about occurring.

Next we'll look at the three frame types and the many different subtypes of each. Let's start by covering the basic three frames we'll typically find roaming our network:

Management   As the name indicates, these frames are there to help manage the connection. The frame control field "type" section shows as "management," and these include beacons, probes, authentication, and so on.

Control Frames The purpose of these frames is to aid communication on the network medium. For example, Request to Send (RTS) frames are used with the control frames.

Data Frames This type of frame contains packets of information, hence its name, but it can also be an empty or a null frame that's commonly called a null function.

These three types of frames all have the same form of header, but with different indicators. The main difference is in their body. This part of the frame can contain specific information, like the allowed speeds in a beacon frame (a management frame type), or nothing. For instance, ACK, RTS, and CTS frames all have an empty body, because all the information needed resides in their headers.

Table 4.5 depicts the various types of frames used with 802.11 networks. Most of these are management frames there for the important purpose of keeping a wireless network working smoothly—or at least a lot smoother than it would without them! We're grading on a curve, of course.

TABLE 4.5 Management, Control, and Data Frames

Management Frames	Control Frames	Data Frames
Association Request	Request to Send (RTS)	Data
		Null Data
Association Response	Clear to Send (CTS)	
Reassociation Request	Acknowledgment (ACK)	
Reassociation Response	Power-Save Poll	
Probe Request		
Probe Response		
Beacon		
ATIM		
Disassociate		
Authentication		
Deauthentication		
Association Request		

First, take a look at Figure 4.15, which simply shows a basic frame. We'll then dissect that frame.

FIGURE 4.15   An 802.11 frame

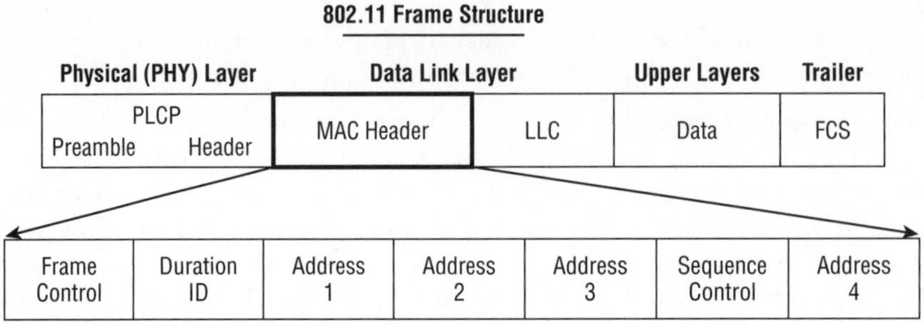

802.11 Frame Structure

This frame begins with a preamble at the Physical layer that's either 72 or 144 bits long. The preamble is followed by the portions at the MAC sublayer of the Data Link layer listed here:

- The "frame control" field (2 bytes long [16 bits]).

- A duration field, expressing how long the medium is reserved for (2 bytes long [16 bits]).

- Up to three MAC addresses (18 bytes total).

- A sequence control field (2 bytes long [16 bits]). The sequence control field is used to show if the frame is a fragment or a complete frame.

- An optional fourth field for a MAC address (6 bytes [48 bits]). Used when a frame goes over a wireless bridge link.

- The LLC header that defines who owns the data at the Network layer the frame is carrying (typically IP, which is 0x800 in hex), which is then followed by these parts:

  - The frame body (2304 bytes or octets)

  - A 4-byte (32-bit) frame check sequence (FCS)

Figure 4.16 shows an example of a data frame from a network analyzer.

The network media gives us information about the Physical layer attributes like signal strength, noise, data rate, and channel, as well as a few other things. The frame control field helps to define the purpose of the frame as well direct where it's sent.

- The first control subfield contains information about the protocol version.

- The second control subfield contains information about the frame type (2 bytes worth). It indicates if the frame type is a data frame, a control frame, or a management frame. (Figure 4.16 shows a data frame.)

- The final subfield contains information about the subtype (4 bytes), and tells us it is a reserved data frame.

- The next part of the control field is 1 byte, or 8 bits, and indicates if the frame is coming from or going toward the distribution system (DS). Our frame just came from the DS. For any client in the cell, the AP represents the DS, whether the frame is supposed to be sent to the cable or back to the wireless network.

FIGURE 4.16   Data frame output from a network analyzer

```
⊟ network media info
    ┈ timestamp : 7/25 13:20:11.000000 microseconds
    ┈ signal strength : 4% (-93 dBm)
    ┈ noise level : 0% (-96 dBm)
    ┈ frame length : 3273
    ┈ data rate : 36 mbps
    ┈ channel : 2
    ┈ CRC error : yes
⊟ 802.11 MAC header
    ⊟ frame control
        ┈ protocol version : 0
        ┈ frame type : 10 data
        ┈ subtype : 1101 reserved data frame
        ⊟ frame control
            ┈ .... ...0   :   to DS : No
            ┈ .... ..1.   :   from DS : Yes
            ┈ .... .0..   :   more frag : No
            ┈ .... 0...   :   retry : Not a retry
            ┈ ...1 ....   :   power management : PS mode
            ┈ ..0. ....   :   more data : No more Data
            ┈ .0.. ....   :   WEP/Protected Frame : Non-Protected Frame
            ┈ 0... ....   :   order : Non-Strict Order
    ┈ duration : 13507 usec
    ┈ dest addr : 2E:A7:DE:05:29:78
    ┈ bssid : 6E:16:9E:D4:74:29
    ┈ src  addr : 73:13:95:92:F6:3C
    ┈ frag number : 6
    ┈ seq number : 2598
    ⊞ QoS control
⊞ 802.11 frame body
```

If the transmission that's taking place is in an infrastructure mode—not ad hoc—there will be multiple MAC addresses in the frame. Although the AP is still like a hub in that it's just basically repeating or forwarding the information, it still uses MAC addresses to communicate. APs work at Layer 2, so our host needs to use more than one destination MAC address in order to send a frame on the network media—one destination to the AP and one to the destination host. It can even use a third destination in some circumstances. In our data frame output in Figure 4.16, there is a source and destination, as well as the AP MAC address that's shown as the basic service set identifier (BSSID).

Before we move on, let's take apart the rest of this data frame. Keep in mind that when you're using a wireless analyzer, you must understand how to use your filters or you'll find yourself lost in a sea of management frames! Figure 4.17 shows that our frame is carrying an IP packet and a UDP segment.

In Figure 4.17's output, the thing I want you to focus on—the main reason I'm showing this output to you—is so you can check out the Logical Link Control (LLC) header output in this frame. I know I brought it up when I discussed the output of Figure 4.15, but I didn't point out that the Subnetwork Architecture Protocol (SNAP) header at the LLC layer is what gives the wireless frame its mojo. SNAP designates control and management, and identifies the Network layer protocol, which in this case is IP. In reality, the frame is carrying 0x800 in hex in this field but the analyzer kindly decoded that for us. And know that if we were carrying IPv6 data, the frame would be carrying a 0x866 SNAP header.

FIGURE 4.17   This data frame is carrying an IP packet and a UDP segment.

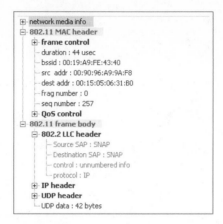

There are some new names used in these fields that are only there to completely confuse you. (I'm kidding… sort of. They do tend to confuse people!) But that doesn't mean you can ignore them—I'll be using them throughout this chapter:

Receiver Address (RA)   The receiver address is the MAC address of the direct station the frame is sent to.

Transmitter Address (TA)   The transmitter address is the address of the station emitting a frame.

Destination Address (DA)   The address of the final recipient of a frame—its final destination. Most of the time, the RA and DA will be the same MAC address.

Source Address (SA)   The address of the original sender of a frame. Usually, the TA and SA will be the same MAC address.

Here are four scenarios that illustrate different ways a frame can be sent and how the four addresses can be used within these frames:

The frame is sent from our host to another host in an infrastructure basic service set. Address 1 is the destination address (RA and DA are the same). Address 2 is our transmitting or source host (TA and SA are the same), and Address 3 is the AP MAC address for this SSID (the BSSID).

The frame is sent from our host to an AP.   In this scenario, Address 1 is the RA (or BSSID, which is the AP Mac address), Address 2 is the TA/SA, Address 3 is the DA, and Address 4 is not used at all.

The frame is sent back from the AP to our host.   Address 1 is the RA/DA, Address 2 is the TA or BSSID, Address 3 is the SA, and Address 4 is not used.

The frame is sent on a wireless link between two APs, in a repeater or bridge configuration. This is the only frame in which all four addresses are used: Address 1 is the RA, Address 2 is the TA, Address 3 is the DA, and Address 4 is the SA.

Now that you have all these new terms straight, let's take a look inside some 802.11 frames.

A Closer Look at Management Frames

Management frames are important to grasp because understanding them is a CCNA Wireless objective—so pay attention! I know that's hard—this is already a long chapter—but this information is critical. In this section, I'll go over the following types of frames (but I'm not going to show every type of frame in an analyzer output):

- Beacon

- Probe request, probe response

- Authentication request, authentication response

- Association request, association response, disassociate

- Deauthentication, reassociation request, reassociation response

We'll start by looking at a *beacon*, which is what the AP sends out announcing its capabilities.

Beacon Frames

APs send out a beacon, if enabled, every 100ms (about 1/10th of a second). This beacon contains useful information a wireless client needs to see, such as the availability status of the AP and its capabilities. Check out the beacon in Figure 4.18 to see all the information an AP sends to our host.

FIGURE 4.18   A beacon from an AP as seen on an analyzer

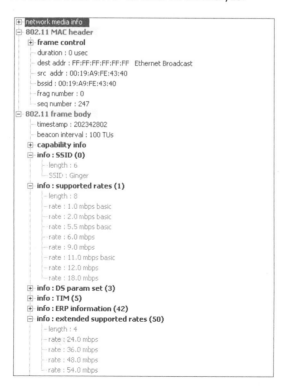

I didn't open all the fields found on the analyzer output—just the ones you really need to see. First, this was a broadcast, as all beacons are, and the source address is the same as the BSSID or AP's MAC address.

- A timestamp (to give a time reference to the cell): 8 bytes

- Indication of how often the beacon is sent: 2 bytes

- A field called capability information, containing specific items such as whether encryption is used, and whether channels can be changed to short or long preambles: 2 bytes

- The SSIDs supported: 2 to 34 bytes. We can see that this AP is broadcasting an SSID of Monica onto the Basic Service Area (BSA).

- The supported rates (speeds): 3 to 10 bytes. Because the basic rates are 1 to 18 Mbps, we know this is an 802.11g frame. 802.11b only supports 1 to 11Mbps and 802.11a starts at 6Mbps.

- The Traffic Indication Map (TIM), which is used to tell whether the AP has traffic buffered for some stations in Power Save mode: 7 to 256 bytes. If this were an ad hoc mode broadcast, stations having a message buffered to send to a station would send a specific message, called ATIM (not TIM), which is an empty message used to ask the receiving host not to switch to Power Save mode to save battery power and to wait for traffic to be sent. We shouldn't see this ATIM frame in our networks today.

- Extended support rates shows that the rates 24 to 54Mbps are available.

Before our host—whom we'll call "Gilligan," tries to send a frame, he's got to determine the optimal speed he can use. He does this by looking at the received signal strength indication (RSSI) and signal-to-noise ratio (SNR) reported in packets received by our AP, "Ginger." As shown earlier in Figure 4.18, Ginger the AP sends the supported rates she can run in the beacon. If a client, such as Gilligan, can run any of those speeds, he'll try to connect using the highest speed possible. Again, this is something that's determined by RSSI and SNR, which can tell the host exactly how far away it is from the AP.

By the way, you can configure an AP to be exclusive and only allow hosts with certain mandatory running speeds available to connect to it. You can even disable specific speeds, or you can just leave the default setting of supported rates on the AP, as the Ginger AP demonstrates back in Figure 4.18.

Probes

Probes are sent when certain events occur, such as when a host doesn't receive a beacon because the AP has the beacons disabled for security reasons, or when the host doesn't want to wait for a beacon (talk about impatient... is 100ms really that long?). If a host is sending a probe, it's called active scanning, and when a host is listening for a beacon on all channels, it's called passive scanning. Figure 4.19 shows a probe from our impatient little host, Gilligan, who's trying to find an AP.

FIGURE 4.19   Probe request

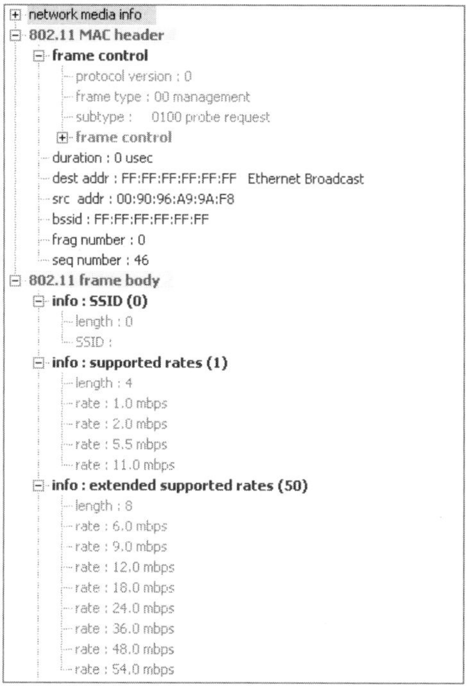

```
[+] network media info
[-] 802.11 MAC header
    [-] frame control
        -- protocol version : 0
        -- frame type : 00 management
        -- subtype :   0100 probe request
        [+] frame control
    -- duration : 0 usec
    -- dest addr : FF:FF:FF:FF:FF:FF  Ethernet Broadcast
    -- src addr : 00:90:96:A9:9A:F8
    -- bssid : FF:FF:FF:FF:FF:FF
    -- frag number : 0
    -- seq number : 46
[-] 802.11 frame body
    [-] info : SSID (0)
        -- length : 0
        -- SSID :
    [-] info : supported rates (1)
        -- length : 4
        -- rate : 1.0 mbps
        -- rate : 2.0 mbps
        -- rate : 5.5 mbps
        -- rate : 11.0 mbps
    [-] info : extended supported rates (50)
        -- length : 8
        -- rate : 6.0 mbps
        -- rate : 9.0 mbps
        -- rate : 12.0 mbps
        -- rate : 18.0 mbps
        -- rate : 24.0 mbps
        -- rate : 36.0 mbps
        -- rate : 48.0 mbps
        -- rate : 54.0 mbps
```

Gilligan sends a probe request along with his wireless capabilities, hoping to find any AP to connect to. He's basically hoping that a good AP will find him and want to set up a connection. So Gilligan sends a probe request discovery management message that contains the following elements:

- The SSID he's looking for (2 to 34 bytes). This field is sometimes left empty (set to the null value) for "any SSID." The probe request shown in Figure 4.19 shows no SSID value, so our host is looking for anyone that will accept his capabilities. He's not being too picky here—just like Gilligan stuck there on a desert island after a three-hour tour with not a whole lot of possibilities to pick from.

- The rates our host supports, which is usually all the 802.11b, 802.11g, or 802.11a rates (3 to 260 bytes). Gilligan will accept a connection from any AP that runs any rate in our example. Again, he's a pretty desperate host when it comes to finding an AP—*any* AP will do at this point!

If the SSID name is specifically mentioned in the request, the AP answers only if it has the relevant SSID. If null, or nothing, is listed, the AP should answer with whatever SSIDs it has available.

The answer is called a probe response, and it's very similar to the beacon in that the beacon contains all the information a client needs to know in order to be able to connect to the wireless network. The only differences are that probe responses do not contain TIM, and they're only sent when the AP receives a probe request. On the other hand, the beacon is sent on a regular basis. Figure 4.20 shows a probe response from our AP Ginger, telling Gilligan all about her capabilities. Since Gilligan isn't all that particular about which AP he connects to, well, we've got a match, don't we?

FIGURE 4.20 Probe response to our host

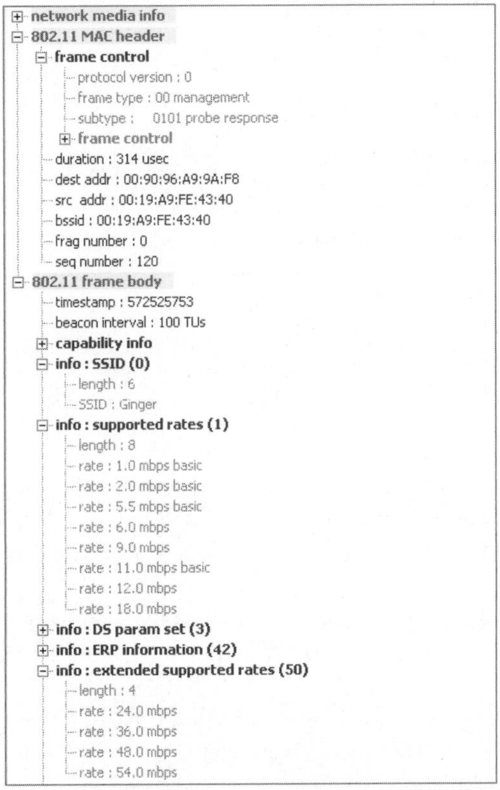

```
⊞ network media info
⊟ 802.11 MAC header
   ⊟ frame control
        ┈ protocol version : 0
        ┈ frame type : 00 management
        ┈ subtype :   0101 probe response
      ⊞ frame control
   ┈ duration : 314 usec
   ┈ dest addr : 00:90:96:A9:9A:F8
   ┈ src addr : 00:19:A9:FE:43:40
   ┈ bssid : 00:19:A9:FE:43:40
   ┈ frag number : 0
   ┈ seq number : 120
⊟ 802.11 frame body
   ┈ timestamp : 572525753
   ┈ beacon interval : 100 TUs
   ⊞ capability info
   ⊟ info : SSID (0)
        ┈ length : 6
        ┈ SSID : Ginger
   ⊟ info : supported rates (1)
        ┈ length : 8
        ┈ rate : 1.0 mbps basic
        ┈ rate : 2.0 mbps basic
        ┈ rate : 5.5 mbps basic
        ┈ rate : 6.0 mbps
        ┈ rate : 9.0 mbps
        ┈ rate : 11.0 mbps basic
        ┈ rate : 12.0 mbps
        ┈ rate : 18.0 mbps
   ⊞ info : DS param set (3)
   ⊞ info : ERP information (42)
   ⊟ info : extended supported rates (50)
        ┈ length : 4
        ┈ rate : 24.0 mbps
        ┈ rate : 36.0 mbps
        ┈ rate : 48.0 mbps
        ┈ rate : 54.0 mbps
```

Remember that an AP could send back "mandatory rates" that would have to be supported by the host seeking to connect, or it would be out of luck and forced to try to find another date. But since our little host and our AP run all the same rates, they're good to go. But, wait, as usual, it's more complicated than that: once our host and AP decide they can communicate, they still need to tango before our host gets to send frames. They must now authenticate and associate. Ginger still needs to make sure that Gilligan has the right key to her heart!

Authentication/Association Request

Now that our host Gilligan and our AP Ginger agree to try to connect (meaning that they're compatible), they need to authenticate to make sure they are who they say they are when they met and exchanged capabilities on www.findmeahotwirelessconnection.com. This is called the authentication phase, and for now, I just want you to get the basic concept of this process down. We'll go way deep into authentication in Chapter 5.

Okay—back to our island drama… At this point our goofy little host Gilligan is essentially saying to Ginger the AP, "Hey, I really am who I say I am—trust me!" Let's take a look at what this host-to-AP exchange really looks like in Figure 4.21.

FIGURE 4.21   Authentication request

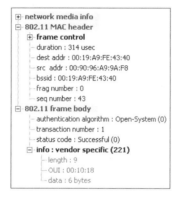

- The authentication algorithm number (2 bytes): This element defines which algorithm to use if the authentication requires a challenge—for example, if Ginger wanted to ask Gilligan for his ID.

- The authentication transaction number (2 bytes): The number 1 is used for the request, the number 2 for the AP answer, and so on. Figure 4.21 shows that Ginger is requesting authentication based on word alone, no ID, nothing—easy as coconut pie.

- The status code (2 bytes): This element is used to indicate if the authentication has been a success or failure. In this case, Ginger will believe Gilligan because she has no security enabled by default.

- Challenge text (3 to 255 bytes): The challenge text is found in certain frames only.

Authentication can be password based by using WEP or WPA (I'll define these terms in Chapter 5), but in our example, we're using open authentication, which is just a way to make sure that Gilligan has the physical ability to connect. As soon as Ginger made sure that our host is the romantic type, likes long walks on the beach, and can go the speeds he said he could in his profile (probe request), Ginger will answer with an authentication response that has a transaction number of 2 and a status code that is set to "success" to validate that Gilligan has the required capability to connect.

All good, but we're still not done. The next step is for Gilligan to ask Ginger on a formal date—the host, once authenticated, sends an association request, as shown in Figure 4.22.

FIGURE 4.22   Association request

This request amounts to nothing more than our host resending (confirming) the same capabilities it sent with its probe request. The association request message contains the following information:

- The client's capabilities (2 bytes): This field is the same type of field as the one found in the AP beacon frame.

- A listen interval field (2 bytes): This field specifies how often (in beacons) the client will listen to AP messages in case it has to turn to Power Save mode. When in this mode, the client turns its radio down to save power and wakes up to listen to see if the AP has traffic for it, like your computer's sleep mode.

- The SSID the client is trying to join (2 to 34 bytes): Unlike probe frames, in this case the name must be mentioned.

- The rates the client supports: 3 to 257 bytes.

Meanwhile, back on the island, AP Ginger answers with an association response frame. This contains exactly the same capability field, except that the listen interval is replaced by a status code (2 bytes), which usually equals "success." Ginger doesn't like to say "no" by default, hence the SSID by an association ID (2 bytes). AP Ginger follows up by adding her own rates to the association response. The answer Ginger gives is a message that says something like "Association succeeded, you are client number 2 in my BSA." Basically, this means that Ginger has added Gilligan to her little black book of hosts she's willing to connect with.

This seems redundant, I know. After all, the probe request and probe response should have been good enough to check each other out, right? The reason they happen here again is because the system just doesn't know if the client went through the probe process or tried to associate directly. It's all good; what's a little more overhead to our already overloaded network medium? But the "supported rates" information is very important because it indicates how fast the devices will be able to connect to each other.

Wow, so that wasn't so hard! The AP basically tried to connect to the host as soon as the host contacted the AP. A password-based authentication would contain a challenge phase, and Ginger really should be more careful these days! We'll come to AP Ginger's rescue and show her how to be more careful out there on the wireless network in Chapter 5 where she'll learn how to tell who is really contacting her, how to make her dates authenticate, and how to make sure all the Gilligans out there are password protected and encrypt their data transfer.

Deauthentication, Disassociation, and Reassociation Message

Once our host is communicating to the AP, we still need to maintain and/or end the connection to the network. That happens through the use of control frames, which I'll talk about in minute, but there are some management frames involved as well. These are called deauthentication, disassociation, and then reassociation, and they're used at times like when we travel out of cell coverage range and back into it.

A host can send a disassociation message, which results in the host and the AP becoming disassociated but still remaining authenticated. The connection would be terminated if either the host or AP sends a deauthentication method. Figure 4.23 shows a host that deauthenticated to an AP.

If the host and AP just lose association, either one can send a reassociation, but if our host disassociated, it can no longer communicate to the AP because it left the BSS. However, all this host would have to do is send a reassociation frame when it came back into the BSS because the AP still had the host in her little black book. At this point, the AP would send a reassociation response, and the host and AP would start communicating again.

FIGURE 4.23 A host deauthentication

Even though our host left the AP for possibly another AP, when our host came back to the AP cell coverage area, the AP didn't say "no" to reestablishing their connection—they reconnected ASAP. And interestingly enough, if this were an extended service set (ESS), the APs would have communicated about our little host buddy as he went from AP to AP, keeping track of our host on the DS (not just on the wireless network!), disassociating and reassociating to him as he roamed around. Even the authentication can be moved from AP to AP in some circumstances.

Before we move on to talking about the control frames that help us maintain our network medium, let's look at a summary figure of what our host looks like when communicating to our AP. Figure 4.24 shows how the two devices communicate, as well as the overhead involved in that communication.

FIGURE 4.24 Host to AP to host communication

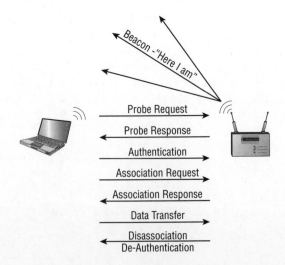

Wow, I know I've alluded to this many times in this chapter, but after looking at all this, it's hard to believe that these two devices can still send data after all the communication that must occur before they can even "date." It's pretty amazing stuff!

A Closer Look at Control Frames

Okay—so our host is up and running and the management frames are making sure the host stays authenticated and associated, but all the actual frames need to be controlled so they don't overwhelm the network medium and the receiving device. And after reading this far into the chapter you probably find it hard to believe that more than one host can communicate on this network at a time. Well, they can't—it only appears that they do.

The illusion that multiple hosts can communicate at the same time happens because of the control frames used in our 802.11 wireless networks that are used to optimize the network. Again, we're still grading on a curve here, but here's a list of the control frames used to create the magic:

- Acknowledgment (ACK)

- Request to Send (RTS)

- Clear to Send (CTS)

- Power-Save Poll

When in normal DCF mode, you'll find a common control frame called the acknowledgment (ACK) message. This message is sent as a response from the destination station to any frame received without a CRC error. It is a 13-byte-long frame, and Figure 4.25 shows you an example.

FIGURE 4.25   ACK frame

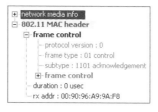

It only contains these fields:

- The usual frame control field (2 bytes).

- The duration field (2 bytes). This field is set to zero to indicate the end of the transmission process.

- The receiver address. This address is the address to which the frame is sent back, Gilligan in our example.

- An FCS.

The ACK frame is basically a blip on the network medium. There's only a DA in the frame and the receiving host assumes that this frame came from the AP where the host sent the frame in the first place. The RTS and CTS are light as well, and as an example, the RTS is used when the host needs to send a frame to an AP.

The RTS frame has both an SA and DA, and the duration field is set to show the time required for the whole transmission, which includes an SIFS, the CTS, another SIFS, the data frame, another SIFS, and finally the ACK. The CTS frame is shown in Figure 4.26.

FIGURE 4.26   CTS frame

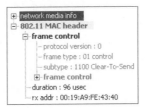

The CTS frame only has a DA to keep the frame as light as possible. The duration field is set to show what is still to come—an SIFS, the data frame, another SIFS, and the ACK. This RTS and CTS are known as protection mechanisms and are used in two different circumstances:

- The first scenario is when you're using 802.11b hosts in a mixed-cell environment with 802.11g hosts. This is not a good idea, as you should know by now, so be sure to turn "b" capability off on all your APs if you can. In an example of a mixed-cell environment, the 802.11g hosts sends an RTS message at 802.11b speed and the AP responds with a CTS at the same speed. Therefore, all the slower 802.11b hosts know that a transmission is about to occur and how long the transmission will last using DSSS. Of course, our 802.11g hosts need to send data at 802.11b speeds in a mixed-cell environment as well. Not so good!

- The second reason your AP would need to use the RTS/CTS is in a hidden node network. This situation occurs when two stations are so far apart in a BSA that they can't hear each other. In this case, even if one station sends data, the two stations could falsely believe that the medium is clear when in fact it's not, thus causing collisions. But since the AP is supposedly centrally located, it can send out a CTS to each host in turn, which both hosts will hear and will then wait until they think the medium is clear before trying to transmit.

Power Save Mode (PS-Poll)

Most wireless hosts, especially power-hungry laptops, have a power-saving mode. To save battery power, a wireless host that has its power-saving mode enabled will peacefully snooze away when it has nothing to send and isn't expecting a frame. It will still wake up periodically to listen to the AP messages, though.

The 802.11 header contains a field in the Frame Control subfield, which has the bit on that shows if the station is turning to Power Save mode. Figure 4.27 shows a host that has its Power Save mode enabled.

So as you can see, this is just an empty frame, called a null function, that's sent to the AP just to show that the machine's power save bit is set to 1. The snoozing machine then shuts its radio off if there's no data to send, and simply keeps a clock running to know when to wake up. The AP responds by buffering all the subsequent incoming traffic destined for this station (remember the Traffic Indication Map?). The AP keeps track of sleeping hosts with a number for each one.

FIGURE 4.27   Power Save mode is enabled

If a TIM is sent from an AP to a host, the host reads this frame, sees its number in the TIM, and sends a control frame called Power Save Poll (PS-Poll), meaning "I was in Power Save mode, but I see you have some traffic for me. I'm awake now, so please send it." The AP answers by sending the buffered packets.

Many vendors consider the Power Save mode inefficient, and I totally agree with them, for these two reasons:

- The mode creates a lot of overhead on the network because multiple messages have to be exchanged.

- The Power Save mode only saves between 10 and 15 minutes of power on a two-hour battery. The gain is not that substantial, so it just isn't worth the overhead it causes.

The default for Cisco is called Constant Awake Mode (CAM), but Power Save can be enabled if you want to go around visiting all the laptops in your company to tuck them in.

Nonstandard Wireless Technologies

Many devices transmit in the 802.11 frequency range, as well as other frequency ranges, all of which makes it important for you to understand how these devices relate to Wi-Fi. So in this section, I'm going to cover things from the everyday familiar to the mysterious and arcane like:

- Bluetooth
- Wireless phones
- ZigBee
- RF interference sources
- WiMAX

Bluetooth

This common word actually refers to a protocol defined in the IEEE 802.15 working group called Wireless Personal Area Network (WPAN). A special interest group (SIG) was also formed around it whose members promote the Bluetooth technology using the 802.15.1 protocol. Bluetooth is meant to be used in small areas with low power to enable users to connect up to seven devices, like wireless keyboards and mice and PDAs, to desktops or laptops, where your PC is known as the master and the satellite devices it discovers are called slaves. (But it has nothing to do with Nietzsche.) And the area that's transmitting around your PC is not called a cell as it is in 802.11—it's called a *piconet*.

Unfortunately for our WLANs, Bluetooth runs in the same frequency range as 802.11b/g, or 2.4GHz. The problem that surrounds Bluetooth results from the fact that it doesn't use DSSS as 22MHz wide channels. Instead, it uses FHSS at 1MHz wide channels and stays on each channel in the band for about 400ms each before moving on. Lucky for everyone, most Bluetooth devices have very low power!

And speaking of power, there are three classes of it:

Class 1 Has a maximum power of 100mW, just like our 802.11 clients and APs. There are seriously few manufactured devices in this power range—something we can all be thankful for!

Class 2 Has a maximum power of 2.5mW, which supports an area of around 33 feet, or 10 meters.

Class 3 Has a maximum power capacity of 1mW, and can go about 1 meter, or around 3 feet. (I like this one the best!)

The latest version of Bluetooth, version 2.1, hums along at around 2Mbps, which is plenty of bandwidth for keyboards and mice, but not everything.

Because Bluetooth uses FHSS, it's not compatible with any 802.11 devices, and since we use mostly Class 3 power, with some Class 2–powered devices, we don't experience too much interference because of the small distance the radios can reach.

Cordless Phones

From garage door openers to our cordless phones, the ISM band is open for business in your home and office. Since the FCC released the frequencies to the public, lots of manufacturers created devices that operate within these ranges. Cordless phones started out in the 900MHz range and evolved into the 2.4 and 5GHz range. They too run frequency hopping, so it's a good idea not to keep your phone on top or around your access point. But you already knew this and that is not what I want to discuss here.

What I want to talk about is another type of cordless phone in use called a Digital Enhanced Cordless Telecommunications (DECT) phone. Since this originated in Europe, the name use to be Digital European Cordless Telephone, but this standard has been adopted by countries all over the world so the name has changed along with its popularity. Chances are you are using one at your home right now.

Unlike 802.11, DECT uses both Time Division Multiple Access (TDMA) and Frequency Division Multiple Access (FDMA) at the Physical layer. These provide time slots for each voice packet. Since voice packets are predictable in that they're the same size every time, DECT phones can allocate more time slots than 802.11 wireless networks can. The reason for this is that the size and source of each packet is anyone's guess when it comes to our WLANs!

Clearly, DECT and Wi-Fi networks are not compatible in any way, so don't get these confused with the 802.11 wireless phones that are becoming increasingly popular in our corporate offices today. DECT uses the old ISDN Link Aggregation Control Protocol (LACP) to provide features like flow control, mobility management, and message services.

The power on a DECT phone is only about 10mW in Europe and 4mW in the United States, but beware—it can burst up to 250mW in Europe and 100mW in the U.S., which might be bad news for our WLANs. But since DECT phones don't normally operate in the 2.4GHz frequency, we're all right. And because they can jump frequencies with amazing agility, tracking these interfering bad boys down would be next to impossible. More evil results from the fact that they can send out a signal on a test channel to find availability even when they're not being used—nice.

ZigBee

This is a relatively new standard and most people have never even seen a ZigBee device yet. But I think you will pretty soon because they run on batteries, with very low power, which makes them a competitor to Bluetooth. ZigBee is part of the IEEE 802.15 protocol, but the working group is called the 802.15.4 WPAN, and their goals revolve around networking, security, and application protocols.

If you have seen a ZigBee device, this is because you've worked in a manufacturer or warehouse that needed sensors and ZigBee is great for applications that need low-power sensors. In fact, ZigBee can run on such extreme low power that you can use a battery in the device for years, not just weeks or months. However, the data rate it can handle is very low as well—up to 250kbps, with most being only around 20 or 40kbps! With its basement-low power, you would think the range would be low too, but it's actually longer than Bluetooth's. ZigBee can run from 10m to 100m, and as you just found out, Bluetooth's maximum is usually only around 10m. Even though ZigBee has an impressive reach, we won't be replacing our Bluetooth headsets with ZigBee because of that low data rate. And we won't see any ZigBee devices replacing our desktop devices any time soon either. However, the future vision of ZigBee is to create an application in a cell phone that can transform it into a universal remote control for your house for use on such devices as garage door openers, TVs, stereos, heaters and air conditioners, and lighting, so we'll just have to wait and see.

Although ZigBee has very low power (up to 60mW, but most offer considerably less), it still uses the ISM band. Therefore, it can interfere with your WLAN because 802.15.4 devices and 802.11 devices are not compatible and just see each other as noise. ZigBee uses up to 16 separate 5MHz channels in the 2.4GHz frequency range.

Non-802.11 Interfering Devices

Since the ISM band is unlicensed, go there and you'll find a crowded frequency range. Some devices to keep an eye on when designing and installing your WLANs are:

- Analog video cameras
- Microwave ovens
- Baby monitors
- Motion detectors
- Florescent lights
- Wireless headphones
- Wireless game controllers
- Wireless video cameras
- Radar
- Outdoor microwave links

Analog video cameras are probably the worst offenders when it comes to our 802.11 networks. These devices saturate the entire range of frequencies by using a constant signal with 100 percent duty cycle on the entire RF range.

Baby monitors are something probably not too many people think about, but they can actually run at 100mW and use several channels. In addition, microwave ovens operate between 800 and 1000W! If a microwave leaks just .0000001 percent, it will cause interference with your WLAN when in proximity of a host or AP.

WiMAX

Most people just say IEEE 802.16 when they mention WiMAX, and that's mostly accurate. WiMAX (Worldwide Interoperability for Microwave Access) has many different generations of protocols, but the two I'll discuss here are Fixed WiMAX (also called 802.16-2004, or *802.16d*), and Mobile WiMAX (which is also called 802.16e-2005, or *802.16e*).

Basic 802.16 had definitions in the 10 to 66GHz range, which, as you should know by now, is a licensed frequency range. It used OFDM that allowed it to use channels larger than 10MHz, and which was supposed to limit line-of-sight and interference issues. But this technology sunk like the Titanic and isn't in use today, mostly because even with OFDM, it had serious line-of-sight and distance issues that made it fizzle badly if used in the frequency range.

802.16a utilizes the 2GHz to 11GHz band, which includes both licensed and unlicensed frequency ranges. 802.16a is able to work in non-line-of-sight implementations, meaning it can, in theory, transmit around a building or over a hill. It can do this by recombining or reforming the signal on the other side of the obstacle. This is called low fading.

802.16b was added to 802.16a, and it allowed for something called time-division multiplexing (TDM) that made time slots available in a way that everyone could transmit in turn. It also used frequency-division multiplexing (FDM), which allowed multiple frequencies to be used—one up and one down, thus providing full-duplex communication.

802.16c was used to define what was mandatory and what was optional in the original 10 to 66GHz WiMAX communication range. It failed miserably; this group created so many options that interoperability became a tangled conundrum of impossibility, ensuring that no vendor's products could ever hope to work together.

802.16d was finally able to put 802.16a, b, and c together in a single protocol and create interoperability. Finally! And they added improvements such as quality of service (QoS) to provide a way to assign priorities to frames.

Lastly, there's 802.16e, which was a published protocol in February 2006, but in reality is still under development. The group created an interesting modulation technique called Scalable Orthogonal Frequency Division Multiplexing Access (SOFDMA). It uses the subcarriers just like OFDM does, but it allows for multiple users by allocating these subcarriers to different usage categories. In turn, this permits the modulation of speeds depending on the number of users and the size of the main carrier. Because several subcarriers can be grouped into fewer tones, it can provide the same speed with a slower modulation to users far away from the antenna. However, SOFDMA is not compatible with the OFDM in 802.16d, which means that 802.16d and 802.16e aren't compatible either.

802.16d can be used in a point-to-point environment (like a T1), up to about 50 miles, and point-to-multipoint environments up to about 70Mbps. The point-to-multipoint configuration can cover about 3,000 square miles using an omnidirectional antenna, covering a fixed location, connecting to last mile connections, and even to mobile users, but the distances available to mobile users' distances are short and limited.

802.16e is typically used in fixed-station environments and can travel about 30 to 50 miles if configured in a line-of-sight, meaning that a high-gain antenna will be placed close to the client. The non-line-of-sight range plummets to about 4 to 6 miles.

Most manufacturers are using the licensed frequency bands (although unlicensed bands can be used), so this makes installing and configuring WiMAX in your network pricey due to licensing costs. But this also means that WiMAX won't interfere with your 802.11 networks—trade-offs as usual!

Summary

In this chapter, I discussed the various regulations and wireless standards that are used in our wireless networks today. Mostly I discussed the IEEE standards because who doesn't use 802.11 in some way?

You learned about the RF spectrum in detail in Chapter 2, but we took off from there and learned how the standards in the RF spectrum led by the IEEE help make our wireless networks work today. It is important that you remember the rules set by the FCC in the United States and the ETSI in Europe, so I covered the FCC rules in this chapter. And don't forget that the Wi-Fi Alliance helps make sure manufacturers are following the IEEE guidelines here in the U.S.

We then discussed how DIFS and SIFS work, and how data, management, and control frames are used in IEEE wireless networks. We used Gilligan and Ginger as an example of how much overhead is involved in one host trying to connect to an AP.

We finished the chapter with a look at the various non-IEEE standards and their effect on the IEEE wireless networks you'll see installed all over the world.

Exam Essentials

Remember the various organizations and what they do to help us build our wireless networks today.   The FCC defines the bands we can use as unlicensed; the IEEE creates the rules manufacturers use to create products, which promotes interoperability (called ETSI in Europe); and the Wi-Fi Alliance tests the manufacturers' products to verify they followed the IEEE rules and are compliant.

Be familiar with the management frames used in an 802.11 network.   There are quite a few management frames used in an 802.11 network, but basically we have a beacon, probe, authentication, association, and then disassociation and deauthentication.

Know the control frames used in an 802.11 network.   These are easy to remember because there are only a few control frames: RTS, CTS, ACK, and PS-Poll.

Know the various nonstandard wireless networks and how they can affect our 802.11 wireless networks.   It is important to remember that analog video can wreak havoc on our 2.4GHz networks. We also need to pay attention to how WiMAX is used and configured, and the different specifications for WiMAX.

Written Lab

1. You have an 802.11g host that is working great, but an 802.11b host connects to the AP your host connected to. What encoding technology are you running?

2. What modulation technique do 802.11g and 802.11a use to get an extended rate?

3. What spread spectrum technology does Bluetooth use and in which frequency range?

4. Which governing body in the U.S. analyzes the applications and environment in which wireless network are used?

5. According to the current ETSI rule, what is the 2.4-GHz maximum transmitter output power for point-to-point installations?

6. Which non-IEEE standard has a constant signal with a 100 percent duty cycle?

7. Which non-IEEE standard is capable of working as a long-range system over several miles?

8. True/False: Typically, fixed WiMAX networks have a higher gain direction antenna installed near the client.

9. According to the current ETSI rule, what is the maximum transmitter output for point-to-point installations?

10. According to the current FCC rule, what is the maximum transmitter output for point-to-point installations?

Review Questions

1. What is the maximum EIRP output for the UNII-1 band?
   A. 17dBm
   B. 20dBm
   C. 22dBm
   D. 36dBm

2. What 802 group is ZigBee part of?
   A. 802.3
   B. 802.11
   C. 802.15.4
   D. 802.16

3. What modulation technique does 802.11b use?
   A. CCK
   B. DSSS
   C. FHSS
   D. OFDM

4. Which of the following were released by the FCC and are considered unlicensed frequencies? (Choose all that apply)
   A. 800MHz
   B. 900MHz
   C. 2400MHz
   D. 5GHz

5. How many channels in the 2.4GHz band are considered nonoverlapping the United States?
   A. One
   B. Two
   C. Three
   D. Four
   E. Five

6. Which UNII band allows an EIRP of 36dBm?
   A. UNII-1
   B. UNII-2
   C. UNII-2 Extended
   D. UNII-3

7. What working group is working on fixed WiMAX?

   A. 802.11j

   B. 802.11.i

   C. 802.16d

   D. 802.16e

8. Which Physical layer modulation technology is common to both the IEEE 802.11g and the IEEE 802.11a standards?

   A. BPSK

   B. CCK

   C. DSSS

   D. OFDM

9. Which of the following describes Bluetooth RF characteristics?

   A. Continuous transmitting— 5GHz range

   B. Frequency hopping—2.4GHz range

   C. Frequency hopping—5GHz range

   D. Continuous transmitting—2.4GHz range

10. Which governing body analyzes the applications and the environments in which wireless networks are used in Europe?

   A. EIRP

   B. ETSI

   C. FCC

   D. IEEE

   E. WiFi Alliance

11. Why are wireless analog video signals that are operating in the 2.4GHz band particularly harmful to Wi-Fi service?

   A. Analog video is a strong signal and increases the SNR.

   B. Analog video is a constant signal with 100 percent duty cycle.

   C. Analog video signals are slow frequency hopping and tend to affect the entire band.

   D. Analog video modulation is the same as Wi-Fi and causes interference.

12. Which are considered management frames on an 802.11 network? (Choose all that apply)

   A. RTS

   B. ACK

   C. Beacons

   D. Probe requests

   E. Deauthentication

13. Which are considered control frames on an 802.11 network? (Choose all that apply)

    A. RTS

    B. CTS

    C. ACK

    D. Probe requests

    E. Deauthentication

14. Which also are considered management frames on an 802.11 network? (Choose all that apply)

    A. CTS

    B. Authentication responses

    C. Association requests

    D. PS-Poll

    E. Probe responses

15. What does PS-Poll use as an empty frame to wake up a sleeping host in an ESS?

    A. RTS

    B. ATIM

    C. TIM

    D. Probe request

16. What is the center frequency in channel 6 of the 2.4GHz frequency range?

    A. 2412

    B. 2417

    C. 2437

    D. 2462

17. Which of the following devices can cause interference on your 802.11 wireless network? (Choose all that apply)

    A. TV remotes

    B. Microwave ovens

    C. Cordless phones

    D. Vista

18. ACKs use what type of CSMA/CA timing to make sure that the AP sends back the ACK to a client in high priority?

    A. DCF

    B. PCF

    C. SIFFS

    D. DIFFS

19. UNII-2 Extended added what two capabilities and is now called 802.11h?

   A. DCF

   B. PCF

   C. SIFFS

   D. DIFFS

   E. TPC

   F. DFS

20. What modulation technique does 802.16e use?

   A. DSSS

   B. FHSS

   C. OFDM

   D. SOFDMA

Answers to Review Questions

1. C. UNII-1 output power should not exceed 50mW (17dBm), with 22dBm EIRP maximum output.

2. C. The working group for ZigBee is called the 802.15.4 WPAN.

3. B. 802.11b uses DSSS, and 802.11g and 802.11a use OFDM; however, when 802.11g is using the 802.11b speeds, 802.11g uses DSSS.

4. B, C, D. To date, the FCC has released three unlicensed bands for public use: 900MHz, 2.4GHz (2400MHz), and 5GHz.

5. C. The U.S. has only three, Japan uses four, and Europe can have five mostly nonoverlapping channels.

6. D. The UNII-3 band is intended for outdoor bridge products and permits the use of external antennas. Output power should not exceed 1W (30dBm), with 36dBm EIRP.

7. C. Fixed WiMAX is also called 802.16-2004, or 802.16d, and Mobile WiMAX is also called 802.16e-2005, or 802.16e.

8. D. 802.11b uses DSSS, and 802.11g and 802.11a use OFDM; however, when 802.11g is using the 802.11b speeds, 802.11g uses DSSS.

9. B. Bluetooth devices use frequency hopping spread spectrum and run in the 2.4GHz band.

10. B. The ETSI is the equivalent to the FCC in the U.S.

11. B. Analog video running in the ISM band is probably the worst type of interference we can have around our wireless networks. It saturates the entire RF band, and this is called a 100 percent duty cycle, which leaves no room for 802.11 frames.

12. C, D, E. Beacons, probe requests, and deauthentication are considered management frames, whereas RTS, CTS, and ACK are control frames.

13. A, B, C. RTS, CTS, and ACK are considered control frames.

14. B, C, E. Authentication responses, association requests, and probe responses are all management frames. CTS and PS-Poll are control frames.

15. C. ATIM is used in peer-to-peer networks only. TIM is used on infrastructure BSS networks to wake a sleeping host.

16. C. Each ISM band channel is 22MHz wide. Each channel is known by its center channel. Channel 1's center channel is 2412, 6 is 2437, and 11 is 2462.

17. B, C. I know, I know, we all want to answer "Vista," but that is not causing interference on our wireless networks, just annoyance. Microwave ovens and cordless phones can cause interference.

18. C. DIFFS is normal priority whereas SIFFS is high priority.

19. E, F. Transmit power control (TPC) and dynamic frequency selection (DFS) are the two new capabilities we get when using 802.11h, or UNII-2 Extended.

20. D. 802.16e was a published protocol in February 2006, but in reality, it's still under development. The modulation technique used is called Scalable Orthogonal Frequency Division Multiplexing Access (SOFDMA).

Answers to Written Lab

1. DSSS

2. OFDM

3. Frequency hopping, 2.4GHz

4. IEEE

5. 20dBm

6. Analog video

7. WiMAX

8. True

9. 20dBm

10. 30dBm. Cisco's maximum is 20dBm, but the FCC allows 30dBm at the transmitter in the U.S.

Chapter

5

Introduction to Wireless Security

THE CCNA WIRELESS EXAM TOPICS COVERED IN THIS CHAPTER ARE:

✓ **Implement basic WLAN Security**

- Describe the general framework of wireless security and security components (authentication, encryption, MFP, IPS)

- Describe and configure authentication methods (Guest, PSK, 802.1X, WPA/WPA2 with EAP-TLS, EAP-FAST, PEAP, LEAP)

- Describe and configure encryption methods (WPA/WPA2 with TKIP, AES)

- Describe and configure the different sources of authentication (PSK, EAP-local or -external, Radius)

✓ **Describe WLAN fundamentals**

- Describe 802.11 authentication and encryption methods (Open, Shared, 802.1X, EAP, TKIP, AES)

Okay, it's true that wireless security is basically nonexistent on access points and clients by default. That's because the original 802.11 committee just didn't imagine that wireless hosts would one day outnumber bounded media hosts—which is actually where we're heading now, and fast! Same thing with the IPv4 routed protocol—unfortunately engineers and scientists didn't include wireless security standards robust enough to work in a corporate environment. This is why we were left to handle this problem with proprietary solution add-ons in our quest to create a secure wireless network for the last decade. However, some new standards provide us with really great wireless security, and they are somewhat easy to implement—with some practice, however, you still need to add some proprietary solutions today.

But don't misunderstand: I'm not just sitting here bashing the standards committees for the last decade, because the security problems we still face aren't completely their collective doing. The issues were compounded by the U.S. government because of export issues with its own security standards. Our world is a complicated place, so it follows that our security solutions would be as well!

In this chapter I am going to discuss the wireless threats that we face, the rudimentary (and insufficient) security methods provided by the 802.11 standard—specifically, the security weaknesses of WEP and the improvements provided by WPA. We will also explore the 802.11i standard and the improvements added with that amendment. When we discuss 802.11i we will examine types of EAP, including EAP-Fast, LEAP, PEAP, and EAP-TLS. With respect to encryption of the data, we will explore the difference between symmetrical and asymmetrical encryption, and we will compare TKIP and AES. Finally, we will cover key management and key caching—both important enhancements to handling those all-important keys used in both authentication and encryption.

Wireless Threats

Protection of data and the authentication process are certainly vitally important factors, but there are other wireless security threats lurking out there as well. We'll dive deeper into the processes and procedures designed to mitigate these dangers in Chapter 10, but let's briefly discuss them here.

Rogue APs

First, there's what we call rogue APs. These are APs that have been connected to your wired infrastructure without your knowledge. They may have been placed there by a determined hacker who snuck into your facility and placed one in an out-of-the-way location, or maybe even by an employee who just wants wireless access and doesn't understand the danger of doing this. Either way, it's just like placing an open Ethernet port out in the parking lot with a sign that says "Corporate LAN access here—no password required!"

Clearly, the worst type of rogue AP is the one some hacker has cleverly slipped into your network. This is because their goal probably doesn't end with simply gaining access to your network. The hacker has done this to entice your wireless clients to associate with his or her rogue AP, and it's accomplished by placing their AP on a different channel from your legitimate APs and setting its SSID in accord with your SSID. Wireless clients identify the network by the SSID, not the MAC address of the AP or the IP address of the AP, so jamming the channel that your AP is on will cause your stations to roam to the bad guy's AP instead. With the proper DHCP software installed on the AP, the bad guy can issue the client an address, and once that's accomplished, the hacker has basically "kidnapped" your client over to their network and can freely perform a peer-to-peer attack. And believe it or not, this can all be achieved from a laptop while the bad guy sits in your parking lot, because there are many types of AP software that will run on a laptop—yikes!

Mitigation

Okay, so one way to keep rogue APs out of the wireless network is to employ a wireless LAN controller (WLC) to manage the APs. This is a nice mitigation technique because APs and controllers communicate using Lightweight Access Point Protocol (LWAPP), and it just so happens that one of the message types they share is called Radio Resource Management (RRM). Basically, your APs monitor all channels by momentarily switching channels from their configured channel and by collecting packets to check for rogue activity. If an AP is detected that's not one usually managed by the controller, it's classified as a rogue, and if a wireless control system is in use, that rogue can be plotted on a floor plan and located. Another great benefit to this mitigation approach is that with it, your APs can also prevent workstations from associating with the newly exposed rogue—nice!

Ad Hoc Networks

As you already know, ad hoc networks are those created peer-to-peer or directly between stations and not through an AP. This can be a dangerous configuration because there's no corporate security in place, and since these networks are often created by unsophisticated users, you end up with the same scenario I just described that's primed for, and wide open to, a peer-to-peer attack. Even uglier, if the laptop happens to connect to the corporate LAN through an Ethernet connection at the same time the ad hoc network is created, the two connections could be bridged by a hacker to gain them access straight up into the wired LAN itself.

Mitigation

When you've got a Cisco Unified Wireless Network (CUWN) in operation, ad hoc networks can be identified over the air by the kind of frames they send, which are different from those belonging to an infrastructure network. When these frames are identified, the CUWN can prevent harm by sending out something known as deauthentication frames to keep your stations from associating via ad hoc.

Denial of Service

Not all attacks are aimed at the goal of stealing information. Sometimes the hacker just wants to cause some major network grief, like jamming the frequency where your WLAN lives to cause a complete interruption of service until you manage to ferret out the jamming signal and disable it. This type of assault is known as a denial-of-service (DoS) attack.

Mitigation

And this is how we deal with them... First, if someone is jamming the frequency, there isn't much, if anything, you can do. However, many DoS, man-in-the-middle, and penetration attacks operate by deauthenticating, or disassociating, stations from their networks. Some DoS attacks take the form of simply flooding the wireless network with probe requests or association frames, which effectively makes the overwhelmed network unavailable for normal transmissions. These types of management frames are sent unauthenticated and unencrypted. Since deauthentication and disassociation frames are classified as management frames, the Management Frame Protection (MFP) mechanism can be used to prevent the deluge. There are two types of MFP you can use, referred to as infrastructure and client. Let's take a look at each.

Infrastructure Mode

This cool strategy doesn't require configuration on the station—only the AP. Controllers generate a specific signature for each WLAN, which is added to each management frame it sends, and any attempt to alter this is detected by the MIC in the frame. Therefore, when an AP receives a management frame from an unknown SSID, it reports the event to the controller and an alarm is generated.

When an AP receives an MFP protected frame from an unknown SSID, it queries the controller for the key. If the BSSID isn't recognized by the controller, it will return an "unknown BSSID" message, which causes the AP to drop the frame. Figure 5.1 demonstrates this process.

FIGURE 5.1   Infrastructure mode

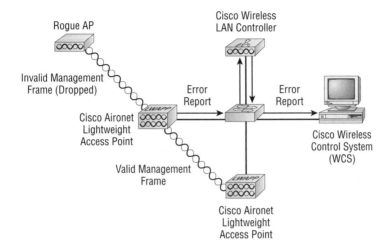

Client Mode

Often rogue APs attempt to impersonate the company AP. With client MFP, all management frames between the AP and the station are protected. Clients can detect and drop spoofed or invalid management frames. To use this feature, stations must support Cisco Client Extensions version 5 and must negotiate WPA2 with either TKIP or AES (I'll discuss these concepts a little later in the chapter). See Figure 5.2.

FIGURE 5.2   Client mode

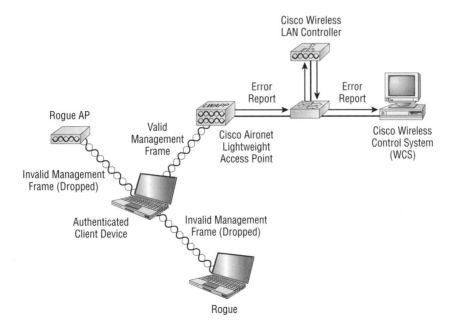

MFP is a feature that requires Cisco Client Extensions v5. The Cisco Compatible Extensions program is discussed in Chapter 6.

Passive Attacks

So far, the attacks I've talked about are in a category referred to as active attacks because in deploying them, the hacker is interacting with stations, the AP, and the network in real time. But there are other ways into the fort.

Passive attacks are most often used to gather information to be used in an active attack a hacker is planning to execute later, and they usually involve wireless sniffing. During a passive attack, the hacker captures large amounts of raw frames to either analyze online with sniffing software used to discover a key and decrypt it "on the fly." Offline simply means the bad guy will take the data away and analyze it later.

Mitigation

In addition to the tools already described, you can use an intrusion detection system (IDS) or an intrusion protection system (IPS) to guard against passive attacks:

IDS An intrusion detection system (IDS) is used to detect several types of malicious behaviors that can compromise the security and trust of your system. These malicious behaviors include network attacks against vulnerable services, data-driven attacks on applications, host-based attacks like privilege escalation, unauthorized logins, access to sensitive files, and malware—viruses, Trojan horses, and worms.

IPS An intrusion prevention system (IPS) is a computer security device that monitors network and/or system activities for malicious or unwanted behavior and can react, in real time, to block or prevent those activities. For example, a network-based IPS will operate inline to monitor all network traffic for malicious code or attacks. When either is detected, it can drop the offending packets while still allowing all other traffic to pass.

Which approach you want to use depends on the size of your wireless network and how tight your security needs to be. The goal of a security mechanism is to provide three features: confidentiality of the data, data integrity, and an assured identification process. The methods that I'm going to describe can be compared in three ways:

- The safety of the authentication process
- The strength of the encryption mechanism
- Its ability to protect the integrity of the data

I'll divide this topic into authentication and encryption and focus on the capabilities of each mechanism with respect to each feature. I'll also cover any integrity features that happen to be present as well.

🌐 Real World Scenario

War Driving

Wireless networks are pretty much everywhere these days—you can get your hands on a wireless access point for less than $100, and they're flying off the shelves. You can find APs in public places like shopping malls, coffee shops, airports, and hotels, and in some cities, you can just hang out in a downtown area and zero in on whole menu of APs operating in almost every nearby business.

Predictably, this proliferation of APs has led to a hobby for some people I met when I was in downtown Boulder, Colorado: it's called war driving. And these people went on to tell me that war drivers are everywhere today. These people told me that war driving (not for the technologically challenged) involves driving around in a car with a laptop, a wireless NIC, and a high-gain antenna, trying to locate open APs. If one with high-speed Internet access is found, it's like hitting the jackpot. These people do this aided by various software programs and global positioning systems (GPSs) to make their game even easier. But to me it's not always innocent—war drivers can be a serious security threat because they can potentially access anything on your wireless LAN, as well as anything it's attached to! Even though the people I met did not appear to be a sinister threat, you should realize that at the very least, they're possibly consuming precious resources from your network. So, if you happen to notice unusually slow-moving vehicles outside your home or business—especially those with computer equipment inside—know that you're the potential target of a war driver.

A good place to start discussing Wi-Fi security is by talking about the standard basic security that was incorporated into the original 802.11 standards and why those standards are still way too flimsy and incomplete to help us create a secure wireless network relevant to today's challenges.

Open Access

All Wi-Fi certified wireless LAN products are shipped in "open access" mode, with their security features turned off. Although open access or no security sounds scary, it can be totally appropriate and acceptable for public hot spots like coffee shops, college campuses, and even airport hot spots. But it's definitely not an option for an enterprise organization, and it's probably not even adequate for your private home network. Check out Figure 5.3.

FIGURE 5.3   Open access process

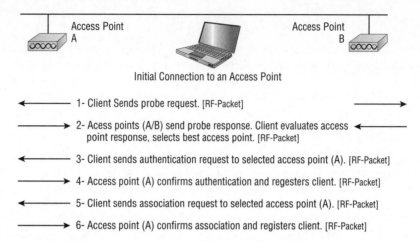

Initial Connection to an Access Point

← ─────── 1- Client Sends probe request. [RF-Packet]   ──────→

─────→ 2- Acess points (A/B) send probe response. Client evaluates access ←──────
          point response, selects best access point. [RF-Packet]

← ─────── 3- Client sends authentication request to selected access point (A). [RF-Packet]

─────→ 4- Access point (A) confirms authentication and regesters client. [RF-Packet]

← ─────── 5- Client sends association request to selected access point (A). [RF-Packet]

─────→ 6- Access point (A) confirms association and registers client. [RF-Packet]

Interestingly enough, you can see that an authentication request is sent and "validated" by the AP. However, when open authentication is used or sometimes set as "none" in the wireless controller (which I'll talk more about later), the request is pretty much guaranteed not to be denied. Understand that this authentication is done at the MAC layer (Layer 2), not to be confused with the higher-layer authentication we'll discuss after the client is associated to the access point.

With what I've told you so far, I'm sure you agree that security seriously needs to be enabled on wireless devices during their installation in enterprise environments. But believe it or not, a surprising number of companies don't enable any WLAN security features, dangerously exposing their valuable data networks and resources to tremendous risk.

The reason that these products are shipped in open access mode is so that anyone—even someone without any IT knowledge—can buy an access point, plug it into their cable or DSL modem, and voilà—they're up and running. It's marketing, plain and simple, and simplicity sells. But that doesn't mean you should leave the default settings—unless you want to allow that network to be open to the public!

Security Measures

After reading about all the major wireless threats that are out there, the question on your mind is likely, "So, how can I protect myself?" Fortunately, effective programs are already in place, as well as several steps you can take to avoid being compromised. A good place to start this topic is with a discussion of SSID and MAC security, straight from the designers of 802.11 standard.

Service Set Identifiers (SSIDs) and Media Access Control (MAC) Address Authentication

To create basic security, the original designers of 802.11 included the use of SSIDs, open or shared-key authentication, static Wired Equivalent Privacy (WEP), and optional Media Access Control (MAC) authentication. Sounds like a lot, but none of these really offers any type of serious security solution—they may be adequate for use on a common home network, but that's it. I'll go over them anyway.

SSID is a common network name for the devices in a WLAN system that creates the wireless LAN. An SSID prevents access by any client device that doesn't have the SSID. The thing is, by default, an access point broadcasts its SSID in its beacon many times a second. And even if SSID broadcasting is turned off, a bad guy can discover the SSID by monitoring the network and just waiting for a client response to the access point. Why? Because, believe it or not, that information, as regulated in the original 802.11 specifications, must be sent in the clear—how secure!

Last, client MAC addresses can be statically typed into each access point, and any of them that show up without a MAC address in the filter table will be denied access. A major benefit of the lightweight approach to WLAN management is that the MAC addresses don't have to be entered into each AP, but rather into the WLC. The MAC address database can also be stored on a RADIUS server—more on that in a bit—for centralized management.

Sounds good, right? Well, there's a catch—all MAC layer information must be sent in the clear, which means that anyone equipped with a free wireless sniffer can just read the client packets sent to the access point and spoof their MAC address.

Wired Equivalent Privacy (WEP) is better than no security if administered correctly. But there are many methods available today to break the static WEP key very quickly. Therefore, basic static WEP keys are no longer a viable option in today's corporate networks without some of the proprietary fixes that run on top of it. Let's look into exactly what we're up against in today's wireless environments.

Authentication

Authentication is essentially the process of identifying yourself. It has no effect on the confidentiality or integrity of the data because it's simply there to prove your identity or, in some cases, a device's identity. However, all authentication methods are not created equally. Depending on the type of authentication mechanism being used, the degree of security the transmitted authentication request is given varies quite a bit. Some methods protect the transmission by sending it through an encrypted tunnel, whereas others don't—they just send away, straight up in clear text. And with that latter, clear text type of transmission, all a hacker needs is a packet sniffer to capture the authentication packet and resend the name and the password.

Authentication can be based on things like:

- Something you know, like a username and a password
- Something you have; for example, a smart card device
- Something you are—biometrics like a retina scan or fingerprint

Furthermore, there's a whole bunch of combinations of authentication requirements that can be employed and enforced. For example, using a smart card plus a PIN, or a fingerprint plus and a name and password, and so on. At any rate, the more authentication methods you include, the safer and more secure the authentication process will be. But remember, not everyone or every network needs Fort Knox–level security, and though it seems that the more secure the better, there's a trade-off to making your network a fortress. The more secure you make your network, the more complicated it becomes for your users to gain access, and performance could be hampered as well. It comes down to striking a good balance between the amount of security imposed and the ease of access to network resources that makes sense based on the specific needs of an individual or corporation.

Okay, so as I mentioned, authentication can be applied to the user as well as the device used to make a remote connection. It can be achieved with a digital certificate issued to the machine or in other ways as well. This type of authentication can occur either at Layer 2 by a switch or at an AP when the connection is first initiated, or it can be achieved later in the connection process at Layer 3. Either way, I highly recommend using Layer 2 authentication only to augment the authentication imposed on a user since there's just no guarantee that some bad guy hasn't gotten a hold of or taken control of the device that's being used to gain access.

Authentication Methods

The authentication methods I'm going to cover vary in the degree of protection they provide, as well as in how complicated they are to administer. I'll start with the least secure and work up to the most secure methods.

Open and Shared Authentication

Two types of authentication were specified by the IEEE 802.11 committee: open and shared-key authentication. Open authentication involves little more than supplying the correct SSID, but it's the most common method in use today. With shared-key authentication, the access point sends the client device a challenge-text packet that the client must then encrypt with the correct WEP key and return to the access point. Without the correct key, authentication will fail and the client won't be allowed to associate with the access point. Figure 5.4 shows shared-key authentication.

Understand that shared-key authentication is still not considered secure because all an intruder has to do to get around it is detect both the clear-text challenge, the same challenge encrypted with a WEP key, and then decipher that WEP key. So it's not a surprise that shared key isn't used in today's WLANs.

With open authentication, even if a client can complete authentication and associate with an access point, the use of WEP prevents the client from sending and receiving data from the access point unless the client has the correct WEP key. A WEP key is composed of either 40 or 128 bits, and in its basic form, it's usually statically defined by the network administrator on the access point, and on all clients that communicate with that access point. When static WEP keys are used, a network administrator must perform the time-consuming task of entering the same keys on every device in the WLAN. Clearly we now have fixes for this because tackling this manually would be administratively impossible in today's huge corporate wireless networks!

FIGURE 5.4   Shared-key authentication

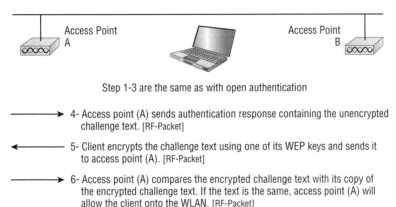

Step 1-3 are the same as with open authentication

4- Access point (A) sends authentication response containing the unencrypted challenge text. [RF-Packet]

5- Client encrypts the challenge text using one of its WEP keys and sends it to access point (A). [RF-Packet]

6- Access point (A) compares the encrypted challenge text with its copy of the encrypted challenge text. If the text is the same, access point (A) will allow the client onto the WLAN. [RF-Packet]

EAP

WPA2 and 802.11i can both use an EAP method for authentication. Extensible Authentication Protocol (EAP) isn't a single method, but a framework that enhances the existing 802.1X framework. The EAP framework describes a basic set of actions that will take place, and each EAP type differs in the specifics of how it operates within the framework. These variables include things like whether they use passwords or certificates and the ultimate level of security provided. Figure 5.5 illustrates this process.

FIGURE 5.5   EAP process

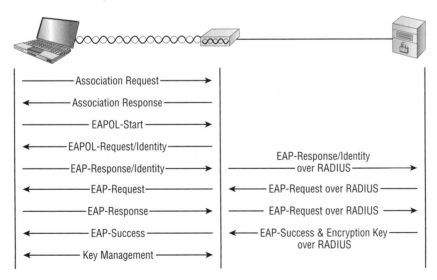

Here are the steps involved:

- The wireless station and the AP perform a normal Layer 2 association. The port to the rest of the network is not open.

- The station indicates that it's configured for EAP and would like to authenticate. This is the EAPOL-START frame.

- The AP challenges the station about its identity with the EAPOL-Request/Identity frame.

- The station responds with its credentials using the EAP-Response/Identify frame, which the AP relays over to the RADIUS server and is protected by RADIUS encryption.

- The RADIUS server makes its own authentication challenge to the station with the EAP-Request over RADIUS frame. This frame is forwarded by the AP back to the station as an EAP frame.

- The station responds with an EAP-Response frame, which is forwarded as a RADIUS message back to the RADIUS server.

- The RADIUS server replies with success and, if configured to do so, also sends the station an encryption key. This frame is finally forwarded back to the station, and the AP opens the port to the rest of the network.

Local EAP

EAP normally uses a RADIUS server as the authentication server in the process, but the AP can be configured as both the authenticator and the authentication server. This process is an arrangement called Local EAP. The user database that's checked to authenticate the users can be local to the AP, or it can be an LDAP server like Active Directory. Local EAP supports Lightweight EAP (LEAP), EAP-FAST, and EAP-TLS authentication between the controller and wireless clients, and I'll cover these in the next section. Local EAP typically is used only as a backup option if the global RADIUS server becomes unavailable for some reason.

Now let's dig into the various flavors of EAP. I'm not going to cover all of the types of EAP that exist because doing that is too much information for this book. I'll cover the most relevant types here, but to understand some of these methods, you must first understand what certificates and PKIs are.

Certificates and PKI

Some of the EAP methods require that certificates be used as the credential used during authentication. This means that to implement those methods you must have a Public Key Infrastructure (PKI) in your network. A PKI requires a certificate server that issues certificates to your users and/or devices. These certificates, which consist of a public/private key pair, must be securely installed on the devices and renewed at regular intervals.

In symmetric encryption, the two encryption keys are the same, just as they are with WEP keys, but in asymmetric encryption, the key used to encrypt is different from the key used to decrypt. In PKI, asymmetric keys are used, and the keys are called a public/private key pair. Certificates are binding regulations of a public/private key pair that are generated by a certificate server to a user or computer. As long as two parties trust the same certificate source, called the trusted certificate authority (CA), they can trust the certificate they're presented with for authentication. These keys can also be used for encryption and as digital signatures.

Despite the other uses of public/private keys, our focus here is the use of the certificates as a form of authentication. And as a means of identifying the device or the user, this is considered the highest form of authentication when compared to names and passwords. What all this means is that as long as the AP or controller and the station or user trust the CA that issued the certificates, the certificate is trusted as a means of identification as well.

EAP-TLS

EAP Transport Layer Security (EAP-TLS) is the most secure method, but it's also the most difficult to configure and maintain. To use EAP-TLS, a certificate must be installed on both the authentication server and the client. An authentication server pair of keys and a client pair of keys need to be generated first, signed using a PKI, and installed on the devices. On the station side, the keys can be issued for the machine itself and/or for the user. The EAP-TLS process is shown in Figure 5.6; as you can see, it follows the EAP framework.

FIGURE 5.6   EAP-TLS process

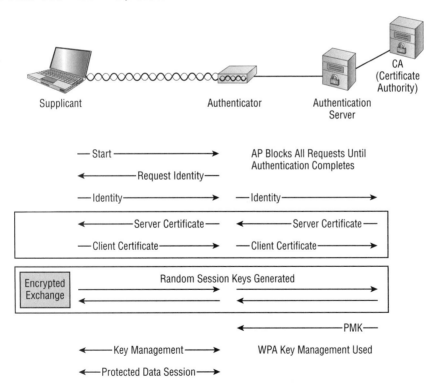

So here, in the authentication stage, the station, along with the authentication server (RADIUS, LDAP, or Local EAP), exchange certificates and identify each other. Mutual authentication is a beneficial feature that ensures the station that it's communicating with is the proper authentication server. After this process is completed, random session keys are created for encryption. The server also sends the pairwise master key and manages the keys, as you'll learn later in this chapter.

EAP-FAST

EAP-Flexible Authentication via Secure Tunneling (EAP-FAST) was first supported in Cisco Client Extensions v3, and is designed to provide the same level of security as EAP-TLS without the difficulty of managing certificates and a PKI. It does this by using a unique process to create an encrypted tunnel, and then using that tunnel to authenticate the client. This process has three phases:

Phase 0   In this phase, the server generates a Protected Access Credential (PAC) for the station. This serves the same purpose later as the key pair used in EAP-TLS. This PAC can be installed manually on the station or can be installed automatically by the server and sent to the client if the connection between the two is secure. The PAC has several key components:

- PAC-key, which you can think of as the "secret" part of the PAC, somewhat like the private key in a certificate.
- PAC-opaque, which is sent from the station to the server to be used to identify the station. The server uses this to retrieve the PAC key.
- PAC-info, which contains information about the server called Authority ID.

Phase 1   These components are used as shown in Figure 5.7 to create a secure tunnel. After the tunnel is established, authentication occurs through the tunnel.

When the station sends its "identity" to the server, it's really only a network access identifier and doesn't have the credentials required for access.

The server sends its authority-ID (A-ID) to the station and the station uses this to choose the proper PAC opaque to return. This serves as authentication of the server for the station.

After the station returns its PAC opaque, the server decrypts it and retrieves the PAC key.

Phase 2   The PAC key is used to create the tunnel. After this is done, the station is authenticated through the tunnel. This is done with either passwords or security tokens.

PEAP

Whereas EAP-TLS requires certificates on both the server and the stations, and EAP-FAST requires certificates on neither, protected EAP (PEAP) requires one on the server but none on the stations. This EAP method was developed in a rare moment of enlightened cooperation between Microsoft, Cisco, and RSA Security—the same bunch who came up with the RC4 algorithm, among others.

FIGURE 5.7   EAP Phase 1

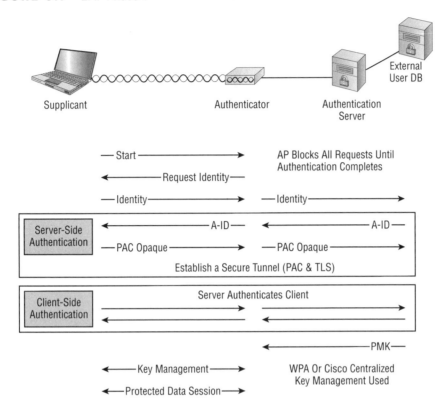

There are two implementations, and the main difference between them is that they differ in the authentication mechanism that's used after a secure tunnel is created:

- PEAP-GTC uses a Generic Token Card (GTC).

- PEAP-MSCHAPv2 uses Microsoft Challenge Handshake Authentication Protocol version 2 (MS-CHAPv2).

The process is depicted in Figure 5.8 and includes the following steps:

1. The process starts with the station identifying itself. Believe it or not, this identification can even be wrong and it will still succeed! In fact, this is quite often purposely configured incorrectly to throw off hackers since this part is vulnerable and sent in the clear. As I mentioned, the server will respond anyway.

2. The server sends back a certificate to the client. The client uses this to verify the identity of the server with the CA.

3. At this point, the client generates a master key and encrypts it using the server's public key. Remember, a certificate consists of a public and private key. To anyone "listening"

that's trying to capture this process, it will appear the same way as what's happening during EAP-TLS when the client authentication phase is taking place. Now a secure tunnel is created with these keys.

4. Through the newly created tunnel, the server requests identity a second time, and now the station responds with its real credentials. As in other EAP methods, all transmissions are now protected within the tunnel.

FIGURE 5.8   PEAP process

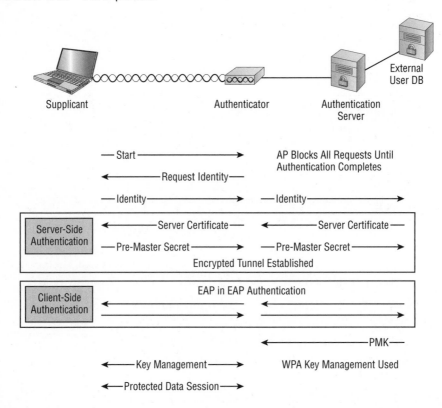

LEAP

Lightweight EAP (LEAP) is a method developed by Cisco early on in the wireless game back in 2000. It's available in many non-Cisco devices through licensing from Cisco, and it uses only usernames and passwords. This method was seriously compromised with the release of a hacking tool called ASLEAP, which could quickly break the LEAP password. With this in mind, I don't recommend implementing LEAP, especially with all the other great nonproprietary options available.

The process, shown in Figure 5.9, follows these steps:

1. The process starts with the AP sending an identity request to the station. The station replies with a username.

2. The AP wraps that in a RADIUS message and then sends it to the server.

3. The server challenges the station and the station responds using MS-CHAPv2.

4. The station challenges the server and the server responds.

5. Using a proprietary algorithm, the server and the station derive a session key to use for encryption.

FIGURE 5.9   LEAP process

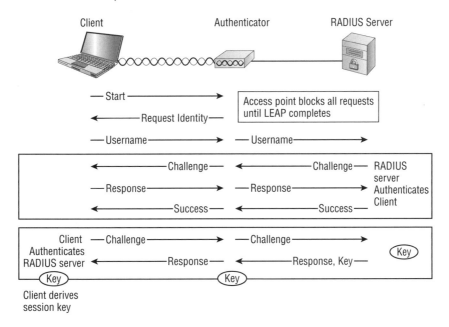

802.1X

To fully understand 802.1X operations, you need to understand the 802.1X framework first. If you haven't ever read the entire IEEE 802.1X standard; which if you ever have trouble falling asleep I highly recommend. Anyway 802.1X isn't used only with wireless networks; it's a framework that you can employ to authenticate and control access to wired networks, VPN connections, and dial-in connections as well. Fundamentally it is the pack mule for extended authentication. By extended authentication I mean authentication that isn't just a username and password that resides locally on the device that is authenticating you. With this process you can use the many types of EAP that I will discuss later in this chapter.

The process requires three components, by the 802.1X standard they are called the:

- Supplicant, is the client or device trying to gain access
- Authenticator, is the device controlling access such as the AP, Switch, or VPN device
- Authentication server, is the central authentication database typically called the RADIUS server

Now as far as 802.1X's use with wireless networks, it can be used with most of the implementation standards I am sure you have heard of: WEP, WPA, WPA2 and 802.11i. Not all of these are the same in regard to their use of 802.1X though. All of the standards except 802.11i use 802.1X as an optional component for authentication. For a vendor's device or implementation of the 802.11i standard, 802.1X is supposed to be required, but not all vendors fully comply with the standard. As I said, there are other methods; this is optional. For WEP and WPA, the use of 802.1X was added as an option after the standard was released, but for WPA2 it was included in the standard as a highly recommended option.

In fact, this is the difference in WPA or WPA2 personal and enterprise that you may have heard of. In the personal implementation, typically a pre-shared key is used, and in enterprise the 802.1X standard is used. These terms are more of a marketing strategy than a real implementation term or standard.

Since the authentication server will typically be a RADIUS server, let me take a brief detour and explain RADIUS before returning to 802.1X.

RADIUS and AAA

Remote Authentication Dial-In User Service (RADIUS) is a networking protocol that offers several nice security benefits:

- Authorization.
- Centralized access.
- Accounting supervision regarding the users and/or computers that connect to and access our network's services. Once RADIUS has been authenticated, it allows us to specify the type of rights a specific user or workstation has.
- Control as to what a device or user can do within the network.
- A record of all access attempts and actions.

The provision of authentication, authorization, and accounting is called AAA, or "Triple A." In this process, authentication takes place first, followed by authorization of any and all actions that can be performed by the security principal, after which the accounting function records all those actions. Once authentication has taken place, the entity with knowledge of actions allowed for the security principal, like a WLC, can then allow access to the resources being requested.

RADIUS has ascended to stardom because of its AAA features and is often employed by ISPs, web servers, wireless networks, and APs, as well as network ports—basically, by anybody who wants or needs an AAA server. These servers are becoming critically important in large corporate environments because they offer security for wireless networks. Now let's return to 802.1X and examine the relationship between the roles of supplicant, authenticator, and the authentication server.

Supplicant, Authenticator, and the Authentication Server

I want you to remember that regardless of the application, the roles remain the same—only the devices involved change. Check out Figure 5.10.

FIGURE 5.10   EAP server

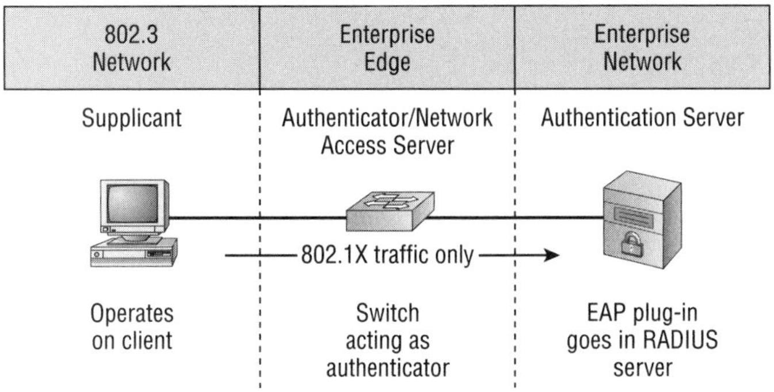

Okay—so here you can see that the supplicant is a computer that's located on the wired portion of the network. The switch is the authenticator, and the RADIUS server is the authentication server. So what does this have to do with wireless? Mostly the concepts, but I just wanted to illustrate its use outside of the wireless environment so you understand how it works. Also, it's important because many networks today are hybrid environments that are wired networks with wireless sections that connect to them.

Anyway, the computer is turned on and accesses the switch port on the switch. It sends an ID to the switch. The switch uses an EAP plug-in to contact the RADIUS server and validate the computer's ID. Once validation is completed, the switch will open the switch port and allow access to the rest of the network.

When applied to a wireless network, only the devices change. The wireless station becomes the supplicant, the AP (or controller) becomes the authenticator, and the RADIUS server remains the authentication server. Figure 5.11 illustrates this nicely.

So once again, the wireless station will not be allowed past the logical port on the AP until authentication is complete, just like the wired station in Figure 5.10.

An additional feature of the RADIUS server is that it can manage encryption keys if you want it to. When the authentication process completes, the RADIUS server can send the station and the AP a session key to use for all wireless encryption. It will also send along the common key that's being used by all stations and the AP for multicast and broadcast traffic. This makes management of the encryption keys much simpler and more secure since no humans really know what they are and they change every session.

FIGURE 5.11   RADIUS server process

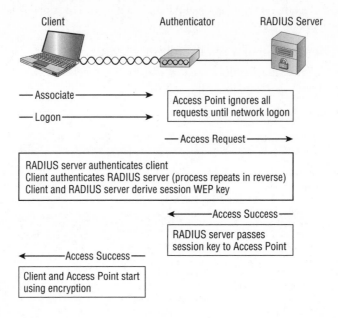

Encryption

Whereas authentication uniquely identifies the user and/or machine, the purpose of encryption is to protect the data or the authentication process by scrambling the information in a way that it becomes unreadable by any party trying to capture the raw frames.

A variety of methods are used to encrypt information, and new methods are always being developed. But whatever the method, it will follow the same basic process. The original data, in a form we call *plain text*, is scrambled with an agreed upon process called the *cipher*. The result is called the *cipher text*. When the cipher text is received, the receiver uses a decryption cipher or key to return the data back to its original *plain text*. The overall process is shown in Figure 5.12.

FIGURE 5.12   Encrypting data

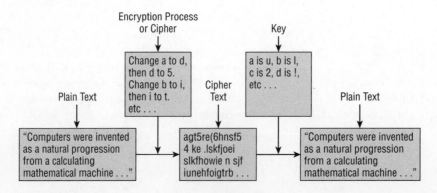

The strength of the encryption mechanism comes from several factors inherent in the encryption process:

The sophistication of the encryption process or encryption algorithm   These algorithms are mathematical formulas used to perform operations on the original data. The operations can include substituting one letter for another, shifting the order of the letters (transposition), and sometimes, using a combination of both. Some algorithms do these operations multiple times to increase the level of confusion and, therefore, the encryption's strength. They also differ in whether they operate on single bits of data (stream ciphers) or on blocks of data (block ciphers).

The length of the key used in conjunction with the algorithm   The key is used as a part of the process and is essentially a string of random characters. The key is what makes the process unique between users and machines that are using the same algorithm. The longer the key, the more secure the process. The trade-off—you knew there had to be a cost, right?— is that longer keys work the processors harder on each device due to the mathematical calculations that must be performed in both the encryption and the decryption process. So the longer the key, the more overhead.

The relationship between the keys used to encrypt and those used to decrypt   We'll cover this in detail in the next section, but for now know that the keys used to encrypt and decrypt can be symmetrical or asymmetrical.

Symmetrical and Asymmetrical Encryption

With symmetrical encryption, the process used to encrypt the data or the authentication process is reversed to decrypt the information. For example, if the process begins with:

1.   Substitute z for a and g for l.

2.   Switch the third character with the fifth and the 10th character with the 15th.

then the reverse process would be:

1.   Switch the third character with the fifth and the 10th character with the 15th.

2.   Substitute a for z and l for g.

On the other hand, with asymmetrical encryption, the keys are not simply the reverse of each other—they're completely different on the surface. Even so, they're still mathematically related in such a way that one can be used to encrypt and the other to decrypt. The difference in these methods is illustrated in Figure 5.13. Notice that the keys are different in asymmetrical encryption. As you learned earlier, the rule is that there's a trade-off that directly reflects the amount of security between ease of use and functionality. Encryption is no different, and there are advantages and disadvantages to using each type:

- Symmetrical isn't considered as secure because the key has to be the same on all devices— like when using static WEP. When the same key is located in a bunch of different places, the odds of that key being compromised increase greatly. The advantage is that symmetric encryption works a whole lot faster. Some encryption processes use both methods and strike a balance between the speed symmetrical encryption offers, while combining the mechanism with a separate round of asymmetrical encryption.

- Asymmetrical encryption is a lot more secure, but it's also much slower to process. Use it when your security needs outweigh the speed of the transaction.

FIGURE 5.13   Encryption types

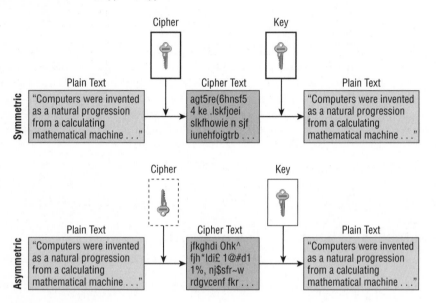

Key Management

Another important factor in encryption centers on keys and managing them, and is also related to the type of encryption used. Generally, there are two methods—the first uses a common key for all users, and in the second method, a unique key is employed for each user.

Common Keys

When common keys are used, the keys are the same everywhere; on the AP and on each station (think static WEP). The dangers are the same as described earlier, only there's an additional administrative headache added to the mix—the keys must periodically change and that has to be done manually on all devices. Check out Figure 5.14.

FIGURE 5.14   Common keys

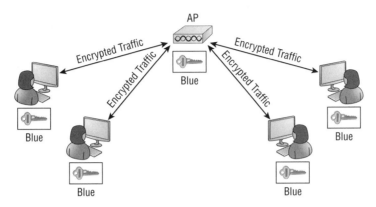

These common keys can be used for various functions and in combinations of functions, such as:

- Authentication only, after which all data is sent in clear text
- Authentication and encryption
- Encryption of the data only

Individual Keys

With individual keys, the keys for each user or machine are unique. This approach provides much tighter security but presents an ugly problem regarding what to do about broadcast and multicast traffic. The good news is that this issue has been solved by using an individual key for unicast communication and a common key for broadcast and multicast transmissions. The individual method is shown in Figure 5.15.

FIGURE 5.15   Individual keys

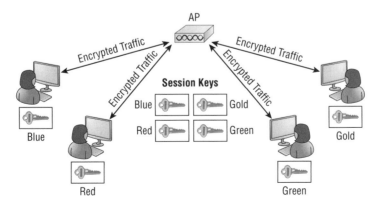

You'll notice in Figure 5.15 that these keys are called *session keys*. This is because they're unique to each user's session with the AP. The keys can be derived in two different ways. First, they can be unique from the outset, meaning that as in seen the figure, either the individual keys must be on the AP and the stations, or each session key must be derived from a common key that's present on the AP. Then, a unique key is generated for each session that the user has with the AP, never to be used again on any other session with the AP. When keys are unique from the outset, they're usually managed from a central location in the network and not on the AP. This type of key management is a feature of WPA, WPA2, and 802.11i.

Encryption Methods

There are two basic types of encryption methods used in most wireless networks today: Temporal Key Integrity Protocol (TKIP) and Advanced Encryption Standard (AES). However, before we had TKIP and AES, our options were limited to using RC4 encryption with static keys. This was mostly implemented using WEP, which is a pretty weak security system and has given wireless networks a bad name in the security arena for almost a decade. TKIP and AES have come to the rescue, and we can safely secure our wireless networks and rebuild the reputation of making good, secure, wireless networks. Let's take a look at these various options.

RC4 and Static Keys

As I mentioned earlier, this type of authentication really means no authentication at all. A static encryption key (like WEP) basically involves configuring a matching encryption key on both the AP and the station. This can run on top of open authentication; the AP responds to an authentication request with an authentication response. Or the AP can use the shared key option by sending a random string of characters or text. The station responds by encrypting that text with the static WEP encryption key and then sends what's known as cipher text back to the AP. The AP then decrypts the text and compares it with what was sent; if it matches, the AP knows that the station has the correct key. This is good because with it, the key isn't just plainly sent across the network.

The hole in shared-key authentication lies in that challenge text packet. Because it's initially sent unencrypted and then returned as an encrypted packet, it's not all that difficult for a bad guy to capture both packets and reverse-engineer the stream cipher.

So it's good to remember that the WEP encryption mechanism can use either an open or a shared key authentication mechanism. After authenticating the client, the AP encrypts the text using the RC4 algorithm. Above and beyond the issue of capturing both the plain text and encrypted text and reverse-engineering the key, the implementation of the RC4 algorithm in WEP leaves it wide open to cracking. Let's check out some of WEP's weaknesses.

First, understand that an encryption mechanism must have an element of randomness to its calculations to be truly safe. What this means is that two packets with the same contents, like a ping packet, shouldn't be the same when encrypted. WEP introduces this randomness with something called an initialization vector (IV). Every new frame gets a 24-bit IV (random value), also known as a key stream.

The RC4 algorithm uses this IV and the key to encrypt the packets, resulting in a unique result even for frames with the same contents. The result is that after the data is encrypted, the IV is included in the frame header so that the receiver can then use it to decrypt the frame. The receiver already knows the key and the algorithm. Take a look at Figure 5.16 to see this process.

FIGURE 5.16   WEP process

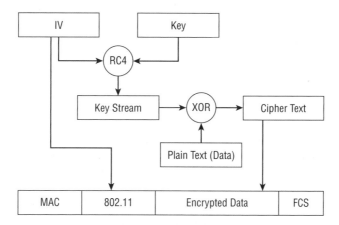

As you can see, anyone capturing the packet already has part of the key used, and since the RC4 algorithm is well known, they actually have two out of three pieces, missing only the key. More ugly problems with WEP include:

- There's no authentication of the packets, making man-in-the-middle attacks possible.
- Due to the nature of the static key, cracking tools can discover a 104-bit key fairly quickly.
- The wireless infrastructure authenticates the station but the station doesn't authenticate the infrastructure, allowing rogue APs to impersonate corporate APs.
- Data encryption is really weak.
- IVs can be repeated, which provides insight into cracking the WEP key.

For all of these reasons, using WEP alone is clearly a bad idea for an enterprise wireless network. Still, as long as it's used in combination with other more secure methods, WEP can still play a role in security.

Temporal Key Integrity Protocol (TKIP)

Put up a fence, and it's only a matter of time until bad guys find a way over, around, and through it. And true to form, they indeed found ways to get through WEP's defenses, leaving our Wi-Fi networks vulnerable—stripped of their Data Link layer security! So someone had to come to the rescue. In this case, it happened to be the IEEE 802.11i task group and the Wi-Fi Alliance, joining forces for the cause. They came up with the solution we discussed earlier called Temporal Key Integrity Protocol (TKIP). We've looked at this with respect to the protections it affords the authentication process, but it is also used afterward to encrypt the data traffic. The Wi-Fi Alliance unveiled TKIP back in late 2002 and introduced it as Wi-Fi Protected Access (WPA). This little beauty even saved us lots of money because TKIP—pronounced "tee kip"—didn't make us upgrade all our legacy hardware equipment in order to use it. Then, in the summer of 2004, the IEEE put their seal of approval on its final version and added even more defensive muscle with goodies like 802.1X and AES-CCMP (AES-Counter Mode CBC-MAC Protocol). Upon publishing IEEE 802.11i-2004, the Wi-Fi Alliance responded positively by embracing the now-complete specification and dubbing it WPA2 for marketing purposes.

A big reason that TKIP doesn't require buying new hardware to run is because it just kind of wrapped around the preexisting WEP encryption key, which was way too short, and upgraded it to a much more impenetrable 128-bit encryption. Another reason for TKIP's innate compatibility is that both its encryption mechanism used to power WEP and the RC4 algorithm used to define WEP remained the same.

But there are still significant differences that help make it the seriously tough shield it is. I mentioned one of them earlier—the fact that it actually changes each packet's key. Let me explain. Packet keys are made up of three things: a base key, the transmitting device's MAC address, and the packet's serial number. It's an elegant design because although it doesn't place a ton of stress on workstations and APs, it serves up some truly formidable cryptographic force. Here's how it works: Remember the packet serial number part of the transmission key? Well, it's not just your average serial number; it's special—very special.

TKIP-governed transmission ensures that each packet gets its very own 48-bit serial number. The serial number is augmented with a sequence number (remember we talked about that) whenever a new packet gets sent out. Not only does the serial number serve as part of the key, but it also acts as the IV. And the good news doesn't end there—because each packet is now uniquely identified, the collision attacks that used to happen on your wireless network using WEP are also history. In addition, the fact that part of the packet's serial number is also the IV prevents something called replay attacks. It takes an ice age for a 48-bit sequence repeat, so replaying packets from some past wireless connection is just not going to happen; those "recycled" packets won't be in sequence, but they will be identified, thus preventing the attack.

Okay—now for what may be the truly coolest thing about TKIP keys: the base key. Because each base key that TKIP creates is unique, no one can recycle a commonly known key over and over again to gain access to a formerly vulnerable WEP wireless LAN. This is because TKIP throws the base key into the mix when it assembles each packet's unique key, meaning that even if a device has connected to a particular access point a bunch of times, it won't be permitted access again unless it has a completely new key granting it permission.

Even the base key itself is a fusion of something called nonces—an assortment of random numbers gleaned from the workstation, the access point, and each of these devices' MAC addresses, referred to as a session secret. So basically, if you've got IEEE 802.1X authentication working for you, rest assured that a session secret absolutely will be transmitted securely to each machine every time it initiates a connection to the wireless LAN by the authentication server—unless you're using preshared keys (PSKs), that is. If you happen to be using PSKs, that important session secret always remains the same. Using TKIP with preshared keys (WPA) is kind of like closing an automatically locking security door but not enabling its security settings and alarm—anyone who knows where the secret latch is can get right in!

AES

Both WPA2 and the 802.11i standard call for the use of 128-bit Advanced Encryption Standard (AES) for data encryption. It's widely considered the best encryption available today, and has been approved by the National Institute of Standards and Technology (NIST). It's also referred to as—okay, first take a deep breath here—Advanced Encryption Standard-Counter Mode with Cipher Block Chaining Message Authentication Code Protocol (AES-CCMP) authentication—and exhale. Now that was quite a mouthful, wasn't it?

AES augments the key stream with initialization vectors. As opposed to RCA, which is a stream cipher and operates on the data bit by bit, AES is a block cipher that operates on blocks of data. The aforementioned initialization vectors increase by one for each block of data. This means each block uses a different key. It also uses a message authentication check to assure integrity using the length of the frame, source address, and data input values.

The only shortcoming of AES is that due to the computational requirements, you need a cryptographic processor to run it. Still, compared to RC4, it's a lot more efficient while at the same time seriously augmenting security compared to what you get with RC4.

A cool possibility for networks that are migrating from WPA to WPA2 or 802.11i is that the same key can be used for both TKIP and AES. This allows you to migrate over time as your network's devices are switched out for those that can support the additional computational requirements of AES.

Try to make this transitional move as quickly as possible, so you don't end up living in this limbo state. You'll want to get to AES and dump the TKIP folks when feasible. For migration from TKIP to AES, Cisco's devices support both encryption types simultaneously on your network.

Centralized Key Management

Another benefit of 802.11i and WPA2 is centralized key management. When wireless clients roam from one access point to another, often the reauthentication that must take place can take long enough to break an application's connection—especially if more complicated authentication mechanisms are in use. Two mechanisms in 802.11i help to mitigate this problem:

Key Caching The AP caches the credentials of the station, and if the station roams away from the AP and then roams back, the reauthentication occurs much faster than if the process were to start from the beginning.

Preauthentication   If a station roams near another AP, but not close enough to associate, it will perform the authentication process. This way, if the station does eventually roam and associate with the new AP, the authentication is much quicker. The only negative to this feature is the additional load it places on the authentication server (RADIUS) because of all the frequent authentications it must perform, with many of them never being used.

The preauthentication process is shown in Figure 5.17.

FIGURE 5.17   Preauthentication

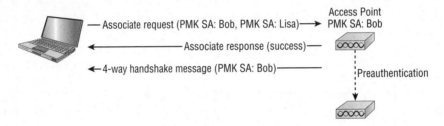

Implementation Standards

So, how can we implement both authentication and encryption easily and effectively? Well, this used to be a hard process—that is, until WPA. First, I would like to define the differences between personal and enterprise modes. The terms *personal* and *enterprise* are not from a specific standard, but are more marketing terms. The difference between personal and enterprise is defined by the authentication method used. Personal mode uses only the preshared key for authentication, and enterprise mode uses the 802.1X and EAP methods of authentication. Many people associate these terms with small business and large business, respectively, but that only depends on the implementation.

Now let's take a look at how WPA and WPA2 are defined.

WPA and WPA2: An Overview

I mentioned that WPA and WPA2 were created in response to the shortcomings of WEP. WPA was a stopgap measure taken by the Wi-Fi Alliance to provide better security until the IEEE finalized the 802.11i standard. When 802.11i was ratified, WPA2 incorporated its improvements, so there are some significant differences between WPA and WPA2.

These are each essentially another form of basic security that's just an add-on to the specifications. Even though you can totally lock the vault, WPA/WPA2 PSK is a better form of wireless security than any other basic wireless security method I've talked about so far. But do note that I did say basic!

Wi-Fi Protected Access (WPA) is a standard developed by the Wi-Fi Alliance. WPA provides a standard for authentication and encryption of WLANs that's intended to solve known security problems. The standard takes into account the well-publicized AirSnort and man-in-the-middle WLAN attacks. So, of course we use WPA2 to help us with today's security issues because we can use AES encryption, which provides for better key caching than WPA could provide. However, WPA is only a software update whereas WPA2 requires a hardware update.

The PSK verifies users via a password or identifying code, also often called a passphrase, on both the client machine and the access point. A client gains access to the network only if its password matches the access point's password. The PSK also provides keying material that TKIP or AES uses to generate an encryption key for each packet of transmitted data.

Although more secure than static WEP, the PSK method still has a lot in common with static WEP in that the PSK is stored on the client station and can be compromised if the client station is lost or stolen (even though finding this key isn't all that easy to do). This is exactly why I definitely recommend using a seriously strong PSK passphrase that includes a mixture of letters, numbers, cases, and nonalphanumeric characters. With WPA, it's still possible to specify the use of dynamic encryption keys that change each time a client establishes a connection.

 The benefit of WPA keys over static WEP keys is that the WPA keys can change dynamically while the system is used.

WPA is a step toward the IEEE 802.11i standard and uses many of the same components, with the exception of encryption. 802.11i (WPA2) uses AES-CCMP encryption. The IEEE 802.11i standard replaced WEP with a specific mode of AES known as Counter Mode with Cipher Block Chaining Message Authentication Code Protocol (CCMP). This allows AES-CCMP to provide both data confidentiality (encryption) and data integrity—now we're getting somewhere!

What's very cool here is that you have a choice of using TKIP or AES as the encryption method, and you can choose up to a 64-character key—pretty tight!

WPA's mechanisms are designed to be implementable by current hardware vendors, meaning that users should be able to implement WPA on their systems with only a firmware/software modification.

Let's look into the details now.

Wi-Fi Protected Access (WPA)

WPA was designed to offer two methods of authentication in implementation. The first, called WPA Personal or WPA (PSK), was designed to work using a passphrase for authentication. However, it improves on the level of protection for authentication and the data encryption as well.

WPA PSK uses the exact same encryption as WPA Enterprise—the PSK just replaces the check to a RADIUS server for the authentication portion. PSK provides us the following benefits:

- The IV is 48 bits and not 24 bits. This increases the number of vector values from over 16 million possibilities to 280 trillion values. Also, they must be used in order and not randomly, which oddly enough increases the security because it eliminates the reuse of IVs—a condition referred to as collisions (not to be confused with collision domains).

- The key for each frame is changed for each packet, hence the term *temporal*, or temporary. A serial number is applied to each frame and the serial number, along with the temporal key, and the IV is used to create a key unique to each frame. Furthermore, each frame undergoes per-packet key hashing as well.

- Centralized key management by the AP including broadcast and unicast keys. The broadcast keys are rotated to ensure that they do not remain the same, even though at any particular point in time, they will be the same for all stations in the Basic Service Set (BSS). When a PSK is used for authentication, it's used to derive the Pairwise Master Key (PMK) as well as the resulting Pairwise Transient Keys (PTKs). (No worries—I'll tell you more about those concepts later.)

- And lastly, we get a new form of frame check sequence (FCS). The FCS refers to the part of any packet that's used to ensure that the integrity of the packet is maintained. It's also used to determine if anything changed in the packet. Here's a scenario: Through an attack called *bit flipping*, a hacker could generate a TCP re-send message. The AP will forward this TCP re-send to the wireless space, thereby generating a new initialization vector. A bit-flipping attack allows the attacker to artificially increase the number of IVs, thus speeding up a WEP attack by increasing the chance of duplicates or collisions occurring. TKIP uses a message integrity code (MIC), instead of a regular FCS. MIC can detect almost all changes to a bit in the frame, so it can bust bit flipping much more readily than FCS. If it detects a MIC failure, it will report this event to the AP. If the AP receives two of these failures in 60 seconds, it will respond by disassociating all stations and stopping all traffic for 60 seconds, thus making it impossible for the hacker to recover the key—sweet!

The only known weakness of WPA PSK lies in the complexity of the password or key used on the AP and the stations. If it happens to be one that's easily guessed, it could be susceptible to something known as a dictionary attack. This type of attack uses a dictionary file that tries out a huge number of passwords until the correct match is found and consequently is very time consuming for the hacker.

Because of this, WPA PSK should mainly be used in a small office, home office (SOHO) environment and in an enterprise environment only when device restrictions, such as voice over IP (VoIP) phones, don't support RADIUS authentication.

WPA2 Enterprise

Regardless of whether WPA or WPA2 is used during the initial connection between the station and the AP, the two agree on common security requirements. Following that agreement, a series of important key related activities occur in this specific order:

1. The authentication server derives a key called the PMK. This key will remain the same for the entire session. The same key is derived on the station. The server moves the PMK to the AP where it's needed.

2. The next step is called the four-way handshake. Its purpose is to derive another key called the PTK. This step occurs between the AP and the station, and as you would think, it requires four steps to complete:

    a. The AP sends a random number known as a nonce to the station.

    b. Using this value along with the PMK, the station creates a key used to encrypt a nonce that's called the snonce, which is then sent to the AP. It includes a reaffirmation of the security parameters that were negotiated earlier. It also protects the integrity of this frame with a MIC. This bidirectional exchange of nonces is a critical part of the key-generation process.

c. Now that the AP has the client nonce, it will generate a key for unicast transmission with the station. It sends the nonce back to the station along with a group key commonly called a group transient key, as well as a confirmation of security parameters.

d. The fourth message simply confirms to the AP that the temporal keys (TKs) are in place.

One final function performed by this four-way handshake is to confirm that the two peers are still "alive."

802.11i

Although WPA2 was built with the upcoming 802.11i standard in mind, some features were added when the standard was ratified:

- A list of EAP methods that can be used with the standard.
- AES-CCMP for encryption instead of RC4.
- Better key management; the master key can be cached, permitting a faster reconnect time for the station.

All good—we've got WPA, WPA2, and now 802.11i covered. But how do they compare? Table 5.1 breaks them down.

TABLE 5.1   WPA, WPA2, and 802.11i Compared

Security TYPE	WPA	WPA2	802.11i
Enterprise Mode: Business, education, government	Authentication: IEEE 802.1X/EAP Encryption: TKIP/MIC	Authentication: IEEE 802.1X/EAP Encryption: AES-CCMP	Authentication: 802.1X/EAP Encryption: AES-CCMP
Personal Mode: SOHO, home, and personal	Authentication: PSK Encryption: TKIP/MIC	Authentication: PSK Encryption: AES-CCMP	
	128-bit RC4 w/TKIP encryption	128-bit AES encryption	128-bit AES encryption
	Ad hoc not supported	Ad hoc not supported	Allowed ad hoc

Summary

This chapter really packed a punch—in it you learned all about new wireless threats and ways to mitigate them. You also now understand the weaknesses of WEP, the improvements provided by WPA and WPA2, and the additional improvements that became available when the 802.11i standard was formalized.

With respect to authentication, you learned about the most common methods of EAP, like EAP-Fast, LEAP, PEAP, and EAP-TLS, and the various levels of security they provide. In the realm of encryption, you learned about TKIP and the AES, the varying degrees of security provided by symmetrical and asymmetrical encryption algorithms and the letter method required by the 802.11i standard.

Finally, we covered key management and key caching—both important enhancements to handling those all-important keys used in both authentication and encryption.

Exam Essentials

Know the three components of the 802.11i framework.   The three components are the authenticator, the authentication server, and the supplicant.

Know the four improvements of WPA.   The improvements are a larger initialization vector (48 bits), a message integrity check protocol to prevent forgeries, key management using 802.1X, and unicast and broadcast key management.

Understand the relationship between TKIP and AES keys.   The same key can be used for both TKIP and AES when performing a gradual migration from TKIP to AES.

Know when TKIP and AES are used.   TKIP is used to encrypt the data in WPA, and AES or TKIP is used in WPA2 and 802.11i.

Understand the purpose of MFP.   Management frame protection helps to prevent man-in-the-middle attacks and denial-of-service attacks.

Written Lab

1. True/False: When using open authentication, the authentication request always succeeds.

2. True/False: Stations identify their WLAN by the MAC address of the AP.

3. Which type(s) of authentication may be employed by static WEP?

4. What type of attack is occurring when a hacker jams the wireless network, disconnecting the stations?

5. True/False: A rogue AP is always the result of a determined hacker.

6. What type of frames are protected by MFP?

7. What types of authentication are examples of something you have?

8. What encryption algorithm is used by both WEP and TKIP?

9. True/False: WPA uses a 24-bit IV.

10. True/False: There is no difference in the functionality of an IPS and IDS.

Review Questions

1. What extensions are required to implement EAP-Fast?
   - **A.** CCXv1
   - **B.** CCXv2
   - **C.** CCXv3
   - **D.** CCXv4

2. What roles are involved in the 802.1X framework? (Choose three.)
   - **A.** Authenticator
   - **B.** Authentication server
   - **C.** Supplicant
   - **D.** None of the above

3. A 48-bit initialization vector is a characteristic of which encryption mechanism?
   - **A.** TKIP
   - **B.** WEP
   - **C.** AES
   - **C.** RADIUS

4. Which of the following are not improvements provided by TKIP over WEP?
   - **A.** 48-bit IV
   - **B.** Message integrity check (MIC)
   - **C.** Static keys
   - **D.** Packet sequence numbers

5. What will be the result of configuring the same key for TKIP and AES in the same WLAN?
   - **A.** The overhead on the AP will degrade performance.
   - **B.** There will be no appreciable impact; this is a common approach to a migration from TKIP to AES.
   - **C.** The configuration is not supported and will generate alarms.
   - **D.** TKIP clients will be unable to associate.

6. Which method supports the following?
   - **A.** WEP
   - **B.** TKIP
   - **C.** Dynamic WEP
   - **D.** DES

7. What is the function of the preshared key when implementing WPA or WPA2?

   A. To act as the pairwise master key

   B. To act as the group transient key

   C. To act as the shared nonce value

   D. To derive the pairwise transient key

8. What process is used to establish the pairwise transient key during the WPA authentication process?

   A. The exchange of nonces

   B. The four-way handshake

   C. The distribution of the group transient key

   D. The exchange of the broadcast keys

9. What encryption algorithm is used with 802.11i?

   A. TKIP

   B. DES

   C. Triple DES

   D. AES-CCMP

10. Which of the following is common to both WPA2 and 802.11i?

    A. Uses AES-CCMP

    B. Uses TKIP

    C. Uses static keys

    D. Uses encrypted management frames

11. Which of the following is not a part of the AAA framework?

    A. Authentication

    B. Authorization

    C. Accounting

    D. Acceptance

12. Which open standard requires EAP and AES encryption?

    A. 802.11i

    B. 802.11x

    C. 802.11n

    D. 802.1q

13. Which authentication method is not common to enterprise implementations?

    A. EAP-FAST

    B. EAP-TLS

    C. WEP

    D. PEAP

14. What method can help to mitigate DoS attacks that flood the wireless network with probe requests and association frames?

    A. MFP

    B. Centralized key management

    C. Preauthentication

    D. Key caching

15. Which of the following authentication mechanisms has fallen from favor and is infrequently used?

    A. EAP-FAST

    B. EAP-TLS

    C. EAP-MD5

    D. LEAP

16. Which EAP method requires a certificate on both the server and the stations?

    A. EAP-MD5

    B. EAP-FAST

    C. EAP-TLS

    D. PEAP

17. Which EAP method requires a certificate on the server but not on the stations?

    A. EAP-MD5

    B. EAP-FAST

    C. EAP-TLS

    D. PEAP

18. Which EAP method uses PACs?

    A. EAP-MD5

    B. EAP-FAST

    C. EAP-TLS

    D. PEAP

19. What capability that becomes available when utilizing wireless controllers allows a station to roam to different APs more quickly with less chance of application breakage?

    A. Key caching

    B. LWAPP

    C. Preauthentication

    D. MFP

20. When using WPA2 with EAP, where are the encryption keys located during an active user session? (Choose two.)

   A. The RADIUS server

   B. The AP

   C. The WLC

   D. The station

Answers to Review Questions

1. C. Implementation of EAP-Fast requires the support for Cisco Client Extensions version 3.

2. A, B, C. The roles in the 802.1X framework and the typical devices performing those roles in a wireless environment are:

    Authenticator: the AP

    Authentication server: the RADIUS server

    Supplicant: the station

3. A. A 48-bit IV is a characteristic of TKIP. WEP uses a 24-bit IV. RADIUS is an authentication server, and AES is an encryption mechanism. Neither is an authentication mechanism.

4. C. Static keys are a characteristic of WEP, not TKIP.

5. B. This is a supported and common approach to a migration from TKIP to AES.

    Broadcast key rotation

    Message integrity check

    Per-packet key hashing

6. B. TKIP supports broadcast key rotation, message integrity checks, and per-packet key hashing. WEP does not support these. There is no Dynamic WEP, and DES is an encryption mechanism.

7. A. The function of the preshared key when implementing WPA or WPA2 is to act as the pairwise master key, which is then used to derive the pairwise transient key. There is no shared nonce value, and it is not used as the group transient key.

8. B. The purpose of the four-way handshake and its result is to establish the pairwise transient key.

9. D. The encryption algorithm used with 802.11i is AES-CCMP.

10. A. Both WPA2 and 802.11i require AES-CCMP.

11. D. AAA includes authentication, authorization, and accounting.

12. A. 802.11i is the standard that requires EAP and AES encryption.

13. C. Most forms of EAP are somewhat common to enterprise implementations. WEP is not common to these type of implementations.

14. A. Management frame protection (MFP) marks management frames with a signature and can mitigate DoS attacks that flood the wireless network with probe requests and association frames.

15. C. EAP-MD5, which uses a hashed password, is rarely used now.

16. C. EAP-TLS requires a certificate on both the server and the stations.

17. D. PEAP requires a certificate on the server but not on the stations.

18. B. EAP-FAST is the only method that creates and uses PACs.

19. C. Preauthentication is the capability that allows a station to roam to different APs more quickly with less chance of application breakage.

20. B and D. When using WPA2 with EAP, the encryption keys are located on the AP and the station.

Answers to Written Lab

1. True

2. False

3. Shared key or open

4. Denial of service

5. False

6. Management frames

7. Smart cards, security tokens, one-time password generators

8. RC4

9. False

10. False

Chapter

6

Wireless Clients and Cisco Extension (CCX)

THE CCNA WIRELESS EXAM TOPICS COVERED IN THIS CHAPTER ARE:

✓ **Install Wireless Clients**

 ▪ Describe client OS WLAN configuration (Windows, Apple, and Linux)

 ▪ Install Cisco ADU

 ▪ Describe basic CSSC

 ▪ Describe CCX versions 1 through 5

How well wireless stations or clients perform when interacting with APs depends on the type of the wireless network adapter and its associated chipset, along with the type of wireless client software being used on the device. Stations can refer to hardware and clients can refer to software, but Cisco uses these terms interchangeably.

Client software can come from several sources:

- The manufacturer of the wireless network adapter
- The manufacturer of wireless infrastructure equipment like APs and controllers (think Cisco)
- The manufacturer of the computer's OS

This chapter covers the client software that comes from these various sources as well as the Cisco Compatible Extensions (CCX) program. The CCX program allows Cisco's partner vendors to build capabilities into wireless adapters and client software that enable them to take advantage of Cisco features like Management Frame Protection (MFP). Keep in mind, however, that some Cisco extensions are standards based.

Wireless Clients

First, I want you to understand that wireless clients are not APs. I know I've referred to wireless clients as stations, and technically, as well as in the standards documents, an AP is also a station. This is why we refer to the non-APs as clients—for clarification purposes.

Some wireless clients are built straight into the underlying OS of a wireless computer. These pieces of software can be used to configure and control the wireless adapter in the computer, but there's a much sweeter feature set that you can access in either the client software provided by the wireless adapter manufacturer or by Cisco. Let's start by getting to know these built-in wireless clients and understanding their respective strengths and weaknesses.

Windows XP

The Windows XP OS includes with a tool called Windows Wireless Zero Configuration that you can use to manage your wireless adapter card. You can also manage it with the utility provided by the manufacturer, but if you do, you're limited in that you can enable only one card at a time.

As is usually the case with any wireless-enabled device, when you first start up the computer, it will scan for possible wireless networks in the area. If a particular network's profile has been either configured or saved, it will be seen by the computer, which will respond by automatically trying to connect to it. Sometimes, a message will pop up that says "Wireless Networks Detected," but typically you only see this message if none of your configured networks are available nearby (as shown in Figure 6.1). If you click on the message, a list of available networks will appear, as you can see in Figure 6.2.

FIGURE 6.1   Wireless Networks Detected

FIGURE 6.2   Choose A Wireless Network

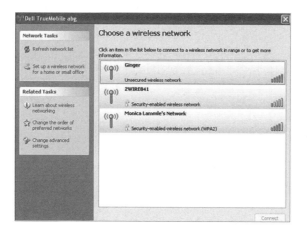

So let's say you missed the pop-up but you still want to view available networks. All you need to do is left-click the icon that represents your wireless network adapter in the system tray, or notification area, and select View Available Wireless Networks, as shown in Figure 6.3.

FIGURE 6.3   Select the View Available Wireless Networks option

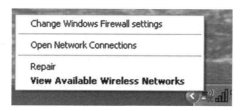

No matter how you access the Choose A Wireless Network dialog box, a list of available networks will appear in it just like the one in Figure 6.2. If the network is broadcasting its SSID, it will be displayed whether or not the network has security configured, but if it is a secure network, it will be designated as such. A network's signal strength (indicated by bars) will also be displayed. Notice that only AP Ginger does not have a lock showing, meaning that AP is not configured with security.

Now that you know what networks are available, just double-click or highlight the desired network, select Connect at the bottom of the page, and you're good to go. But if you've chosen a network that requires security, you'll be prompted for credentials at this point. Always remember that connections happen in two phases: first at Layer 2 (association), and then at Layer 3 when you get your IP address from the AP or DHCP server.

Creating Profiles

Profiles are just collections of wireless settings, such as the security required, name, password, and so on that you can save and access when you want to connect to a particular wireless network. They're created manually or by the device itself. When you connect to a network for the first time, the utility will ask you if you want to save the connection. If you answer yes, it will save the profile.

To create a profile manually, click Change Advanced Settings at the bottom of the menu on the left side of the Choose A Wireless Network dialog box. Doing this will open the wireless card configuration page shown in Figure 6.4. You just click the Wireless Networks tab to access the main wireless configuration settings.

FIGURE 6.4   Wireless Networks tab

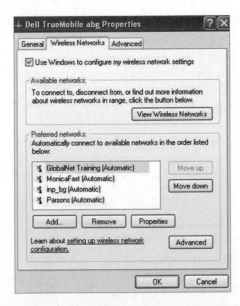

Before going any further, I want to point out a very important setting at the top of this page: the Use Windows To Configure My Wireless Network Settings check box determines whether Windows Zero Configuration will be used to manage the wireless adapter or if another client utility will be used. Remember: you can only use one at a time, so if you've installed a Cisco ADU (which I'll talk about soon) and you want to use that instead, make sure this option is deselected. Clearly, if you decide to go back to using the Windows client, check this box.

All existing profiles, whether they've been created manually or automatically, will be displayed, and the order in which they appear is important. Let's take a quick detour and talk about that for a minute.

Preferred Networks

When you boot up your computer, it will automatically scan for networks and attempt to connect to any network it sees for which it has a configured profile. This can result in connecting to a network that you didn't want to connect to. You can avoid that by designating a preferred network. Do this by using the up and down arrows on the right side of the Preferred Networks box that holds a list of profiles so you can change their order and priority. Connection attempts to the networks you've listed will be deployed in the order in which they're listed.

Let's get back to profile creation... Click Add, and the Properties dialog box will appear, which will allow you to configure all necessary parameters to connect to a network, including SSID and security, as shown in Figure 6.5.

FIGURE 6.5   The Properties dialog box, Association tab

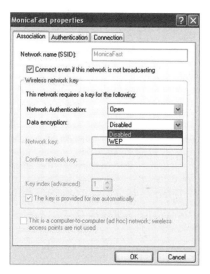

The three tabs and their functions are:

Association   This tab is where you set the SSID. Drop-down menus are provided for selecting the authentication type and data encryption, as shown in Figure 6.6.

FIGURE 6.6   The Network Authentication options

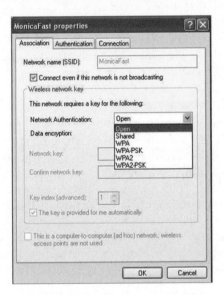

When you're selecting PSK-based authentication like WPA-PSK, the Network Key field becomes active, allowing you to enter the proper PSK. If choosing a non-PSK-based authentication, you have the option of selecting the check box The Key Is Provided For Me Automatically. It's vital that this matches the key defined on the AP!

Authentication   This tab is grayed out since it isn't active when using PSK-based authentication because you've already set this on the Association tab. You use it when non-PSK authentication is being employed, like with types of EAP. For example, to configure PEAP, set the network authentication on the Association tab to Open, WPA, or even WPA2, and the data encryption to TKIP (or AES if you're using WPA2). The Authentication tab will then become available for you to specify PEAP or smart card (EAP-TLS), as shown in Figure 6.7.

After selecting PEAP, click the Properties box and complete the configuration.

Connection   This tab displays information about the current connection. This tab is used if you want to prevent the client from attempting to connect automatically to the network you are configuring.

Now let's take a look at Windows Vista.

FIGURE 6.7   The Properties dialog box, Authentication tab

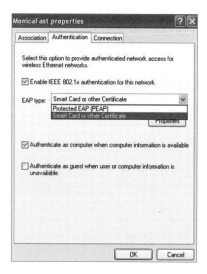

Windows Vista

The Windows Vista OS includes a tool called WLAN Auto Configuration that provides the same functions as Windows Wireless Zero Configuration does. The only real difference is that some of the features are accessed from different locations. As long as the computer is set to display the icon in the notification area, you gain access through the Control Panel, or by left-clicking the icon that represents your network's adapter and selecting Network And Sharing Center. You are offered another option when you do this called Connect To A Network. This selection will lead you to a page that allows you to scan for networks and connect to available ones, but it won't get you to the full utility, which is where you need to be to make configuration changes. The Network And Sharing Center is shown in Figure 6.8.

FIGURE 6.8   Network And Sharing Center

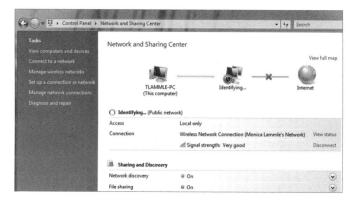

On the left hand side, under Tools, are some selections that relate to wireless networking:

Connect To A Network This option allows you to view available networks and connect to them if possible.

Manage Wireless Networks This option displays all created wireless network profiles and allows you to add, edit, and delete them. As in XP, these profiles can be created either manually or by the system, so when you connect to network for the first time the utility will ask you if you want to save the connection. Answering yes will save the profile (this link takes you to the Vista equivalent of the Wireless Networks tab in XP that was shown in Figure 6.4).

Set Up A Connection Or Network This option allows you to create profiles as well as connect manually to a network when you know the required parameters but you have not created a profile. This is exactly what you're doing when you stay in a hotel that gives you the password to connect to their wireless network. You can also create an ad hoc network from here and use a wizard to configure your home wireless network. To do this, you either connect to the AP directly or connect to the computer and then configure it via this utility. You can even create the settings you want and transfer them to the AP with a USB device!

Manage Network Connections This option allows you to set properties, such as the IP address, of your wireless network adapter. Most often, you would just set it to use DHCP. You can also enable and disable the adapter from here.

As in XP, if a network profile has been configured or saved and the network is seen, the computer will automatically attempt to connect. Otherwise, you'll get the Wireless Networks Are Available pop-up shown in Figure 6.9.

FIGURE 6.9 Wireless Networks Are Available

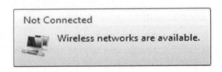

If you click on the message in Figure 6.9, you'll get a list of available networks, as shown in Figure 6.10.

If the network is broadcasting its SSID, it will be displayed. If not, it will simply be listed as Unnamed Network. Again, you'll also get to see whether or not security is configured on a network and Figure 6.10 shows that it is. The signal strength is again indicated by bars, and wow, this Usecured Network has a really strong signal!

Double-click or highlight the network and select Connect at the bottom of the page, and you'll initiate an attempt to connect. If the network requires security, you'll be prompted for credentials. In places that don't have security configured (like hotspots), the client will simply associate or connect.

And again, the same as in XP, the connection occurs in two phases: first at Layer 2 and then at Layer 3, when you receive your IP address from the AP.

FIGURE 6.10   Selecting a wireless network

Preferred Networks

By clicking Manage Wireless Networks in the Network And Sharing Center, you'll open the screen shown in Figure 6.11. Here you can change the order of the networks using the up and down arrows. The system will attempt connections in the order they're displayed (which is basically the same as the Preferred Networks list in XP).

FIGURE 6.11   Manage Wireless Networks

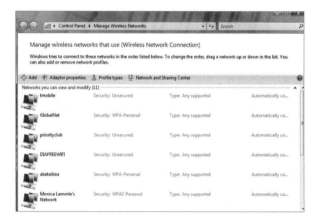

A setting that was available in XP that has vanished in Vista is a check box that specifies the client utility that will be used to control the network adapter. So, if you're using Vista, you must follow these steps:

1. Turn off or disable the other program.

2. Click to open the command prompt window.

3. Type `netsh wlan show settings`.

If automatic wireless network configuration is enabled, you'll see `Auto configuration logic is enabled on interface "Interface name"`. If you want to disable autoconfiguration, type **`set autoconfig enabled=no interface="<Interface name>"`**, or you can disable the service.

Profile Creation

Profiles can be created in two different places in Windows Vista; both approaches get you to the same dialog box. If you select Manage Wireless Networks in the Network And Sharing Center, you can click the Add button on the toolbar, as shown in Figure 6.11. If you do this, the dialog box in Figure 6.12 will appear. You can access the same dialog box by clicking Set Up A Connection Or Network in the Network And Sharing Center—refer back to Figure 6.8. The first selection is Add A Network That Is In Range Of This Computer, which lets you automatically add a profile for a network. The second option lets you create a profile manually, including any desired security parameters. The third option is for creating an ad hoc network.

FIGURE 6.12   Choose how you want to add a network

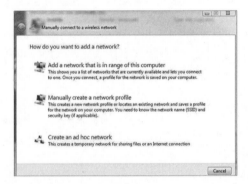

If you select Manually Create A Network Profile, you'll launch the wizard shown in Figure 6.13. This wizard will allow you to complete the configuration.

FIGURE 6.13   You can enter information manually

Clicking the Security Type drop-down list displays your possible options, as shown in Figure 6.14.

FIGURE 6.14   Security Type drop-down options

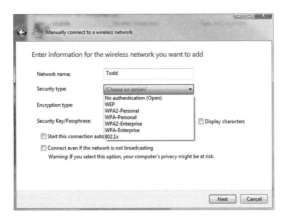

The Encryption Type drop-down list reflects the security type you select. For example, if you select WPA2 Enterprise, you'll see the options shown in Figure 6.15.

FIGURE 6.15   Encryption Type drop-down options

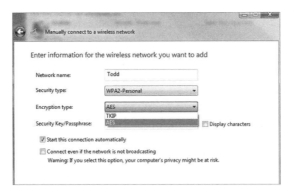

Using this box, you can set all the same parameters I covered in the section on XP—the only differences are that the Security-Type drop-down list uses the terms WPA-Personal and WPA2-Personal (instead of WPA-PSK and WPA2-PSK, respectively), and that 802.1X has been added to XP. To use 802.1X with WEP in XP, you just select the option The Key Is Provided For Me Automatically.

Windows 7

This probably won't come as a huge surprise: wireless networking procedures in Windows 7 are remarkably similar to those in Windows Vista. Although some of the dialog boxes look different cosmetically, the approach is basically unchanged. You can access wireless configuration through the Network And Sharing Center when you need to create a profile and then complete the job in Connect To A Network, or you can choose Set Up A Connection Or Network.

You can also scan for networks or view available ones by hovering over the icon that represents your wireless adapter in the system tray. If you've set one of your profiles to connect automatically and it has done so, the icon will be nicely lit up. You can still select the options from the Connect to menu that will appear just as in Vista, and the choices you get are basically the same as well. You have similar options for checking out your available network's security (or lack thereof) and signal strength. So basically, if you know how to configure wireless in Vista, then you should be fine with Windows 7.

Using the default client to control your wireless adapter (like a Cisco ADU) is also unchanged:

1. Turn off or disable the other program.

2. Click to open the command prompt window.

3. Type `netsh wlan show settings`.

If automatic wireless network configuration is enabled, you'll see `Auto configuration logic is enabled on interface "Interface name"`. To disable autoconfiguration, just type `set autoconfig enabled=no interface="<Interface name>"`.

Apple

Mac OS allows you to use two wireless hardware utilities: AirPort and AirPort Extreme (shown in Figure 6.16). Airport supports legacy 802.11b, and AirPort Extreme supports 802.11a/b/g/n. All the work is done from these two tools, which are now the same tool. To view detected networks, click the Network Name drop-down to choose from the list of detected networks, as shown in Figure 6.16.

To create a profile, click the Network Name drop-down and select Join Other Network, which is on the AirPort main window.

In the pop-up window, enter the network in the Network Name box and specify the security type, as shown in Figure 6.17. You can configure the 802.1X security requirements by clicking the Advanced button on the main page. Then select the previously created profile and select the 802.1X option, as shown in Figure 6.17.

FIGURE 6.16   Mac AirPort

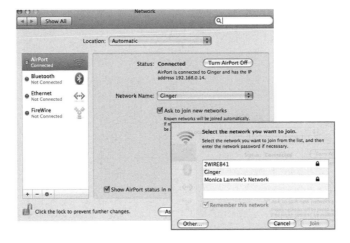

FIGURE 6.17   Mac AirPort configuration

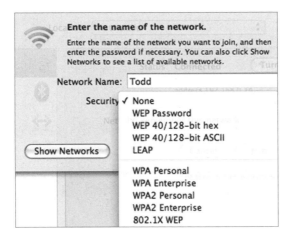

By clicking the Advanced button on the main page, you can access other options. At the top of the resulting screen is a list of tabs:

Airport   Lists the configured profiles. Click on one to edit it. You can also change the connection order here.

TCP/IP   Allows you to configure the IP address.

DNS   Allows you to configure the DNS server address.

WINS   Allows you to configure the WINS server address.

Appletalk Allows you to enable Appletalk.

802.1X Lets you configure parameters for a server-based (RADIUS) network.

Proxies Lets you configure a proxy server if required.

And that's that—you're good to go!

Linux

Wireless networking can be controlled in the Linux OS by using the `iwconfig` command-line utility, and in many versions, with graphical utilities. These tools are:

NetworkManager NetworkManager interacts directly with the hardware, so it will work on various versions (distributions) of Linux. Fedora, Ubuntu, Gnome, and KDE are among the distributions that support it.

NetworkManagerDispatcher NetworkManagerDispatcher is a supplemental tool that allows you to script the automation of actions when the computer boots up or a particular SSID is encountered. But that's beyond the scope of this book.

NetworkManager is used to configure all of the same settings in WLAN Auto Configuration and Windows Wireless Zero Configuration (WZC). Just as in WZC, the tool icon appears at the bottom of the desktop, and it even gets you similar menus if you roll the mouse across it. It will tell you whether you are connected and what the SSID of the network is. If you click the box, it will let you view detected networks, as shown in Figure 6.18. To create an ad hoc network, select Create New Wireless Network, and to create a new profile, click Connect To Other Wireless Network.

FIGURE 6.18 Linux wireless networks

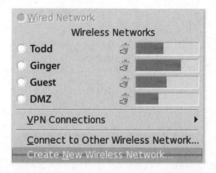

The profile configuration box, shown in Figure 6.19, also works pretty much the same way as in Windows WZC. The one difference is that you don't enter the password here. Instead, you enter it when the first connection is made or by scripting with NetworkManagerDispatcher.

FIGURE 6.19   Linux wireless security

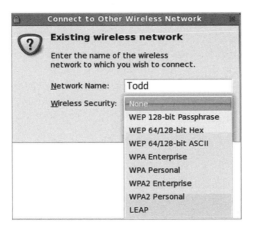

If you choose an EAP method when you enter the security type, the box expands to give you several more settings, as shown in Figure 6.20. Other than that, configuration is the same as in Windows, and you access additional features by using the `iwconfig` command-line utility as well. This is what it looks like:

FIGURE 6.20   Security options

Cisco's Supplicants

Like many other companies, Cisco makes wireless network adapters, and some of these cards are now looking toward the enterprise level so they support lots of advanced features. These cards can be managed with the default wireless tools provided in the operating systems I talked about earlier (except the Mac). But to take advantage of all the supercool new features available today, you've just got to use a Cisco utility. I'm going to focus on two of them: the Aironet Desktop Utility (ADU) and the Cisco Secure Services Client.

Cisco ADU

The Cisco ADU provides all the features of the default wireless clients discussed earlier, with the advantage of additional features supported by Cisco adapters and Cisco infrastructure. It also allows the following:

- Scanning of different channels
- Identification of APs seen on each channel, including SSID, type of authentication, and encryption
- Ability to analyze the current network connection, including the RSSI, SNR, packet statistics, and control frame information on both the send and receive sides

It follows that in order for you to use the utility, a Cisco adapter must be present in the device on which you plan to use the ADU. After the adapter is physically installed as a PC Card placed in a slot, the drivers for the adapter can be installed simultaneously with or separately from the ADU.

Installation

After downloading the ADU setup file from Cisco—which of course requires an account (you may get a CD with the software as well)—you can execute the setup program. A wizard launches with a number of steps for you to complete. During these steps, you've got to answer questions to guide the installation, as well as choose and decline the available options. The first page of the wizard offers you three choices of action, shown in Figure 6.21.

If you choose to install the client utility and the driver, then you'll always have the option to use either the ADU or the default client utility in the OS. But if you only install the driver, you'll only have the default client utility available to manage the adapter with. A third option is to extract the driver from the setup program.

If the ADU version is 2.0 or higher, the next page of the wizard will offer the option to install the Site Survey utility. Just to be clear on this, it's not something you would use to perform a serious site survey, but it's seriously handy for troubleshooting. This utility also happens to be available as a separate download, and you can use it separately from the ADU if the driver has been installed—nice!

FIGURE 6.21   ADU installation wizard, Setup Type page

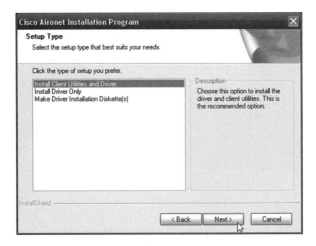

Moving on, if you choose to install the driver and the ADU, the next page will require you to specify whether the ADU or a third-party tool (like WZC in Windows XP or Vista) will be used to manage the adapter. If you decide to install the ADU but use the OS default client adapter, you can always change your mind by deselecting the Use Windows To Configure My Wireless Network Settings check box in WZC in XP, by executing the `set autoconfig enabled=no interface="<Interface name>"` command in Vista, or by changing the setting to Third-Party Tool. For our examples, let's use the ADU, so select the top radio button, as shown in Figure 6.22.

FIGURE 6.22   Choose the Cisco ADU to configure your adapter

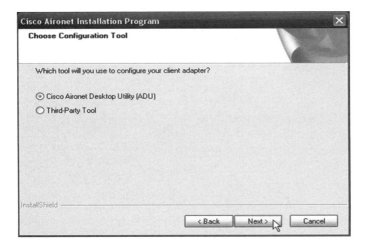

The installation is completed with a request to reboot the computer, which you should definitely do. After installation, an icon will appear on the system tray representing the Aironet System Tray Utility (ASTU). If you're connected to a network and you scroll over it, it will give you basic information about the connection, as shown in Figure 6.23.

FIGURE 6.23   Scrolling over the ADU icon

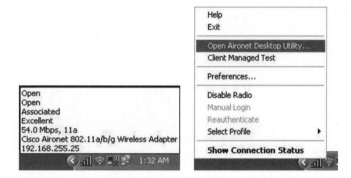

Right-clicking the icon will open a menu like the one shown in Figure 6.21. The color of the icon itself is important and gives you an indication of the adapter's condition—intuitively, green indicates a good connection. To open the main ADU utility, you can select it from this menu, as in Figure 6.21, or you can access it from Start ➢ All Programs ➢ Cisco Aironet ➢ Aironet Desktop Utility. The main page shows more complete information on connection status, as you can see in Figure 6.24.

FIGURE 6.24   ADU main page

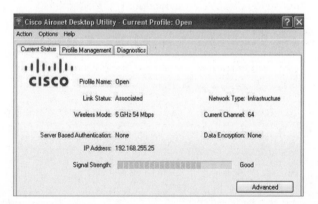

If you still want more information about the current connection, just click the Advanced button, and the page in Figure 6.25 will open. This page includes information about RSSI, SNR, the type of security in use, and more.

FIGURE 6.25   ADU Advanced page

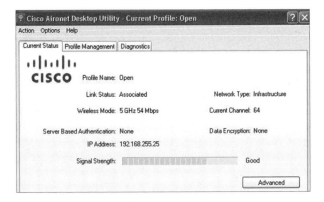

Profile Creation

You create profiles by selecting the Profile Management tab, as seen in Figure 6.26. Any existing profiles created either manually or automatically will appear. To use one of the existing profiles in the list, simply select Activate. To create a new profile, select New. To import profiles, select Import, and to export profiles from the ADU—you've got it, select Export. The oh-so-aptly named Scan button will scan for networks and display a list of networks it finds, as shown in Figure 6.26.

FIGURE 6.26   ADU profiles

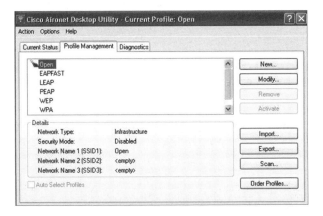

Clicking New on the main Profile Management page will open the Profile Management dialog box, as shown in Figure 6.27, where you can enter the profile name, client name, and up to three SSIDs. Keep in mind that the same security will have to used for all SSIDs. Also note that any time any of the listed networks are in range, the same profile will be used.

FIGURE 6.27 ADU profile management

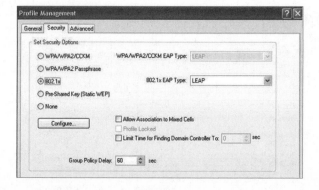

Security in ADU

Take a look at Figure 6.28. When creating a new profile, you use the Security tab to specify the appropriate settings. Anything not available to you is grayed out and depends on the radio button that you selected in the row right under Set Security Options. Notice that in Figure 6.28, no security (None) is selected, so no security options are available. I'm going to take you step by step through the possible options, moving from least to most secure:

FIGURE 6.28 ADU security

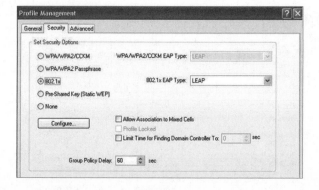

Pre-Shared Key (Static WEP)   This option is the simplest to configure—well, other than opting for None. All you do is click the Pre-Shared Key (Static WEP) radio button, then the Configure button, and then type in the WEP key. You also have to specify whether it is Open or Shared WEP after clicking the Configure button.

802.1X   Selecting this radio button will make the 802.1X EAP Type drop-down box available. Your choices will be LEAP (the default), EAP-TLS, PEAP, EAP-GTC, EAP MS-CHAP v2, EAP-FAST, and host-based EAP. Common sense dictates that you must choose the same method employed on the AP and the authentication server or things won't be compatible. You can also click Configure to add a username and password when you choose WEP as the encryption method.

WPA/WPA2 Passphrase   Configuring this option is pretty much like configuring WEP, but it offers better security. After selecting the radio button, just click Configure and type in the passphrase.

WPA/WPA2/CCKM   When you select this option, the WPA/WPA2/CCKM EAP Type drop-down box becomes available and you get to choose from the same options that were available in 802.1X, with the exception of host-based EAP. Again, that list includes LEAP (the default), EAP-TLS, PEAP, EAP-GTC, EAP MS-CHAP v2, and EAP-FAST (which you choose when TKIP or AES-CCMP is your encryption method).

Let's discuss a Cisco proprietary client that is not a free utility: the Cisco Secure Services Client.

Cisco Secure Services Client

Even though the Cisco Secure Services Client (CSSC) can be used for wireless connections and will certainly be our focus here, you can use it for wired clients too. Either way, CSSC makes Cisco security features available to both implementations. It can be downloaded and installed like the ADU, and it includes three tools: the basic client, the administration utility used to create and distribute profiles, and a logging function that can also be installed on network clients to collect information on them for troubleshooting. However, unlike the ADU, the wireless adapter doesn't have to be Cisco.

Installation

Some good news is that the installation is more straightforward than when installing ADU, but it does require administrative privileges. This is why the fact that it comes as an .msi file is so cool—if you distribute it with a Group Policy from Active Directory, the installation will have those privileges without even touching the device!

Creating Profiles

After installation, the CSSC will appear as an icon in the system tray. If you right-click it, the context menu displays the names of existing profiles along with those that have been detected. If you click More, the SSC utility opens (SSC will also appear on the Start menu). One of the finest features for administrators is the ability to create and distribute profile packages with the management utility and deploy them to the proper end-user computers, making life so much easier. When you use this approach, the configuration file is distributed along with the .msi file as an .xml file. How sweet is that!

When you open the main window of the SSC by selecting More from the context menu of the connection icon or by selecting the utility from the Start menu, all current profiles and all available WLANs within range will be displayed. Connections can be organized into groups, with each one consisting of multiple wireless profiles. You can see an example of this page on the left in Figure 6.29.

FIGURE 6.29   Creating profiles

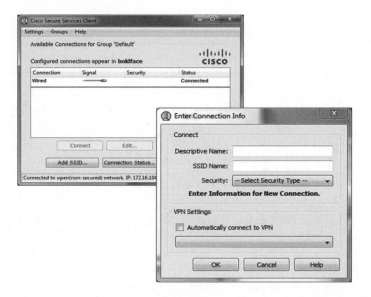

To add a profile or network, just select Add SSID. In the box shown on the right in Figure 6.29, you enter the SSID and choose the security type from the Security drop-down list—starting to sound familiar? Good! When you select a security type, the box will change to allow you to enter the information specifically required for it.

The options are:

- Open (unsecured)

- WEP or Shared WEP (each a separate selection)

- WPA Personal using either TKIP or AES (each a separate selection)

- WPA Enterprise using either TKIP or AES (each a separate selection)

- WPA 2 Personal using either TKIP or AES (each a separate selection)

- WPA 2 Enterprise using either TKIP or AES (each a separate selection)

- CCKM Enterprise using either TKIP or AES (each a separate selection)

Yes, that's 13 different choices in the drop-down list! Now let's check out the selections that affect the dialog box for each type:

Open   Well, as you would guess, when you choose Open, the box doesn't change at all because there's nothing to configure.

WEP and Shared WEP   If you select WEP or Shared WEP, the box will change as shown on the left in Figure 6.30. All you configure is the WEP key.

FIGURE 6.30   Security in SSC

WPA/WPA2 Personal TKIP/AES   For any variant of WPA or WPA2 Personal, the box will change to what you see on the right in Figure 6.30, and all you enter is the personal key (PSK).

WPA/WPA2 Enterprise and CCKM Enterprise   Choose any of these and the box the will change to what's shown in Figure 6.31. You can now pick the EAP type in the EAP drop-down list, and depending on which type you've chosen, the options in the corresponding drop-down list on the right (regarding the form of authentication) will reflect what's then available.

FIGURE 6.31   Choosing the EAP type

The EAP types available are EAP-FAST, LEAP, and PEAP. If you select LEAP, the only option in the corresponding drop-down list will be Password. But if you select either EAP-FAST or PEAP, your options will include Password, Token, and Certificate.

Remember that when using the ADU, you must also use a Cisco adapter, but when using the SSC, it doesn't matter.

Cisco-Compatible Extensions

One of the challenges we face with standards-oriented organizations is they move like glaciers when it comes to adapting to new threats—a sad fact of life with the 802.11 committee. In an effort to more quickly incorporate innovations for providing increased security and different ones aimed at optimizing performance from Cisco and their partners, Cisco created a program called the Cisco-Compatible Extensions (CCX) program. This program allows for partners to take advantage of and implement Cisco proprietary features, and just as operating systems have versions, the CCX has evolved through five versions as of this writing, with each one building on the features and benefits afforded by the last version.

An important thing about CCX is that vendors that participate in it are required to implement all the features. Even so, many features required on laptops aren't required on application-specific devices like PDAs.

Let's look at some of the features these versions have made available.

CCX Versions 1 Through 5

There are five versions of Cisco-Compatible Extensions. Here's a bit about each.

Version 1

The debut version added support for WEP, IEEE 802.1X, LEAP, and Cisco TKIP. It also made it possible to have Version 1 products that are also interoperable with WLANs that use multiple SSIDS/VLANs on the APs as well.

Version 2

The second version included everything that version 1 did and added PEAP-GTC, WPA, and Enhanced Distributed Coordination Function (eDCF). eDCF is a method of managing access to all channels, including to the AP. Version 2 featured AP-assisted roaming, which enables a client to roam from one AP to another quickly by reducing the time that the client spends scanning for available APs. Version 2 also introduced centralized key management, available when you're using LEAP.

Version 3

In version 3, WPA2, EAP-FAST, Wi-Fi multimedia (a type of QoS from the Wi-Fi alliance), and centralized key management with EAP_FAST were added into the mix.

Version 4

Version 4 added network access control (NAC), which is a method of keeping devices off the network until they pass certain tests and/or remediation. This version also included EAP-TLS, PEAP-MSCHAP, and new support for voice over IP (VoIP) and expanded centralized key management for other EAP types.

Version 5

The latest version gave us Management Frame Protection (see Chapter 5), more enhancements to key management, and some other nice improvements.

Summary

This chapter examined the client software that comes from various sources, including:

- The manufacturer of the wireless network adapter
- The manufacturer of the wireless infrastructure equipment (APs, controllers, etc.— think Cisco)
- The manufacturer of the operating system of the computer

Important topics we covered related to the Cisco Aironet Desktop Utility (ADU) and the Cisco Secure Services Client (CSSC), as well the Cisco-Compatible Extensions program.

Exam Essentials

Know how to configure a wireless profile in the Cisco ADU.   Make sure you understand the options that are available with each security type. WEP and WPA/WPA passphrase require only the key or passphrase whereas WPA, WPA2, CCKM, and 802.1X require selecting an EAP type.

Understand the importance of selecting the correct EAP type.   Ensure that the EAP type you select for the client is supported by the authentication server. Otherwise, connection will not be possible. More importantly, know what method of authentication (password, OTP, smart card, certificate, etc.) is supported by each EAP type.

Know the improvements supplied by each version of Cisco-Compatible Extensions.   For example, EAP-FAST was first supported in version 3. Also know that there are two sets of requirements for vendors that participate in the program: one set for laptops and another for application-specific devices.

Define the various CCX versions.   Version 1 featured PEAP, version 2 introduced WPA and Cisco's PEAP; version 3 featured QoS, WPA2, and EAP-FAST (an upgrade from LEAP); version 4 introduced VoIP, NAC, and Microsoft's EAP types (PEAP, MS-CHAPv2, and EAP-TLS); and version 5 featured MFP.

Be able to set a system to use either a default wireless client or a Cisco supplicant.   In XP you deselect Use Windows To Configure My Wireless Network Settings. In Vista and Windows 7 you disable autoconfiguration and type **set autoconfig enabled=no interface="<Interface name>"**.

Know the two places where you can create profiles when using CSSC.   You can create profiles from the client or by using the CSSC management utility. These configurations exist as XML files that can be distributed to your users, thus ensuring consistency.

Written Lab

1. True/False: When selecting WPA, WPA2, or CCKM as the security type in the ADU, length and value of the key must be configured.

2. True/False: The SSID is configured on the same page as the security type in the ADU.

3. Other than the CSSC client and the CSSC management utility, what else is part of the SSC suite?

4. What is the name of the wireless utility in XP?

5. True/False: The wireless connection process starts at Layer 3 and then proceeds to Layer 2.

6. True/False: The order of the networks listed in the Manage Wireless Networks dialog box in Vista is unimportant.

7. True/False: When a preferred network is configured, the system will stop attempting to connect to networks if the preferred network is not available.

8. In Windows XP, which tab in the Wireless Network Properties dialog box do you select to configure the EAP type?

9. True/False: The process of disabling Windows native OS clients is the same in XP and Vista.

10. Which Cisco supplicant does not require a Cisco adapter to function?

Hands-on Labs

To complete the lab in this section, you need at least one Cisco AIR-CB21AG-X-K9 card bus adapter (this is a PC Card) or a Cisco AIR-P12AG-A-K9 adapter (this is a card you install into a PCI slot in the computer). You also need a copy of the Cisco ADU installation program, which can be downloaded from the Cisco site with a valid Cisco account.

There are two labs in this chapter:

Lab 6.1: Installing the Cisco ADU

Lab 6.2: Creating a Profile

Hands-on Lab 6.1: Installing the ADU

In this lab, you will install the Cisco ADU.

1. Copy the Cisco ADU installation program to your desktop or to another location.

2. Insert the PC Card or physically install the PCI card before you start the installation program. When the Add hardware wizard appears, close it. You will not need to use it.

3. Browse to the location of the program and click on it. If you're running an operating system that has User Account Control, allow the installation, if necessary. If logged on as a standard user, right-click the installation program and select Run As Administrator.

4. When the Setup Type dialog box appears, select Install Client Utilities And Driver. Click Next.

5. In the Install Cisco Aironet Site Survey Utility dialog box, select Install Cisco Aironet Site Survey Utility if desired and click Next.

6. If you are running XP, in the Cisco Aironet Installation Program dialog box, click Next. On the Choose Configuration Tool dialog box, select Cisco Aironet Desktop Utility (ADU).

7. In the Enable Tray Icon dialog box, select Enable Cisco Aironet System Tray Utility (ASTU).

8. The installation will proceed and direct you to reboot. Do so.

9. When the computer reboots, if the Found New Hardware Wizard starts, allow the wizard to locate and install the software for the card. When this is done, installation is complete.

Hands-on Lab 6.2: Creating a Profile

In this lab, you will create a profile that uses LEAP:

1. Locate and click on the Cisco ADU icon on your desktop.

2. When the Cisco Aironet Utility dialog box appears, select the Profile Management tab.

3. Click the New button on the Profile Management tab and the Profile Management dialog box appears.

4. On the General tab of the Profile Management dialog box, enter the SSID of the network to which you will be connecting with this profile. In this case, enter **Testnet**.

5. Select the Security tab and click the 802.1X radio button. This will enable the 802.1X/EAP drop-down list. From this list select LEAP. Click OK and you are done!

Review Questions

1. In the Choose A Wireless Network dialog box in XP, which of the following is not shown for each network?

   A. SSID, if it's being broadcast

   B. Security, if configured

   C. Signal strength

   D. Number of connected stations

2. During profile creation, on which tab of the Wireless Network Properties dialog box in XP is the SSID set?

   A. Authentication

   B. Association

   C. Connection

   D. Network

3. Which of the following selections in the Network And Sharing Center would be used to assign an IP address to the wireless network card?

   A. Connect To A Network

   B. Set Up A Connection Or Network

   C. Manage Network Connections

   D. Manage Wireless Networks

4. In Vista and Windows 7, which tool is used to disable Windows native OS clients?

   A. Control Panel

   B. Command line

   C. Manage Network Connections

   D. Device Manager

5. Which wireless tool in Linux allows scripting or automating actions when the computer boots up or when a particular SSID is encountered?

   A. NetworkManager

   B. iwconfig

   C. NetworkManagerDispatcher

   D. AirPort Extreme

6. Which two of the following are Cisco supplicants?

   A. WZC

   B. CSSC

   C. ADU

   D. ASTU

7. Which capability does the ADU have that Windows wireless clients do not?

    A. Displays signal strength of each network

    B. Displays SSID, if broadcast

    C. Can determine RSSI

    D. Preferred networks can be set.

8. During the installation of the ADU, three options are offered. Which of the following is not an option?

    A. Install the client utilities and the driver

    B. Install the client utilities only

    C. Install the driver only

    D. Make a driver diskette

9. What is the name of the tool that resides on the system tray after the installation of the ADU that can report basic information about the state of the wireless connection?

    A. CSSC

    B. ASTU

    C. WZC

    D. NetworkManager

10. Using the ADU, where can you learn information about the RSSI of the current connection?

    A. ASTU

    B. Advanced tab of the ADU

    C. Advanced button on the ADU Current Status page

    D. Diagnostics tab of the ADU

11. What option is selected to use a profile listed on the General tab of the Profile Management page in the ADU?

    A. Activate

    B. Connect

    C. Import

    D. Install

12. What is the relationship between the SSIDs entered on the General tab of the wizard invoked when you select to create a new profile in the ADU?

    A. The SSIDs can use different profiles.

    B. The SSIDS will all be used by the same profile.

    C. The SSIDs must be the same.

    D. Only the first SSID listed will be active.

13. Which of the following security types will require the selection of an EAP type while creating a profile in the ADU? (Choose all that apply.)

  A. Pre-Shared Key (static WEP)

  B. 802.1X

  C. WPA/WPA2 passphrase

  D. WPA, WPA2, and CCKM

14. Which of the following security types is the only type that can be configured to use host-based EAP in the ADU?

  A. Pre-Shared Key (static WEP)

  B. 802.1X

  C. WPA/WPA2 passphrase

  D. WPA, WPA2, and CCKM

15. Which of the following Cisco supplicants can be used to manage non-Cisco adapters?

  A. CSSC

  B. ASTU

  C. ADU

  D. NetworkManager

16. Which of the following statements is true of the CSSC?

  A. Profiles and connections are the same thing.

  B. Connections can be organized into groups.

  C. Profiles are organized into connections.

  D. Connections are organized into profiles.

17. In the CSSC, which of the following security types do not allow you to choose AES or TKIP?

  A. WPA Personal

  B. WPA Enterprise

  C. CCKM Enterprise

  D. Shared WEP

18. In the CSSC, which of the security types allows you to use a passphrase? (Choose all that apply.)

  A. WPA Personal

  B. WPA2 Enterprise

  C. CCKM Enterprise

  D. WPA 2 Personal

19. Which type of EAP is not available in the CSSC?

    A. LEAP

    B. PEAP

    C. EAP-FAST

    D. EAP-SIM

20. Which of the following security types will *not* require the selection of an EAP type while creating a profile in the ADU? (Choose two.)

    A. Pre-Shared Key (static WEP)

    B. 802.1X

    C. WPA/WPA2 passphrase

    D. WPA, WPA2, and CCKM

Answers to Review Questions

1. D. The SSID will be shown if it is not hidden; if hidden, it will say Unnamed Network. If security is required, it will be indicated and the signal strength will be shown. The number of connected stations will not be shown.

2. B. The Association tab is used to set the SSID. The Authentication tab is used to set the EAP type when EAP is used. The Connection tab allows you to choose whether the client will automatically attempt to connect or if you will have to connect manually.

3. C. The Manage Network Connections option is used to assign an IP address to the wireless network card, or it can be set to DHCP here as well.

4. B. Disabling Wireless Zero Configuration is done with the following command in Vista and Windows 7: `set autoconfig enabled=no interface="<Interface name>"`.

5. C. NetworkManagerDispatcher allows scripting or automating actions when the computer boots up or when a particular SSID is encountered.

6. B, C. The Cisco Secure Services Client (CSSC) and the Aironet Desktop Utility (ADU) are Cisco supplicants.

7. C. Windows wireless clients have all these capabilities except the ability to determine RSSI.

8. B. All of the choices are options except installing the client utilities only. The client utilities cannot be used without the driver.

9. B. When the ADU is installed, the Aironet System Tray Utility (ASTU) will appear in the system tray and can be used to monitor the state of the wireless connection.

10. C. The Advanced button on the ADU Current Status page is where information on the RSSI and SNR of the current wireless connection can be found.

11. A. The Activate button is selected to use a profile listed on the General tab of the Profile Management page in the ADU.

12. B. The SSIDs will use the same profile and a connection attempt will be made whenever any of the listed SSIDs come in range.

13. B, D. 802.1X and WPA, WPA2, and CCKM will require the selection of an EAP type when creating a profile in the ADU.

14. B. 802.1X is the only type that supports host-based EAP.

15. A. The Cisco Secure Services Client (CSSC) is the only Cisco supplicant that can be used to manage non-Cisco adapters.

16. B. In the CSSC, connections can be organized into groups, each consisting of multiple profiles.

17. D. Shared WEP and WEP are the only options that do not allow you to choose AES or TKIP.

18. A, D. Any variant of WPA/WPA2 Personal uses a passphrase. All Enterprise versions use EAP.

19. D. EAP-SIM is not available in the CSSC.

20. A, C. 802.1X and WPA, WPA2, and CCKM will require the selection of an EAP type when creating a profile in the ADU, pre-shared key and WPA types do not.

Answers to Written Lab

1. False

2. False

3. The SSC Log Packager

4. Wireless Zero Configuration

5. False

6. False

7. False

8. The Authentication tab

9. False

10. The Cisco Secure Services Client (CSSC) does not require a Cisco adapter to function.

Chapter

7

Introduction to the Cisco Unified Wireless Network (CUWN)

THE CCNA WIRELESS EXAM TOPICS COVERED IN THIS CHAPTER ARE:

✓ **Install a basic Cisco wireless LAN**

- Describe the basics of the Cisco Unified Wireless Network architecture (Split MAC, LWAPP, stand-alone AP versus controller-based AP, specific hardware examples)

- Describe the modes of controller-based AP deployment (local, monitor, HREAP, sniffer, rogue detector, bridge)

- Describe controller-based AP discovery and association (OTAP, DHCP, DNS, Master-Controller, Primary-Secondary-Tertiary, n+1 redundancy)

- Describe roaming (Layer 2 and Layer 3, intra-controller and inter-controller, mobility groups)

- Describe RRM

Moving on from our exploration of Cisco client devices, we're going to jump to the next logical step by talking about their specific places and tasks within the Cisco Unified Wireless Network (CUWN) architecture. I'll begin with a discussion about both the stand-alone and lightweight WLAN implementation models and how each affects the actual network's implementation. Diving deeper, I'll cover how Access Points (APs) discover and associate with their controller in the lightweight solution, plus demonstrate approaches that provide us with redundancy. I'll wrap this chapter up with a survey on roaming and also explain why you'll find a capacity called Radio Resource Management (RRM), available via the lightweight model, so helpful.

For up-to-the-minute updates on this chapter, check out www.lammle.com or www.sybex.com/go/ccnawireless.

WLAN Deployment Models

CUWN was brought into this world to address grief-inducing WLAN management issues like these:

- Integrating disparate devices types into your WLAN while making them play nicely and work well together

- Maintaining a consistent security configuration with an ever-increasing number of APs being added into the enterprise

- Monitoring the environment for new sources of interference and redeploying existing devices as necessary

- Properly managing channel allocation to minimize co-channel and adjacent channel interference, while ensuring that enough APs are deployed in areas requiring high capacity

Just to complicate matters further, keep in mind that all these issues must be managed in a three-dimensional environment that's changing constantly. The good news about this conundrum is that most of the challenges listed above are a result of the deployment model utilized back in the day known as the stand-alone model, now also called the autonomous model or design. I'll describe this model in more detail soon, but for now just keep in mind that APs operate as separate entities with no centralized management capabilities—so it's not a stretch to imagine the inherent weaknesses of the stand-alone model.

A typical stand-alone design begins with a static site survey that's basically a snapshot of the radio frequency (RF) environment at a particular point in time. Based on this snapshot, you would then deploy devices to mitigate any existing interference and provide coverage where you need it. The problem lies in the word *static*, because you now know that change is the constant within the RF space. A good example of a commonly occurring change is a new company moving into the unoccupied office next door. Clearly, that would probably change pretty much everything, but even simple little things like adding a new metal object in the area can give you some surprisingly serious issues to deal with!

The new lightweight model (*lightweight* is also used to describe the type of APs used within it) not only puts the power of centralized administration in our hands, but also brings some sweet new capabilities for addressing each of the issues listed at the beginning of this section. Even more wonderful, this model can create an infrastructure that is able to react to changes in real time. So let's take some time to compare these two models now.

Stand-alone Model

Not just any kind of AP can operate in the stand-alone model—only the autonomous variety of APs can do this—and I'll give you a list of all these types soon.

Autonomous APs have their own internetworking operating system (IOS). You configure them individually, and there's no centralized administration point, as shown in Figure 7.1.

FIGURE 7.1   Stand-alone model

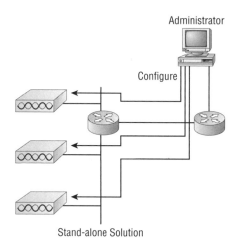

Cisco came up with a couple of solutions that focused on helping with configuration and management issues, but those fixes are nothing compared with the lightweight solution. We'll only discuss them briefly here.

Basically, you can configure a feature called Wireless Domain Services (WDS) on an AP or Cisco switch that will allow for at least some centralization of services for autonomous APs.

There's also a device called the Wireless Solution Engine (WLSE) that can give you limited centralized control and monitoring.

Lightweight Model

The CUWN lightweight model definitely requires centralized control, which is gained via Cisco WLAN controllers (WLCs; more on these in a bit). APs are controlled and monitored by the WLC. All clients and APs transmit information—including stats about coverage, interference, and even client data—back to the WLC. Figure 7.2 illustrates the lightweight model.

FIGURE 7.2   Lightweight model

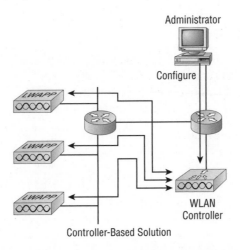

All transmitted data is sent between the APs and the WLCs via an encapsulation protocol called Lightweight Access Point Protocol (LWAPP). LWAPP carries and encapsulates control information between the APs and the WLC over an encrypted tunnel. Client data is encapsulated with an LWAPP header that contains vital information about the client's received signal strength indicator (RSSI) and signal-to-noise ratio (SNR). Once the data has arrived at the WLC, it can be forwarded as needed, which is how the real-time processes I talked about earlier become available. A couple of great benefits gained through this kind of centralized control are improved security and traffic conditioning.

Physical and logical security is a lot tighter in the CUWN because to ensure only authorized APs connect to the WLC, both devices exchange a certificate and mutually authenticate. Any APs found not to be LWAPP capable are classified as rouges. So the network forces LWAPP-capable APs to be authenticated before they'll be permitted to download any configuration from a WLC—which helps mitigate rogue APs. For physical security reasons, the configuration of the AP resides only in RAM while in operation and connected to the WLC. That way, the configuration can't be snagged from the AP once that device has been removed from the network.

The CUWN consists of five elements that work together to provide a unified enterprise solution:

- Client devices
- APs
- Network unification
- Network management
- Mobility services

A variety of devices are available that support these elements, among them Cisco Aironet client devices, the Cisco Secure Services Client (CSSC), and other Cisco-compatible devices. For APs, we can choose between the type configured and managed by a WLC, and those that operate in stand-alone mode.

While it's good to know that a single Cisco WLC can manage many APs, understand that you'll enjoy a serious increase in capacity with a few additional Cisco WLCs in the mix. You can incorporate other devices into your basic CUWN to add more features and management capabilities, too, such as the Cisco Wireless Control System (WCS), which facilitates the centralized management of multiple WLCs. You also need WCS in order to add a Cisco Wireless Location Appliance, which is a very cool tool that provides features like real-time location tracking of clients, and RFID tags.

Split MAC

Another good thing about lightweight architecture is that it allows for the splitting of 802.11 Data Link layer functions between the lightweight AP and the WLC. The lightweight AP handles real-time portions of the communication, and the Cisco WLC handles the items that aren't time-sensitive. This technology is typically referred to as split MAC.

The real-time portions of the protocol that are handled by the AP include the following:

- Frame exchange handshake between the client and AP performed during each frame transfer
- Beacon frame transmission
- Handling of frames for clients operating in power save mode (including both buffering and transmission)
- Responses to probe request frames from clients, and the relaying of received probe requests to the controller
- Transmission to the controller of real-time signal quality information for every received frame

- RF channel monitoring for noise, interference, other WLANs, and rogue APs

- Encryption and decryption (Layer 2 wireless only), with the exception of VPN and IPSec clients

The remaining tasks that aren't time-sensitive are handled by the WLC. Some of the MAC-layer functions provided by WLC include:

- 802.11 authentication

- 802.11 association and reassociation (mobility)

- 802.11 to 802.3 frame translation and bridging

- The termination of all 802.11 frames at the controller

Although the controller handles the authentication, wireless encryption keys for WPA2 or EAP will remain in both the AP and the client. This is an important CCNA Wireless objective to remember.

Lightweight Access Point Protocol (LWAPP)

Lightweight Access Point Protocol (LWAPP) runs between the AP and the WLC and performs some important tasks. One of its jobs is to encapsulate and encrypt information called *control data*. Control data is information about the wireless environment that's vital to the wireless infrastructure. LWAPP also encapsulates client data coming from client stations. It works by encapsulating data frames received from a station with a 6-byte LWAPP header that contains the SNR and the RSSI (which pinpoint exactly where the client was seen). LWAPP also includes a fragment field that signals that the last fragment of a frame is imminent, although frame fragmentation is rare in today's networks. Then a new header is added with the source and destination address set to the AP and the WLC, respectively. LWAPP can operate in Layer 2 and Layer 3 modes, but when it's in Layer 2 mode, only the MAC addresses are written in the outer header. In Layer 3 mode, both the Layer 3 and Layer 2 addresses are added. While outside of the objectives for the CCNA Wireless exam, note that the use of Layer 3 mode is used almost exclusively for LWAPP, and in later versions of the WLC code, Layer 3 is the only option.

With all this additional encapsulation, the new wireless frame can often grow larger than the maximum size allowed by the 1,500-byte maximum transmission unit (MTU) of an Ethernet segment. The wireless MTU is 2,346 bytes, exceeding the 1,500 bytes allowed on Ethernet networks. When this happens, the 802.11 frame is fragmented into manageable mouthfuls we call segments (not to be confused with segments of data at the Transport layer). The fragment field of the LWAPP header is there to count these segments.

The LWAPP protocol is a useful protocol that offers many enhancements to the management of the RF environment; I'll tell you all about those coming up later in Radio Resource Management (RRM) at the end of this chapter. This feature-filled, handy protocol also enables the WLC to support wireless VLANs, multiple SSIDs, and the 802.1Q trunking protocol.

Cisco Unified Network Devices

All of the unified network services I've been telling you about are provided by devices like stand-alone WLCs and integrated switches and routers. You can integrate WLCs into existing enterprise networks to gain advanced management capabilities and enhanced performance. They communicate with lightweight APs over any Layer 2 (Ethernet) or Layer 3 (IP) infrastructure and are responsible for handling system-wide functions.

With wireless integrated switches and routers, you get cost-effective support for converged networks that integrate wireless connectivity. Integrated platforms can lower your cost on hardware as well as simplify remote management.

These hardware devices and services are formally described by Cisco as *elements* in the Cisco United Wireless Network. They fall into one of five classes:

Client Devices   Includes Cisco Aironet devices, Cisco-compatible devices, and Cisco Secure Services Clients (CSSC)

Access Point   Includes both autonomous and lightweight APs

Network Unification   Includes devices that pull the wired and wireless network together—for example, adding wireless capability to a device such as the wireless services module (WiSM) and the Wireless LAN Controller Module (WLCM)

Network Management   Includes devices that allow for broad network management like the Cisco Wireless LAN Controller Module (WLCM).

Network Services   Includes services that help make the Cisco self-defending network a reality—services like intrusion detection and admission control

Access Points

Most Cisco APs—including the 1130AG series AP, 1140AG series AP, 1240AG series AP, or 1250AG series AP—can work in either stand-alone or lightweight mode. The 1140 and 1250 are the newest APs that support the IEEE 802.11n draft v2.0 specifications. APs like the 1300 series and the 1400 series wireless bridges are specifically designed to work in an outdoor environment. The 1300 will accept clients, but the 1400 only functions as a bridge. All the others are indoor APs designed to connect clients to the WLAN.

Some APs, like the 1500 series wireless mesh AP, only operate with LWAPP, but most of the other models can be migrated from one mode to the other. Let's take a look:

1130AG Series AP   The 1130AG series AP supports dual IEEE 802.11a and IEEE 802.11g radios and local or inline Power over Ethernet (PoE). It's compliant with IEEE 802.11i, WPA2, WPA, and most variations of EAP. It has 32MB of RAM and 16MB of flash memory. This AP can be migrated to and from both stand-alone and lightweight modes.

The 1130AG, shown in Figure 7.3, is designed for indoor use, usually in an office environment. You can commonly find it installed on the ceiling in halls or rooms, but it can also work mounted on a wall.

FIGURE 7.3 1130AG series AP

The limitation of the 1130AG is that it uses only internal antennas and does not have an external antenna interface, which reduces of the number of places where it can be deployed.

1240AG Series AP Like the 1130, the 1240AG series AP provides dual IEEE 802.11a and IEEE 802.11g radios and supports local or inline PoE. It's also compliant with IEEE 802.11i, WPA2, WPA, and most types of EAP. This AP has 32MB of RAM and 16MB of flash memory. It can be migrated between stand-alone and lightweight modes.

But that's where the similarities end—the 1240AG has two 802.11b/g and two 802.11a external connectors that not only make it a lot more versatile, but also extend your coverage possibilities. The AP can also be installed in a rugged metal housing if you need to use it in areas where the temperature fluctuates (such as in an industrial setting).

This AP gives you more flexibility when it comes to installation. You can place it above ceilings or suspended ceilings, and its antenna can be camouflaged and placed below the drop ceilings. This means you can even deploy the AP in a safe place while deploying the antenna in hazardous locations by connecting the two with a low-loss antenna cable. Figure 7.4 gives you a look at the 1240AG.

FIGURE 7.4 1240AG Series AP

1250AG Series AP   The 1250AG series AP is the first enterprise-class AP to be Wi-Fi 802.11n draft 2.0 certified. The 1250AG provides coverage for existing 802.11a/b/g clients and new 802.11n clients as well. The 1250 is also one of the first APs that's modular, making field upgrades so much easier than ever before. Standards evolve, and the AP is flexible in supporting future radio modules. The 1250AG is a rugged indoor AP designed for offices as well as more difficult RF environments, such as factories, warehouses, hospitals, and large retail outlets. It has an external antenna and a rugged metal enclosure. It has 64MB of DRAM and 32MB of flash memory. Additionally, it provides data rates of 300Mbps per radio, 2/3 multiple input, multiple output, 2.4GHz and 5GHz radio modules, and interoperability with many WiFi-certified 802.11n devices. This AP (shown in Figure 7.5) can be migrated between stand-alone and lightweight modes.

FIGURE 7.5   1250AG Series AP

1300 Series Bridge   The 1300 series bridge can operate as an AP, a bridge, or a workgroup bridge, but it only operates in the 2.4GHz frequency bank. It's also good for outdoor applications and comes with the option for using either an integrated antenna or connectors for a wide array of Cisco antennas.

The 1300 bridges can be used for network connections in a campus area, for mobile networks and users, in outdoor public access networks, and in temporary networks for portable operations. Although it requires a power injector, it offers a wide range of DC power inputs like those for solar or vehicle power (+10 to +48 volts direct current [VDC]). This AP can be purchased or migrated to and from both stand-alone and lightweight modes.

1400 Series Bridge   The 1400 series wireless bridge operates only in the 5GHz frequency range. Because of its rugged nature, you can place it in an outdoor environment, and you don't need a National Electrical Manufacturers Association (NEMA) enclosure for it. This bridge allows for point-to-point or point-to-multipoint bridge connections.

The 1400 bridge comes in two different setups, with and without integrated antenna. The integrated high-gain antenna version makes it possible for you to install point-to-point links and act as the nonroot side of a point-to-multipoint network.

The external antenna version supplies you with an N-type connector, which allows for the deployment of root nodes of point-to-multipoint networks with omni-directional, sector, or high-gain dish antennas. The 1400 is only available in stand-alone mode and does not support LWAPP.

Wireless LAN Controllers

When you are implementing the lightweight model, the centralized control system is the WLC. All device configurations are done at the WLC and then simply downloaded to the appropriate device. WLCs come with various features and price tags. They come in multiple form factors that allow either stand-alone alliances or modules that integrate into routers and multilayer switches. WLCs can support from 6 to 300 APs!

Impressively, you can configure and control up to 16 WLANs for each AP on a single WLC. A WLAN is defined in the WLC somewhat like a profile. The WLAN has a separate WLAN ID (1–16) and a separate WLAN SSID (WLAN name). The WLAN SSID is where you configure unique security and quality of service (QoS) settings. If you have clients that are connected to one AP, they'll share the same RF space and channel, but if they're connected to different SSIDs, they're in a different logical network. This means that clients in different SSIDs can be isolated from one another in the RF space and can have different VLAN and QoS tags. However, they will still be in the same collision domain, just as in autonomous AP configurations with VLANs. The SSIDs will be mapped to the VLANs in the WLC configuration.

The WLC can support up to 512 VLANs, but you will rarely need that many in order to separate your wireless traffic—you typically would isolate your data, VoIP, guest access, and network management.

Let's look at some of the Cisco WLCs:

4400 Series WLC   The 4400 series WLC is the most commonly implemented WLC device. It's a standard 19-inch rack-mount 1RU device. The two models of the 4400 series available as of this writing are the 4402 and the 4404. The 2 and the 4 specify the number of small form-factor pluggable (SFP) ports installed in the device. The 4402 can support a maximum of 50 APs and the 4404 can support up to 100 APs.

The 4400 series uses SFP mini-gigabit interface converter (GBIC) ports as their primary network connection. The GBIC ports support copper or fiber-optic interfaces, and will load-balance APs across all available ports configured as AP-Manager interfaces.

This series has two separate ports for management and configuration, including a DB-9 console port for a command-line interface (CLI) and an RJ-45 service port for GUI management, Telnet, and Secure Shell (SSH) access. You'll also find a strange RJ-45 port on the front of the device that's labeled "utility port," this is reserved for future use.

As with all WLCs, when you upgrade the code on the WLC, each AP that's associated or becomes associated with that WLC will be upgraded as well. The controller will upgrade four APs at a time until all APs are upgraded. Figure 7.6 shows the 4400 series WLC.

2100 Series WLC   The 2100 series WLCs are designed for small office locations and will support six APs. The Cisco 2100 WLCs have eight built-in switch ports, two of which are PoE capable. It also has an RJ-45 console port for CLI access.

FIGURE 7.6   4400 series WLC

As a replacement for the Cisco 2006 WLC, the 2100 maintains all the features of the 2006, while improving performance and providing additional switch ports for directly connecting APs or other network devices. Figure 7.7 shows the 2106 WLC.

FIGURE 7.7   2106 WLC

WLC Module (WLCM)   The Cisco WLCM (shown in Figure 7.8) and the Cisco WLAN Controller Module Enhanced (WLCM-E) extend the capabilities of an integrated services router (ISR), and provide small offices with unified wireless functionality nearly equal to the Cisco 2100 WLC (with the exception of directly connected APs and the console port). The WLCM supports 6 APs and the WLCM-E supports 6, 8, 12, or 25 APs, depending on the model. These modules provide many of the same features as the 4400 Series controllers.

FIGURE 7.8   The Cisco WLCM

3750G Integrated WLC   The Cisco Catalyst 3750G WLC combines all the functionality of a Cisco Catalyst 3750 Series switch and a Cisco 4402 WLC into a single 2RU chassis. These switches maintain separate processing and storage capabilities. An advantage gained by the backplane integration of the WLC is that you save ports that can be utilized for connecting additional devices to the network. This also eliminates having to configure multiple ports, which could be required on the stand-alone 4400 series controllers.

The 3750G WLC can be combined in a stack with other Catalyst 3750G switches (in an arrangement called the Cisco StackWise), either with or without the WLC built in. The StackWise interface allows for a 32GB high-speed stack link. Other than the absence of external Gigabit ports, the feature set of the integrated controller is identical to the Cisco 4402 WLC.

6500 Integrated Module (WiSM)   The Cisco Catalyst 6500 Wireless Services Module (WiSM) is essentially a blade that's installed into the Catalyst 6500 Series chassis to provide power and network connectivity. This WiSM has the features and functionality of the 4400 series controllers and supports a larger number of APs.

The Cisco WiSM supports 150 APs per controller, but the cool thing is that each blade contains two separate controllers. A single blade can support 300 APs!

Also cool is that by clustering up to 12 modules in a single mobility domain, you can control 3,600 APs in a single mobility group. There's a catch, though—because you can only put five blades into a single chassis, achieving this would require three switches.

You can install the WiSM into any of the following: Cisco Catalyst 6509, 6506, 6503, 6504, and 6513 switches (enhanced and unenhanced versions). This blade must be used with the Cisco Catalyst 6500 Series Supervisor Engine 720 since it's built on 40GB-per-slot hardware. The Catalyst 6500 Series Supervisor Engine 2 supports only 8GB-per-slot line cards.

Wireless Control Systems

I know I've mentioned WCS quite a bit in this chapter, and I'm going to cover it in great detail in Chapter 11. But I really want to give you a very brief introduction here.

The WCS tool is used to manage multiple WLCs. In the same way that a WLC can send a configuration to APs, the WCS can send configurations to multiple WLCs. WCS also include other features like RF prediction, troubleshooting, graphical user tracking, and security monitoring.

WCS is management software that you install on a Linux or Windows server. You configure it through HTTPS, and it gives you the ability to manage hundreds of WLCs. The WLCs don't even have to be on the same LAN—they can be physically located in offices in different countries if necessary!

This is clearly the top of the line for wireless management. In addition, the Cisco WCS Navigator can manage several instances of WCS—pretty much anything you need it to. To summarize: APs are managed by controllers, controllers are managed by WCS, and if you have lots of WCS servers, they are managed by WCS Navigator.

It would be rare that you would need a WCS Navigator, and as of this writing, I've heard that are only a handful of networks that use it. Those particular networks are worldwide operations with tens of thousands of APs and controllers. The Cisco WCS Navigator has the ability to manage up to 30,000 APs.

Lightweight AP Operation and Maintenance

Lightweight APs associate with a specified WLC that's used to control them and can also provide them with firmware upgrades. As you've probably guessed, an AP has to locate its particular WLC before it can associate with it—a process called discovery and association, which can be done at different layers as well as in different operational modes. Let's take some time to survey the various modes that affect AP operations during the discovery and association process.

AP Discovery and Association

When lightweight APs initially boot up, they attempt to locate a controller. How they go about doing this reflects any prior configuration in the AP, the actual network configuration in which it resides, and the configuration of the WLC. Depending on these factors, the AP will use either Layer 2 frames or Layer 3 packets, and may also even utilize a higher-layer function like DHCP or DNS to locate the controller. These various modes of discovery are also called LWAPP modes, which we'll take a look at next.

Discovery Phase

The goal of the initial discovery process is to detect as many controllers as possible because the more controllers found, the better the odds are of locating a controller. From the responding controllers the AP will associate with the one with the least number of APs currently associated.

But what if the AP and the WLC aren't on the same subnet? Well, the AP definitely won't get an answer from a controller at Layer 2, so it will then attempt a Layer 3 discovery. Cisco IOS-based APs only go with Layer 3 LWAPP discovery, and they have several options for locating controllers, each giving you different choices based on what works best on your network. A good thing to remember is that the AP will try all methods before choosing the best controller. Here's a description of those methods, all attempted at Layer 3:

Subnetwork Broadcast Mode   This is the default mode of discovery. The AP sends out a subnet broadcast discovery request on the local subnet. Any WLCs on the local subnet that receive this packet will respond with a discovery response, much like how DHCP servers respond to a DHCP broadcast. The AP will also attempt contact with the IP addresses of previously associated controllers because it stores this information even after it's rebooted.

Over-the-Air Provisioning (OTAP) Mode   Typically, APs that are joined to the network transmit neighbor packets for over-the-air Radio Resource Management (RRM) that include the IP addresses of their associated WLC. After an initial boot or reboot, an AP will listen for these packets to obtain the IP address of a controller and will use the information it gains to send a directed packet discovery request. Be warned that this approach is not exactly a secure solution because this information can be read by anyone. Worse, in some code versions it's the default, which is why I recommend disabling it and using a clearly defined method of reaching the WLC. OTAP provisioning wastes bandwidth, and I can't stress enough the security hole it creates.

AP Priming   AP priming is the process of connecting the AP and its controller together before the AP is deployed so that it can learn the address of the WLC. The lightweight AP will retain the WLC's address even when rebooted. A major benefit of this is for an AP that must be installed in a hard-to-reach or remote location where physical access to it would be difficult to gain. If the controller is a part of a mobility group—a set of WLCs—it will learn all of these addresses as well, and will send a subnet broadcast for each of them when deployed.

DHCP Vendor Option Mode   APs can also get WLC addresses when they receive their configuration from DHCP, but this is something that must be set as a scope or server option within DHCP itself. Multiple addresses are entered as a comma-separated string, and depending on the type of DHCP implementation, they can be in either dotted decimal or hexadecimal format. Once the address of the proper WLC is obtained, the AP will then send a unicast discovery message to it. This configuration is important to understand, and I'll show you in Chapter 9 how to create and implement the DHCP vendor option.

DNS/DHCP Vendor Option Mode   A Cisco AP can also obtain the Cisco WLC IP address from DNS. Once the AP receives its configuration from DHCP, including the address of a DNS server, it will use the information to conduct a hostname lookup via a CISCO-LWAPP-CONTROLLER record in DNS that should be associated with the available controller management interface IP addresses. The AP will then be able to perform a unicast query to this address and associate with responsive WLAN controllers. If you're not using DHCP, you should manually set the DNS server address in the AP when entering the IP address.

An important factor that influences the entire process is the WLC's configuration. For now, understand that you can set the LWAPP Transport mode to either Layer 2 or 3 in the General menu of the Controller page because the WLC will only respond at the layer that it's configured for. Check out Figure 7.9.

FIGURE 7.9   LWAPP Transport mode

Controller	General	
General	802.3x Flow Control Mode	Disabled ▼
Inventory	LWAPP Transport Mode	Layer 3 ▼
Interfaces		Layer 2
Network Routes	LAG Mode on next reboot	Layer 3
Internal DHCP Server	Ethernet Multicast Mode	Disabled ▼
▶ Mobility Management	Broadcast Forwarding	Disabled ▼
Spanning Tree	Aggressive Load Balancing	Disabled ▼
Ports	Peer to Peer Blocking Mode	Disabled ▼
	Over The Air Provisioning of AP	Enabled ▼

> The newest code for the controllers only allows Layer 3 LWAPP, but the CCNA Wireless exam objectives still cover Layer 2 and Layer 3 LWAPP.

After you complete the necessary discovery steps and send out a discovery message, it's possible an AP can sometimes get a bunch of responses from controllers. Because of this, there's a specific order an AP uses to select the WLC to register with. If there isn't any controller information primed in the AP, it will simply look for a master controller, which is defined when you create a mobility domain. But if the AP has been primed, it will try to associate with its primary controller first; if that fails, it will proceed to try its secondary, and then its tertiary. Each mobility group can have a master controller designated for it, and if so, that specific controller will be the WLC that any unprimed APs will use once the discovery process finds it. Finally, if all else fails, an AP will resort to choosing the least loaded AP-Manager interface from all controllers that have responded to it.

Good to know is that in the last scenario, APs will ultimately load-balance between all available AP-Manager interfaces from any controller. The first AP will register to controller 1, the second to controller 2, and then the process will repeat. This is very cool, but how do APs determine which controller has the smallest load? They don't determine this based only on the number of APs associated with a given WLC, but by the percentage of the capacity already used on the controller, which it learns during the discovery phase.

To clarify this, let's say an AP finds two controllers—one with 10 APs associated with it and another one with only 5. You would think that the AP would go for the controller with only 5 APs associated with, but that's not necessarily the case. If the one with 10 has a total capacity of 100 (meaning that only 10 percent of its capacity is being utilized) but the AP with 5 only has the capacity for 20 APs (meaning it's 25 percent utilized), the AP will choose the first one because the WLC is carrying the least amount of load. If our AP finds two WLCs with the same percentage of their total capacity in use, it will simply opt for the first one that answers.

But things change if there happens to be a master controller configured on the network. Unprimed APs that were not configured ahead of time with an IP address of the controller and that are accessing the controller via a Layer 2 or Layer 3 broadcast will automatically join the controller marked as master. This allows us to easily assign the APs to specific controllers, be aware of which APs have been joined to the network, and then finally locate and reconfigure each AP to associate with its correct final destination controller.

Primary, secondary, and tertiary controller names are defined in each AP and stored in the AP flash memory. If a controller name is recognized in the controller discovery response, the AP will join that controller. Priming the AP first requires it to be registered with a controller before it can receive the whole list of controllers (Chapter 9 will show you how to configure AP priming in detail).

Join Phase

The LWAPP join request sent by the AP includes:

- The type of controller and its MAC address that it would like to associate with.

- The AP's hardware and software version, its name and the number and type of radios present on the request-issuing AP

- The AP's X.509 certificate that's used to initiate a secure LWAPP connection

Another important fact an AP needs to find out is whether or not the network supports jumbo frames. To do this, it will create two different-sized join request packets—one composed of 1,596 bytes and one of 1,500 bytes. The larger packet is a test payload to pad the packet size and test the network's ability to support jumbo frames.

Okay, so after receiving a join request from an AP, the controller will send a join reply that includes:

- A result code that's either a 0 for success or a 1 for failure. If there's a failure, a status message will indicate why.

- The controller's X.509 certificate.

- A test payload to check for the support of jumbo frames.

If all goes well, the AP will move on to either the Image Data state to download code or to the Config state to download its configuration. If the AP and the WLC are unable to create

the trusted relationship required, the AP will transition back to the discovery
over. Let's move along and talk about the Image Data and Config states now.

Image Data State

If the code version on the AP isn't in sync with the code on the WLC, the Al
Image Data state, which doesn't always mean its code will be upgraded. Tha
the WLC's version is lower than the AP's, the AP will downgrade its code version to sync
with the WLC's. It does this by downloading the code from the WLC in an LWAPP control
message. Once downloaded, it will be executed by the AP, followed by a reboot. The discovery and join phases then repeat, only at a much faster rate this time around because the
AP has retained the address of the WLC in flash memory.

By the way, you can update the WLC's code from Cisco. If the code you're updating to
is release 4.1 or higher, Cisco recommends that you use TFTP software daemon Tftpd32
version 3.0 or later for the transfer because this version supports TFTP transfers of 32MB
and larger.

So, finally, now that the AP and the WLC code match, revised or not, the Image Data
state is complete, and the AP will then begin the Config state. This is where the AP downloads its configuration from the WLC and is initiated with a configuration request from
the AP that includes the parameters that need to be set and their current values (which will
probably be 0). The WLC will respond by supplying proper values for all the parameters,
after which the AP will execute them just like a router would execute a set of commands
sent from the Cisco GUI interface called Security Device Manager (SDM).

You can see an illustration of the complete process from initial boot to reboot in
Figure 7.10.

FIGURE 7.10 AP states

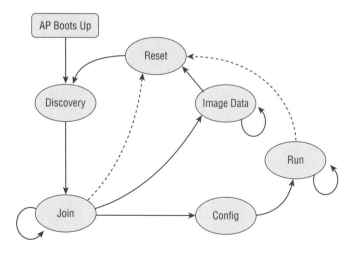

Much like the running configuration on a router or switch, this information resides in RAM, meaning if power to the AP is lost, it will need to start the discovery stage all over again. But since the IP address of the controller is retained in flash memory, the process will happen much faster after initial contact with any of the controllers has already been made.

 WLC Management should be carried out over a wired connection. You can use the Cisco WLAN Solution Management over Wireless feature to do this wirelessly from a client, but if you do, uploads and downloads from the client on the wireless network to the WLC will not be allowed.

Redundancy

Redundancy is always a good idea and should be built into any system. The good news is that it can be implemented in the CUWN architecture at several levels. Two levels of those pertain to APs:

RF Level   If one AP is lost, the WLC will raise the power levels of neighboring APs to cover the hole. Power level 1 is the highest and equals the highest level allowed in the country in which the AP is operating. Each level down decreases the power by 50 percent. So to go from power level 1 to 3 would be a 6dB difference. For this to work well, your APs can't be set to the highest power level for normal coverage or it will clearly be impossible to go to a higher level when necessary. For this reason, I recommend leaving two available higher power levels on each AP. But do understand that this will mean it will require more APs to cover the same area, something that Cisco is quite okay with. This process is shown in Figure 7.11.

FIGURE 7.11   AP redundancy

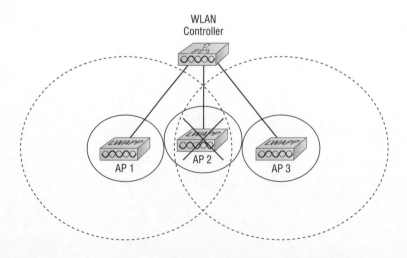

The Port Level   This refers to using multiple AP-Managers or link aggregation groups on the controller. Device level-multiple WLCs can be configured to provide backup to each other, somewhat like clustering servers for fault tolerance. And remember that if DHCP provides the addresses of multiple WLCs to the AP, it will retain all of them in case the controller the AP is associated with goes down.

Using a WLC redundancy strategy gains a number of failover options to select from. This is similar to failover options in server clustering. Let's explore these options now.

N+1 Solution

In the N+1 solution, one WLC is used as a backup. All of the APs would have this backup device configured as secondary on their lists of available controllers. In the list on each AP, the primary would be its local WLC and the secondary would be the redundant controller. This allows the redundant WLC to provide backup to multiple local WLCs.

If you opt for this solution, know that if more than the WLC were to be lost, the backup will become oversubscribed. And when it reaches its limit, it is possible that some APs could be left out in the cold with no controller.

N+N Solution

The N+N solution doesn't require a passive WLC. In this solution, live WLCs are set to back each other up if a failure occurs. There are two important considerations when using this solution. The first is to make sure the normal load is balanced between the two. Second, for this arrangement to work, each WLC should only be operating at or near half capacity during normal operation. That way, either one will be able to handle the load of the other if it fails.

To make this work, just set all APs to use the local WLC as primary and the other as secondary. This is the most common configuration.

N+N+1 Solution

This solution looks and is configured a lot like N +1 with one more level of safety—and more cost. Again, the WLCs are set to back each other up as in N+1, but you also have a third WLC in the mix that's not active as tertiary. In the N+N+1 solution, there's only one pair of APs set to use this third WLC, but you can opt to have multiple blocks of two sets of APs to use the same tertiary WLC.

By now, you probably get that there's a direct relationship between the cost of the solution and the safety it provides—as usual, the more redundancy you have in place, the higher the cost. In addition, your choices should be based on the parameters of the service level agreement (SLA), so it is no surprise that SLAs that provide more average uptime cost more money. You get what you pay for!

AP Modes

Basically, the mode of an AP describes the task that it's fulfilling. Normal operation is called Local Mode, but five more operational modes are possible. The model number of the AP tells you how many of the six potential modes can be supported. As with all other settings when using lightweight APs, this is carried out in the controller per AP. The six modes are:

- Local
- Monitor
- Sniffer
- Rouge Detection
- H-REAP
- Bridge

Local Mode

In local mode, the AP performs the data transfer for clients and monitors all channels. This mode can really come in handy when performing a basic site survey! When you're using it for this purpose, data will be sent and received via the AP, and the surveyor (you) will move about the expected cell area checking for RSSI and SNR values at various locations.

To properly service the stations and monitor all channels, the AP has to split time between the two duties. It does so using a 180-second cycle. In the 2.4GHz frequency, it will spend 13 seconds on the assigned channel, scan the next channel for 60ms, and then return to the assigned channel for 13 seconds. It will continue this pattern until all channels have been scanned. In the 5GHz frequency, it will spend only 10 seconds on the assigned channel due to the higher number of channels to scan. These two patterns are illustrated in Figure 7.12.

FIGURE 7.12   Channel monitoring

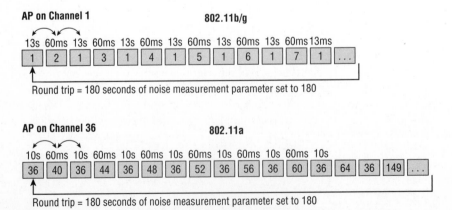

The round-trip time (RTT) and the channels to scan can be set in the WLC.

Monitor Mode

As the name implies, monitor mode only allows monitoring and no regular client servicing. Here's a list of some important tasks an AP operating in this mode can be used for:

- As a sensor for a WLC acting as an intrusion protection device (IDS) scanning for rogue APs and rogue clients
- As a data gatherer to troubleshoot a performance issue related to changes in the RF environment
- As a site survey tool
- As an additional triangulation point when using a Cisco Wireless Location Appliance

In monitor mode, all channels are scanned but the scanning algorithm is different from the one that's used in normal mode. Each channel receives 1.1ms of time, resulting in an RTT of 1.1ms / the number of channels. The channels scanned can be set from the command line with the following commands:

```
Config advanced 802.11b monitor channel-list all
```

(which monitors all channels)

```
Config advanced 802.11b monitor channel-list country
```

(which monitors all channels available in a country)

```
Config advanced 802.11b monitor channel-list dca
```

(which monitors all channels assigned by the dynamic channel assignment).

Sniffer Mode

Sniffer mode allows the AP to capture all frames on a specific channel and sends the frames to a station running an analyzer like OmniPeek, AirMagnet, or Wireshark. You configure it by setting the AP to sniffer mode, which will result in the AP rebooting. Once it does, the WLC will specify to the AP the channel it needs to scan as well as the IP address to send the data to via the settings on the AP configuration page. When the AP sends the data, it will be framed with a header specific to the sniffer program, and the corresponding sniffer program on the collection station will be used to examine it.

Rogue Detection Mode

In rouge detection mode, the AP operates on the wired side without the radio. Therefore, it should be connected to a trunk where it can hear all VLANs. The controller continually updates an AP operating in this node with the addresses of all rogue AP and client MAC addresses. Remember—this information comes from all the other APs that are listening on the wireless side.

The AP in this mode listens on the wired network for ARP packets. When it sees a rogue AP or client MAC address, it will generate an alarm indicating that not only has a rogue been detected, it's been found on the wired side! Remember that when your AP is in monitor, sniffer, or rogue detection mode, stations are not allowed to associate.

H-REAP Mode

Hybrid remote-edge access point, known as H-REAP, is used when the AP is placed a remote location via a WAN link but positioned where it doesn't warrant an onsite WLC. Unlike in normal mode, an AP in H-REAP can lose contact with its WLC and still function. Here's a list of some restrictions regarding the link between the AP and the WLC:

- The link cannot be less than 128kbps.
- Round-trip latency cannot exceed 100ms.
- A minimum of 500 bytes of MTUs must be supported.
- Code updates over 4MB cannot be received by the AP.

The AP can switch locally between wireless clients and even authenticate clients when the connection is lost. In addition, when it's connected again, it can start sending traffic back to the WLC. Dynamic Frequency Selection (DFS), required on some channels in 802.11a, will also function in either connected or disconnected mode. An AP working in this mode must have at least 32MB of memory since it will need to be able to store important information like the following:

DTIM Period (Delivery Traffic Indication Message)   Determines how often a beacon contains broadcast and multicast traffic. Affects how long stations in power save mode are allowed to sleep.

Beacon Period   Specifies the frequency of beacons.

Time between Beacon Frames   Measured in kilo-microseconds.

Preambles   Determines whether short or longer preambles (compatible with legacy 802.11) will be used; however, this only applies to 802.11b stations.

Power Level   Set by the WLC.

Country Code   Determines the allowable power level and channels.

Channel Number   Again, set by the WLC.

Black List   Forbidden station MACs.

An important point to remember is that an AP in H-REAP mode can't use Layer 2 or 3 broadcasts to locate its WLC. It must use DHCP Option 43, DNS/DHCP, or OTAP via an AP that's already connected to the controller.

Earlier, I talked about an AP being able to perform authentication if disconnected from the WLC when in stand-alone mode, but there are some limits. IPSec and PPTP won't work because they both require access to the controller. Further, during a disconnection, central-switched WLANs will be shut down and local WLANs will continue to operate.

Any existing sessions that were created using these mechanisms prior to the disconnection will remain functional until the next time an authentication must occur (as when roaming). A few other normal features, like RRM, will become unavailable as well.

But the good news is that if your controller's software is version 5.0 or later, you get new features that can help mitigate some of these functional losses during an outage:

- Backup RADIUS, a feature that allows you to set the AP to use a backup RADIUS server that will allow it to continue using 802.1X authentications

- Local authentication, which enables the AP to perform LEAP and EAP-FAST for 20 statically configured users, can be used in concert with the backup RADIUS server

- QoS, which allows the AP to tag frames with priorities

 If a controller loses power and a remote location is configured for H-REAP mode, up to 20 users will be allowed to locally authenticate using EAP.

Bridge Mode

Yep, you guessed it. An AP can be even be used as a bridge in a point-to-point or point-to-multipoint link when deployed in bridge mode. But not all models can handle this job; only the Cisco Aironet 1130AG series, Cisco Aironet 1240 series, and Cisco Aironet 1500 series APs can. These kinds of APs also function well for mesh networking solutions—since some APs in this type of design don't have a wired connection, bridge mode allows them to use Adaptive Wireless Path Protocol (AWPP) to find the best radio path to an AP, thus affording wired connectivity to the WLAN controller.

Roaming

Back at the beginning of this chapter, I told you about a very cool functional benefit you gain by having APs managed by controllers: seriously improved roaming capabilities! Why is this so important? Well, if you think about it, roaming is what happens when a station moves out of range of one AP and into the range of another AP with the same SSID. Using controllers has a huge impact on roaming, but to fully understand how, you first need a solid grasp of exactly how controllers can be arranged to optimize the network's performance.

Mobility Groups

As I briefly touched upon earlier, a mobility group is essentially a set of WLCs that have been grouped together to enhance roaming capability. You start by setting a global parameter on each WLC. WLCs in the same mobility group can exchange information about their associated clients, and you can take this to the next level by organizing mobility groups into mobility domains. Something to keep in mind is that clients can only roam between mobility groups if those mobility groups are part of the same mobility domain. If they aren't, a complete reauthentication process has to happen before clients can enter any new mobility group. To get a picture of this, take a look at Figure 7.13.

FIGURE 7.13 Mobility groups

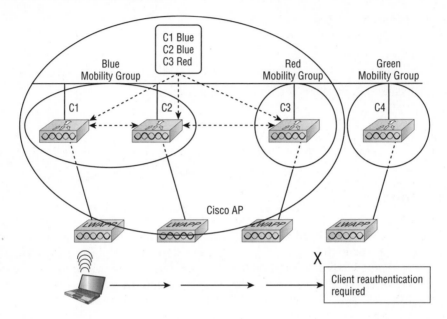

So how do we do this? Well, to enable a new controller to be included in the same mobility domain with any other WLCs, on the new WLC you must configure the MAC and IP addresses that map to the management interfaces of the WLCs already grouped. Equally important is that all WLCs in the same mobility group be set with same domain name, and they all must be set with the same virtual gateway address, which will be discussed further in Chapter 9.

Keep in mind that you can include up to 24 controllers in a group. Since that's quite a few controllers to keep the information just floating around in your head, it's a good idea to create a template that you can refer to that accurately depicts all members in the group.

Roaming can occur at Layer 2 or at Layer 3 without changes in the subnet, and therefore, to the IP address. You know that roaming can happen between APs that are controlled by different controllers provided they're part of the same group and domain. This all sounds simple, but just as it is with most everything; it's not as easy as it sounds. For instance, all controllers in a group must also share:

- The same code version

- The same LWAPP mode

- The same Access Control Lists (ACLs)

- The same WLANs (SSIDs)

During a roaming event, either AP connections can be handled by the new controller (asymmetric tunneling), or all traffic can be sent back to the old controller, a process known as symmetric tunneling.

Layer 2 and Layer 3 Roaming

When Layer 2 roaming occurs on the same subnet, the client will attempt reauthentication with the new AP, and its request will be sent back to its old controller. If it's a controller the AP has already met and has the AP in memory, this process takes less than 10ms and is called *intracontroller* roaming. But if it's a controller that happens to be a stranger to the AP, the controllers involved will then exchange information that effectively moves the client over to the new controller. This process takes less than 20ms and is called *intercontroller* roaming. During this process, the client is unaware of any activity going on in the background, even if it moves to a new controller. Check out Figure 7.14 to clarify this kind of event.

FIGURE 7.14   Layer 2 roaming

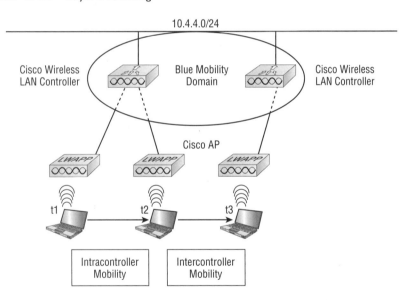

During Layer 3 roaming, either the client changes subnets but retains its old IP address or it reauthenticates. Again, this process is transparent to the client, although more processing and activity is done in the background than with Layer 2 roaming. Layer 3 roaming is made possible via a process wherein the controller creates a tunnel that tricks the network and the client into believing that the subnet hasn't changed at all. This can be set up two ways:

- If the traffic both to and from the client is tunneled between the new and old controllers, we call it symmetric roaming.
- If the traffic from the client uses normal IP routing and only the return traffic is tunneled between the new and old controllers, it's known as asymmetric tunneling.

That Layer 3 controller handoff I talked about takes only 30ms—pretty quick considering the process. An example is shown in Figure 7.15.

FIGURE 7.15   Layer 3 roaming

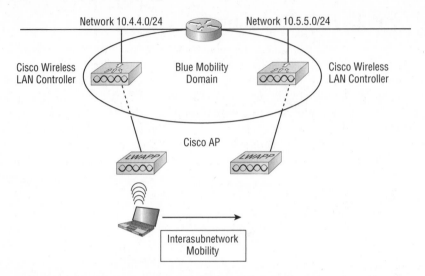

Layer 3 roaming can happen quickly because unlike with Layer 2 roaming the full amount of client information isn't handed off to a new controller, so there's no time required for that to take place. Instead, the client data is marked with something referred to as an *anchor entry* in the old controller and a *foreign entry* in the new controller. The only really new thing that happens is that the client is re-authenticated with a new security context.

The manner in which the frames are moved between the client and the computer to which it is communicating occurs differently based on the type of roaming at Layer 3. When asymmetric is used, the path to and from the destination computer is:

- From client to foreign (new) controller to router to destination computer

- From destination computer to anchor (old) controller to foreign controller to client

The return trip uses the tunnel that is created between the anchor and the foreign controller.

When symmetric roaming is used, the path to and from the destination computer is:

- From client to foreign (new) controller to anchor (old) controller to destination computer

- From destination computer to anchor (old) controller to foreign controller to client

The tunnel that is created between the anchor and the foreign controller is used in both directions in this case.

The roaming type is set in the controller and is called the Symmetric Mobility Tunneling mode. If it is enabled, the mode is symmetric; if it is disabled, the mode is asymmetric. This setting is a global parameter shared by all WLANs on the controller. However, sometimes it becomes necessary to perform symmetric on one while leaving the others asymmetric. A commonly cited example would be when a guest WLAN needs to be restricted in its access so users can only get to the Internet and not the internal company network. To do this, a special type of anchor called a mobility anchor must be designated.

The tunneling operation with a mobility anchor operates differently. *All* traffic to and from the clients will go through the mobility anchor. This is the case without regard to where the client is located. This is also where the client will get its IP address and security configuration. For redundancy, more than one mobility anchor can be designated for a WLAN. Don't forget that the anchor must be connected to a VLAN trunk port to allow all stations to keep their IP addresses when roaming.

The controllers that will be available to the mobility anchor are designated when the mobility group is designated. If more than one mobility anchor is designated, the local controller will try to load-balance. Status messages are sent from the mobility anchor every 100 seconds to keep the local controllers aware if a mobility anchor becomes unavailable.

Radio Resource Management

The Radio Resource Management (RRM) engine is the component of the WLC that makes the magic of RF environment management possible. Through the use of dynamic algorithms, the WLC creates an environment that is completely self-configuring, self-optimizing, and self-healing. The RRM performs these functions:

- Radio resource monitoring
- Client and network load balancing
- Dynamic channel assignment
- Coverage hole detection and correction
- Dynamic transmit power control
- Interference detection and avoidance

By receiving information constantly from the APs under its control, the WLC maintains a broad and comprehensive view of the RF environment. The controller considers a number of RF characteristics in real time to efficiently handle channel assignments. These include the following:

- Noise
- Client load
- 802.11 interference
- Utilization
- Access point received energy

The WLC can digest all this information and, through the use of algorithms, make decisions on the behalf of the entire system. This optimizes channel configuration, taking into account a three-dimensional view of the environment, where APs on the floor above and below must be taken into consideration.

The WLC is also capable of managing the power output of the individual APs in such a manner that it can react to changing conditions. Whereas normally it may keep power low in an area with many APs to reduce inference among the APs where extra capacity is needed, it may need to selectively increase power output on certain APs in the event of a failed AP. It will attempt to balance the APs so that they see their neighbors at −65dBm (best practice).

Moreover, it can reduce congestion in areas where many stations are using the same AP (with disastrous performance results). It can influence the choice of AP by the stations by instructing the closest AP (this is usually the one the station chooses, regardless of how busy it is) to refuse the association in order to encourage the use of a more distant yet less busy AP. If the station insists, the association with the closer AP will be allowed, but the net result is a better distribution of stations among the APs.

Roaming can also be enhanced by the WLC. By comparing the RSSI and SNR of the stations with respect to each AP (remember that information is in the header of each station's data), the WLC can anticipate when roaming is about to occur, making the process smoother.

Summary

In this chapter, we discussed the position that various devices hold in the Cisco Unified Wireless Network (CUWN) architecture and the roles the devices play. We also examined the two models that can be used when implementing WLANs—the stand-alone and the lightweight model—and how the two models impact the implementation of the network. In addition, we explored how APs discover and associate with their controller in the lightweight solution, as well as approaches to providing redundancy. Finally, we examined roaming and how one of the functions that becomes available in the lightweight model, Radio Resource Management (RRM), can make this a smoother process.

Exam Essentials

Identify the types of communications that occur between APs and their controllers after deployment. Among these are client transfers, code downloads, and configuration downloads.

Know the methods used to manage the controller. These include HTTPS, console port and service port for GUI management, Telnet, and SSH. You also use the Cisco WLAN Solution Management over Wireless feature, but when you use this method, uploads and downloads to the WLC are not allowed.

Know the order of methods an AP will use to discover its controller. The order is Layer 2 broadcast, and then Layer 3 broadcast unless the AP has been primed. If it has been primed, the AP will try its primary WLC, secondary, and tertiary, and then will attempt to contact the WLC designated as the master controller.

Know the functions that Radio Resource Management (RRM) performs. These include channel assignment, power-level control radio resource monitoring, client and network load balancing, dynamic channel assignment, coverage hole detection and correction, dynamic transmit power control, and interference detection and avoidance.

Understand how a controller-based network can deal with sources of interference in real time. The controller can mitigate interference by adjusting power levels and by changing operating channels to avoid the interference.

Written Lab

1. True/False: LWAPP is used for communication between the AP and the client.

2. True/False: The AP and the Cisco WLC verify one another's certificates before establishing a secure connection.

3. When using WPA2 or EAP authentication, where are the wireless encryption keys kept during the session?

4. What function makes the identification of rogue APs possible?

5. True/False: Autonomous APs send information back to the WLC.

6. What is a group of APs that share information about their clients called?

7. True/False: Mobility group members can use different versions of code.

8. In dB, what is the net gain in power going from power level 2 to 1?

9. True/False: EAP-TLS is supported by the Cisco Unified Wireless Network.

10. How many WiSMs are supported in a mobility group?

Review Questions

1. Which AP mode allows client connections?

    A. H-REAP

    B. Sniffer

    C. Monitor

    D. Rogue detection

2. When an AP operating as H-REAP loses connectivity with the WLC, which of the following items can still continue to function? (Choose two.)

    A. Locally switched WLANs

    B. RRM

    C. Clients using WPA or WPA2 with PSK

    D. Clients using EAP-TLS

3. Which of the following is *not* an advantage of using a controller-based WLAN?

    A. Easier to maintain consistent configurations

    B. Availability of new channels

    C. Real-time interference mitigation

    D. Easier deployment

4. Which of the following describes the path used when asymmetric roaming is in use?

    A. Client > foreign controller > router > destination computer > anchor controller > foreign controller > client

    B. Client > foreign controller > destination computer > anchor controller > foreign controller > client

    C. Client > foreign controller > anchor controller > destination computer > anchor controller > foreign controller > client

    D. Client > foreign controller > anchor controller > destination computer > router > foreign controller > client

5. When all WLANs are operating in asymmetric roaming mode except for one (which is in symmetric mode), what type of WLC will the client operating in symmetric roaming mode use?

    A. Anchor

    B. Mobility anchor

    C. Master controller

    D. Secondary controller

6. How long does it take for a client to complete an intracontroller roam?

   A. 10ms

   B. 60ms

   C. 30ms

   D. 20ms

7. Which of the following is *not* required to be the same on all members of a mobility group?

   A. Code version

   B. Subnet ID

   C. LWAPP mode

   D. ACLs

8. What is the maximum number of controllers that can be in a mobility group?

   A. 16

   B. 20

   C. 24

   D. 32

9. What is a collection of mobility groups called?

   A. Mobility tree

   B. Mobility domain

   C. Mobility organization

   D. Mobility realm

10. How much memory is required for the AP to operate as H-REAP?

    A. 16MB

    B. 20MB

    C. 24MB

    D. 32MB

11. Which discovery method cannot be used by an H-REAP to locate the WLC?

    A. DHCP

    B. Over-the-air provisioning

    C. Layer 2 broadcast

    D. DNS

12. In which mode does the AP operate on the wired side of the network?

    A. Local

    B. Rouge detection

    C. Sniffer

    D. Monitor

13. Which DHCP option can be used to provide the address of the WLC to the AP?

   A. Option 46

   B. Option 44

   C. Option 43

   D. Option 40

14. What is the minimum link capacity required for an H-REAP implementation?

   A. 128Kbps

   B. 64Kbps

   C. 256Kbps

   D. 512Kbps

15. Which AP mode spends 1.1ms on each channel when scanning?

   A. Rouge detection

   B. Local

   C. Monitor

   D. Sniffer

16. Which redundancy solution for WLCs uses no passive WLCs?

   A. N+1

   B. N+1+1

   C. N+N

   D. N+N+1

17. What does the AP receive from the WLC during the Image Data state?

   A. Code revision

   B. AP configuration

   C. List of WLCs

   D. Network configuration

18. How many join request packets will the AP create?

   A. 1

   B. 2

   C. 3

   D. 4

19. What is the last state an AP cycles through to locate the WLC and to become fully functional?

   A. Join

   B. Run

   C. Image Data

   D. Config

20. What is the process called when an AP is connected to the WLC, disconnected, deployed, and then successfully completes discovery?

   A. Staging

   B. Priming

   C. Prepping

   D. Loading

Answers to Review Questions

1. A. The modes that do *not* allow client connections are monitor, sniffer, and rogue detection modes.

2. A, C. Clients using WPA or WPA2 with PSK and locally switched WLANs will continue to operate. Additionally, when operating in a locally switched WLAN, clients using Local-EAP for EAP-LEAP and EAP-FAST will also continue for up to 20 users if the users have accounts in the AP.

3. B. Using a controller-based WLAN will not make any new channels available.

4. A. Asymmetric roaming uses IP routing to the destination computer but uses a secure tunnel between the anchor and foreign APs for the return traffic.

5. B. When a single WLAN is operating in symmetric roaming mode while the others are in asymmetric roaming mode, those clients will use a mobility anchor regardless of where they roam.

6. A. When Layer 2 roaming occurs (same subnet), the client will attempt reauthentication with the new AP, which will send the packets back to its old controller. If it is the same controller, this process takes less than 10ms and is called intracontroller roaming. If it is a different controller, the controllers exchange information, moving the client to the new controller. This process will take less than 20ms and is called intercontroller roaming.

7. B. It is not required that all mobility members be in the same subnet.

8. C. Twenty-four APs can be in a mobility group.

9. B. A collection of mobility groups is called a mobility domain.

10. D. Because of the amount of information it must store, an AP operating as H-REAP must have 32MB of memory.

11. C. Neither Layer 2 or Layer3 broadcasting can be used by H-REAP to locate the WLC.

12. B. In rouge detection mode, the AP operates on the wired side.

13. C. DHCP option 43 can be used to provide the address of the WLC to the AP.

14. A. The minimum link capacity required for an H-REAP implementation is 128Kbps.

15. C. In monitor mode, each channel is scanned for 1.1ms.

16. C. All methods use a passive or inactive backup except N+N.

17. A. In the Image Data state, the code is upgraded or downgraded to match the WLC.

18. B. Two packets are created, one 1,500 and one 1,596 bytes. This serves the purpose of testing for jumbo frame support in the network.

19. B. The order of states is Discovery, Join, Image Data, Config, and Run.

20. B. The priming process allows the AP to know its WLC when it boots up after deployment.

Answers to Written Lab

1. False

2. True

3. On the AP and the client

4. Radio Resource Management

5. False

6. Mobility group

7. False

8. +3dB

9. True. You need certificates on the server and all the clients to run this.

10. 12

Chapter

8

Introduction to the Cisco Mobility Express Wireless Architecture

---

THE CCNA WIRELESS EXAM TOPICS COVERED IN THIS CHAPTER ARE:

✓ **Install a basic Cisco wireless LAN**

  ▪ Describe the Cisco Mobility Express Wireless architecture
  (Smart Business Communication System—SBCS, Cisco
  Config Agent—CCA, 526WLC, 521AP—stand-alone and
  controller-based)

After the previous chapter's lengthy discussion on solutions fit for a large enterprise environment that can support hundreds of access points (APs) and a potential legion of wireless LAN controllers (WLCs), it's a good time to fill you in on Cisco's effective solutions for small and medium businesses (SMBs). I'm going to describe SMB solutions like Cisco Mobility Express devices as well as compare them to the Enterprise versions you just learned about. After that, I'll thoroughly cover how to configure these Express devices using the Cisco Configuration Assistant (CCA) and by a direct method through the web interface. You'll also learn how to configure Cisco's 526WLC controller through the management ports on the front panel.

For up-to-the-minute updates on this chapter, check out www.lammle.com or www.sybex.com/go/ccnawireless.

Cisco Mobility Express

The actual architecture of the Cisco Mobility Express solution isn't all that different from the Cisco Unified Wireless Network (CUWN) solution, except for one key distinction—scale. While it's definitely true that far fewer devices can be managed with this system, that's exactly what makes it great for businesses for which the CUWN's massive capacity would just be sheer overkill. Not to mention its budget-threatening price tag! Cisco Mobility Express essentially provides a subset of the functions and features supported by the CUWN, so it's vital for you to grasp the similarities as well as the differences in order to ensure you've got everything needed for your solid and final solution.

Cisco Mobility Express is part of a complete system called the Cisco Smart Business Communication System (SBCS), which includes voice, data, video, and wireless networking products tailored for small businesses. To place Cisco Mobility Express in perspective, let's take a quick look at the products that make up the SBCS.

Small Business Communication System

There are plenty of large to ginormous organizations and corporations that truly need super-sized CUWN capability and can also pony up for it without selling body parts, but for the legions of mere-mortal businesses, the streamlined, cost-effective SBCS was created. It consists of a number of components that can be used together or individually, making it so its owner can create a personalized solution that's perfectly suited to their specific needs. All that's required is to strategically combine the scaled-down versions of the larger, more costly, and robust Cisco devices.

First, there are several models of the Cisco Unified Communications 500 Series that provide voice and video for small businesses. There's a rack-mount version as well as a desktop version that can also include an integrated AP. And depending on the model, it can support 8, 16, 32, or 48 users and even provide DHCP, which is especially handy because a number of the other devices in SBCS don't support DHCP. The back panel of a 500 series desktop model is shown in Figure 8.1. It has a nice variety of connection types, including ISDN, Basic Rate Interface (BRI), Power-over-Ethernet (PoE), WAN, and a console port. As an added benefit, this model includes the built-in AP I mentioned.

FIGURE 8.1   UC500 example

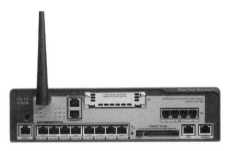

For VOIP endpoints, the Cisco Unified Wireless IP Phone and Cisco IP Communicator SoftPhone can be used with the UC500. These models include a single number reach feature.

For connecting IP phones to the UC500, the CE520 series switches provide 8 ports in a desktop model and 24 ports in a rack-mount version. Cisco considers this to be the companion switch to the UC500. To extend access to a telecommuting employee or small branch office, routing, VPN, and security features are provided by the 800 series Integrated Services Routers. The 871W wireless router shines here because it has an integrated AP for wireless access to devices.

Finally, the Cisco Mobility Express, consisting of the Cisco 521 Wireless Express Lightweight Access Point and the Cisco 526 Wireless Mobility Express Controller, provides wireless access plus a tie-in to the wired network. This is critical, so I'll be placing a lot of focus on it in this chapter.

There's also a feature specifically geared to ease the configuration of the 500 series suite of products called the Cisco Configuration Assistant (CCA). It's cool mostly because it's free, but you still should be familiar with it, so I'll talk about that in detail soon.

Cisco Monitor Director gives us enhanced network monitoring and troubleshooting capabilities to further tighten up dependable network performance of all networking devices and IP phones in the SMB market. But of course, it's not free. See the Cisco website for more information on Monitor Director (http://www.cisco.com/en/US/products/ps7246/index.html).

> **Cisco Configuration Assistant**
>
> CCA is a GUI-based application that runs on a PC. The CCA software is available as a free download at www.cisco.com/go/configassist. The download does require a CiscoConnection Online (CCO) login.

Express Wireless Architecture

A big reason that the design of the Cisco Mobility Express solution provides flexibility regarding system architecture is because the APs can be deployed in either stand-alone or lightweight mode. If you choose not to deploy a controller and use the APs in stand-alone mode, you can use the CCA to manage three APs.

But by adding a Cisco 526 WLC controller and managing the APs in controller-based mode, you can manage up to six APs per controller and combine up to two WLCs to form a mobility group, which gives you a grand total of 12 APs. I know this doesn't sound like very many, but 12 APs can cover some serious real estate if you plan well and install everything correctly.

Even though the 500 series is not as robust a solution as those I described in the previous chapter, it still offers some cool advanced features you would otherwise not get at all without using a controller. Some of these features are:

- Radio Resource Management (RRM)
- Mobility management
- Guest access

Remember, RRM affords the benefits of self-configuration, self-optimization, and self-healing. Mobility management can be carried out at the AP level using the local web interface of each AP or achieved globally using the CCA. But you don't get WCS. Now let's take a look at the components of the Mobility Express solution, starting with the APs.

521 Series Express AP

The Cisco 521 AP comes in a stand-alone and a controller-based model. The controller-based variety is designed to be managed by the Cisco 526 controller and uses a protocol similar to Lightweight Access Point Protocol (LWAPP) to communicate with the controller. But it doesn't support LWAPP so you can't deploy it in the Enterprise solutions covered in the previous chapter.

Here's a list of the functional limitations of the 521 that you need to know to be prepared for the exam:

- Offers no support for LWAPP
- Offers no support for 802.11a or 802.11n (b/g only)

- Uses a subset of the CLI commands available in the 1130 (which it resembles in appearance)

- Offers no support for local EAP

- Offers no support for H-REAP mode

- Offers no support for multiple SSIDs or broadcast SSIDs

- Offers no support for Cisco fast secure roaming

- Offers no support for SNMP control

- Offers no support for multiple RADIUS servers

- Offers no support for IPsec

In addition, RADIUS servers created in CCA must be deleted from the web interface.

Remember, when using stand-alone mode, you can manage three APs through the CCA and you can do so individually via CLI, telnet, a web interface, or a console port. The Cisco 521AP looks quite a bit like the 1130, as you can see in Figure 8.2.

FIGURE 8.2   521AP

526 Series Express WLC

Since the 526WLC is designed to work with 521APs, you probably guessed correctly that it would also be based on a similar architecture and have some of the same limitations. It supports six APs per controller, and only two 526s can be combined in a mobility group. In addition, it unfortunately doesn't support LWAPP, making it incompatible with large Enterprise solutions and so this limits scalability. This is a huge downside: you're basically making a commitment that you'll never grow to need more than 12 APs, because if you do, you'll have to buy all new equipment. That's right: all new APs and controllers, which as I mentioned, is a painfully pricey thing and a definite downside to going with the 500 series SMB solution.

Because it uses an LWAPP-like protocol to communicate just like the 521APs do, the 526WLC will only work with these APs. You can configure the 526 through its local web interface or with the CCA and I'll show you some other ways you can do so as well later in the chapter.

Just as the 521AP is similar to the 1130AP in appearance and functionality but does not support all the features an 1130AP does, the 526 controller is similar in functionality to the 2106WLC. Here's a list of key differences you should commit to memory:

- Offers no current support for rogue AP and client detection (support is planned for future versions)
- Offers no support for a location service
- Offers limited support for voice and video
- Provides no local RADIUS or DHCP
- Provides no VLAN for AP groups
- Offers no support for spanning trees
- Offers no support for Layer 3 wireless protection policies
- Offers no support for SNMP
- Offers no support for 802.11a, 802.11n, or 802.11h
- Offers no support for ACLs
- Specifies maximum of eight dynamic interfaces and eight SSIDs
- Specifies maximum of two RADIUS servers

But even with these negatives, the 526 still offers us some great features. Think about it—for a SMB that doesn't need the features in this list, it's a marked upgrade in functionality to the alternative option of simply utilizing multiple stand-alone APs.

Cisco Mobility Express vs. CUWN Features Comparison

Because of everything I've talked about, you can see that it's absolutely vital to have a solid grasp of the differences between the Enterprise solution and the SMB solution so you can correctly determine what you need during the design phase of a wireless infrastructure and avoid costly mistakes. Table 8.1 lists the features of the two systems for easy comparison.

TABLE 8.1   Cisco Mobility Express vs. CUWN

	Cisco Mobility Express	CUWN
Management Platform	CCA	Wireless control systems
Roaming	2 WLCs, 1 mobility group Layers 2 and 3	48 WLCs, 48 mobility groups Layers 2 and 3
Capacity	6 APs per WLC, 2 WLCs per network Limited to 500 series devices only	150 APs per WLC, H-REAP supported All APs support all controllers

TABLE 8.1   Cisco Mobility Express vs. CUWN *(continued)*

	Cisco Mobility Express	**CUWN**
Security	Encryption and authentication	Encryption and authentication Uses IDS and IPS
Mobility	Very simplified Voice over Wi-Fi Guest access No location services	Full Voice over Wi-Fi Full guest access Location services
Integration	Shared management with SBCS elements (all technologies)	Some features share management with the wired infrastructure (security)

Using the Cisco Configuration Assistant

Earlier I mentioned that the Cisco Configuration Assistant (CCA) is a GUI tool that can be downloaded for free from Cisco with a Cisco CCO account and password that you can create for free as well. The tool is installed on a PC and used to connect to various Cisco devices, including routers, switches, wireless APs, and controllers, as well as Cisco Unified Communications call-routing and voicemail systems.

After it downloads to your computer, the installation file will be named something like Cisco-config-assistant-win-k9-1_8-en. Let's walk through the installation now.

Click on the file and setup will begin. After accepting the license agreement, you'll be asked to choose a location for the installation, as shown in Figure 8.3.

FIGURE 8.3   Providing a directory name for the CCA installation

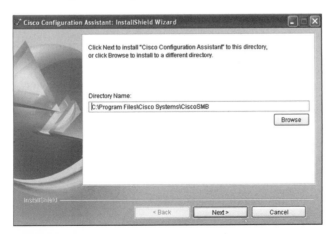

Once you've chosen an installation location, files will be extracted to it and then executed. A finish screen will then appear, and when you dismiss it, the installation is complete. Once the software is installed and you open it, you'll see the screen shown in Figure 8.4.

FIGURE 8.4   Loading the Cisco Configuration Assistant

After that, you'll get the initial configuration screen shown in Figure 8.5.

FIGURE 8.5   Initial CCA configuration screen

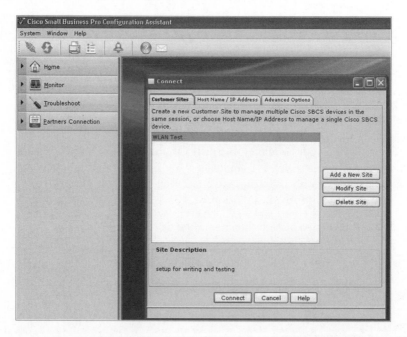

Click the Customer Sites tab, and then enter the IP address of the device that you would like to connect to and manage. When you connect, you'll also be prompted for the username and password. The default password on Cisco devices is typically "Cisco" until you change it. Once you're at the Customer Sites page, select the customer you created and click Connect. You'll then be presented with the screen in Figure 8.6.

FIGURE 8.6   New customer network layout

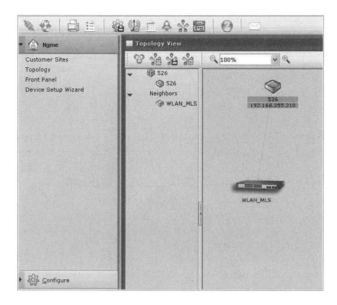

Even though this tool can be used to manage myriad devices, it's meant specifically as part of the tool set used to manage those included in the Cisco Mobility Express solution. Wizards guide you through the initial setup for the 526, 521, 520, UC500, and CE520, as shown in Figure 8.7.

FIGURE 8.7   Device Setup Wizard

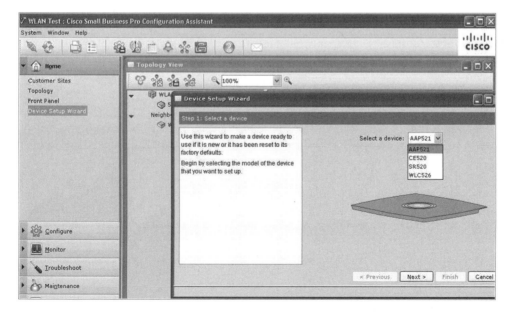

The best way to learn about the CCA is to download it and play with it yourself, but if you don't have any 500 series devices or aren't using the SMB wireless solution, you should just move on to the WCS section.

 Real World Scenario

When to Recommend the 500 Series

I was sitting in a coffee shop in downtown Boulder, Colorado, a few weeks ago complaining to a friend about how much work I have to do on my CCNA Wireless book, and how demanding my editors are being about it, when my friend, who happened to own the shop, asked me how to control the wireless users in his business. I asked him to clarify what he meant, and he told me that the students from the university come in, buy a single cup of coffee, and hunker down for hours upon hours studying and doing their homework. Since I had a 526 series controller with a 521 series AP that I had bought to check out before I started writing the book, I told him I'd bring it down and let him try it out.

I explained to him how he could not only manage the amount of time and bandwidth users were allotted on his wireless system, he could also control what they're allowed to connect to in the first place. The next day, I connected the system and showed him how to use the CCA, which made administration a breeze for him. When I went back this week, he told me how much he loves the product and offered me free coffee for the year. Free coffee for the year is truly awesome, yes, but what I really wanted was my controller back! I could've threatened to hold a wireless hacking class in his coffee shop soon, but well, he *is* my friend and hacking is definitely illegal, so I decided to take him up on his free coffee offer instead... every day, all day long. In fact, I am sitting in that coffee shop right now as I write this chapter.

The moral of this story is that you only recommend the 500 series to a small business that you know will never become an enterprise network, does not need the WCS for administration, and has really, really good coffee!

After your network is configured and you want to open the CCA tool, you must then connect to a device by entering its IP address. If the device hasn't been configured previously, you can use the wizard to do that. The wizard will instruct you where to connect to the device and walk you through the initial configuration of any of the devices in the Select A Device drop-down box in Figure 8.7.

If you are working with stand-alone APs, the CCA (well, version 1.5 and later) also has the ability to migrate a stand-alone Cisco Mobility Express AP to Lightweight mode.

The Discovery Process with the CCA

Now at this point, some final words about requirements for the discovery process are in order. The process can be performed using IP discovery or via Cisco Discovery Protocol (CDP), so this is a good spot to start troubleshooting if the CCA won't cooperate. If all devices support CDP, after the seed device is entered, any other devices will be discovered as well. If this doesn't happen, you'll need to discover them one by one.

Using the CCA to connect to a WLC is no different from connecting to a stand-alone AP. As a matter of fact, if the device hosting the CCA and the WLC are connected to the same switch and the switch and the WLC have CDP enabled, everything relevant will be discovered as soon as the first device is discovered.

When the WLC appears in the Topology view as a result of discovery after entering the address of an AP—meaning,—you can right-click the WLC in the Topology view and see the configuration options, as illustrated in Figure 8.8.

FIGURE 8.8   Configuring the 526 with the CCA

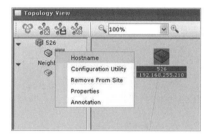

If you need to configure certain parameters on the APs that are not available via the CCA, you can click the AP icon to get the IP address of the AP. The properties box for an 871 router is shown in Figure 8.9. The only difference for an AP is the exclusion of the Device Type and Software Version fields.

FIGURE 8.9   Device Properties

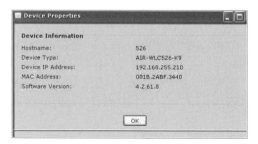

Once you have determined the IP address, you can open your browser and enter the AP's IP address where the URL goes and then connect to the web interface of the AP. You can make more settings here than from the CCA.

Some final words about requirements for the discovery process are in order. The process can be performed using either IP discovery or using CDP. If all devices support CDP, after the seed device is entered, all other devices will be discovered as well. If this is not the case, you will need to discover them one by one.

After the controller has been configured, you can select Properties. The Properties dialog box lets you determine the IP address of the WLC for the purpose of connecting to its web interface. At this point, the Cisco 526 controller can be configured using the web interface, or you can continue to use the CCA.

Configuring the Express 526WLC Without the CCA

If you need to configure the 526WLC without the CCA, you can do this by connecting a PC to the controller management port shown in Figure 8.10. This is the port on the right of the two RJ45 connectors. The following process will work even if the WLC is brand-new, out of the box.

FIGURE 8.10   526 controller

The controller will provide an IP address in the 192.168.1.0/24 range, and will be accessible at http://192.168.1.1. Once connected to the web interface, you can work with the settings, which I personally like more than the CCA, but this is a personal preference and remember, this HTTP screen is only managing the controller, not the mobility wireless network as the CCA can do. The setup screen is shown in Figure 8.11.

Again, the best way to learn about the 500 series is to connect through both the setup and configuration using the HTTP screen or through CCA and you're good to go.

For more information regarding the Mobility Express controller and AP, go to:

```
http://www.cisco.com/en/US/prod/collateral/wireless/ps7306/ps7319/ps7338/
product_solution_overview0900aecd8060c84b_ps7320_Product_Solution_Overview
.html
```

Although this site has great information, links on Cisco change all the time, so it's a good idea to periodically search for Cisco 500 Series Mobility Express Solution.

FIGURE 8.11   526 setup screen

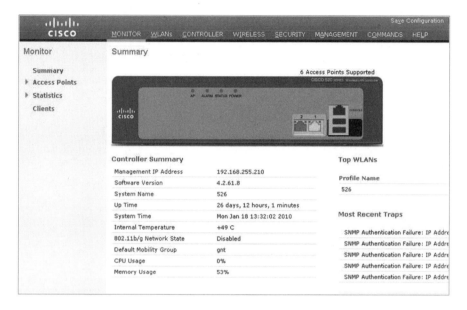

Summary

In this chapter we discussed solutions for small and medium businesses (SMBs). We explored solutions that include Cisco Mobility Express devices.

After we discussed how the devices compare to the Enterprise versions described in the previous chapter, we looked at the configuration of the Express devices both through the use of the Cisco Configuration Assistant (CCA) and directly through the web interface and, in the case of the 526WLC, through the management ports on the front panel.

Exam Essentials

Know the limitations inherent in using the Cisco 521AP.   The 521AP does not support 802.11a; it does not support 802.11n or 802.11h. It also cannot support local EAP or IPsec, nor can it act as an H-REAP device. Moreover, the 521APs cannot be managed by any of the solutions in the CUWN family such as the 2106WLC.

Know the limitations inherent in using the Cisco 526WLC.   Limitations include very limited support for VoWLAN, Location servers, and no support for 802.11a, 802.11n, or 802.11h. Moreover, the maximum configuration capacity of a Cisco Mobility Express controller using v4.2 is one controller with six APs.

Understand the methods available to set up the Cisco 526WLC.   Setup methods include using the web interface (when the IP address is known), using the discovery process when using the CCA, and by connecting directly to the management port and opening the browser to 192.168.1.1 I if set to the defaults).

Know the devices that fit into the Cisco Smart Business Communications System.   These devices include the Cisco Unified Communications 500 Series for Small Business, Cisco Unified Wireless IP Phones and Cisco Communicator SoftPhone, CE520 series switches, Cisco 521 Wireless Express Lightweight Access Point, and the Cisco 526 Wireless Mobility Express controller.

Written Lab

1. True/False: The primary methods of configuration management for the Mobility Express solution are CCA, the web GUI, and the CLI.

2. True/False: The 521AP does not support 5GHz wireless networking.

3. What IEEE standards are not supported by the 521AP?

4. True/False: The 526 controller does not support the use of location services.

5. What is the default IP address of the management web GUI on a 526 controller?

6. True/False: The Cisco Mobility Express controller supports one controller and 12 APs.

7. True/False: Cisco 521APs do not use LWAPP.

8. What methods can be used to discover devices with the CCA?

9. True/False: A login is required before the CCA will display a device in the Topology view.

10. Where is the port located that can be used to directly configure a 526WLC?

Hands-On Labs

To complete the labs in this section, you will need a copy of the Cisco Configuration Assistant (CCA) and a Cisco 526WLC. We also assume that the two devices are connected to the same switch.

Here is a list of labs in this chapter:

Lab 8.1: Installing the CCA and Connecting to the 526WLC

Lab 8.2: Connecting Directly to the 526WLC Through the Management Port

Hands-on Lab 8.1: Installing the CCA and Connecting to the 526WLC

1. Copy the CCA installation program to your desktop or another location.

2. Click on the file and setup will begin. After accepting the license agreement, you will be asked to choose a location for the installation. Accept the default or select a different location.

3. Files will be extracted to the location and executed. When the Finish screen appears, click Finish.

4. Click Start ➤ Programs ➤ Cisco Configuration Assistant ➤ Cisco Configuration Assistant.

5. The CCA will open and display a Connect dialog box. Select the Connect To radio button and type the IP address of the 526WLC. Click OK.

6. When the Authentication dialog box appears, type the username and password required to connect to the 526WLC.

7. It may take a few moments for the CCA to locate the 526. When it does, the CCA will open in the Topology view, showing the 526. It may display the switch as well, and it may indicate Unsupported Device.

8. Right-click the 526 and select Properties. Note the name, device type, IP address, MAC address, and software version.

9. Browse some of the tabs on the left side of the display and explore the functions that you can use.

Hands-on Lab 8.2: Connecting Directly to the 526WLC Through the Management Port

1. Connect an Ethernet cable from your PC to the management port on the Cisco 526. This port is located on the front panel. It is one of two ports surrounded by yellow and is the one on the right side.

2. Set the computer to obtain an IP address automatically.

3. The PC will receive an IP address from the DHCP server in the 526WLC. The address will be 192.168.1.100. You can verify this by typing **ipconfig** at the command prompt on the PC.

4. Open Internet Explorer and type **http://192.168.1.1** in the browser.

5. When the network password screen appears, type the username and password. If the 526WLC is new or is set to the defaults, type **admin** for both the username and the password.

6. You are now connected to the GUI interface, specifically the Configuration Wizard. Here you can edit the IP address and other information. Feel free to explore the wizard. You can always return to the factory defaults if needed.

Review Questions

1. Which of the following devices is not a member of the Cisco Smart Business Communications System?
   A. UC500
   B. Cisco Aironet 1130
   C. CE520
   D. 526WLC

2. How many users can the UC500 manage?
   A. 48
   B. 64
   C. 72
   D. 100

3. Which of the Cisco Mobility Express solution devices perform DHCP? (Choose all that apply.)
   A. UC500
   B. Cisco 870W
   C. 521AP
   D. 526WLC

4. Which of the following is not a part of the feature set in the Cisco Mobility Express solution?
   A. Guest access
   B. RRM
   C. LWAPP
   D. Mobility management

5. How many APs are supported in the Cisco Mobility Express solution when the APs are in stand-alone mode?
   A. Two
   B. Three
   C. Four
   D. Five

6. What standards do the 521AP support?
   A. 802.11b/g
   B. 802.11a
   C. 802.11n
   D. 802.11h

7. Which of the following AP(s) is supported by the 526WLC?

A. 1130AG

B. 521

C. 1240AG

D. 1300

8. Which of the following ports is not present on the 526WLC?

A. Console port

B. Management port

C. USB

D. Service port for out-of-band management

9. What is the factory IP address on the Cisco 521AP?

A. 192.168.1.1

B. 192.168.1.100

C. It is set as a DHCP client.

D. It must be statically configured.

10. What is the name used to describe a set of devices in the Cisco Mobility Express network?

A. Domain

B. Community

C. Mobility group

D. Neighborhood

11. How can a Cisco Mobility Express solution be upgraded to the CUWN solution?

A. Code upgrade

B. Service patch

C. No upgrade is possible

D. Code upgrade and firmware upgrade

12. Which controller/AP combination is supported?

A. 2106AP/526WLC

B. 521AP/526WLC

C. 1130AP/521WLC

D. 526AP/521WLC

13. What is the default username/password combination on the Cisco Mobility Express APs?

A. admin/admin

B. admin/Cisco

C. tsunami/Cisco

D. Cisco/Cisco

14. What is the default username/password combination on the 526WLC?

    A. admin/admin

    B. admin/Cisco

    C. tsunami/Cisco

    D. Cisco/Cisco

15. In the CCA, what is the view called that displays discovered devices and the manner in which they are connected?

    A. Network view

    B. Map view

    C. Topology view

    D. Logical view

16. What is the name given to the IP address that is entered in the Connect To dialog box that is used to locate the first device in CCA?

    A. Anchor address

    B. Prime address

    C. Seed address

    D. Root address

17. You just entered the seed address of the first device in the CCA and after entering the username and password combination, the device displays in the Topology view. Shortly afterward you are prompted for the credentials for a second device and after that another. What protocol is locating these other devices?

    A. ICMP

    B. TCP

    C. IP

    D. CDP

18. In the Topology view of the CCA, what is the easiest way to obtain more details about a device in the display?

    A. Right-click and select Properties.

    B. Highlight the device and select Monitor from the task list.

    C. Double-click the device.

    D. Connect to it through the browser for more details.

19. Which of the following cannot be set up out of the box in the CCA?

    A. 521AP

    B. CE520

    C. 1130AP

    D. 526WLC

20. You would like to synchronize the passwords on three devices in the Cisco Mobility Express solution. Which tool would allow you to do this with the least amount of work?

   A. Web interface

   B. Console port

   C. Management port

   D. CCA

21. Which if the following statements are true with regard to the Cisco 521AP?

   A. Only five 521APs can be managed in the CCA in controller mode.

   B. Three 521APs can be managed in the CCA in stand-alone mode.

   C. 521APs can associate with either the 526WLC or an LWAPP-based WLC.

   D. 521APs support 802.11a.

Answers to Review Questions

1. B. The Cisco 1130 runs LWAPP and is part of the CUWN.

2. A. The UC500 can support up to 48 users.

3. A, B. Only the UC500 and the 870W router provide DHCP.

4. C. LWAPP is not supported in the Cisco Mobility Express solution.

5. B. In stand-alone mode, only three APs are supported by the CCA.

6. A. The 521 does not support 802.11a, 802.11n, or 802.11h.

7. B. Only the Cisco 521AP is supported. All of the others use LWAPP when managed by a WLC, which is not supported by the 526.

8. D. All of the ports are present except a service port for out-of-band management.

9. C. The 521 is set as a DHCP client by default.

10. B. A set of devices in the Cisco Mobility Express network is called a community.

11. C. There is no upgrade path from Cisco Mobility Express to the CUWN.

12. B. The 526WLC can work with the 521AP. The other combinations are not supported. Moreover, the 521 is not a WLC and the 526 is not an AP.

13. B. The default username on the Cisco Mobility Express APs is admin and the password is Cisco.

14. A. The default username on the 526WLC is admin and the password is admin.

15. C. The Topology view shows all devices that have been discovered as well as the connections between the devices.

16. C. The initial IP address entered is called the seed address.

17. D. Cisco Discovery Protocol (CDP) will discover any devices that have it enabled.

18. A. By right-clicking and selecting Properties, you will be able to view the IP address, MAC address, version, and name of the device.

19. C. The only device listed that cannot be set up out of the box with the CCA is the 1130AP. Don't get confused here; the 1130 is not even part of Cisco Mobility Express.

20. D. All of the methods would work, but this could be done to all three at once with the CCA.

21. B. Only three 521APs can be managed in the CCA in stand-alone mode. In controller mode six can be managed. The 521 can only associate with Cisco Mobility Express controllers. Finally, 521APs do not support 802.11a.

Answers to Written Lab

1. True

2. True

3. 802.11a, 802.11n, and 802.11h

4. True

5. 192.168.1.1

6. False. You can have two controllers with up to 12 APs.

7. True

8. CDP and IP discovery

9. True

10. On the front panel. It is one of two ports surrounded by yellow and is the one on the right side.

Chapter 9

Installing the Cisco Unified Wireless Network (CUWN)

THE CCNA WIRELESS EXAM TOPICS COVERED IN THIS CHAPTER ARE:

✓ **Install a basic Cisco wireless LAN**

- Configure a WLAN controller and access points WLC: ports, interfaces, WLANs, NTP, CLI and Web UI, CLI wizard, LAG AP: Channel, Power

- Configure the basics of a stand-alone access point (no lab) (Express setup, basic security)

After exploring solutions for small and medium businesses (SMBs) based on the Cisco Mobility Express platform, you're ready to learn how to implement the Cisco Unified Wireless Network (CUWN). I'll begin by showing you how to install and configure the heart of the CUWN—the controller. I'll introduce you to the entire menu of ports and interfaces and explain how they're used; then we'll move on to demonstrating the possible ways to implement an initial setup of the WLAN controller (WLC). After that, we'll delve into the creation of WLANs. I'll also brief you on the management of configuration and code files on the controller, as well as management of stand-alone APs, with a special focus on the migration from autonomous APs to lightweight APs.

To find dynamic updates to this chapter, please go to www.lammle.com or www.sybex.com/go/ccnawireless.

Understanding Controller Interfaces

When you start up a WLC fresh out of the box for the first time, you will find... nothing much. This is because it has no default configuration and needs you to provide one for it—something you can do in a variety of ways. But before you start configuring anything, you really need to have a solid grasp of the terminology of ports and interfaces specific to the controller first. When I say specific, I do mean specific, because some of these terms' meanings only apply when they're used in reference to WLCs. Believe me, this one fact can confuse things in many ways, so let's get some of that highly specialized WLC terminology nailed down tight!

Ports

On the WLC, a port is the physical representation of an interface. If you survey the front of a WLC like the one pictured in Figure 9.1, you'll see the following port types:

Service Port This is an RJ-45 connection that can be used for out-of-band management of the controller, and it's the only port that's functional when the WLC is in boot mode. Because it cannot carry 802.1q VLAN tags, it must be connected to an access port on a switch. Since it's not autosensing, you've got to make sure that you use the correct cable type. For instance, if you want to connect this port to another controller, a hub, or a switch, you must use a straight-through cable. But if you want to connect to a workstation or a router, you've got to use a crossover cable. And a really important thing to remember is that you can't set this interface with a default gateway, which means that if your management station is in a different subnet, you'll probably have to add a static route to the management station on the controller.

The Cisco WiSM 4404 controllers use this port for internal communication between controllers. The Cisco 2100 and WLCM series controllers do not have this port!

Console Port Serial   This is the standard female DB-9 port used to establish a terminal emulation connection that's used as a console port.

Utility Port   Another RJ-45 connection, but one that's currently nonoperational and for possible future use.

Distribution Ports 1–4   How many ports you'll find here depends on the model. The 4404 has four and the 4402 only has two, but in both cases, these ports are used for controlling the associated APs and providing connectivity between the distribution and Enterprise networks. They also supply a connection for interfaces—multiple logical entities that can be assigned to a single port of this type. But this doesn't work in reverse because you can't assign multiple ports to a single interface. Another important point is that in order to support multiple VLANs on the same port, data must be tagged or untagged, as I talked about way back in Chapter 1. With software release 3.2 or later you can bundle these ports together, which is known as link aggregation (LAG).

FIGURE 9.1   WLC port

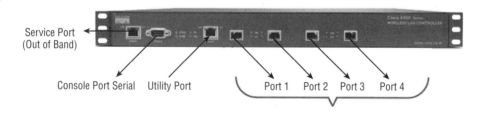

Types of Interfaces

Interfaces are logical entities that are either predefined or user defined, which must be mapped to a physical port. User-defined interfaces are dynamic and are used to define VLANs for WLAN access, whereas predefined interfaces are static. Let's get into a little more detail about this.

Static Interfaces

Types of static interfaces include:

Management Use this interface for in-band management, for connections to enterprise services like AAA, and for Layer 2 communication with the associated controllers. It can be tagged or untagged, but if it's untagged, the value is 0. This interface must also be in a different subnet from a service port that's in use, and its address will be the one used to connect to the GUI interface from the browser of a management station.

AP Manager Use the AP manager interface(s) for controller-to-AP communications at Layer 3. Its address will be the tunnel source address when packets are sent from the WLC to the AP, as well as the tunnel destination address for packets being received, so it should be in the same subnet as the management interface.

All Layer 3 LWAPP communication runs through this interface and if all distribution ports have been aggregated (LAG), then only a single AP management interface will be employed. If the distribution ports operate separately, the AP management interface can be attached to each one.

 Every interface needs to be defined on all controllers within a mobility group or seamless roaming just won't happen. The result? Clients will drop out of the network and have to reauthenticate and reassociate when roaming.

Virtual The virtual interface is used to support these tasks:

Mobility Management The mobile client uses the same virtual IP address, which can be any unused gateway IP address, across multiple controllers. It's only seen on the wireless side of the network and does not need to be routable, but all controllers in the same mobility group should have the same virtual gateway address.

DHCP Relay Clients use this address for the DHCP server.

Layer 3 Security Serves as a redirect for the web authentication login page.

Service Port The service port interface controls and is statically mapped to the service port we just talked about.

Dynamic Interfaces

These interfaces, also known as VLAN interfaces, are user defined and intended for wireless client data. They're configured with these vital details upon their creation:

- VLAN ID
- Physical port assignment
- DHCP server support
- ACL support

Dynamic interfaces can be assigned to distribution ports, WLANs, Layer 2, management, Layer 3, and AP management interfaces. When a WLAN is initially created, it's associated with an SSID and assigned to a dynamic interface. You can create up to 512 dynamic interfaces on a WLC.

So basically, you need to remember that static interfaces are used for management and dynamic interfaces are created to represent the WLANS, their associated SSIDs, and VLANS. Figure 9.2 portrays the relationship between ports, interfaces, and WLANs. In Figure 9.2, you can see that the three dynamic interfaces that are associated with WLANs, and the two management interfaces, are all using a single distribution port. Also notice that each dynamic interface/WLAN is on its own VLAN.

FIGURE 9.2   Ports and interfaces

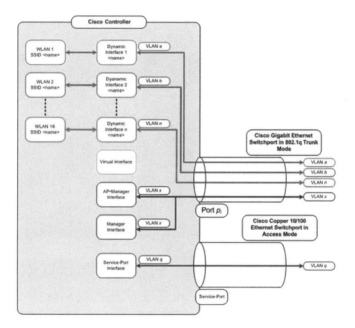

Configuration

Let's start by talking about the configuration of the three possible static interfaces (only two on the 2100 WLC), and then move on to dynamic interfaces.

Static Interfaces

You can view and edit static interfaces on the Interfaces page in the WLC, as illustrated in Figure 9.3. When you click on an interface, you get the dialog boxes required to configure each one, as shown in the figures that follow shortly.

FIGURE 9.3   Controller interfaces

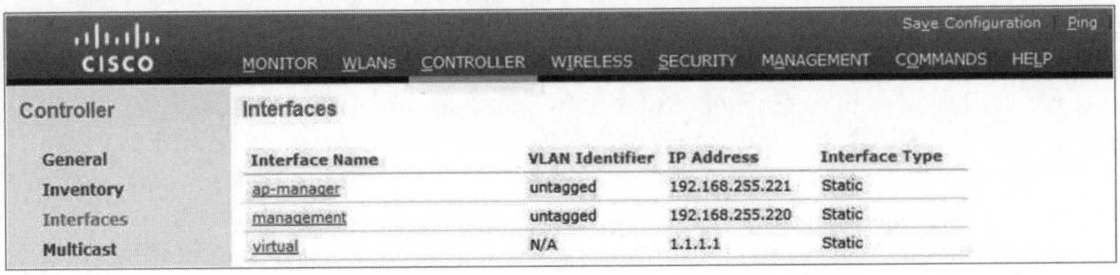

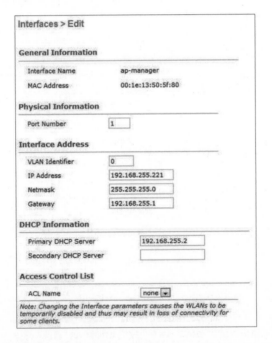

Management Interfaces   The management and AP management interfaces are configured as shown in Figure 9.4 and should be in the same subnet. Since I see this problem a lot, I need to mention one more time that if the controller isn't set for Layer 3 LWAPP, the AP management interface won't show up!

FIGURE 9.4   Management interfaces

Controllers running the latest code only run Layer 3 LWAPP.

Virtual Interface   This interface serves as the gateway for wireless clients. If you want to enable seamless roaming, set all controllers within a mobility group with the same virtual gateway address. Figure 9.5 shows the only settings available for this interface—the IP address and the DNS host name.

FIGURE 9.5   Virtual interface

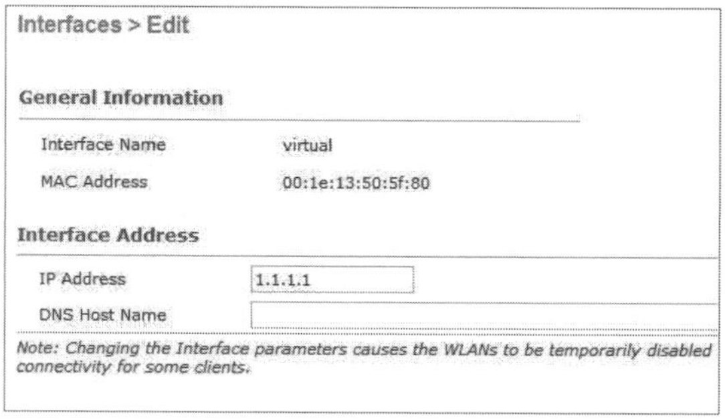

Interfaces > Edit

General Information

| Interface Name | virtual |
| MAC Address | 00:1e:13:50:5f:80 |

Interface Address

| IP Address | 1.1.1.1 |
| DNS Host Name | |

Note: Changing the Interface parameters causes the WLANs to be temporarily disabled connectivity for some clients.

Service Port Interface   This is used for out-of-band management and should be in a different subnet from the other management interfaces. Importantly, if the remote management station is in a different subnet you'll need to add a route to that station on the controller in the Network Routes section via Controller ➢ Network Routes.

 Not all controllers have a service port.

Dynamic Interfaces

As I've said, it is highly recommended that you create the dynamic interfaces before you configure a WLAN. You can configure multiple dynamic interfaces on a single distribution port. If this is the case, and that port is tagged, all of the interfaces must be in different VLANs. If you've got a bunch of dynamic interfaces configured on an untagged distribution port, all interfaces must be in separate subnets.

WLC Management

Okay—here's where I'm going to guide you through creating that nonexistent, initial WLC configuration. Remember, there's no default, so you begin bringing your new WLC to life via an initial setup that's either carried out through the serial connection with the CLI or by using the service interface port and connecting to the web interface. Once the initial configuration is out of the way, you can then configure your WLANs. So let's move on and tackle that initial setup, first via the CLI and next with the web interface. After that, we'll configure some WLANs.

Initial Setup Options

Let's start with the CLI and then I'll show you the web interface.

CLI

The first step in the initial setup through the CLI is to connect a computer to the serial port with a DB-9 female-to-female null-modem cable. On the latest WLCs, you'll need an RJ-45 connector (which the Cisco console cable has). You'll also require a terminal emulation program like HyperTerminal on a Windows machine. The terminal emulation program should be set to:

- 9600 baud
- 8 data bits
- 1 stop bit
- No parity
- No hardware flow control

It's good to know that you can also use this same kind of connection to the controller when other methods aren't working, like during a network failure.

Initial Configuration

When you first start up the controller to perform the initial configuration with this method, the boot process will load the OS image and start up services. When these services start up, the management interfaces will also be started, and if the controller hasn't been configured yet, the secure web interface will give you an error message saying, "Web authentication certificate not found." This message only shows up when no configuration exists or if an upgrade has been performed on the image file:

```
Starting Client Troubleshooting Service: ok
Starting Management Frame Protection: ok
Starting LWAPP: ok
Starting Certificate Database: ok
Starting VPN Services: ok
Starting Security Services: ok
Starting Policy Manager: ok
Starting Authentication Engine: ok
Starting Mobility Management: ok
Starting LOCP: ok
Starting Virtual AP Services: ok
Starting AireWave Director: ok
Starting Network Time Services: ok
Starting Cisco Discovery Protocol: ok
```

```
Starting Broadcast Services: ok
Starting Power Over Ethernet Services: ok
Starting Logging Services: ok
Starting DHCP Server: ok
Starting IDS Signature Manager: ok
Starting RFID Tag Tracking: ok
Starting Mesh Services: ok
Starting TSM: ok
Starting CIDS Services: ok
Starting Ethernet-over-IP: ok
Starting FMC HS: ok
Starting Management Services:
    Web Server: ok
    CLI: ok
    Secure Web: Web Authentication Certificate not found (error). If you
cannot access management interface via HTTPS please reconfigure Virtual
Interface.

(Cisco Controller)
(Cisco Controller)
Welcome to the Cisco Wizard Configuration Tool
Use the '-' character to backup
Would you like to terminate autoinstall? [yes]:
AUTO-INSTALL: starting now...
```

Another unmistakable clue marking a controller with no configuration is the appearance of the "Welcome to the Cisco Wizard Configuration Tool" message that follows shortly thereafter. This menu-based tool will look a little familiar to you if you've configured routers. At any rate, it's pretty straightforward and starts automatically when you boot the controller for the first time:

```
Welcome to the Cisco Wizard Configuration Tool
Use the '-' character to backup
Would you like to terminate autoinstall? [yes]:
AUTO-INSTALL: starting now...
```

Here's a partial list of items that the wizard will prompt you for, which can be different for each controller model:

- System name
- Administrator username
- Administrator password

- Service interface IP address configuration—set to either None or DHCP
- Service interface IP address—IP address of the service port. By default, this is set to 192.168.1.1 and is the address used for connection to the web interface if you chose to do the initial setup with that method. If the service interface IP address configuration is set to DHCP, then it is not configured. If it is set to None, then it must be configured during the CLI setup.
- Service interface net mask—subnet mask for the service port
- Enable LAG, which you use to aggregate the distribution ports (not available on the 2100)
- Management interface IP address
- Management interface net mask
- Management interface default router, which is the gateway for the management interface
- Management interface VLAN ID
- Management interface port number
- Management interface DHCP server address
- Virtual gateway IP address
- Mobility/RF group name—must be the same on all WLCs in a mobility group

    Let's take a look at this setup wizard:

```
Would you like to terminate autoinstall? [yes]: yes
System Name [Cisco_50:5f:80] (31 characters max): 2106-1
Enter Administrative User Name (24 characters max): 2106-1
Enter Administrative Password (24 characters max): ******
Re-enter Administrative Password              : ******
Management Interface IP Address: 192.168.255.210
Management Interface Netmask: 255.255.255.0
Management Interface Default Router: 192.168.255.1
Management Interface VLAN Identifier (0 = untagged): [enter]
Management Interface Port Num [1 to 8]: 1
Management Interface DHCP Server IP Address: 192.168.255.2
AP Manager Interface IP Address: 192.168.255.211
AP-Manager is on Management subnet, using same values
AP Manager Interface DHCP Server (192.168.255.2): [enter]
Virtual Gateway IP Address: 1.1.1.1
Mobility/RF Group Name: Todd
Enable Symmetric Mobility Tunneling [yes][NO]: [enter]
Network Name (SSID): Todd
Allow Static IP Addresses [YES][no]: no
Configure a RADIUS Server now? [YES][no]: no
```

```
Warning! The default WLAN security policy requires a RADIUS server.
Please see documentation for more details.
Enter Country Code list (enter 'help' for a list of countries) [US]: [enter]
Enable 802.11b Network [YES][no]: [enter]
Enable 802.11a Network [YES][no]: [enter]
Enable 802.11g Network [YES][no]: [enter]
Enable Auto-RF [YES][no]: [enter]
Configure a NTP server now? [YES][no]: no
Configure the system time now? [YES][no]: no
Warning! No AP will come up unless the time is set.
Please see documentation for more details.
Configuration correct? If yes, system will save it and reset. [yes][NO]: yes
Configuration saved!
Resetting system with new configuration...
```

Did you notice that you can also enable symmetric mobility tunneling here and create an SSID too? You can also determine if static addresses are allowed, configure a RADIUS server, enable the radios, and configure an NTP server. You know you're done with the configuration when you get to the part at the end where you're asked if you want to save the configuration and reset the controller. One last important piece to notice: "Warning! No AP will come up unless the time is set." It's important that you set the time on your production WLC.

CLI Command Set

Of course, you can still make configuration changes after the reboot by using the ? option to find out which commands are available and what they're used for. For instance, you would choose the config commands to make changes and the debug commands to conveniently troubleshoot in real time. I'll get into these extensively in Chapter 12, but here's an important command you'll want to commit to memory now that assigns the management interface of the WLC to the switch's native VLAN:

```
Config interface vlan management vlan 0
```

Controller Boot Options

Understanding the image files that can be used when booting the controller helps you make sense of the boot options available to you, so let's explore the boot options menu and the image files associated with it now.

If you're connected through the CLI, you'll get a brief opportunity to access the boot options menu when you see this message as the WLC is booted up:

```
Launching BootLoader...
 Cisco Bootloader (Version 4.0.191.0)
 Booting Primary Image...
Press <ESC> now for additional boot options...
```

```
Boot Options
Please choose an option from below:
 1. Run primary image (Version 5.1.163.0) (active)
 2. Run backup image  (Version 5.1.163.0)
 3. Manually upgrade primary image
 4. Change active boot image
 5. Clear Configuration
Please enter your choice:
```

Pressing Esc will get you these five options:

1. Run Primary Image (Active) (it will also show the current version number)

2. Run Backup Image (it will also show the version number)

3. Manually Upgrade Primary Image

4. Change Active Boot Image

5. Clear Configuration

Predictably, not pressing Esc will boot the WLC to the image specified in option 1. The controller maintains two image files, a primary file and a backup. When you upgrade the code version, the older version gets saved as the backup, the older image moves to selection 2 in the menu, and the new code becomes number 1. In any situation where the primary image fails to boot (like when it's corrupted), just hit Esc and then choose the backup.

Either manually by hitting Esc or by default (by ignoring it), when an image has been chosen the WLC will proceed to boot to it. Option 5 allows you to clear the configuration, but you can also clear the configuration from the CLI using these two commands:

```
Cisco Controller) >clear config
Are you sure you want to clear the configuration? (y/n) y
Configuration Cleared!
```

```
(Cisco Controller) >reset system
The system has unsaved changes.
Would you like to save them now? (y/N) n
Configuration Not Saved!
Are you sure you would like to reset the system? (y/N) y
System will now restart!
```

Initial Configuration with the Web Interface

If you opt for using the web interface to tackle the initial setup, you need to connect a cross-over cable to the service port from a workstation on the 4400 or newer series. It's also important to make sure the computer's IP address is in the same subnet. If an initial configuration has already been done through the CLI, the service port's IP address could've been changed, but if this is the actual, initial configuration, the default IP address will be 192.168.1.1, which you place into the computer's browser. When you connect you'll be asked for a username and password, which are both admin by default.

Note that you can't perform the initial configuration with HTTPS. If you try, you'll receive an error. It must be done with HTTP.

Web Wizard Configuration Tool

The Web Wizard Configuration Tool will magically appear after you log in. It will prompt you first for a system name, administrative username and password, and then for the selection of the SNMP version(s). After that, the wizard will require another login using the newly created administrator account.

The settings on the 4400 series you'll be configuring will essentially follow the CLI wizard. The main difference is that you'll be presented with dialog boxes instead of prompts.

When you've made your way through all dialog boxes, you'll be asked if you would like to save the configuration changes and reboot. Saving the changes commits the configuration to non-volatile random access memory (NVRAM). After the controller reboots, connections via the web interface will then be required to be HTTPS, and you will be redirected if you try to use HTTP.

Ongoing Administration with Web Interface

I've got to say once you've got the web interface set up it really is the most convenient way to administer the WLC. Just connect to the WLC and you'll get to the controller's home page complete with a menu bar across the top of the screen used to access and choose among various options. Each tab is displayed and described in Figure 9.6:

FIGURE 9.6   Web menu bar

Monitor   View the status of the WLC, APs, and the clients attached to the APs.

WLANs   Configure and manage the WLANs (SSIDs).

Controller   Configure system-wide general settings, as well as the interfaces.

Wireless   Configure and manage the APs, the AP radios, and all the RF aspects.

Security   Control local and remote security settings.

Management   Perform local management of the system and manage interfaces, Telnet, SSH, and SNMP settings.

Commands   Control file management and system status, and reset controls.

Help   Access system-wide help pages.

Additionally, above and to the right of Help are four more administrative commands available as shown in Figure 9.7—Save Configuration, Ping, Logout, and Refresh. Use Save Configuration to keep changes made during a session to NVRAM, Ping when you want to ping a device from the controller's management interface when troubleshooting, and Logout to end an administrative session. The Refresh button can come in handy when you want to check out statistics and if you need immediate updates but know that controller pages refresh automatically every 30 seconds anyway. The Save Configuration and refresh options are circled as I have found that I use these the most when configuring my CUWNs.

FIGURE 9.7 Admin controls

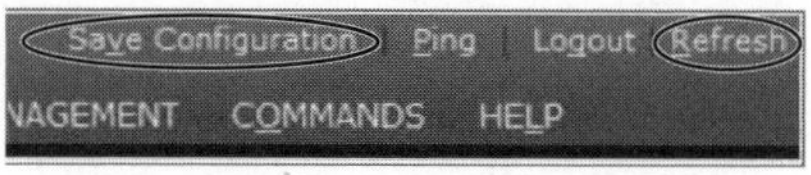

Creating Accounts

If you want to create additional local accounts on the WLC for management, just navigate to Management ➤ Local and add new users by clicking the New button. If you want to get rid of them, use the Remove button located just to the right of the user's account to delete at will.

New users can be given Read/Write, Read Only, or LobbyAdmin permissions, but I want to make it clear that LobbyAdmin users can only create temporary credentials for guest SSIDs, and are obviously used for Lobby personal to create temporary access to a WLAN only. They can't create WLANs. Take a look at Figure 9.8:

FIGURE 9.8 Creating admin accounts

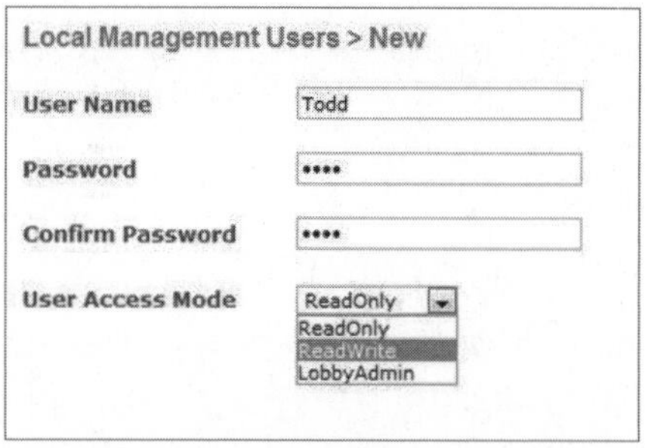

Any accounts created here will be valid when accessing the web interface or the CLI. You can even offload the authentication of management users to a RADIUS or Terminal Access Controller Access Control System Plus (TACACS+) server. You do this on the Security tab by choosing TACACS+ in the AAA section on the left side of the Security page. Figure 9.9 shows the information about the RADIUS server that you can delimit.

FIGURE 9.9   Configuring RADIUS authentication servers

Security	RADIUS Authentication Servers > New	< Back	Apply

Security

- ▼ **AAA**
  - General
  - ▼ RADIUS
    - Authentication
    - Accounting
    - Fallback
  - ▼ TACACS+
    - Authentication
    - Accounting
    - Authorization
  - LDAP
  - Local Net Users
  - MAC Filtering
  - Disabled Clients
  - User Login Policies
  - AP Policies
- ▶ **Local EAP**
- ▶ **Priority Order**
- ▶ **Access Control Lists**
- ▶ **Wireless Protection Policies**
- ▶ **Web Auth**
- ▶ **Advanced**

Server Index (Priority)   1 ▾

Server IPAddress   [   ]

Shared Secret Format   ASCII ▾

Shared Secret   [   ]

Confirm Shared Secret   [   ]

Key Wrap   ☐ (Designed for FIPS customers and requires a key wrap compliant RADIUS server)

Port Number   [1812]

Server Status   Enabled ▾

Support for RFC 3576   Enabled ▾

Server Timeout   [2] seconds

Network User   ☑ Enable

Management   ☑ Enable

IPSec   ☐ Enable

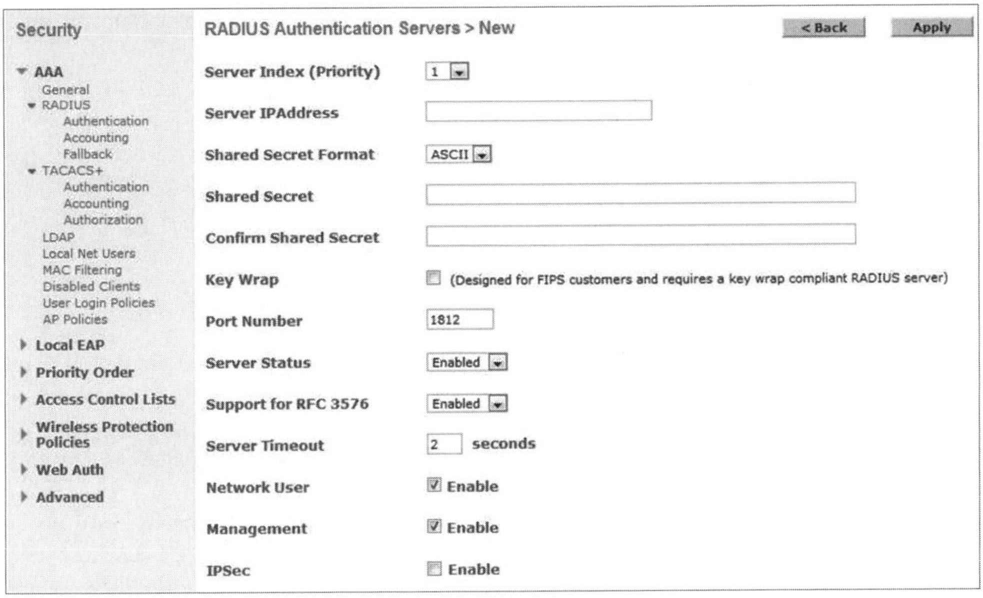

Administration via Wireless

This feature is disabled by default and definitely has its limitations, but the controller can be managed with a wireless connection to a degree via the Management tab. There's a selection available called Mgmt Via Wireless on the bottom left. When you select it, a check box appears in the details pane where you can enable it, as shown in Figure 9.10.

FIGURE 9.10   Managing the controller from the wireless network

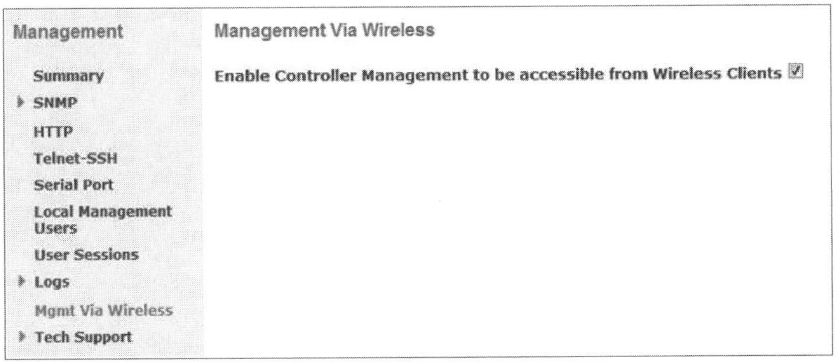

Management

- Summary
- ▶ SNMP
- HTTP
- Telnet-SSH
- Serial Port
- Local Management Users
- User Sessions
- ▶ Logs
- Mgmt Via Wireless
- ▶ Tech Support

Management Via Wireless

Enable Controller Management to be accessible from Wireless Clients ☑

WARNING

I do not recommend enabling this function, mostly because of possible serious security ramifications. But at least it won't allow uploading of files to the WLC from the WLAN!

Creating WLANs

Here's the four-step process of creating a WLAN:

1. Creating the interface
2. Creating the WLAN
3. Mapping the WLAN to the interface
4. Optionally mapping the WLAN to an AP

NOTE

In the newest code, this has changed. You now associate WLANs to AP groups. That's what determines which SSIDs are used by which APs.

Okay—let me guide you through the creation of a WLAN. First, go to the Controller ➢ Interfaces and click New to create an interface. Then give your newborn interface a name and a VLAN number, as shown in Figure 9.11. Typically (but not always) you will create an interface for each VLAN, so your traffic will be tagged when it goes out the trunk link to the switch connection.

FIGURE 9.11   Creating an interface

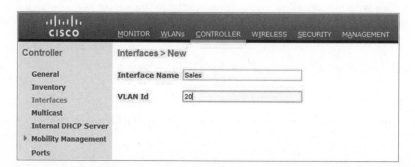

When the interface details options appear, fill in the distribution port number, the interface's IP address, mask, and gateway, plus its primary and secondary DHCP servers. When you're done, just click Apply to save it, as demonstrated in Figure 9.12.

Now you're ready to make a new WLAN and map it to your newly created interface. Go to the WLAN menu and simply choose New to create the WLAN. When the new WLAN dialog box pops up, fill in the profile name of the WLAN plus the SSID as shown in Figure 9.13.

FIGURE 9.12   Configuring the interface

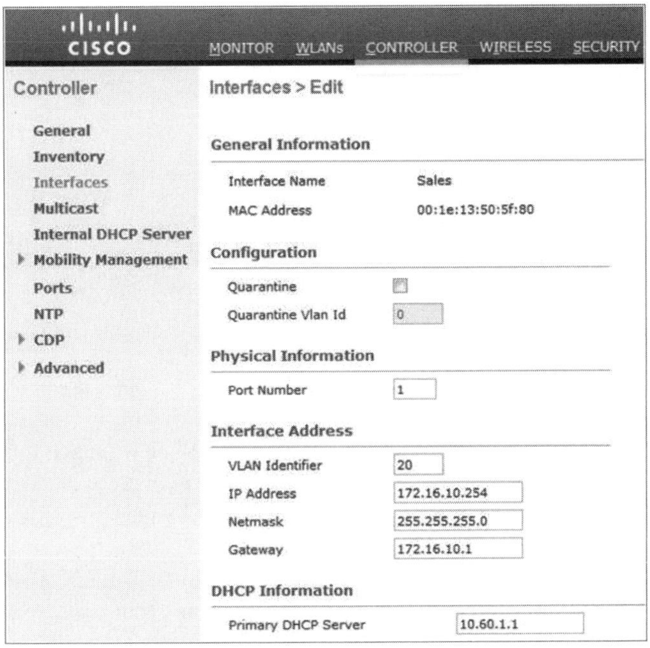

FIGURE 9.13   Creating the WLAN

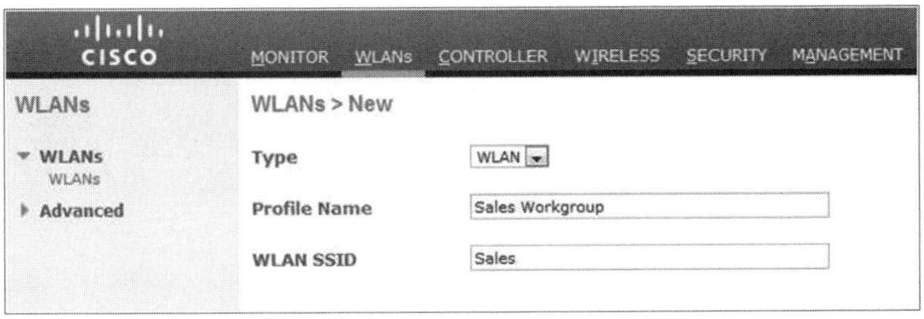

After clicking Apply a new window will appear as shown in figure 9.14, that will allow you to enable the WLAN (WLANs are not enabled by default) and specify the radio policy, such as 802.11a/b/g. In Figure 9.14 you can see that this VLAN is configured as 802.11g only. Your final step is to map the WLAN to the new interface you just created by selecting the interface from the Interface drop-down list. Now, just click Apply to save the WLAN; remember that multiple WLANs can be configured for one interface.

FIGURE 9.14 Enabling the new WLAN

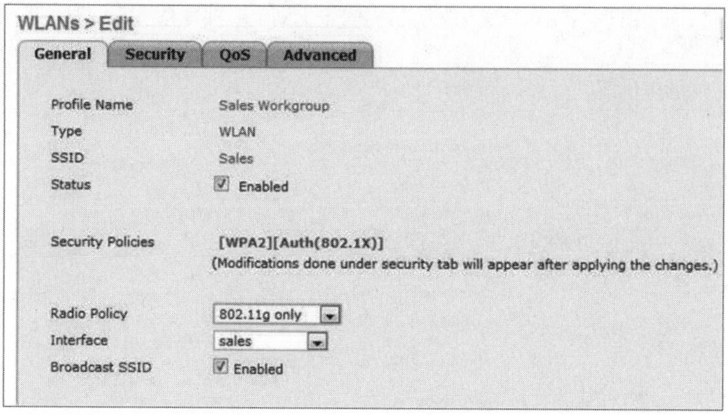

WLANs > Edit

| General | Security | QoS | Advanced |

Profile Name   Sales Workgroup

Type   WLAN

SSID   Sales

Status   ☑ Enabled

Security Policies   [WPA2][Auth(802.1X)]
(Modifications done under security tab will appear after applying the changes.)

Radio Policy   802.11g only ▼

Interface   sales ▼

Broadcast SSID   ☑ Enabled

In reality, you wouldn't stop here—your next move would be to apply appropriate security settings, but I'll be covering that in the next chapter. However, by default, security policies for all WLANs are set to WPA/802.1X, so unless you change this setting, your clients would not be able to be connect to the WLAN by default.

Anyway, if you actually did stop at this point, your newborn WLAN would be available to all APs managed by the controller. If you want things that way, you're all good. But if you want a few limits and boundaries in place, you can optionally map the WLAN to a specific AP by selecting the APs that you want restricted and unable to offer the WLAN to clients. To make this happen, just go to the Wireless tab on the WLC and select 802.11*xx* Radios (where *xx* is the radio type used in the WLAN), which will cause all APs using this radio type to appear. Now, you just go through the list and choose the AP you want to restrict by selecting Configure in the drop-down box next to its name, shown in Figure 9.15.

This process is known as overriding; you can get a picture of it in Figure 9.16.

FIGURE 9.15 Configuring the VLANs that associate with an AP

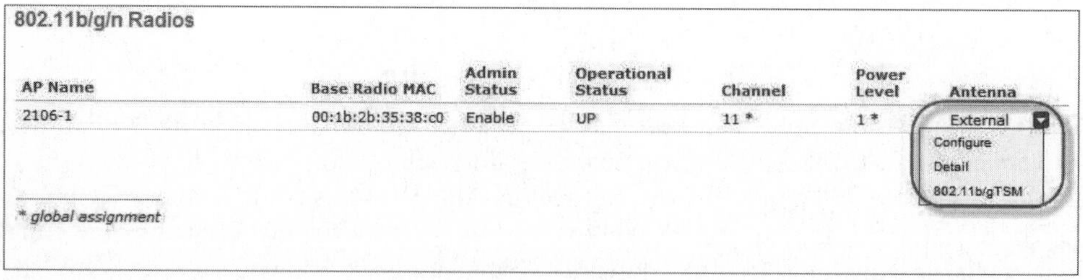

802.11b/g/n Radios

AP Name	Base Radio MAC	Admin Status	Operational Status	Channel	Power Level	Antenna
2106-1	00:1b:2b:35:38:c0	Enable	UP	11 *	1 *	External ▼
						Configure
						Detail
						802.11b/gTSM

* global assignment

WLAN Override is no longer part of the newest code. Instead AP groups are created and you can assign certain WLANs to certain AP groups. Remember, even though I mention "the new code," it is not part of the exam objectives. This is for informational purposes only.

FIGURE 9.16   Overriding VLANs

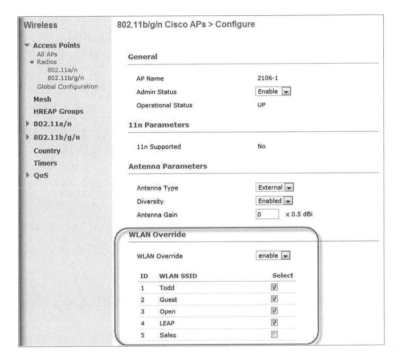

Continue by selecting enable and disable WLANs for each AP connected to your controller. Repeat as desired for each AP you want enabled or restricted. An AP will reboot whenever WLANs associated with them change.

Managing Stand-alone APs

Sometimes you'll find stand-alone APs that you have to manage without the help of a controller. Wireless networks often evolve from little ones with only a few stand-alone APs to jumbo networks that must have controllers involved for management. It's true that stand-alone APs can be migrated to become lightweight APs, but no matter what, you still need to know how to manage stand-alone APs.

Connecting To and Managing a Stand-alone AP

There are three ways to connect to a stand-alone AP to manage it:

- Through the web interface, which requires an IP address
- Through the CLI via Telnet, which also requires an IP address
- Through the CLI via the console port, which requires a rolled cable

As you can plainly see, two of these methods require an IP address that, by default, the AP will try DHCP to obtain. If DHCP isn't available, the most common alternative is to connect through the console cable, set the IP address, and then complete the configuration via the web interface. An AP can get an address with the Cisco Aironet IP setup utility too.

To use the CLI to set an address, add a gateway on the AP to connect with the console cable using the instructions I gave you back in the WLC CLI section to create a terminal session. Once you're connected to the Bridge Virtual Interface 1 (BVI1), execute these commands:

```
Config t
interface BVI1
ip address 10.0.0.24  255.255.255.224
exit
ip default-gateway 10.0.0.1
```

Doing this would set the AP with an IP address of 10.0.0.24 with a 27-bit subnet mask and a gateway of 10.0.0.1.

Clearly, you've got to know the default usernames and passwords for each connection method:

- Web browser: leave blank/Cisco
- Telnet: Cisco/Cisco
- Console port: enable password (Cisco)

As I said, I really like going with the web interface for management, and because most other people do too, that's the method I'm going focus on. Remember, you're basically doing the same thing with CLI commands, so no worries—once you understand the steps you need to take, you're good!

So with that, let's get started… After you connect to the web interface, the first page you will see is the AP's Home page right? If you think back, you'll recall that this page is a summary of information about the AP as well as the platform to jump off into other pages listed in a menu at the upper-left as shown in Figure 9.17.

FIGURE 9.17   AP home page

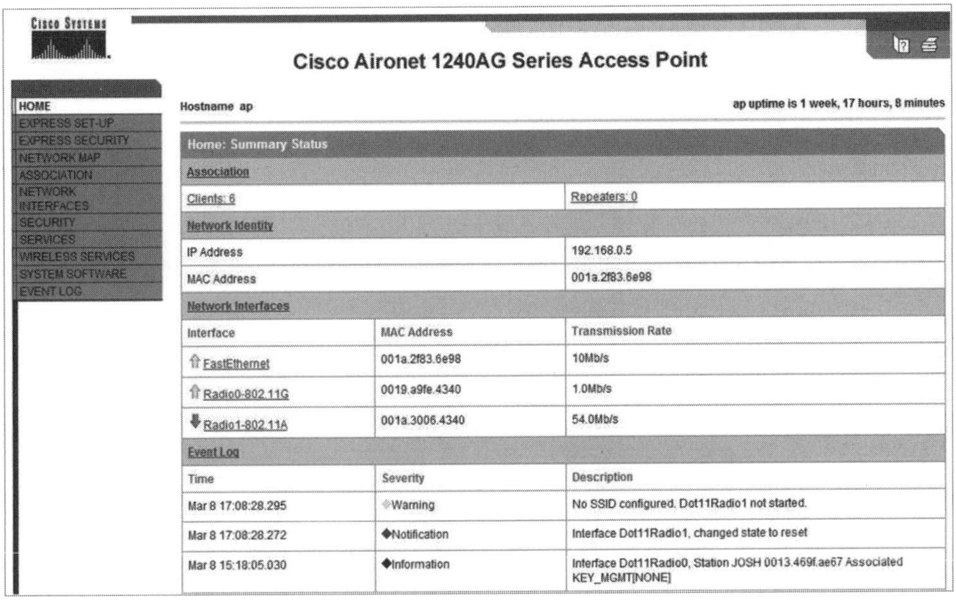

Here we see the number of clients associated, the network identity, (IP and MAC address), and links to network interfaces and the event log. If you click on Network Interfaces or select Network Interfaces from that menu I mentioned, you'll get to the Network Interfaces page that will show you the current configuration and status of each interface, as you can see in Figure 9.18.

FIGURE 9.18   Clicking Network Interfaces opens this page

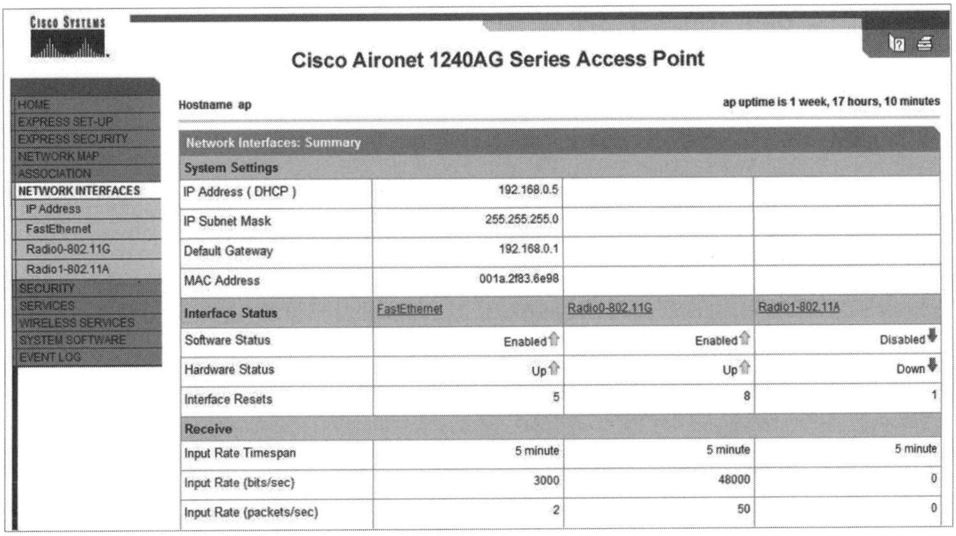

By the way, this particular AP happens to be a Cisco 1240AG that has three interfaces: one for the wired connection (Fast Ethernet), one for the 802.11a radio, and one for the 802.11b/g radio. You can see the Transmit and Receive status for each interface here too. If you click on the respective radio type in the details pane (or choose it from the menu), you can isolate each radio for configuration in the page shown in Figures 9.19 and 9.20. Radio interfaces are disabled by default, so once a WLAN has been configured, you've got to enable the radio used by that specific WLAN.

FIGURE 9.19 802.11a interface

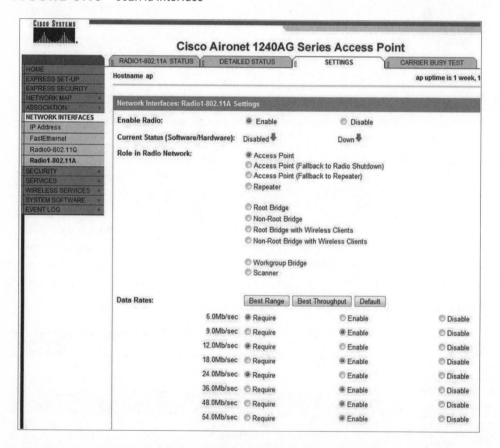

Here's a list of other settings that really need to be set here as well:

Role In Radio Network Specify AP, bridge, or workgroup bridge.

Data Rates Specify data rates allowed or required to be used in this network.

Transmit Power The default is the highest setting allowed in the regulatory domain.

Power Translation Table   Power settings can be either in milliwatts (mW) or decibels (db). The table translates between the two.

Limit Client Power   Can be used to set a ceiling on client power settings.

FIGURE 9.20   Interface configuration

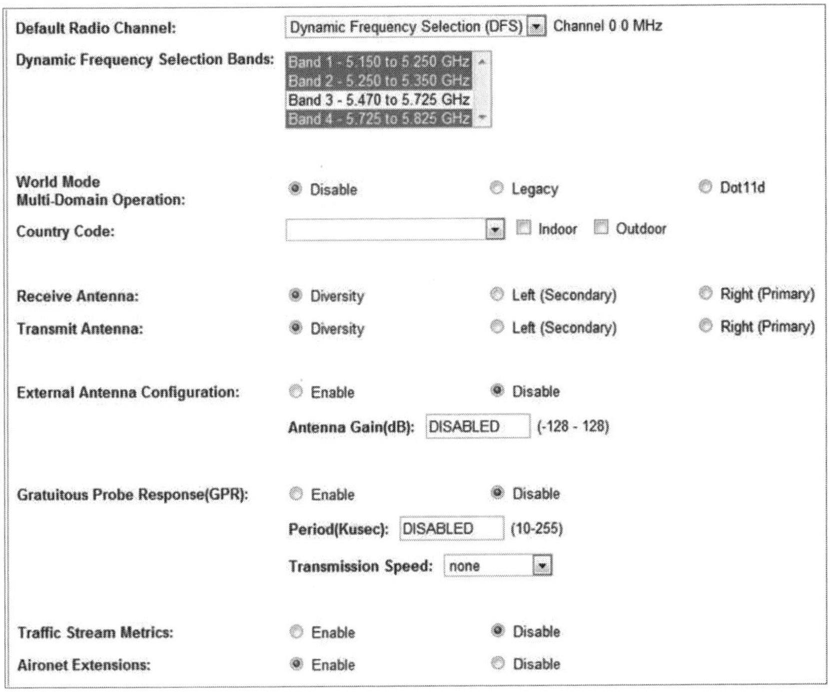

Default Radio Channel   Can be set to a specific channel or set to Least Congested. For example, for the 5GHz Band 2 or Band 3 (actually UNII-2 or UNII-2e, respectively), you must use DFS and a channel cannot be chosen (which is why DFS is not recommended).

Least Congested Channel Search   Select the channels you want to search.

Receive Antenna   Can be set to Right, Left, or Diversity.

Transmit Antenna   Can be set to Right, Left, or Diversity.

External Antenna Configuration   Not currently supported, but may be in the future.

Express Setup and Security

The home page contains two menus: Express Setup and Express Security. You can use these menus to configure a stand-alone AP with minimum settings.

The Express Setup page allows you to configure basic settings relevant to the AP itself, like the hostname, configuration server protocol (either DHCP or static addressing), the IP address, mask, gateway, and SNMP Admin community, as shown in Figure 9.21.

FIGURE 9.21   Express Setup

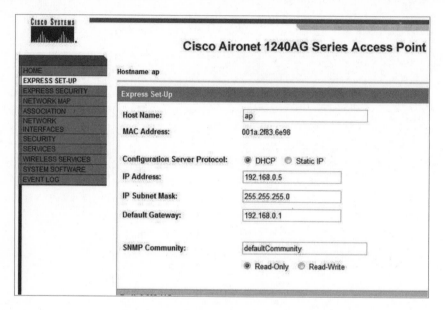

The Express Security page is where you can configure an SSID, VLAN, and a security mechanism for the SSID. If you don't use VLANs in your network, your options here are pretty limited. For instance, the encryption and authentication mechanisms are linked. With no VLANs around, these settings then apply to the interface and must be the same for all SSIDs. And since the Express Security page is designed for simple configurations, you'll find other limitations there, too, like these:

- SSIDs can be created and deleted but not edited.

- SSIDs you create are enabled on all radio interfaces. To assign an SSID to a specific interface, you must use the SSID Manager page.

- You can't configure multiple authentication servers here; you have to go to the Security Server Manager page instead.

- You cannot set multiple WEP keys. This must be done on the Security Encryption Manager page.

- You cannot assign an SSID to a VLAN that's already configured on the AP—you've got to do it on the Security SSID Manager page.

- You cannot configure combinations of authentication types on the same SSID. This must be done on the Security SSID Manager page as well.

Migrating Stand-alone APs

Technology does tend to evolve whether we're ready or not, so it's best just to accept that and be ready for change. For instance, it's more than likely that at some point, you'll need to incorporate a WLC into your wireless network and convert stand-alone APs to lightweight APs. And what if you need to return an AP that's been migrated to use LWAPP back to using the Cisco IOS? Well, you can take on these conversions in one of two ways.

Using a Conversion Utility

The Cisco IOS-to-LWAPP conversion utility is a software tool that runs on Windows. The catch is that it doesn't have a reverse gear so you can't use it to change an already converted AP back to IOS from LWAPP. Going back there must be done through either the CLI of the controller or by physically resetting the AP to the factory defaults.

Anyway, the utility and the LWAPP image can be downloaded from Cisco, and installation in Windows is pretty straightforward. Once you've got it installed, follow these four steps to use the utility for a conversion:

1. Before you do anything else, make sure the AP meets the minimum Cisco IOS version requirements and that it's in the same subnet as the controller. If the AP isn't on the same subnet with its expected controller, make sure that it has a way to discover its controller—for example, through DHCP option 43.

2. Configure the controller to accept Telnet connections.

3. Make sure the Windows PC's time matches the controller's and either turn off the firewall or allow TFTP. Also ensure that the PC is within range of the controller and the AP.

4. Start the utility. First create a flat text file shown in Figure 9.22 that has the following information in this format: AP IP address, Telnet username, Telnet password, enable password. The main screen will present you with the options in Figure 9.23.

FIGURE 9.22   Migration.txt

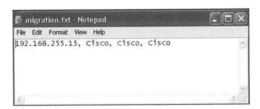

Open the Upgrade tool, shown in Figure 9.23, and enter the path to this migration text file that I created in Figure 9.22 in the IP File field on the main page. Here are the rest of the steps to configure the Upgrade tool:

1. Click the ellipses (...) button to browse to the file or enter the path to the migration file.

2. The image can be served from the local machine by browsing to it or from a TFTP server on the network. If using a TFTP server, enter the address in the System IP Addr field.

FIGURE 9.23 Upgrade utility

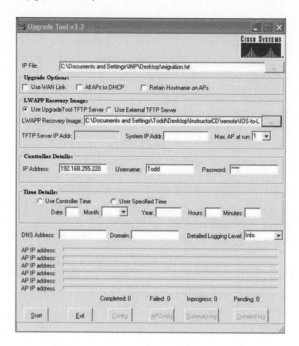

3. Enter the controller details: management IP address, administrative username, and password.

4. Specify the time source: Controller or External Source.

5. Specify the DNS server if used.

After you've completed these steps, just click Start to begin the conversion. The utility checks all parameters and will then begin converting the AP. When the conversion is complete, the AP reboots and attempts to discover its controller.

Using a WCS for Migration Using a Template

If you have a WCS in your wireless infrastructure, you can use it to migrate an autonomous AP to LWAPP using a template following these steps:

1. On the WCS, choose Configure ➢ Access Points. In the drop-down list in the upper-right corner, choose Add Autonomous AP. In the resulting dialog box, enter the credentials for both Telnet and SNMP. Click OK and the AP will be added to the list.

2. Choose Configure ➢ Migration. In the drop-down list in the upper-right corner, choose Add Template and then click Go.

3. When the template box appears, enter a name and all other relevant information (like the DNS address and controller IP address). Click Save to validate.

4. When you click Save, a new button will appear called Select APs. Click it, and a list of all current stand-alone APs will appear. Select the one you want to migrate and click Convert. Once the process is done, you will have an LWAPP AP—simple, right?

Reverting Back to Cisco IOS

There are two ways to return the AP to the Cisco IOS without a WCS: you can do so from a PC (if the PC is in the same subnet as the AP) or it can be done from the command line of the WLC that's managing the AP. Either way, you'll need a default Cisco IOS image, which should follow a precise naming convention of the form `cplatform_name-k9w7-tar.default`, such as `c1250--k9w7-tar.default`. Just download the correct code version from Cisco and rename it to fit this naming convention.

To do this reversion from the controller, make the renamed code file available on a TFTP server. Then log into the WLC CLI and enter the following command:

```
Config ap tftp-downgrade tftp-server-address filename access-point-name
```

The AP will download the code and revert back to the Cisco IOS. This same process can be done from a PC that also serves as the TFTP server if the PC and the AP are in the same subnet. For this to work, set the PC IP address in the 10.0.0.0/27 network but do *not* use 10.1.1.1. Then disconnect power to the AP. Hold the Mode button while you reconnect the power until the status LED turns red, and then release it. The AP will use the default address of 10.1.1.1, broadcast a query for the code file, download the file, and then revert back to the IOS. However, most APs can only be converted back to stand-alone via the downgrade command.

 Real World Scenario

When to Recommend the Enterprise CUWN

Remember my buddy who owns the coffee house I mentioned back in Chapter 8? Well, in spite of our ugly economy, he has managed to expand by opening four more coffee shops in the Greater Boulder area. Predictably, he asked me how he could use my 526/521 series wireless products to cover and provide control over his entire new empire!

This is actually good news for me but not so much for him because well, he can't, which means I get my controllers and APs back! I wasn't joking when I said that the Cisco Mobility Express has limits, and my pal's new need for dozens of new access points most certainly exceeds them. The cold coffee doesn't end there either... My bean buddy's main problem is that he wants to control this whole legion of access points from his corporate office in Boulder, so if you're thinking that what he really needs is an enterprise CUWN, you've nailed it—he does! Having enough caffeine in my veins to make the Energizer Bunny look like a slacker, I enthusiastically offered to dash home and bring him my 2106 plus my new 1142 APs to save the day.

The solution I came up with included two 2106 WLCs for redundancy. I created a cost-effective point-to-multipoint VPN network between shops, and then configured the APs at the other stores with H-REAP. H-REAP mode is the real jewel in this design because even if my buddy loses the WAN connection to his new corporate office, up to 20 users will still be able to authenticate locally using Local-EAP at each specific shop. Even though the people at the shops won't be able to connect, this effectively keeps his shops up and profitably selling coffee because all his merchant services are completely wireless now. This is pretty typical today, making this kind of CUWN configuration more important than ever. Another option would be to place a controller plus a AAA server at each location, but that's not really cost effective at all!

I had a great time setting up this network for my pal. But while he finally gave me back my 500 series products and passed me free coffee for life, he kept my 2106s, which I really need back because I've still got to write three more chapters!

Summary

In this chapter you learned how to implement the Cisco Unified Wireless Network (CUWN), beginning with the installation and configuration of the heart of the CUWN—the controller. This included a survey of the types of ports and interfaces and how they're used, the possible ways to implement the initial setup of the WLC, and the creation of WLANs. We also briefly explored the management of configuration and code files on the controller and the management of stand-alone APs, focusing mainly on their migration from autonomous APs to lightweight APs.

Exam Essentials

Know the methods of connecting to a WLC to manage it. Methods include Telnet, CLI, web interface wired, and wirelessly. Be aware that when managing the WLC wirelessly, uploads and downloads of files are not allowed.

Know which interfaces on the WLC are static and which are dynamic. The static interfaces are the virtual, AP management, management, and service port interfaces. The dynamic interfaces are user-defined and are used as data interfaces for the WLAN clients.

Understand the functions of each interface type on the WLC. The AP management interface is used for Layer 3 communication between the AP and the WLC; the dynamic interface is designed to be analogous to VLANs for wireless LAN client devices; the management interface is the only consistently "pingable" in-band interface IP address on the Cisco WLC; the virtual interface is used to support mobility management, DHCP relay, and guest authentication; and the service port interface is the only port that is active when the controller is in boot mode.

Understand the relationship between ports, interfaces, SSIDs, and WLANs on the WLC. Multiple interfaces (logical) can use the same port (physical). WLANs are mapped to SSIDs, which represent WLANs.

Written Lab

1. Which interface type is designed to be analogous to VLANs for wireless LAN client devices?

2. True/False: The Management interface should be in the same subnet with the service port interface.

3. Which interface is used for Layer 3 communication between the WLC and the APs?

4. True/False: The AP management interface will not be present if the controller is not set for Layer 3 LWAPP.

5. Which interface should have the same IP address for all APs in a mobility group?

6. True/False: The service port can autosense the cable type of a cable to which it is connected.

7. How many dynamic interfaces can a WLC support?

8. What type of interface is required before a WLAN can be created?

9. True/False: A WLAN can be mapped to the management interface.

10. True/False: Initial setup cannot be done through the serial connection.

Hands-On Labs

To complete the labs in this section, you will need a Cisco WLC, a switch. and a computer. The WLC should be returned to the factory defaults. The computer should have an IP address of 192.168.1.2/24.

Here is a list of the labs in this chapter:

Lab 9.1: Performing the Initial Setup via the Service Port

Lab 9.2: Creating a WLAN

Lab 9.3: Performing the Initial Setup via the Serial Port

Lab 9.4: Adding an Administrative User on the WLC

Lab 9.5: Executing the Express Setup on a Stand-alone AP

Lab 9.1: Performing the Initial Setup via the Service Port

Before beginning this lab, connect the WLC to the switch via the service port using a straight-through cable. Connect the PC to the switch with a straight-through cable and ensure that the PC's IP address is 192.168.1.2/24. Also ensure that the WLC has been returned to the factory defaults.

Use the following values to set up the WLC:

System Name: Atlanta

Administrator Username: Padmin

Administrator Username: Peach

SNMP Mode: Enable V2

Service Port Address: 192.168.1.1/24

Management Interface: 10.10.10.10/24, gateway 10.10.10.1, No DHCP

LWAPP Transport Mode: Layer 3, country code US if required

AP Management Interface: 10.10.10.4/24, gateway 10.10.10.1, No DHCP, port #1, VLAN ID 2

Virtual Interface: 1.1.1.1

Leave all other settings unconfigured.

1. On the PC, open the browser and enter **1920.168.1.1** in the browser window.

2. When prompted for a username and password, enter **admin** for both.

3. On the System information page, enter the information provided in the bulleted items.

4. When prompted a second time, enter the new username (**Padmin**) and the new password (**Peach**).

5. Using the settings provided, complete each dialog box as it is presented. For items where no information was provided, leave the box blank.

6. When prompted, select to save the configuration changes. The WLC will reboot with the new settings in effect.

Lab 9.2: Creating a WLAN

1. Enter the address **https:\\192.168.1.1** in the browser window of the PC.

2. When prompted, enter the new username (**Padmin**) and the new password (**Peach**).

3. On the home page, select Interfaces from the task list.

4. Click New to create a new interface. Enter **Fuzzy** as the name and **56** as the VLAN ID.

5. When the interface details page appears, select port 1 and use the IP address 10.5.1.2/24. Use a gateway of 10.5.1.1/24. Specify No DHCP and No ACL.

6. Select WLAN ➤ Go. When the new WLAN box appears, set the profile name to **Public_SSID** and the SSID to **Navel**.

7. Click Apply. When the new window appears, on the first tab set the WLAN status to Enabled. Set the radio policy to 802.11a Only. Set the interface to Fuzzy from the drop-down list.

8. On the Security tab, in Layer 2 Security select None. Click Apply. The configuration is complete.

Lab 9.3: Performing the Initial Setup via the Serial Port

1. Connect a null modem cable to the serial port on the WLC from the serial port on the PC.
2. Open Hyper Terminal on the PC from Accessories ➤ Communications. Set it to use the following settings:
    - 9600 baud
    - 8 data bits
    - 1 stop bit
    - No parity
    - No hardware flow control
3. Select Connect to start the terminal session.
4. After the session begins, reboot the WLC.
5. As the WLC reboots, hit Esc when presented with this message:

```
Launching BootLoader...
 Cisco Bootloader (Version 4.0.191.0)
 Booting Primary Image...
Press <ESC> now for additional boot options...
```

6. When you see the boot menu, select Clear Configuration.
7. When the WLC reboots and the services start, you should see this message:

```
Welcome to the Cisco Wizard Configuration Tool.
```

   When prompted, use the information provided for Lab 9.2 to answer the prompts.
8. When you are asked if you would like to save the configuration and reset the controller, click Yes. When the WLC reboots, the configuration should be complete.

Lab 9.4: Adding an Administrative User on the WLC

This lab assumes that the configuration from Lab 9.3 is still in effect.

1. Enter **https:\\192.168.1.1** in the browser of the PC.
2. When the log-on box appears, enter a user name of **Padmin** and a password of **Peach**.
3. When the home page appears, select Management from the task list on the left side of the page.

4. On the Management page, select Local Management Users from the task list.

5. Click the New button and when the Local Management ➢ New Users dialog box appears, set the user name to **Jadmin** and the password to **Juicy**.

6. Select Read Only from the drop-down box.

7. Close the browser window. Reopen the browser window and enter `https:\\192.168.1.1`. Log in as Jadmin with a password of Juicy. Ensure that you can view but not change settings.

Lab 9.5: Executing the Express Setup on a Stand-alone AP

This lab assumes that the AP has been cleared of the configuration or reset to the factory defaults. It also should be connected to the same switch as the PC. The PC should be set to an IP address of 10.0.0.2/8.

1. Open the browser window on the PC and enter `http:\\10.0.0.1`.

2. When prompted for a username and password, leave blank for the username and **Cisco** for the password.

3. On the home page, select Express Setup from the menu on the left side of the page.

4. When the Express Setup menu appears, enter the following information where required:

    ▪ Host Name: warehouse

    ▪ Configuration Server Protocol: Static IP

    ▪ IP Address: 10.0.0.3

    ▪ Subnet Mask: 255.0.0.0

    ▪ Default Gateway: 10.0.0.1

    ▪ SNMP Admin Community: Cisco

5. Click Apply.

6. Close the browser window. Reopen the window and enter `10.0.0.3` (the new address).

7. When prompted for a username and password, leave blank for the username and **Cisco** for the password. Verify that the changes you made are still effective.

Review Questions

1. Which versions of Cisco WCS support adding autonomous access points to the system?
    A. 3.2 and later
    B. 4.0 and later
    C. 4.2 and later
    D. 5.0 and later

2. Which two of the following are methods that can be used to migrate an LWAPP AP back to the Cisco IOS?
    A. Cisco conversion utility
    B. From the command line of its controller
    C. By returning the AP to its factory defaults
    D. From another autonomous AP in the same subnet
    `Config ap tftp-downgrade` *tftp-server-address filename*
    access-point-name

3. What is the format of the file that must be created for use in the IP File field with the Cisco IOS-to-LWAPP conversion utility?
    A. Telnet username, Telnet user password, AP IP address, enable password
    B. Telnet user password, AP IP address, enable password, Telnet username
    C. AP IP address, enable password, Telnet username, Telnet user password
    D. AP IP address, Telnet username, Telnet user password, enable password

4. Which of the following statements is *not* true about the Cisco IOS-to-LWAPP conversion process?
    A. Telnet must be enabled on the WCS if using the WCS for the conversion.
    B. Multiple APs can be converted at the same time.
    C. The conversion cannot be reversed.
    D. Upgraded APs will only support Layer 3 LWAPP.

5. Which of the following is *not* a limitation of using the Express Security page to configure security?
    A. You cannot delete SSIDs.
    B. You cannot edit SSIDs.
    C. You cannot assign SSIDs to specific interfaces.
    D. You cannot configure multiple authentication servers.

6. What is the default IP address of a stand-alone AP?

   A. 10.0.0.1

   B. Set As A DHCP Client

   C. 192.168.1

   D. 172.168.6.1

7. Which port is used to connect to the web interface on a WLC by default?

   A. Service port

   B. Console serial port

   C. Port 1

   D. Port 2

8. Which of the followings statements is true about the ports and interfaces on the WLC?

   A. Multiple interfaces can be mapped to a port.

   B. Multiple ports can be mapped to an interface.

   C. An interface is a physical connection.

   D. A port is a logical connection.

9. Which interface is used as the default interface for in-band management of the WLC?

   A. Management interface

   B. AP management interface

   C. Virtual interface

   D. Dynamic interface

10. Which of the following describes the AP management interface?

    A. Used as the default interface for in-band management of the WLC

    B. Used as the source IP address for communications with the APs

    C. Used to support mobility, DHCP, and Layer 3 security

    D. Dedicated to out-of-band management of the WLC

11. Which of the following interface types should have the same IP address on all APs in a mobility group?

    A. Management interface

    B. AP management interface

    C. Virtual interface

    D. Dynamic interface

12. Which of the following is the correct cable/device combination when connecting to the service port on the WLC?

    A. Straight-through cable to a PC

    B. Crossover cable to a router

    C. Crossover cable to a switch

    D. Crossover cable to a controller

13. Which of the following interface types is also known as a VLAN interface?

    A. Management interface

    B. AP management interface

    C. Virtual interface

    D. Dynamic interface

14. Which ports can be used to connect to perform the initial setup of a WLC? (Choose two.)

    A. Service port

    B. Console serial port

    C. Port 1

    D. Port 2

15. What key is used to invoke the Boot Options menu during startup on a controller?

    A. F8

    B. Delete

    C. Esc

    D. Alt/Tab

16. What is the default IP address of the web interface on a WLC?

    A. Set As A DHCP Client

    B. 192.168.1.1

    C. 10.0.0.1

    D. 172.150.1

17. Which statement is correct about saving configurations on the WLC?

    A. Clicking Apply saves the configuration to NVRAM.

    B. Clicking Save Configuration saves the configuration to NVRAM.

    C. Clicking Apply saves the configuration to RAM.

    D. Clicking Save Configuration saves the configuration to RAM only.

18. Which is *not* a permission that can be assigned in the WLC?

    A. Read Only

    B. Full Control

    C. Read/Write

    D. LobbyAdmin

19. How many TACACS+ servers can be defined in the WLC?

    A. 2

    B. 3

    C. 4

    D. 5

20. Which management method will not allow you to upload or download to or from the WLC?

    A. Console port

    B. Wireless management

    C. Service port

    D. Ethernet interface

Answers to Review Questions

1. **C.** Although autonomous access points can be added to the system with version 4.2 or later, they will offer limited support.

2. **B.** An LWAPP AP can be migrated back to the IOS from the CLI of the controller by executing the command

3. **D.** A file must be created to be used in the IP File field in the Cisco IOS-to-LWAPP conversion utility. This file must contain the AP IP address, Telnet username, Telnet user password, enable password, in this order. Save this file on the same machine that hosts the Upgrade tool.

4. **C.** The conversion process *can* be reversed from the command line of its controller, by returning the AP to its factory defaults, or from a PC in the same subnet.

5. **A.** You cannot edit SSIDs using the Express Security page, but you can delete them.

6. **B.** A stand-alone AP will make DHCP requests indefinitely by default.

7. **A.** The service port is used to connect to the web interface on a WLC.

8. **A.** Ports are physical interfaces. Interfaces are logical, and multiple interfaces can be mapped to a port.

9. **A.** The management interface is used as the default interface for in-band management of the WLC.

10. **B.** The AP management interface is used as the source IP address for communications with APs.

11. **C.** Unless all APs in a mobility group have the same IP address set for the virtual interface, seamless roaming cannot occur.

12. **B.** The service port on the WLC is not autosensing, so you must use the correct cable type. If you are connecting this port to another controller or to a hub or switch, it must be a straight-through cable. If you are connecting to a workstation or a router, it must be a crossover cable.

13. **D.** Dynamic interfaces are user defined and are also known as VLAN interfaces. These interfaces are intended for wireless client data.

14. **A, B.** Either the service port or the console serial port can be used to connect to perform the initial setup of a WLC.

15. **C.** The Esc key is used to invoke the Boot Options menu during startup on a controller.

16. **B.** The default IP address of the web interface on a WLC is 192.168.1.1.

17. B. Clicking Apply only saves the configuration to RAM, whereas clicking Save Configuration saves the configuration to NVRAM.

18. B. The three permissions that can be assigned in the WLC are Read Only, Read/Write, and LobbyAdmin.

19. B. Three TACACS+ servers can be defined in the WLC.

20. B. When managing the WLC wirelessly, you cannot upload or download to or from the WLC.

Answers to Written Lab

1. Dynamic

2. False

3. AP management interface

4. True

5. Virtual interface

6. False

7. 512

8. Dynamic

9. True

10. False

Chapter

10

Configuring Wireless Security on the CUWN

THE CCNA WIRELESS EXAM TOPICS COVERED IN THIS CHAPTER ARE:

✓ **Implement basic WLAN Security**

- Describe the general framework of wireless security and security components (authentication, encryption, MFP, IPS)

- Describe and configure authentication methods (Guest, PSK, 802.1X, WPA/WPA2 with EAP- TLS, EAP-FAST, PEAP, LEAP)

- Describe and configure encryption methods (WPA/WPA2 with TKIP, AES)

- Describe and configure the different sources of authentication (PSK, EAP-local or -external, RADIUS)

True, I just sounded off an entire chapter's worth about configuring controllers and stand-alone APs, but we didn't get into
one essential aspect regarding these components—securing
them! We discussed the always-critical subject of security when we explored 802.1X, WEP,
and WPA/WPA2 back in Chapter 5, but this chapter takes it much further. With the knowledge you've gained at this point in the book, you're ready to learn how to configure these
security options, both on the controller and on the clients. We'll cover it all—from the connection process on, and configure authentication mechanisms like Guest, PSK, 802.1X, WPA/
WPA2 with EAP- TLS, EAP-FAST, PEAP, and LEAP. I'll end our journey with a talk on
some developing security concepts and strategies using PSK, EAP-local or -external, and
RADIUS.

To find dynamic updates to this chapter, please go to www.lammle.com or
www.sybex.com/go/ccnawireless.

Security and the Connection Process

The process wireless clients go through when they connect to an AP and gain access to the
network is a consistent one that consists of four phases. You can see the footprints of these
phases if you check out the logs on the AP or the controller, or if you're viewing status fields
in packet captures. These phases are:

Start The first phase involves the initial connection between the client and the AP. It's also
when Layer 2 security mechanisms like None, Static WEP, 802.1X, WPA, and WPA2 come
into play. If these mechanisms are employed and in place, the client will be forced to enter
the appropriate password or have the required certificates or smart card in order to proceed
and successfully make the connection.

DHCP This phase is when Layer 3 operations begin—IP addresses are acquired and Layer 3
security (such as web authentication or IPSec passthrough, like at a hotspot or a hotel) is
deployed. Keep in mind that it's possible for security to skip Layer 2 entirely and begin
here. When it does, it allows the client to connect at Layer 2 and then pass along to Layer 3,
get an IP address, and then be presented with an authentication web page (when using web
authentication, of course).

Mobility   Here's when the client receives its final IP address, which makes it fully functional at Layer 3. At this phase, the client gets its final approval to access the WLAN. Clients could change IP addresses if web authentication is used.

Run   In this final stage, the client is sending live data on the network and passing data to the wired network, if allowed.

These four phases happen the same way each and every time a client connects; it's only the details of the overall process that differ based on the type and combination of security mechanisms in place. I'll be referring back to these phases as we explore the security options available at both Layer 2 and Layer 3.

Configuring Security on the WLC

When you configure on the WLC, some settings are carried out on a per-SSID or WLAN basis and others are set globally. Sometimes, you can configure settings globally and then set them again on a specific WLAN; in that case, the per-WLAN settings override the global ones. Let's start with what you can do on a per-WLAN basis.

Settings per WLAN

During WLAN creation is typically when you determine the security settings that will apply specifically to it. But you can still do this after a WLAN has been created. Either way, you begin by choosing WLANs from the top menu and selecting the WLAN you want to focus on. You'll see a Security tab when the WLANs ➢ Edit dialog box opens; click that tab, as shown in Figure 10.1.

FIGURE 10.1   Security tab

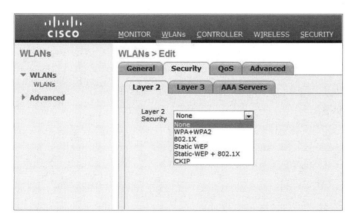

The Security tab has three subtabs: Layer 2, Layer 3, and AAA Servers. Let's expand on those next.

Layer 2

This tab gives you two options for defining the type of Layer 2 encryption and the related authentication mechanism:

Authentication   802.1X or preshared key (PSK)

Encryption   None, WEP, or WPA/WPA2 (remember the encryption methods used with WPA/WPA2 are TKIP and/or AES)

Making a selection on the Layer 2 tab in the Layer 2 Security drop-down box gives you even more selections. We'll review the options next.

Static WEP

If you choose Static WEP from the Layer 2 Security drop-down box, the only additional parameter that will appear is an option to provide the WEP key. Select the parameter, and you're choosing WEP for data encryption. If you want to use it for authentication too, just select the Allow Shared Key Authentication check box at the bottom of the page. This is the least secure setting, so I don't recommend it for an enterprise WLAN.

802.1X

Selecting 802.1X directs the controller to relay client authentication requests to an AAA server—it doesn't specify any particular type of authentication. The AP will block the client's port until a success status message is returned from the authentication server. This means that you should pay a fair amount of attention to which encryption mechanism you choose and remember: the controller must be set with the same encryption mechanism used on the AP. It's also important to keep in mind that if you've selected 802.1X, clients won't be able to use Static WEP, WPA-PSK, or WPA2-PSK for encryption or authentication.

However, after you've chosen 802.X, a section called 802.1X Parameters will pop up, which does allow you to use WEP encryption. When you specify settings this way, the WEP key is generated by the AP from the master key returned by the authentication server. For this to work, the only setting the controller needs is the key length. Don't forget that when you choose this option you'll need to proceed to the AAA Servers tab and define a RADIUS server as well.

802.1X+Static WEP

When you select 802.1X+Static WEP, you get the option to allow clients to use 802.1X or static WEP encryption. If you opt for the former, either a dynamically created WEP key will be created for the controller or the client can use 802.1X authentication along with that key. Again, if you're going to have any clients using 802.1X, you'll need to move on to the AAA Servers tab and define a RADIUS server for them.

The real benefit of going with this option is when you need to simultaneously support clients that can run 802.1X and others that can't support this feature. For instance, if a client starts the connection process with an EAP over Wireless (EAPOW) hello, the 802.1X process begins. Otherwise, the controller will expect the client to use WEP. You must have a WEP key configured on the controller to support this dual capacity.

WPA+WPA2

If you pick WPA+WPA2 from the Layer 2 Security drop-down box, you'll use the WPA+WPA2 parameters section that will appear below it to specify if you want to enable WPA, WPA2, or both. To opt for WPA, just check the WPA Policy check box and select the encryption types you want to allow—TKIP, AES, or both. In Figure 10.2, I have configured WPA2 with AES encryption.

FIGURE 10.2 WPA2 with AES Encryption

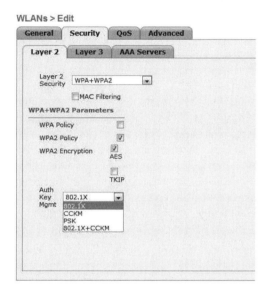

Okay, now realize that the WPA/WPA2 settings we have covered so far only apply to data encryption, but WPA and WPA2 are different key management methods, so key management has been covered as well. But coming up in the next sections, you'll see that the authentication method you choose also affects the key generation. Before we get into authentication, study the following options:

802.1X   A RADIUS server will be employed as the authentication server holding a master key. The master key is negotiated by the AAA server and the station. Then the server passes the master key to the WLC. The AP and the station negotiate encryption keys using the master key as part of the process. Don't forget that this selection means that you've got to go to the AAA Servers tab to specify the RADIUS server.

CCKM   When this is selected, the controller will only support Cisco centralized key management.

PSK   A preshared key will be used; when this option is chosen, an additional section will appear to specify the passphrase or key. The passphrase or key is 8–63 characters and is dictionary crackable.

CCKM+802.1X   This will enable either CCKM or 802.1X authentication and also requires a visit to the AAA Servers tab to specify the RADIUS server.

Layer 3

This tab allows you to define Layer 3 security mechanisms, which include:

- Web-based authentication
- IPSec or VPN passthrough

Web Authentication

Since web authentication doesn't factor in until the client gets to Layer 3, configuring it involves using the Layer 3 tab. As I mentioned, opting for this type of authentication means that the client will bypass Layer 2 authentication completely. So when the user makes their first HTTP request, they'll be directed to a preconfigured web authentication form. You can customize this page in many ways. Also, if you have a WCS in the infrastructure, it can be directed to download your custom page to all controllers, thus ensuring a consistent interface across all APs—nice!

But there are some limitations having to do with a given controller's actual capacity. The maximum number of simultaneous web authentication requests is 21. The username and password will be passed from the AP back to the controller. At that point, the authentication can occur locally on the controller or via an external authentication service that's been configured. If the local user database on the WLC is used, the maximum number of users is 2,048, although by default, that value is set to 512. To raise the default limit, select Security ➤ General and increase the limit to meet your needs.

Before going through the configuration steps for web authentication and options on the Layer 3 tab, it's helpful to understand the web authentication process:

1. When the client attempts a connection, the Layer 2 authentication and association process will be Open. The AP will create a virtual port for the client.

2. Proceeding to Layer 3, the client requests and receives an IP address from the DHCP server. Receiving DNS information as a result of the DHCP process, the client opens the browser and creates an HTTP get request in order to proceed.

3. After the HTTP request is received by the controller, it's cached, and the client is redirected to the HTTP login page. An SSL session is then opened and the server certificate is presented to the client.

4. The client is asked to provide credentials—a username, room number, etc.

5. Authentication is attempted and compared against the local database. If no username is found, a RADIUS server is then attempted for authentication. After successful authentication, the SSL session is torn down and the user is redirected to the original URL entered.

Web authentication is configured on the Layer 3 tab. The Layer 3 Security drop-down provides two choices: VPN Passthrough and None. Select None and click the Web Policy check box, and the options relevant to the setting appear below the Layer 3 Security drop-down box, as shown in Figure 10.3.

FIGURE 10.3   Web authentication

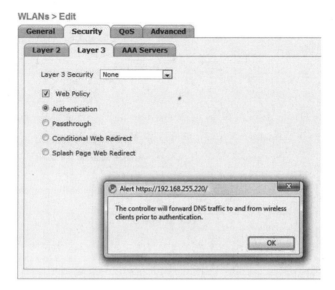

If basic web authentication is what you're after, simply check the Web Policy box and the Authentication radio button (notice that with this choice, the controller passes DNS traffic before authentication). The other radio buttons are as follows:

Passthrough   Allows access to the network with no username and password.

Conditional Web Redirect   The user can be redirected to a particular web page after 802.1X authentication occurs. The web page and the conditions under which this occurs are configured on the RADIUS server.

Splash PageWeb Redirect   The user is redirected to a web page after 802.1X authentication occurs and gains full access to the network. The web page is specified on the RADIUS server.

Customizing the Web Login

You have options for customizing the web page or pointing to an external page. It can be done on the controller or in a WCS if there's one available, but you won't find this setting on the Layer 3 tab. To access this setting, navigate to Security ➢ Web Auth ➢ Web Login, as shown in Figure 10.4. From the Web Authentication Type drop-down box, choose Internal (Default), and the web page that you're customizing here will be used. Choose Customize to download a different page or External to redirect the user to a web server that will offer the page.

FIGURE 10.4   Creating a customized web login page

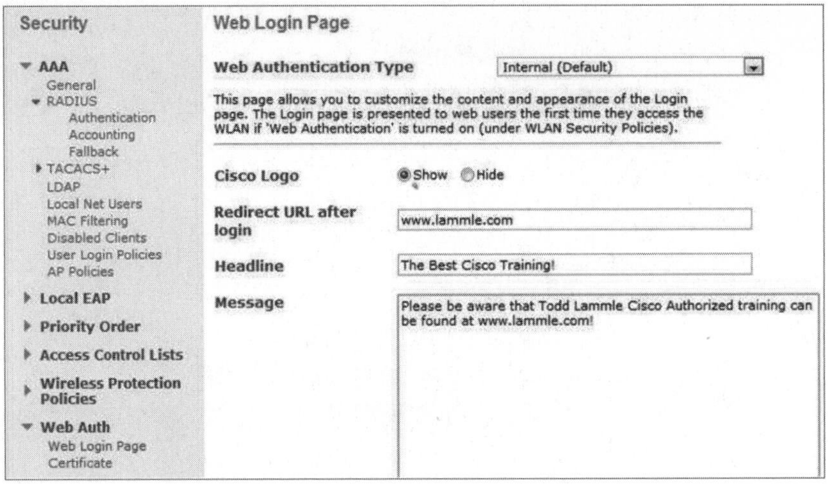

The Redirect URL After Login box allows you to specify a second web page that will appear to the user after the web authentication process has been completed. In the bottom sections, you can determine whether the Cisco logo will appear on the page or enter a headline and custom message for the page instead.

Since SSL will be used for the web authentication, the server will send the client a certificate for the session. This certificate can be self-signed or provided by a certificate authority, something that's determined in the Web Auth area as well but on a separate Certificate page that you can choose from the menu on the left. When you select Web Auth, the self-signed certificate will be displayed. To download a certificate from an authority, select the Download SSL Certificate check box, which opens a second box where you can specify the TFTP server that will provide the certificate and its exact location on the TFTP server.

AAA Servers

This tab is where you can specify authentication, authorization, and accounting (AAA) options specific to your chosen WLAN, including:

AAA Server For This WLAN   This will override any AAA server that's been set globally on the controller.

Local EAP   This option is used for 802.1X or web authentication.

Lightweight Directory Access Protocol (LDAP) Server   This option is used for web authentication only.

Location Of User Credentials When Using Web Authentication   Your options are Local List, RADIUS Server, or LDAP Database. However, keep in mind that the passwords for users aren't here—just the ability to select which place (AAA, Local EAP, or LDAP) passwords are configured.

Global Settings

Global settings are configured on the Security tab from the main page of the controller. These settings affect all WLANs. There are seven items on the tab, and each one has subtabs. The tab layout is shown in Figure 10.5.

FIGURE 10.5   Main Security tab

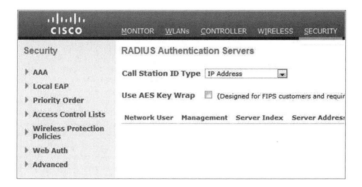

Here's a description of the seven areas:

AAA   Here is where the IP addresses and credentials needed to establish connections with the AAA server(s) are. When specifying the RADIUS server, you must configure a shared secret (sometimes called a server secret) that matches on both the RADIUS server and the WLC. There's also a submenu here for specifying LDAP servers, implementing MAC filtering, and creating the Local Net users list.

Local EAP   This is where EAP can be directed to happen on the controller rather than a configured RADIUS server.

When configuring Local EAP-FAST on the controller, you've got to set four parameters: Server Key, Time To Live For The PAC, Authority ID, and Authority ID Information (see Figure 10.6). It's vital to remember which setting is the appropriate one to configure here! I circled them to help you remember them. The reason these extra parameters must be configured is that EAP-FAST establishes an encryption tunnel for the username and password whereas EAP-LEAP does not.

FIGURE 10.6   Configuring Local EAP-FAST parameters

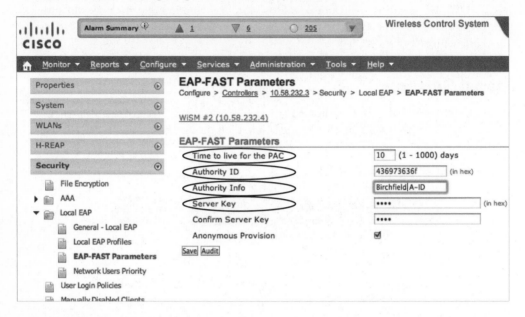

Priority Order   The place where management users are created.

Access Control Lists   Where ACLs are created and applied.

Wireless Protection Policies   The location where items relevant to AP authentication, management frame protection, and attack detection are configured.

Web Auth   This is where you configure that custom web page I've been talking about, as well as the repository for an SSL certificate.

Advanced   Lets you apply intrusion detection settings and IPSec certificate configurations.

Some of the per-WLAN settings I described earlier will require a trip to items in this menu to complete your configuration. For instance, to set up 802.1X authentication, you must also select the AAA tab here and specify the RADIUS server.

Configuring the Clients

As you recall from Chapter 6, the security settings on the controller must agree with the settings on the client. We're going to review those settings briefly before moving on to some more advanced topics. The clients that I'll be including are Windows Zero Configuration, Linux Network Manager, Mac AirPort Extreme, and the Cisco ADU.

Windows Zero Configuration

Likely the most common type of client that you'll encounter is the Microsoft Windows Zero Configuration Windows utility. Security configuration is carried out on the Association and the Authentication tabs.

Association Tab

The options on the Association tab let you set the SSID and select the authentication type and data encryption, as shown in Figure 10.7.

FIGURE 10.7   Association tab

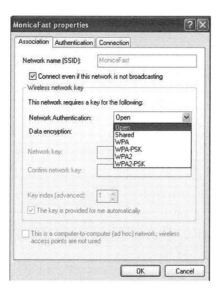

When you select PSK-based authentication like WPA-PSK, the Network Key field becomes active, and you can enter the proper PSK. If you want it to be provided automatically, select the check box The Key Is Provided For Me Automatically for types that support it. Just remember this has got to match the one defined on the WLC.

It's really important for you to understand the relationship between the settings in the Network Authentication drop-down box and the Data Encryption drop-down box. When Open or Shared is selected in the Network Authentication drop-down box, the only options available in the Data Encryption drop-down box will be Disabled (no encryption) and WEP. On the other hand, if any versions of WPA (like WPA, WPA-PSK, WPA2, or WPA2-PSK) are selected in the Network Authentication drop-down box, the only options available in the Data Encryption drop-down box will be TKIP or AES.

Because of this, only certain combinations of these settings are possible if you want things to work well, so it's imperative to understand each combination. Table 10.1 covers these important combinations.

TABLE 10.1   WZC Association Options

Network Authentication value	Data Encryption value	Consequences
Open	Disabled	No encryption, open authentication, no 802.1X.
Open	WEP	WEP encryption, open authentication; 802.1X is possible if the Authentication tab is correctly filled out.
Shared	Disabled	Static WEP key for authentication, no encryption.
Shared	WEP	WEP used for authentication and encryption. 802.1X is possible if the Authentication tab is correctly filled out. Otherwise the key will be static.
WPA/WPA2	AES/TKIP	Can be any combination of these. 802.1X must be configured on the Authentication tab.
WPA-PSK/WPA2-PSK	AES/TKIP	Can be any combination, but key must be pre-shared; 802.1X is not possible.

Authentication Tab

For any setting on the Association tab that requires 802.1X, you'll also need to configure the Authentication tab. This tab remains grayed out (unavailable) for PSK-based authentication because you've already set authentication on the Association tab. But you do need it when you use non-PSK authentication. With any 802.1X configuration, the first step is to select the Enable IEEE 802.1X Authentication On The Network check box. Once you've done this, the EAP Type drop-down box becomes available, as shown in Figure 10.8.

WZC supports two forms of EAP—Smart Card/Certificate (EAP-TLS) and PEAP—but it doesn't natively support LEAP or EAP-FAST. Selecting either Smart card/Certificate or PEAP usually requires additional configuration by clicking on the Properties button on this page. Before we get to those dialog boxes, notice the two check boxes at the bottom of the Authentication tab. The first one, Authenticate As Computer When Computer Information Is Available, will send the computer name and credentials for device authentication, sending the computer name and credentials also must be checked to allow domain users to log in wirelessly without having to connect with a wire first. The second option, Authenticate As Guest When User Or Computer Information Is Unavailable, sends a name of Guest with no credentials when no user or computer information is available.

FIGURE 10.8   Authentication tab

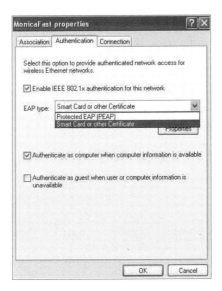

Properties of Smart Card or Certificate

Okay—so you've got two choices to make here. First, select either the Use My Smart Card or the Use A Certificate On This Computer radio button. Choosing either of these implies that you're using an EAP variant that requires certificates such as EAP-TLS. As you can see in Figure 10.9, you can choose to validate the server certificate as well.

FIGURE 10.9   Server certificate

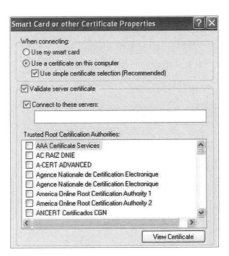

If you go with Use My Smart Card, the smart card will be located on your computer. If you choose Use A Certificate On This Computer, you must install a certificate on the computer. You can do so by connecting to a certificate authority (CA) and requesting a certificate, or by using a Group Policy that automatically installs a certificate.

Important to note is that a user may have multiple certificates installed that come from various certificate authorities. By selecting a CA in the Trusted Root Certification Authorities pane and then clicking the View Certificate button, you display the details of the certificate. Checking the box next to the CA will cause the certificate issued by that CA to be used for the connection. On the RADIUS server, EAP-TLS will have to be enabled for this to work.

Protected EAP Properties

When you've chosen PEAP on the Authentication tab (see Figure 10.10) and clicked the Properties button, you'll need to configure a different set of options. As shown in Figure 10.11, you can select to verify the server certificate. Selecting Validate Server Certificate means that the certificate will be used to create a tunnel and validate the server. If you uncheck it, the certificate is only used to create a tunnel. You can also select the trusted CA for validating the certificate, but if you do, you may have to import the public key of the CA in order to validate the certificate.

The bottom of this page is where you choose an authentication method—EAP-MSCHAP v2 (which is password based) or Smart Card Or Other Certificate. If you select EAP-MSCHAP v2 and click Configure, you'll be prompted to specify whether the domain username and password will be used for this credential, as shown in Figure 10.11. Otherwise the user will be prompted each time they connect.

If you choose PEAP, the authentication can be based on either Generic Token Card (GTC) or MSCHAPv2. If you choose MSCHAPv2, you can either use Windows credentials or select to be prompted for credentials. If selecting GTC, you can configure it for an input token (extra software is required) or use a certificate embedded in the card.

FIGURE 10.10   Choosing PEAP

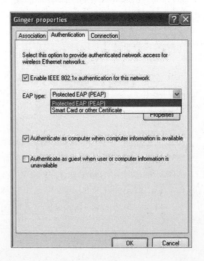

FIGURE 10.11   PEAP options

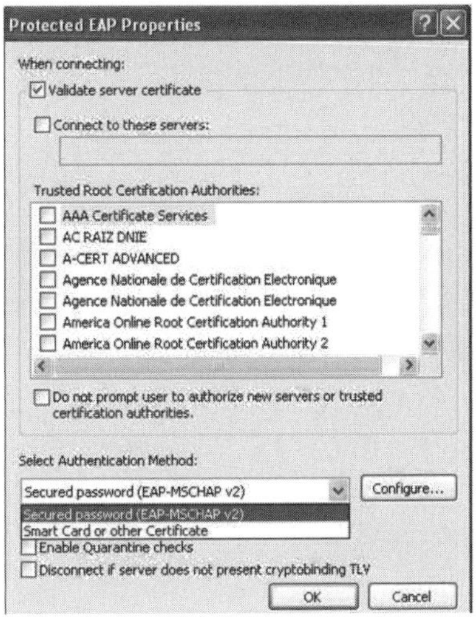

Linux Network Manager

Back in Chapter 6, you learned that to begin configuration of a new wireless profile in Linux Network Manager, you hover your mouse over the icon at the bottom of the desktop and select Connect To Other Wireless Networks. The resulting dialog box appears in Figure 10.12. After you choose a security type, the box will expand and offer you more settings reflecting your selection. Let's take a closer look:

None   Open authentication with no encryption.

WEP 128-Bit Passphrase, WEP 64/128-Bit ASCII, or WEP 64/128-Bit Hex   Choose any of these and the window will expand to allow you to enter the password, which must be 104 bits long if you're using 128-bit. It should be 40 bits long for 64-bit. When choosing these options, you must also decide between open authentication or shared-key authentication.

WPA Personal/WPA2 Personal   For these two, the window expands to allow you to enter the PSK. You can set the encryption type to Automatic, meaning the client will conform to the AP, TKIP, or AES.

WPA Enterprise/WPA2 Enterprise   When you select either of these options, WPA/WPA2 will be used for encryption and 802.1X for authentication. A drop-down list will be provided where you select the EAP type for 802.1X from the following choices: PEAP, TTLS, or TLS. If you choose PEAP, an option will become available to select a second phase that can be set to GTC or MSCHAPv2. Regardless of the type selected, you can select options specific to your chosen EAP type—like username and certificate.

FIGURE 10.12   Network Manager Security settings

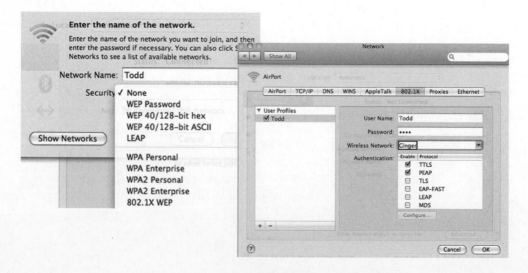

Mac AirPort Extreme

As you also learned in Chapter 6, you can create a new wireless profile in one of two ways with Mac's AirPort Extreme Utility. When scanning for networks, click the Join button in the None Of Your Wireless Networks Are Available dialog box, or choose Join Another Network and select the Network Name you want from the main window. In either case you'll see the Network dialog box in Figure 10.13.

FIGURE 10.13   Mac AirPort 802.1X

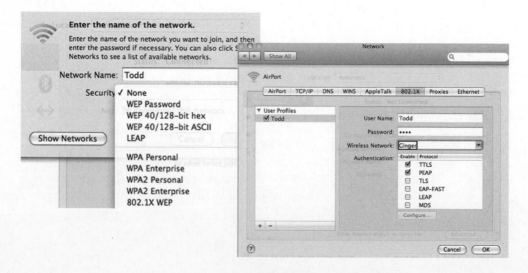

Real World Scenario

What Type of Security Do I Need Now?

Okay... back to my bean buddy in Boulder who, free coffee notwithstanding, is going to get himself tagged all over my blog if he doesn't start buying his own gear soon!

Anyway, as you know, he's all up and running with my latest CUWN gear, and when I ventured into his shop yesterday, he just happened to walk up as I was writing this chapter on Wireless Security. Not surprisingly, he had a boatload of questions that describe a familiar dilemma: How do we provide first class security while permitting free access? In my buddy's case, he needed to support sensitive merchant services on a separate, super secure WLAN, while simultaneously allowing his customers to access the very same wireless network and freely surf the wide-open Internet.

I'm not really sure what he puts in his coffee, but there I was, ready and willing to come to his rescue once again! Digging in, I knew that since he now has a distributed wireless network, I had some options for security. The solution I went for was to set up multiple SSIDs with different levels of security set for them and then I configured the wireless stations so that they would only connect to certain SSID's. This translated to merchant services being set to utilize a SSID with tight RADIUS and AES security, while all the customers are using only basic web authentication concurrently.

This lightweight solution offers up an easy configuration to create, manage, and distribute throughout the entire network—nice!

In the Network dialog box, enter the network name and choose the security type, as shown in Figure 10.13. Your possible security options are:

WEP   Options are WEP Password, WEP 40/128-Bit Hex, or WEP 40/128-Bit ASCII. If you choose WEP, you must enter the password or key.

LEAP   Selecting LEAP displays a box for you to enter the username and password into. You must choose 802.1X/EAP-LEAP with WEP encryption. To use LEAP with TKIP or AES encryption, you choose WPA/WPA2 Personal.

WPA Personal/WPA2 Personal   Selecting either of these will get you to a window for the password. You can set the encryption to Automatic, which means the client will conform to the AP, TKIP, or AES.

WPA Enterprise/WPA2 Enterprise   With this selection WPA/WPA2 will be used for encryption and 802.1X for authentication. You'll have to navigate to Network ➢ Advanced Configuration in the OS X System Preferences to fill in the details for the 802.1X settings.

In the Network dialog box, you choose the network you created from the drop-down box next to Wireless Networks and select the authentication type from the Authentication drop-down box. Your choices are PEAP, TTLS or TLS, EAP-FAST, LEAP, and MD5. If the type you select requires it, a Configure button becomes active that allows you to define a username and password. Or if necessary, a list of certificates installed will appear so you can choose the correct certificate for the credentials. If a certificate needs to be installed, you can download it and then select it by clicking the Get Certificates button.

Cisco ADU

As you've learned, you create profiles in the Cisco Aironet Desktop Utility (ADU) by selecting the Profile Management tab. Any existing profiles will appear, but to create a new one, just select New from the main menu. Doing this will open the Profile Management dialog box, where the profile name, client name and up to three SSIDs can be entered. Simply use the Security tab, shown in Figure 10.14, to specify the appropriate settings.

FIGURE 10.14 ADU Security tab

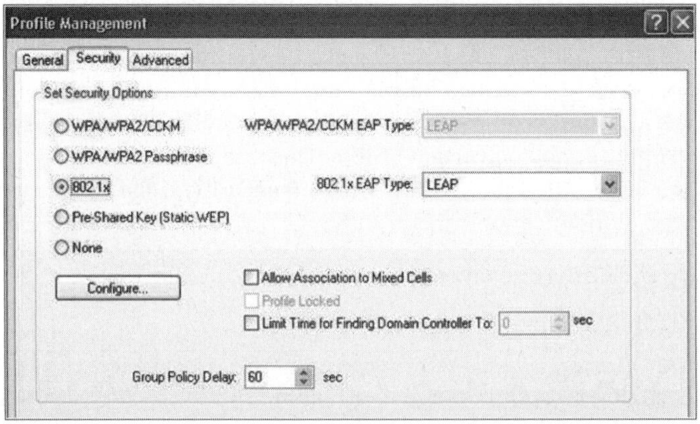

The items that become available to you depend on the radio button that you select in the Set Security Options section. For instance, in Figure 10.14, I selected 802.1X, which gives me several options. Let's step through these choices, moving from least secure to most secure:

Pre-Shared Key (Static WEP)   Other than None, this is the easiest option to configure. All you do is check the Pre-Shared Key (Static WEP) radio button; then click the Configure button and type the WEP key. Notice the Allow Association To Mixed Cells check box on this page. Some APs allow WEP clients to be on the WLAN concurrently with clients with no security. Clearly, if you want to allow this, check this box.

802.1X   Selecting this radio button will make WEP your encryption method and make available the 802.1X EAP Type drop-down box. Your choices are LEAP (the default), EAP-TLS, PEAP, EAP-GTC, EAP MS-CHAPv2, EAP-FAST, and host-based EAP. Remember, you must choose the method employed on the authentication server because they have to match.

Once you've chosen the EAP type, click Configure to complete the details. The box that appears and the options you need to set reflect the type of EAP you selected. Choosing password-based EAP will require a username and password, for LEAP, PEAP, EAP-GTC,

EAP MS-CHAPv2 and EAP-FAST, for example. And if you are using EAP types based on certificates (EAP-TLS and PEAP) for example, this will require the location of the certificate as well as the location of the CA.

There are two check boxes with associated drop-down boxes on the Security tab that apply to 802.1X. The Limit Time For Finding Domain Controller To option allows you to set a time limit for the search, which is sometimes performed by EAP-FAST or LEAP. The option Group Policy Delay is used to delay the application of Group Polices and permits the authentication process to be completed before they're applied. The default is 60 seconds, which usually is plenty of time.

WPA/WPA2 Passphrase   Configuring this option is a lot like configuring WEP, but it gives you better security. After you have selected the radio button, click Configure and type the passphrase, which is the same as WPA/WPA2 PSK or WPA/WPA2 Personal.

WPA/WPA2/CCKM   If you choose this option, the WPA/WPA2/CCKM EAP Type drop-down box becomes available to you. From it, you can select from the same options that were available in 802.1X with the exception of host-based EAP. The difference here is that when you choose 802.1X, WEP is the encryption method. When you choose WPA/WPA2/CCKM, TKIP or AES are the encryption options. Again, these are LEAP (the default), EAP-TLS, PEAP, EAP-GTC, EAP MS-CHAPv2, or EAP-FAST.

Summary

Okay, sweet—you now know how to configure security options on the controller as well as on clients. We covered the connection process and how security fits into it, and we dove deeper into the configuration of authentication methods like Guest, PSK, 802.1X, and WPA/WPA2 with EAP-TLS, EAP-FAST, PEAP, and LEAP. Finally we explored the potential sources of authentication like PSK, EAP-local or -external, and RADIUS.

Exam Essentials

Know the interface of the Cisco ADU and the WLC and how to configure security. Specifically, know where to configure the encryption method and where to set the authentication. On the ADU, security options are organized in three tabs: Layer 2, Layer 3, and AAA. On the WLC there is a single page that expands to allow for additional settings based on the Security option you select.

Understand where to configure the details of the EAP type.   On the WLC, you select 802.1X but not the exact EAP implementation. You configure the details on the client and the authentication server. Moreover, the settings must match on these two devices.

Be familiar with the three authentication methods most widely used in Enterprise WLANs and the objects used as credentials for each type.   The three methods are EAP-FAST, EAP-TLS, and PEAP. Also remember that EAP-FAST uses a protected access credential (PAC), PEAP requires a certificate on the server but not on the client, and EAP-TLS requires certificates on both client and server.

Know the four parameters required to configure Local EAP-FAST on the WLC.   These parameters are the Authority ID, Authority ID Information, Server Key, and Time To Live For The PAC.

Written Lab

1. True/False: The local user database on the WLC can contain 2,048 entries by default.

2. When a client is using either WPA2 or EAP, where are the encryption keys located during the active session?

3. True/False: When configuring RADIUS, you configure the server or shared secret on the AP and the RADIUS server.

4. Which Extensible Authentication Protocol types are supported by the Cisco Unified Wireless Network?

5. True/False: The second phase of client security is the mobility phase.

6. What is the last phase of client security?

7. True/False: Layer 2 security policies are carried out in the Start phase of client security.

8. In which phase of client security does Layer 3 security occur?

9. True/False: To select 802.1X security on the WLC, you use the Layer 3 tab on the Security page.

10. Which tab in the Security page is used to configure static WEP?

Hands-On Labs

To complete the labs in this section, you will need a Cisco Wireless LAN controller and a PC. Here is a list of the labs in this chapter:

Lab 10.1: Configuring the WLC for WPA PSK

Lab 10.2: Configuring the WLC for 802.1X

Lab 10.1: Configuring the WLC for WPA PSK

Before beginning this lab, connect the WLC to the switch via the service port using a straight-through cable. Connect the PC to the switch with a straight-through cable. You can use the setup instructions in Lab 9.1 in Chapter 9 if you need to perform the initial setup. Make note of the IP address. In the lab, we will refer to the IP address of the WLC as 192.168.1.1. If your IP address is different, use that IP address.

1. On the PC, open the browser and enter **192.168.1.1** in the browser.

2. When prompted for username and password, enter **admin** for both (or your username and password if not set to the default).

3. On the home page, select Interfaces from the Task list.

4. Click New to create a new interface. Enter **South** as the name and **49** as the VLAN ID.

5. When the interface details page appears, select port 1 and use the IP address **10.5.1.2/24**. Use a gateway of **10.5.1.1/24**. Don't worry about DHCP or ACL.

6. Navigate to the WLAN menu and then select New. When the new WLAN box appears, set the profile name to **Public_SSID** and the SSID to **Lobby**.

7. Click Apply. When the new window appears on the first tab, set the WLAN status to Enabled. Set the radio policy to 802.11a Only. Set the interface to South using the drop-down list.

8. On the Security page, on the Layer 2 Security tab, select WPA+WPA2. In the WPA+WPA2 Parameters section, check WPA Policy. Also check TKIP in the WPA Encryption section. Leave all WPA2 boxes unchecked.

9. In the Auth Key Mgmt section, select PSK. When the subsection appears, set the PSK format to ASII and enter a key.

10. Click Apply and the configuration is complete.

Lab 10.2: Configuring the WLC for 802.1X

Before beginning this lab, connect the WLC to the switch via the service port using a straight-through cable. Connect the PC to the switch with a straight-through cable. You can use the setup instructions in Lab 9.1 in Chapter 9 if you need to perform the initial setup. Make note of the IP address. In the lab, we will refer to the IP address of the WLC as 192.168.1.1. If your IP address is different, use that IP address.

1. On the PC, open the browser and enter **192.168.1.1** in the browser.

2. When prompted for username and password, enter **admin** for both (or your username and password if not set to the default).

3. On the home page, select Interfaces from the Task list.

4. Click New to create a new interface. Enter **North** as the name and **69** as the VLAN ID.

5. When the Interface Details page appears, select port 2 and use the IP address **10.5.6.2/24**. Use a gateway of **10.5.6.1/24**. Don't worry about DHCP or ACL.

6. Navigate to the WLAN menu and select New. When the new WLAN box appears, set the profile name to **Private_SSID** and the SSID to **Main**.

7. Click Apply. When the new window appears on the first tab, set the WLAN status to Enabled. Set the radio policy to 802.11a Only. Set the interface to North using the drop-down list.

8. Select Security from the menu at the top of the page. When the Security page opens, select RADIUS And Authentication from the Task list on the left side of the page.

9. In the New RADIUS Server page, set the Server Index to 1, enter an IP address of **192.168.1.60** for the RADIUS server, set Shared Secret Format to ASCII, and set Secret to Hoedown. Set Server Status, Network User, and Management to Enabled. Click Apply.

10. Select the WLAN option from the menu at the top of the page. When the WLANs page opens, select the Main WLAN and select the Security page in its properties. On the Layer 2 tab, select 802.1X.

11. Select the AAA tab and click Apply. In the Authentication Server drop-down box labeled Server 1, select the server at 192.168.1.60. Click Apply and the configuration is complete.

Review Questions

1. On which subtab of the Security tab for a WLAN do you configure the RADIUS server?

   A. Layer 2

   B. Layer 3

   C. Layer 4

   D. AAA

2. Which of the following is not configured on the global Security menu at the top of the Main page in the WLC?

   A. IP addresses of the AAA servers

   B. MAC filter list

   C. Encryption type

   D. ACLs

3. When you're using 802.1X security, which statement is correct about the configuration of the EAP type?

   A. It is done on the Security subtab of the Security page of the WLAN.

   B. It is done on the Security page from the Main menu.

   C. It is done on the client and the authentication server.

   D. It is done on the client and the AP.

4. If security for a WLAN is set to Static-WEP + 802.1X, how does the system know which process to invoke when a client is attempting to connect?

   A. If the client starts with an EAPOW hello, the 802.1X process starts.

   B. If the client starts with an EAPOL hello, the 802.1X process starts.

   C. If the client fails the WEP process, the 802.1X process begins.

   D. If the client fails the 802.1X process, the static WEP process begins.

5. Which of the following is not an Auth key management mechanism that can be selected on the Layer 2 subtab when using WPA+WPA2?

   A. PSK

   B. 802.1X

   C. CCKM

   D. WCS

6. On which tab in the WZC utility do you configure the encryption mechanism?

   A. Association

   B. Authentication

   C. Connection

   D. Security

7. Which Network Authentication/Encryption settings combination does not allow for 802.1X when setting the Association tab on the WZC?

   A. Open/WEP

   B. Open/Disabled

   C. Shared/WEP

   D. WPA-WPA2/AES-TKIP

8. What EAP type(s) are not supported on the WZC? (Choose two.)

   A. PEAP

   B. LEAP

   C. Smart card or EAP-TLS

   D. EAP-FAST

9. In the Cisco ADU, what does it allow when you select the option Allow Association To Mixed Cells?

   A. Allows a mix of WEP clients and 802.1X clients

   B. Allows a mix of WEP clients and clients with no security configured

   C. Allows a mix of 802.1X clients and clients with no security configured

   D. Allows a mix of WPA and WPA2 clients

10. When web authentication is configured on the WLC, what is the maximum number of simultaneous authentication requests?

   A. 15

   B. 21

   C. 36

   D. 55

11. Which component in the CUWN solution can provide a common web page to all web authentication clients regardless of the AP and controller to which they are connected?

   A. WLC

   B. WCS

   C. WZC

   D. ADU

12. Which of the following statements are true with regard to web authentication?

   A. The client begins the connection process using shared-key authentication.

   B. The client cannot receive an IP address until after authentication.

   C. Prior to authentication, DNS requests are not allowed to pass.

   D. When the client issues an HTTP request, the client is redirected to the web login page.

13. Which of the following options on the Layer 3 subtab of the Security page for a particular WLAN in the WLC allows for requesting an email address from the client when connecting?

    A. Authentication

    B. Passthrough

    C. Conditional Web Redirect

    D. Splash Page Redirect

14. On which menu in the WLC is MAC filtering enabled?

    A. Security menu on the Main page

    B. Security page on a WLAN

    C. Connection menu

    D. Layer 2 subtab of the Security page on a WLAN

15. Which of the following is the final phase of client security?

    A. Run

    B. DHCP

    C. Mobility

    D. Affirm

16. Which of the following correctly describes the limits of the local user database in the WLC?

    A. 1,024 maximum, 512 by default

    B. 2,048 maximum, 512 by default

    C. 2,048 maximum, 1,024 by default

    D. 1,024 maximum, 256 by default

17. Which of the following security types require the additional configuration of a RADIUS server? (Choose two.)

    A. WPA2 Enterprise

    B. WPA PSK

    C. 802.1X

    D. WEP

18. Where is local EAP configured on the WLC?

    A. Security menu on the main page

    B. Security page on a WLAN

    C. AAA subtab of the Security page on a WLAN

    D. Layer 2 subtab of the Security page on a WLAN

19. When you are configuring Local EAP-FAST on the controller, four parameters must be set. Which of the following is not one of the parameters?

A. Authority ID

B. Server Key

C. Time To Live For The PAC

D. Certificate Authority

20. Where is management frame protection configured on the WLC?

A. Security menu on the main page

B. Security page on a WLAN

C. AAA subtab of the Security page on a WLAN

D. Layer 2 subtab of the Security page on a WLAN

Answers to Review Questions

1. D. The AAA tab is used to specify the RADIUS server for a WLAN. Layer 2 is used to specify the security type, the Layer 3 tab is used to set web authentication or passthrough, and there is no Layer 4 tab.

2. C. The encryption type is a per-WLAN setting that is set on the Security page of the WLAN, not in global Security.

3. C. The EAP type is not configured on the WLC; it is set on the client and the authentication server.

4. A. If the client starts with an EAPOW hello (EAP over Wireless) the 802.1X process starts. An EAPOL (EAP over LAN) frame would not originate from the wireless network.

5. D. Wireless Control System (WCS) is not an Auth key management mechanism that can be selected on the Layer 2 subtab when using WPA+WPA2.

6. A. You configure the encryption mechanism on the Association tab. The Authentication tab is used to define authentication for 802.1X. The Connection tab does not contain security settings, and there is no Security tab.

7. B. All of the above either require or allow 802.1X except for Open Authentication and Disable For Encryption.

8. B, D. Only PEAP and Smart card or other certificate are options in the WZC.

9. B. When Pre-Shared (Static WEP) is selected, the option Allow Association To Mixed Cells becomes available. This option allows a mix of WEP clients and clients with no security configured.

10. B. When web authentication is configured on the WLC, the maximum number of simultaneous authentication requests is 21.

11. B. The Wireless Control System (WCS) can provide a common web page to all web authentication clients regardless of the AP and controller to which they are connected.

12. D. When the client issues an HTTP request, the client is redirected to the web login page. The client begins the connection process using open authentication. The client does receive an IP address and is able to pass DNS requests prior to authentication.

13. B. When you select the Passthrough option, no authentication is required and an option exists to request an email address from the client.

14. A. MAC filtering is enabled on the Security menu on the Main page.

15. A. The four phases, in order are Start, DHCP, Mobility, and Run.

16. B. The limit of the local user database in the WLC is 2,048, but it is set by default to 512.

17. A, C. WEP and WPA-PSK use static passwords or keys whereas 802.1X and WPA2 require an authentication server.

18. C. Local EAP is configured on the AAA subtab of the Security page on a WLAN.

19. D. The four parameters to be set are Authority ID, Authority ID Information, Server Fey, and the Time To Live For The PAC.

20. A. Management Frame Protection (MFP) is configured on the Security menu on the main page.

Answers to Written Lab

1. False

2. The keys are located on the client and the AP.

3. False

4. EAP-TLS, PEAP-MSCHAPv2, PEAP-GTC, LEAP, and EAP-FAST

5. False

6. Run phase

7. True

8. DHCP phase

9. False

10. Layer 2 tab

Chapter

11

Wireless Control System (WCS)

THE CCNA WIRELESS EXAM TOPICS COVERED IN THIS CHAPTER ARE:

✓ **Operate basics WCS**

- Describe key features of WCS and Navigator (versions and licensing)
- Install/upgrade WCS and configure basic administration parameters (ports, O/S version, strong passwords, service vs. application)
- Configure controllers and APs (using the Configuration tab, not templates)
- Configure and use maps in the WCS (add campus, building, floor, maps, position AP)
- Use the WCS monitor tab and alarm summary to verify the WLAN operations

The focus of this chapter will be to zoom in on the most important optional component of the CUWN—the Wireless Control System, or WCS. In it, not only am I going to introduce you to the variety of WCS species that you can populate your network with, I'm going to jam as many impressively cool, time saving features of the program that I can into this chapter! You're going to learn about truly remarkable, innovative tools and methods like centralized control, maps, configuration with and without templates, monitoring, and location tracking. We'll be covering a lot of exciting ground, so get ready!

To find dynamic updates to this chapter, please go to www.lammle.com or www.sybex.com/go/ccnawireless.

Basics of WCS

You know by now that WCS software is an optional part of the CUWN and that I'm an I.T. guy not a salesman, but if there's anything I actually do try to talk my wireless network clients into shelling out for it's some version of a WCS platform. This is because having it around just makes the life of anyone who must deal with the wireless network so much better!

For starters, the WCS communicates with WLCs via SNMP instead LWAPP. Even better, when you make changes on the WCS, they trickle down from it to your controllers, to your APs, all the way to your clients. And then there's that marvelous interface that has the look and feel of the WCS itself! The interface is laid out in a hierarchy, as shown in Figure 11.1.

So here's how that hierarchy works. All clients are organized by the AP that they're associated with, all APs are organized by their associated WLC, and all WLCs are organized by the WCS that manages them. You can compare the current configuration on the WCS to that of any WLC, and if needed, you can push a change or synchronize with the WLC. Controller upgrades, and consequently AP upgrades, can be applied from the WCS in the same way.

You can also use the information gathered from this hierarchy for WLAN monitoring as well for planning things like capacity. Each profile can be examined for noise and interference per channel to pinpoint performance issues and fix them. When using planning mode, you can input assumptions like wall absorption values and create a prospective initial layout using a map of the area to be covered.

FIGURE 11.1   CUWN hierarchy

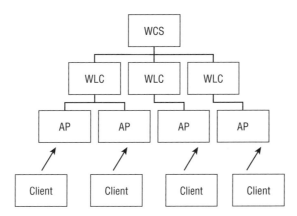

Another great benefit is that you can obtain real-time reporting of any new sources of interference that can be sent to the WCS by incorporating Cisco Spectrum Expert sensors (which I'll cover in detail in Chapter 12).

With all that in mind, let's talk about the various WCS flavors, cover the related licenses and the steps required for you to get the one you need from Cisco.

WCS Versions

Understanding the different versions of WCS that exist used to be a bigger deal than it is today because you had to positively make sure that you downloaded the right software from Cisco's site. But Cisco has since created unified installation packages, meaning that you only have to download one file to get all the functionality you need, which is based upon the license you buy. We'll get to licenses next, but for now, know that in the past, there were really only two forms of the software: WCS Base and WCS Location. Nowadays there are three different ways to use WCS:

WCS Base   The biggest difference between this WCS version and the next one, WCS Location, are location services, as the name suggests. The Base version of the software can only provide on-demand or manual user-prompted location of a client or a rogue AP.

However, the Base version is capable of doing all the rest of the things that I mentioned. Those features include automatically adding the APs to the database when a new AP joins a controller, discovering and containing rogue APs, and taking advantage of user-supplied and -configured maps for your campus, buildings, and the floors.

WCS Location   When you have the Location version of the software, you get all the features in the Base version plus a few more, like on-demand location of rogue APs and location of clients to within 33 feet. You also get the use of those very cool Cisco Spectrum Expert sensors, Cisco Location Appliances, and the Cisco Mobility Solution Engines—at an additional charge, of course.

WCS Location + Location Appliance   This really doesn't qualify as another complete version of the software—it's a third deployment option. This means that if you combine the WLC Location software with a location appliance, even more features become available. This increased functionality includes things like real time tracking, simultaneous support of 2500 clients, asset and inventory management, network modeling and capacity planning—wow!

The WCS application can be installed on Microsoft Windows Server 2003 or on Red Hat Linux. System requirements are as follows:

- Low-end system, 500 APs/50 WLCs
  - Pentium 4/3.06GHz
- Standard system, 2,000 APs/150 WLCs
  - Intel Dual Core 3.2GHz
- High-end system, 3,000 APs/250 WLCs
  - Intel Xeon Quad 3.15GHz

 There is no difference in functionality between the two server versions.

WCS Licensing

As I said, it's actually the licensing for WCS that determines the features you get. There are two major categories: Standard and Enterprise. Standard licenses limit you to only a single server installed with WCS. An Enterprise license allows you to have multiple WCS servers and also includes a WCS Navigator license that will manage 20 WCS instances.

SKU Families

WCS-STANDARD-K9

Base version

Single server only

Up to 500 APs

Uses Closest AP Location tracking

WCS-LOC-UPG-K9

Base version

Single server only

Up to 500 APs

Uses RF Fingerprinting Location tracking

WCS-ENT-K9

  Enterprise version

  Supports up to 50,000 APs

  Multiple servers

  Uses RF Fingerprinting Location tracking

  Includes Navigator for managing 20 WCS instances

WCS-WLSE-UPG-K9

  Single version

  For migration from the 113X WLSE

  Supports 2,500 APs

  Base and Location versions

AIR-WCS-DEMO-K9

  Fully functional 30-day license

  Includes location

  Single server

  10 APs

There are additional licenses you'll need for your WCS, depending on the products you buy with WCS. Cisco's analyzer is one of the most popular and I wanted to provide the licensing options for you.

Cisco Spectrum Intelligence Licenses

I'll cover the Cisco Spectrum Expert, which is a spectrum analyzer used to identify sources of interference, in detail in Chapter 12. In brief, this device can send information to the WCS, but you must obtain special additional licenses for it. The SKUs and their descriptions are as follows:

WCS-ADV-K9

  For one sensor

  Single server

  Includes location capabilities

WCS-ADV-SI-SE-10

  Up to 10 sensors

  Includes location capabilities

  Can be used as a spare when deploying to multiple servers

Cisco WCS Navigator

If your infrastructure is large and complicated, you can use the Cisco WCS Navigator to monitor up to 20 WCS instances. It allows for reporting across all instances of WCS, allows single sign-on, and permits the centralized monitoring of the entire system from a single location. Even though it provides links to any individual WCS, you don't actually apply any configuration from the Navigator. Clicking the links transfers operations to the WCS, where the actual configurations are performed. Here are some important factors to keep in mind regarding the Navigator:

- It must be installed on a server, even though it can be managed from the browser of any computer.
- WCS and the WCS Navigator must be installed on independent servers.
- To support all features like client troubleshooting, the controllers must be version 4.2 or later. I'll discuss this in detail later in the chapter and also in Chapter 12.

Adding WCSs to the Navigator is done in much the same way that you would add a controller to the console of a WLC. When a WCS is added—commonly referred to as a regional WCS, the WCS will populate the database of the Navigator with all of its relevant information like its APs, clients, etc. At the time, the credentials are added as well so that this won't be required later.

An important factor that's not readily apparent here is that the username required to contact the WCS must be given "northbound API" rights. This API will be used for integration with third party utilities and because the WCS and the Navigator are on different hardware platforms, rights to this API must be granted when you add the WCS to the Navigator.

Installing and Upgrading WCS

Installing WCS is pretty straightforward, but there are a few things I'd like to point out that will make future operation and configuration a bit easier for you. I admit that the items on my personal tips list were pretty much learned the hard way, so paying attention to these things will make it a whole lot easier for you to handle backups and perform an upgrade later.

So here we go—it's time to walk you through the process of installing and upgrading WCS, which will be reasonably close to step by step. I'll begin with the pre-setup steps that I use that will really help you to succeed in the long run.

Configuring Ports

You're probably aware of the concept known as "hardening a device" that includes closing all unnecessary ports. The flip side to this is that you need to know which ports the WCS must have opened to function correctly. These ports, which shouldn't be blocked by any firewall between the WCS and the WLCs, are listed in Table 11.1.

TABLE 11.1   WCS Ports

Port Name	Port Number
Advent Net	2000
Database	1315
FTP	21
HTTP connector	8456
HTTP connector redirector	8457
HTTP	80
HTTPS	443
RMI	1299
TFTP	69
Trap	162
Web connector	8009

You can change some of these ports if you want or need to. The HTTP, HTTPS, FTP, and TFTP ports can be set differently during the installation since these functions are built into the WCS. Keep in mind that the WCS is a web server that uses Apache and one of its main components is Apache Tomcat, which is a web container. Tomcat uses Java, and the Java component uses TCP 1299 for the Remote Method Invocation (RMI), as shown in Table 11.1.

Performing a New WCS Install

Clearly, the first thing on your to-do list is to download the particular version of WCS that you want to install and use. You can do this from Cisco's website in the Software Center and a good thing to know is that you can download a 30-day trial of the software to play with and evaluate the functions it provides before committing to it—nice!

Tips for a Successful WCS Deployment

Okay, now for that list of tips... If you plan to use the WCS permanently and actually buy the software, here are a few important things you really need to know. Again, I had to learn these the hard way when setting this product up for my clients, so commit these to memory to prevent unnecessary grief!

- WCS can be a greedy beast in terms of the resources it consumes on a server. So if you're planning to use maps, monitor multiple WLCs, and especially if you intend to perform location services, I definitely recommend that you have more than the minimum requirements for the server hardware at your disposal.

- This may seem obvious, but you must know the operating system you're going to run on the server before you download. This is because you download different software depending on whether your server is running Windows Server 2003 or Linux.

- Once you've purchased a license for the WCS from your local Cisco vendor, you have to contact the Cisco licensing team so that the license file for your software can be created. For this to happen, you must have either already built the server or at least know what the hostname of the server is going to be. This is because when you contact the licensing team, they need that server name to create the license file for it and you don't want to look like an idiot, right? The license file is tied to a single server with that name and that name only!

- If you're upgrading the WCS, make sure you back up the FTP and TFTP server files in the root directories on the WCS server—those files can be deleted during the installation process. Don't miss this one—the results can be really ugly!

Now, assuming you've got your server ready and have downloaded the software to it, it's time to get on with the installation. Let's move through this process step by step:

1. Double-click the WCS software file to begin the installer program and wait for the initial setup screen to appear; this could take a couple of minutes. You will see the initial configuration screen as shown in Figure 11.2. Read the information and then click Next to continue.

2. Read and agree to the software license and then click Next.

3. When the Check Ports dialog depicted in Figure 11.3 opens, enter the HTTP and HTTPS ports for your server. The default is HTTP port 80 and HTTPS port 443. Once you've done this, click Next again to continue.

4. When the Password Restrictions screen appears, read the restrictions, enter a root password that meets all the requirements, and then click Next.

5. Enter the root password and again click Next to continue.

FIGURE 11.2   WCS initial setup screen

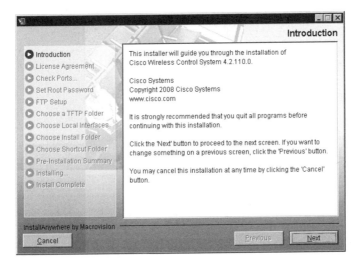

FIGURE 11.3   Check Ports screen

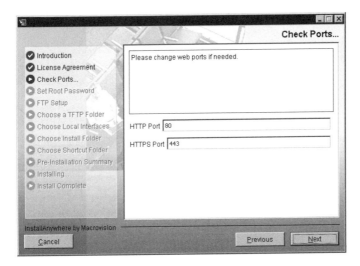

6.   Verify the root password by reentering it. Figure 11.4 shows the Verify Root Password screen.

FIGURE 11.4   Verify Root Password screen

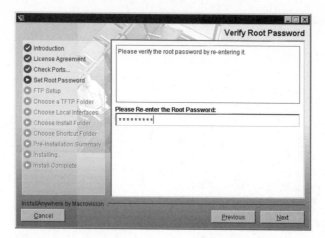

7.   Come up with a new password that meets all the password restrictions. This will be the password that secures the root FTP server. Enter the FTP password on the Enter FTP Password screen, shown in Figure 11.5, and then click Next.

FIGURE 11.5   Enter FTP Password screen

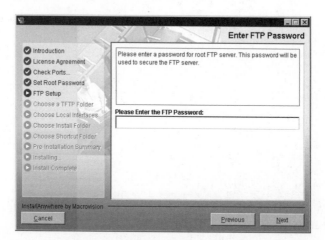

8.   The next screen is where you specify the folder that will be used for the FTP server files. Cisco recommends that this folder be located on a path different from that of the WCS installation. Doing this preserves your FTP server files in case you ever uninstall WCS. The default path, shown in Figure 11.6, is C:\. Click Choose and then specify a different path—one that's appropriate for your particular system. When you're finished, click Next.

FIGURE 11.6   FTP server file location

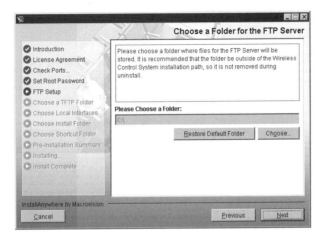

9. Determine the folder you're going to use for TFTP server files. Here again, Cisco rec-
    ommends that you place this folder on a different path from the one used for the WCS
    installation; that way, any files uploaded from or downloaded to controllers will be safe
    if you ever uninstall WCS. The default path, as shown in Figure 11.7, is C:\. Again you
    just click Choose, specify a different and system-appropriate path, and then click Next.

FIGURE 11.7   TFTP server file location

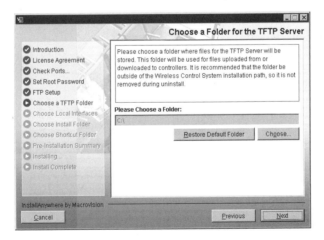

If your machine is multihoned, you'll see an additional screen where you can choose
the interface used to host the WCS.

10. Now it's time to define the installation path for the WCS software. You'll again want
    to go with the default installation path that's shown in Figure 11.8, because it works

well for most systems. But if the default doesn't work for you, click Choose to change the path for your system and then click Next.

FIGURE 11.8   WCS installation path

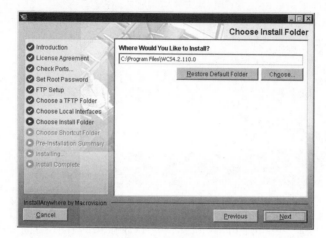

11. Define the shortcut folder for the WCS software, which is usually the default new program group that's shown in Figure 11.9. Again, this is because it's appropriate for most systems, but you have other options for where you can drop this shortcut:

- An existing program group
- The Start menu
- The Quick Launch bar
- Another location you specify

FIGURE 11.9   WCS shortcut options

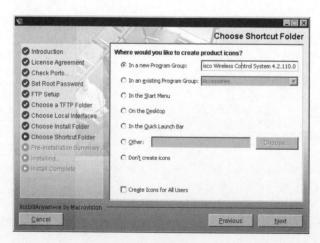

You can also choose not to create icons or to create distinct icons for all users. When you're done, click Next.

12. When the Pre-Installation Summary screen opens, double-check your settings and make sure that your system has enough disk space for the installation. Figure 11.10 shows the settings for the system in my test network. If it all looks good, click Next to begin the software installation.

FIGURE 11.10   Pre-Installation Summary screen

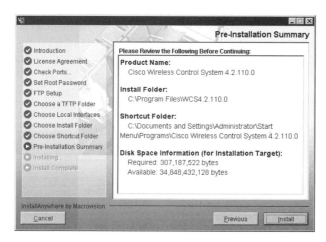

13. Wait while the software installs. Installation messages and a progress bar like the one in Figure 11.11 allow you to monitor the installation. If necessary, you can click the Cancel button to cancel the installation at any time.

FIGURE 11.11   Monitoring the software installation

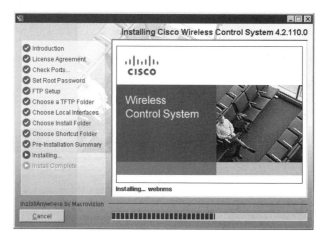

14. Once the installation is complete, you'll see a dialog box like the one in Figure 11.12. Here you choose whether to begin service immediately or not. Click Yes.

FIGURE 11.12 Starting the WCS

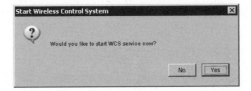

15. Wait while the WCS starts. Once it does, you'll be returned to the installer. Review the on-screen information shown in Figure 11.13, and then click Done to exit the installer.

FIGURE 11.13 Install Complete screen

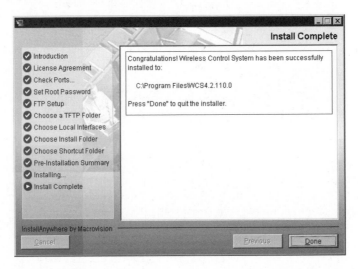

Upgrading WCS

How much trouble upgrading the WCS will give you depends on the version you're upgrading from. Prior to version 4.2.62 you had to back up your previous installation database, stop WCS, uninstall, install the new version, and then restore the database. Lucky for us, all this grunt work is no longer required with the newer versions. Now when you run the installation it will recognize the previous one, tell you it has detected it, and ask you if you want to upgrade rather than run a totally new installation. If you choose to upgrade, all those laborious steps are done automatically. However, I definitely recommend backing up your prior installation because it truly is better to be safe than sorry.

Verifying the Upgrade/Installation

Whether you're performing an upgrade or new installation, it's good to know what to look for to see if the process went well. Here are a couple of things to look for to ensure all is well:

- An installation log will be created in `system root\program file/WCSversion`. Check this log for error messages.

- In the Start menu, the Cisco Wireless Control System item will lead to a submenu that contains six more items. One of these is called WCSStatus, which you use to test the server components. If all is good, it will return a result message indicating things are normal.

Basic WCS Setup

Your next step is to log into the WCS interface, which is an entirely web-based application. Just open a browser and navigate to the IP address of the server where you just installed the software. Check out Figure 11.14 to see an example of the login page. The default username is root and the password is whatever you set during the installation process.

FIGURE 11.14   WCS login page

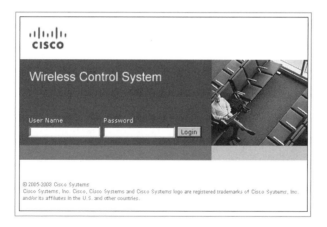

You'll run into a snag if the installation isn't licensed. When you log in, you'll be informed of this immediately and until you add the license, the WCS won't function correctly. To remedy this situation, choose Help ➤ Licensing and select Add License. When the Add A License file dialog box appears, browse to the file's location. Remember, you must get this from Cisco and your server name in their file must match the name of the server.

With that out of the way, simply log in and the WCS interface will notify you that the interface is completely customizable. This is very cool because it means you get to modify the interface to provide easy access to the most important information for your specific network and environment. Read through this and then close the message box.

Now that the interface is open, you can begin to explore the WCS software. Notice there's not a stitch of information about your wireless network—or in fact, about anything at all. This is because WCS is a management suite and by default it isn't connected to any of the devices that populate your network. We'll get to this soon.

Configuring Passwords

The password created during the installation is called the root password. You can continue to use that account and password, but it's a much better idea to create additional administrative accounts as a backup just in case you space that account password and it gets forgotten!

Administration Tasks

Before attempting to understand all the navigational instructions we'll move through soon, it's really helpful to become familiar with the initial screen you'll see when you first log into the WCS. So here's a snapshot of the Home screen to help you get acquainted in Figure 11.15:

FIGURE 11.15 WCS initial screen

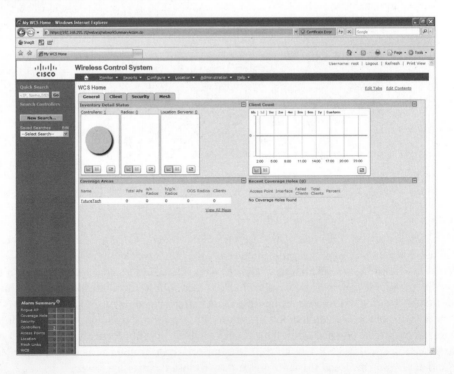

As you can see, there are three sets of menus: a vertical one on the left border used for searching and monitoring the Alarm Summary; a horizontal one at the top in the middle that leads to configuration sections like Monitor, Reports, and Configure; and a smaller status menu in the upper right used to view the current logged-on user, log out, refresh the screen, or access a print view.

You can also see four tabs in the middle of the page. These tabs and what they do are:

General   This tab displays a summary about inventory, coverage, and client count.

Client   This tab gives you more detail about the clients organized by AP; details include the client count, associated clients, disabled clients, and per-client traffic volume.

Security   This tab offers important information about attacks, signatures, rogue APs, and alarms.

Mesh   This tab displays information relevant to mesh networks, including node hop count, backhaul link SNR, and error rate.

When it comes to administrative tasks, that item in the horizontal menu at the top of the screen called Administration is your key to most of the configuration tasks you'll need to perform. This menu has seven items, as shown in Figure 11.16.

FIGURE 11.16   Administration menu

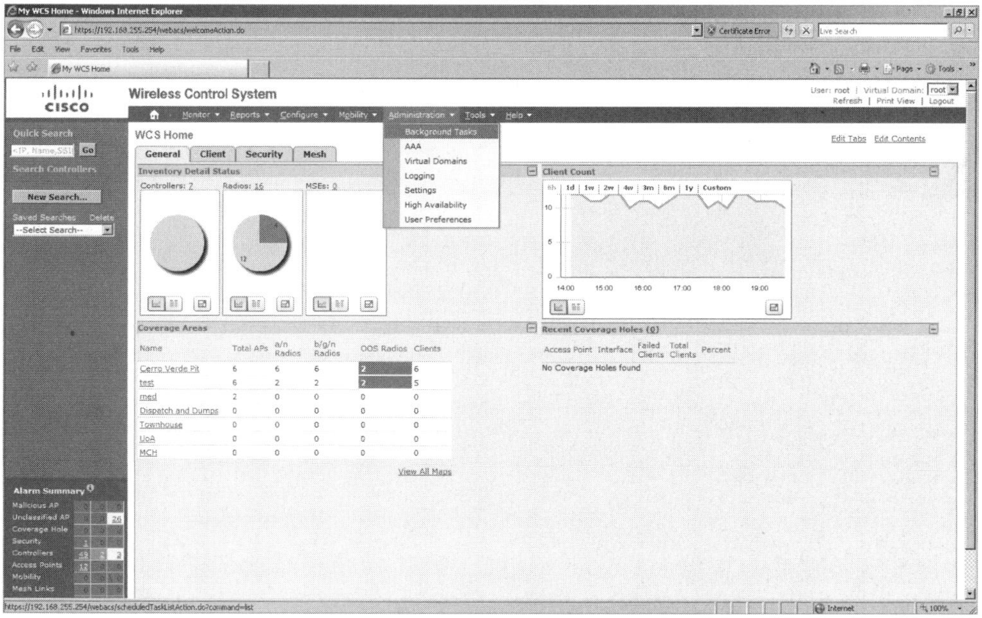

It would be a good idea to bookmark this page because as we progress through the main functions, I'll refer back to this menu fairly often to show you how to get to the various screens required to carry out upcoming tasks. Here are the seven Administration menu tasks you can perform:

- Background Tasks
- AAA
- Virtual Domains
- Logging
- Settings
- High Availability
- User Preferences

Let's take a look at some of the options you'll use the most, which are on the first two pages.

Background Tasks

I'll be exploring this area in much greater detail in Chapter 12, but I want to introduce it here first. This page allows you to enable and disable functions and processes that occur automatically in the background and are relevant to the main WCS activities. Each task can be set to Enable, Disable, or Execute Now. As you would guess, except for the Execute Now choice, all functions will be scheduled at the interval you determine on this page. The data that's collected can be aggregated or nonaggregated, as depicted in Figure 11.17.

FIGURE 11.17 Background Tasks

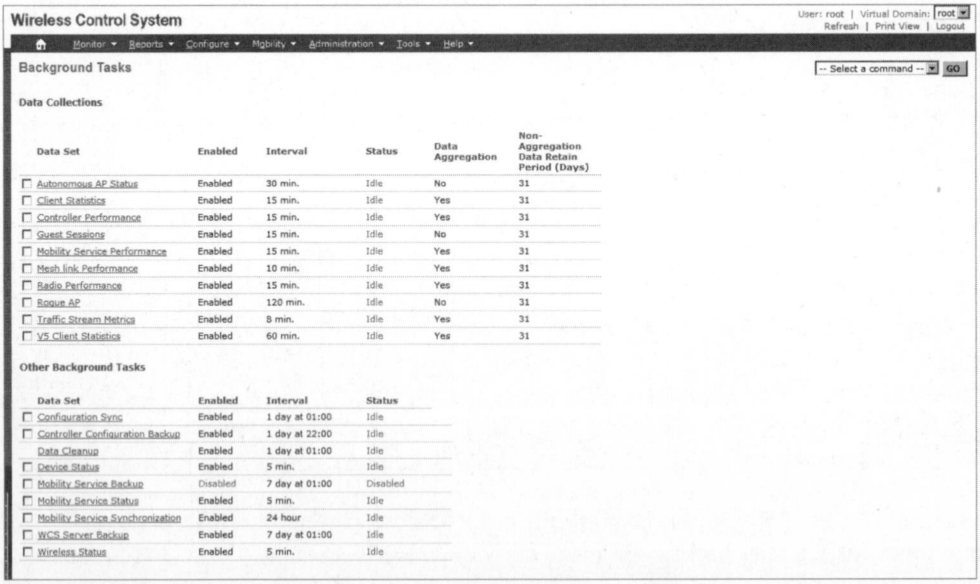

Clicking on any individual task opens a dialog box that offers a veritable buffet of parameters you can set concerning the specific activity you're scheduling.

AAA

This page is where you'll find the settings related to user accounts, access, and RADIUS and TACACS+ servers, and it's also where you can choose to create a group. Once the page is selected, these items, plus a few others, will appear in a task list on the left side of the page, as shown in Figure 11.18. Importantly, in this particular shot, the Change Password item has been clicked, allowing us to change that root password—something you should definitely do!

FIGURE 11.18   Changing the root password

Okay, so to create a new user or group, just choose either Users or Groups from the list on the left, understanding that you're creating locally configured users who will be allowed to manage the WCS, which is different from users configured on your RADIUS or TACACS+ server. In either case, the page will change to one very similar to Figure 11.19. This figure shows the new user's page, which allows you to set the name and password and add the user to a group if you want. This is important because each of the various groups you see listed here have different privileges associated with them. So, make sure you know exactly who the user you're creating settings for is and choose accordingly to limit them to only the permissions you're sure they should have. Take a good look at Figure 11.19.

FIGURE 11.19 New Users page, General tab

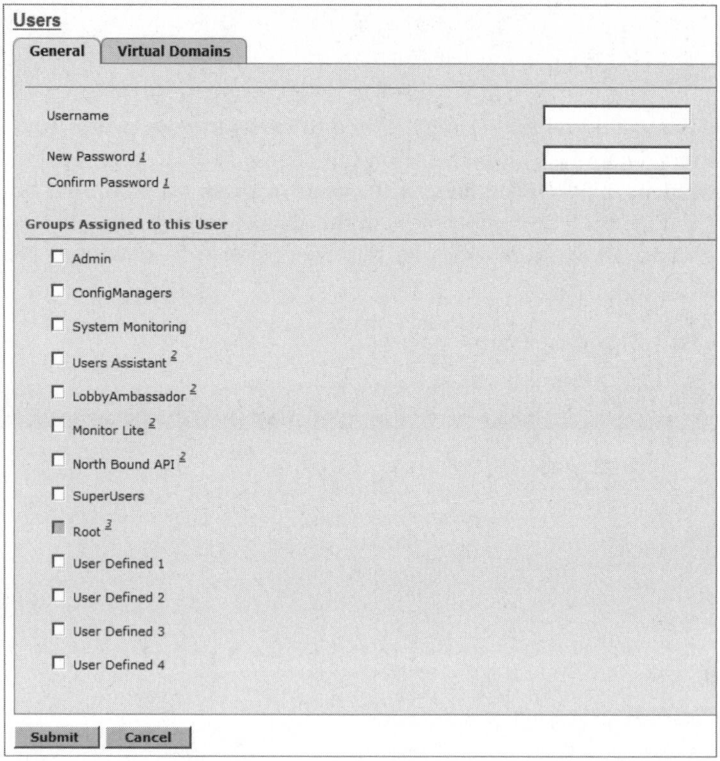

The Groups page is there to allow you to add and subtract to the rights that are granted by default to user groups. In Figure 11.20, I've selected a certain group by clicking on it in the Group page, giving me the ability to control its rights. Even though what you see here seems like a lot of choices, it's only a partial list of the tasks you can select or deselect.

Auditing

Whenever you grant rights to users, it's wise to monitor how they're using those rights. To do this, select Administration ➢ AAA. On the AAA page, select Users to audit individual users, or click Groups to audit a whole group. Next to the user or group name is the Audit Trail button, as shown in Figure 11.21. When you click it, all actions taken by the group or a user account are displayed for your viewing pleasure in the bottom pane, as shown in Figure 11.22.

FIGURE 11.20 Rights to user groups

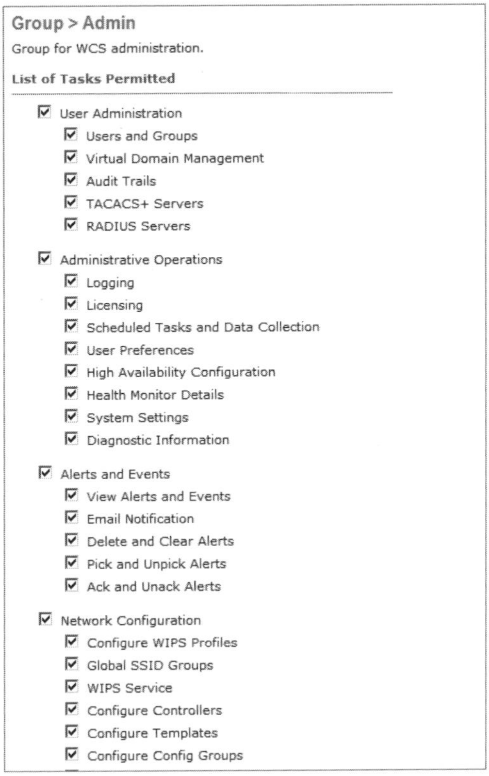
Group > Admin
Group for WCS administration.
List of Tasks Permitted
User Administration
Users and Groups
Virtual Domain Management
Audit Trails
TACACS+ Servers
RADIUS Servers
Administrative Operations
Logging
Licensing
Scheduled Tasks and Data Collection
User Preferences
High Availability Configuration
Health Monitor Details
System Settings
Diagnostic Information
Alerts and Events
View Alerts and Events
Email Notification
Delete and Clear Alerts
Pick and Unpick Alerts
Ack and Unack Alerts
Network Configuration
Configure WIPS Profiles
Global SSID Groups
WIPS Service
Configure Controllers
Configure Templates
Configure Config Groups

FIGURE 11.21 Auditing users

Users
User Name
Member Of
Audit Trail
root
Root

FIGURE 11.22 Auditing user actions

Group Audit Trail > root
-- Select a command --
GO
User
Operation
Time
Status
root Authentication Feb 7, 2010 4:08:24 PM Success
root Authentication Feb 7, 2010 4:05:30 PM Success
root Authentication Feb 7, 2010 4:05:30 PM Success
root Authentication Feb 5, 2010 12:40:16 PM Success
root Authentication Feb 5, 2010 12:40:15 PM Success

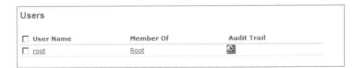

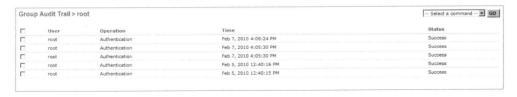

Managing Logs

Because the WCS tracks all activities, it creates a massive amount of data related to all these events. You can manage this legion of information by choosing Administration ➢ Logging to regulate the data you want to log and then selecting Administration Settings ➢ Data Management to determine exactly how the data will be logged. Here you can do the following:

- Select items to log.

- Set retention period (entered in days) for hourly, daily, and weekly aggregate data.

- Specify the path on which to send report data files.

    All of this can be seen in Figures 11.23 and 11.24.

FIGURE 11.23   Managing logs

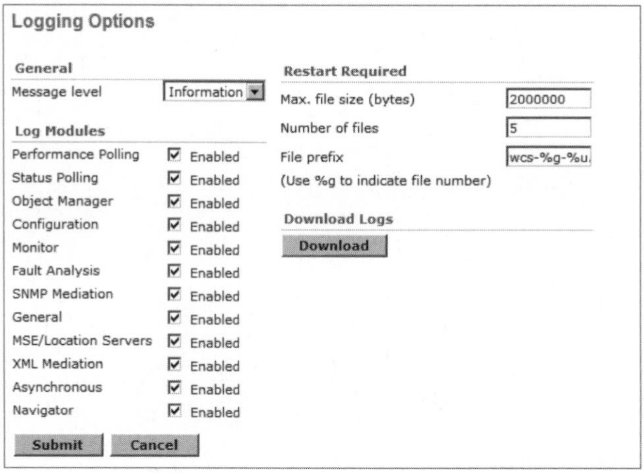

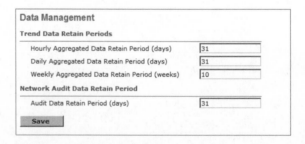

FIGURE 11.24   Continuing to manage logs

Alerts

WCS can use SMTP to send alert emails if you configure it to do so. Choose Administration ➢ Settings ➢ Mail Server and in the resulting screen, define the primary and secondary email servers, complete the To and From fields that determine where the alert mails will be sent, and make a few more relevant settings, as shown in Figure 11.25.

FIGURE 11.25   Configuring alerts

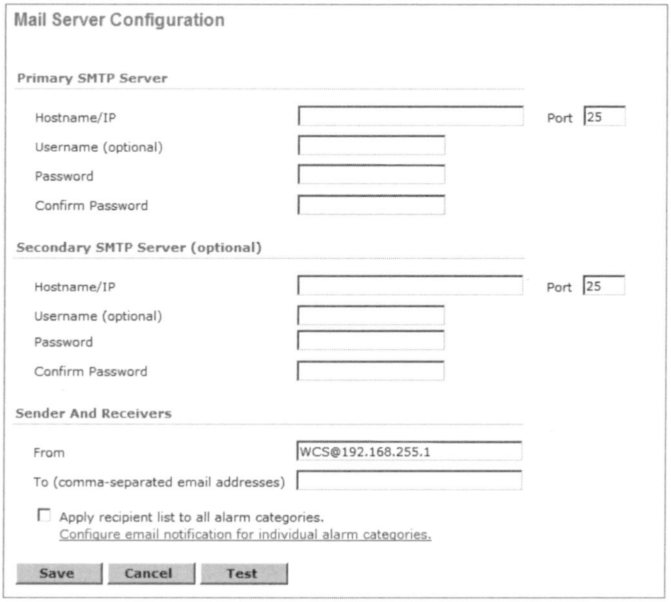

Mail Server Configuration

Primary SMTP Server

Hostname/IP _____ Port [25]
Username (optional) _____
Password _____
Confirm Password _____

Secondary SMTP Server (optional)

Hostname/IP _____ Port [25]
Username (optional) _____
Password _____
Confirm Password _____

Sender And Receivers

From [WCS@192.168.255.1]
To (comma-separated email addresses) [_____]

☐ Apply recipient list to all alarm categories.
  Configure email notification for individual alarm categories.

[Save]   [Cancel]   [Test]

User Preferences

Once you know your way around the console, you'll probably want to customize how it will be displayed to you. Choose Administration ➢ User Preferences to access settings such as the number of items you want shown on a page and the refresh intervals (see Figure 11.26).

FIGURE 11.26   Users Preferences

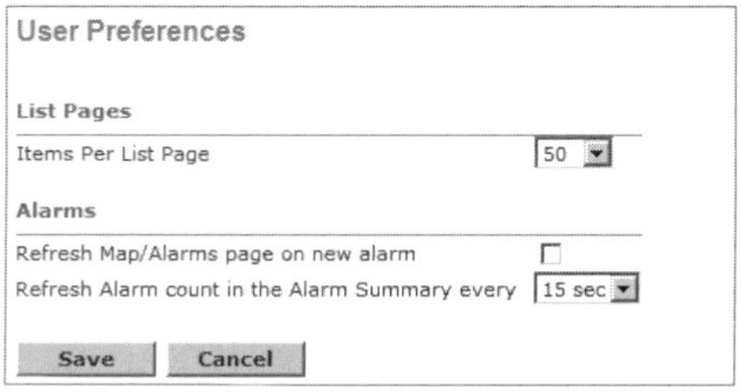

User Preferences

List Pages

Items Per List Page   [50 ▾]

Alarms

Refresh Map/Alarms page on new alarm   ☐
Refresh Alarm count in the Alarm Summary every [15 sec ▾]

[Save]   [Cancel]

Configuring WLCs and APs

The first thing we're going to do with WCS after configuring administration is add a WLC to it so the WLC and the WCS can begin sharing information. This is important because WCS gets most of its data from the WLCs on the network. To demonstrate how, I'm going to walk you through the process of configuring and adding devices and information to the WCS interface. Clearly, the first device we'll add to the WCS interface is the WLC, and doing so is really easy. By looking at Figure 11.27, you can see that I'm on the Home page of the WCS server, which is the place to start when you want to add a WLC.

1. As shown in Figure 11.28, select Controllers from the Configure menu, which brings you to the All Controllers page.

FIGURE 11.27   Home page of the WCS server

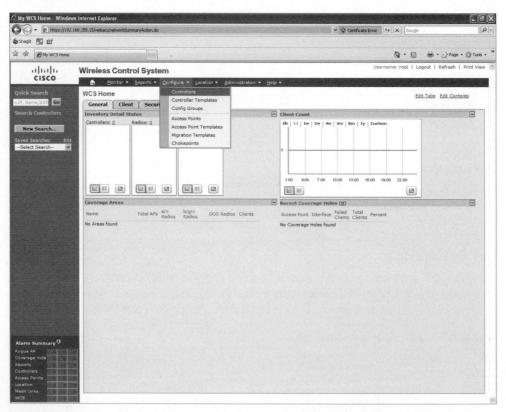

FIGURE 11.28   All Controllers page

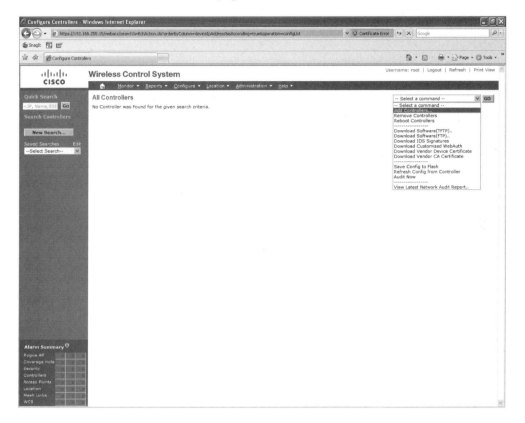

2. Choose Add Controllers from the Action drop-down list box, and then click Go. Below the menu bar on the right, find the Action drop-down list box. This box always contains a list of the actions you can take from whatever page you're currently on.

3. When the Add Controllers page opens, as shown in Figure 11.29, enter the IP address and subnet mask for the WLC you want to add and click OK to add the WLC to WCS.

The address that you enter is the address of the management interface.

FIGURE 11.29   Add Controllers page

It's important for you to know that the IP address and subnet mask provide the minimum information required to add a WLC.

On this screen, you also see the option to change the Simple Network Management Protocol (SNMP) version to match your implementation and further tweak SNMP options. These options are displayed in Figure 11.30.

 The WCS defaults to the current and most secure version of SNMP. Unless you have an older server that only supports an earlier version, it's best to just leave the default version in place.

4.   Once the WLC has been successfully added, you'll see it listed at the top of the Add Controllers page, as shown in Figure 11.30.

FIGURE 11.30   Successfully added WLC

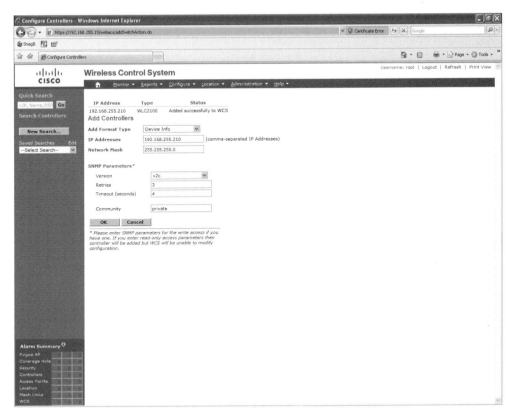

Congratulations—you did it! Now notice that you're still on the Add Controllers page, which is a great place to be if you have another controller to add because if so, you just enter the IP address and subnet mask of the next controller and click OK again. But if you don't need to enter another WLC and click OK, thinking it will get you to another page, it won't—you'll just get a message saying that the controller has already been added. To get out of here you need to move on to step 5…

5. Go back up to the Configure menu and click Controllers again. When the All Controllers page opens, you'll see the WLC that you added. Figure 11.31 shows the All Controllers page with the WLC that we've added.

FIGURE 11.31   All Controllers with a WLC

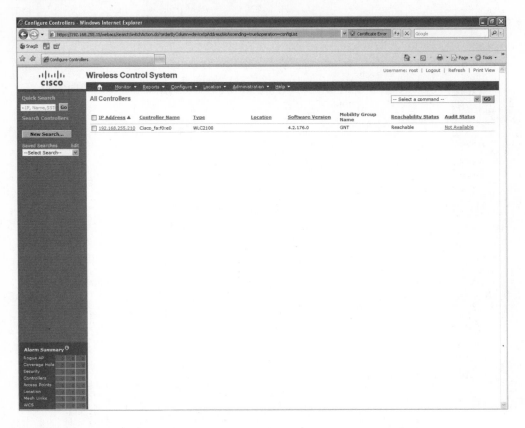

6. Click the hyperlinked IP address to bring up the WLC's Controller Properties page (shown in Figure 11.32).

7. On this page, you add the hostname, location, and contact information for your WLC. Again, you have an opportunity to modify the SNMP details. When you're finished, click OK.

FIGURE 11.32   Controller Properties page

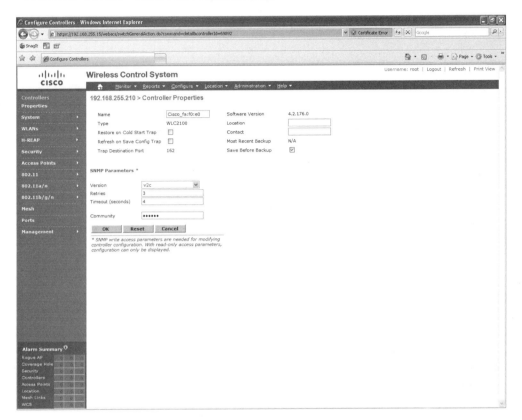

8. To access the WLC, view the summary, and make configuration changes, select the Controllers from the Monitor menu.

9. When the Search Results page opens—it looks pretty much the same as the All Controllers page—click the WLC IP address hyperlink. The WLCs summary page will be similar to the one shown in Figure 11.33. Notice how similar this is to the Monitor screen when configuring a WLC directly through its web-based GUI.

FIGURE 11.33 Controller Summary page

Managing the Controllers

You can manage controllers two ways after they've been added into the console. You can either select each one individually to make changes or you can create configuration templates and push the settings down to multiple controllers. If you're just dealing with a single controller, go with the manual method by navigating to Configure ➤ Controllers, as shown in Figure 11.34. Just click the controller you want to open the configuration page for to make any changes and then click Save at the bottom of the page.

If you have more than one controller in the mix, using templates is the way to go because you can save configurations and apply them as needed for new WLCs, or refresh existing ones. You can also use templates to pull in settings from an existing WLC that you like so much you want to duplicate it. Sounds great, but be aware that even though template settings can be applied to a WLC, those settings can always be overridden manually on any specific controller.

FIGURE 11.34   Configuring controllers

I probably don't need to tell you this but just in case, some settings like IP addresses that must be unique cannot be made a part of a template. What's great is that you can apply a template to all controllers, a single controller, or a preconfigured controller group. Remember that the reason you create templates is to address sections of the configuration and when they're saved, they'll be grouped by the specific configuration section that your template's design pertains to, as shown in Figure 11.35, and reached via Configure ➢ Controller Templates.

FIGURE 11.35   WLAN template

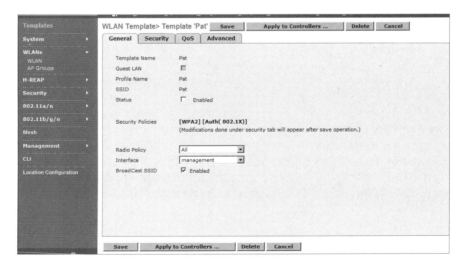

Setting Up APs

You can't add APs directly into the WCS interface because all APs require a WLC to operate on the network. Why? Because all the APs associate to a WLC, so when you add an WLC to the WCS interface, all its associated APs and network data will be passed by the WLCs up to the WCS. You end up with a hierarchical structure and that's when WCS truly becomes a central management application—sweet!

Let's take a look at some templates that will help us configure our APs.

A special type of template worth mentioning is called a radio template (see Figure 11.36). It's applied through the controller to the APs. When you want to create this template, just select the 802.11a or 802.11b/g section in the task list on the left.

FIGURE 11.36   Radio template configuration

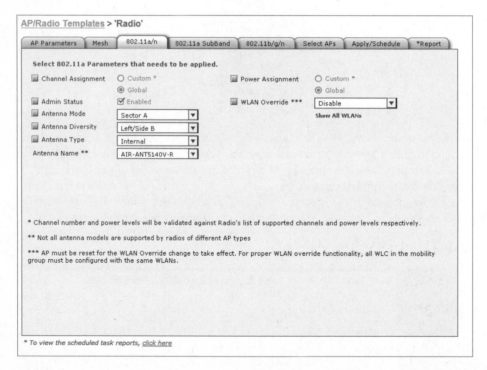

You can apply radio templates by selecting them from a list of APs, by controller or controller group, and even via a map hierarchy, which I'll get into later in the chapter. For now, understand that when applied to a map, the template will be applied to all APs of the same type on that map. To edit a radio template, just navigate to Configure AP Templates, select the template, and use the tabs to make changes, as you can see in Figure 11.37.

FIGURE 11.37 Radio Templates tabs

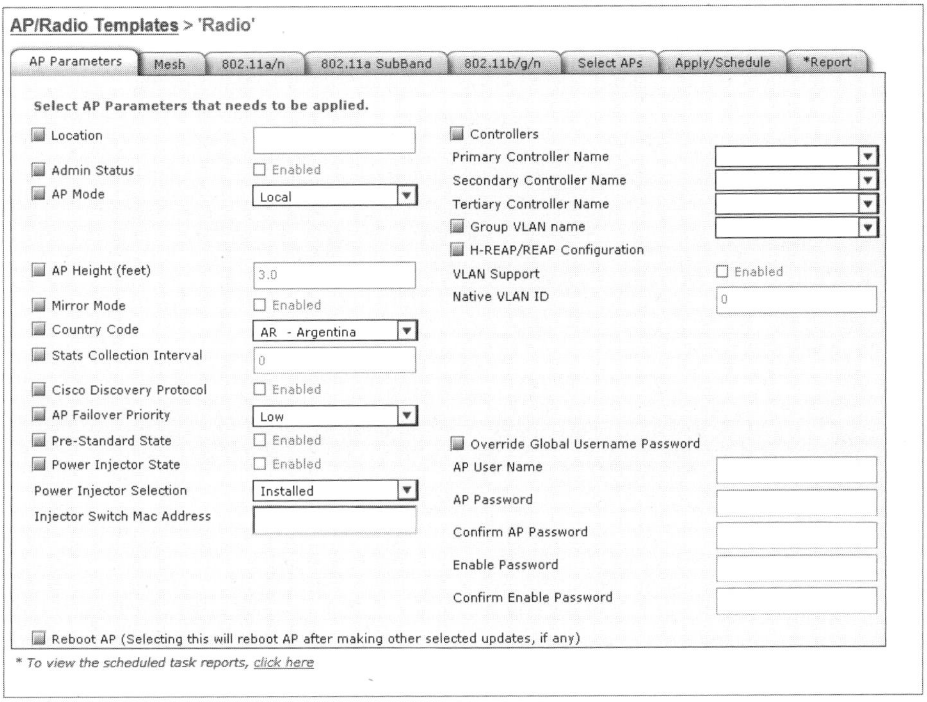

Creating Controller Groups

Controller groups can come in super handy when you want to make a change to a whole bunch of controllers at once. Keep in mind that all controllers in a group should also be in the same mobility group. Using templates for a controller group avoids messes that occur because of inconsistent information, so they can keep you out of trouble!

To create controller groups, choose Configure ➢ Config Groups, and all existing groups will appear. Use the Select A Command drop-down box to create a new group.

After you create a new group, you'll be guided through pages that allow you to set the mobility group name and country. You can also apply templates to the group, add controllers to it, and so forth. Know that once you've created the group, you can always return to the same location, select the group, and edit any settings by accessing the tabs for the group, as shown in Figure 11.38.

FIGURE 11.38   Config Groups

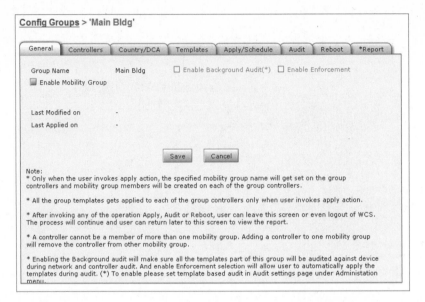

Audits

No matter how the controller(s) was initially added to the console of the WCS, know that one copy of the WLC configuration exists in the local database of the WLC and another one exists in the database of the WCS. It can be a good idea to compare the configuration on the controller to the one held in the WCS database now and then because inconsistencies can develop when and if changes are made to individual devices. To check and make sure your devices all agree, you need the Audit feature. Running an audit creates a report that will identify any inconsistencies. To conduct one, choose Configure ➢ Controllers ➢ Controller Name ➢ System ➢ Commands ➢ Audit Config ➢ Go. An example of an audit result appears in Figure 11.39.

In the drop-down box where you select Audit Config, notice that two more commands are available that need your attention before you execute the audit:

Refresh Config From Controller   This replaces the configuration in the WCS database with the one held locally on the WLC.

Restore Config To Controller   This replaces the configuration held locally on the WLC with the one in the WCS database.

After running your audit, the commands available to repair any inconsistency are:

Restore WCS Values   This replaces the configuration held locally on the WLC with the one held in the WCS database.

Refresh Controller Values   This replaces the configuration in the WCS database with the one held locally on the WLC.

FIGURE 11.39   An audit result

Auto Provisioning

You use the Auto Provisioning feature to push a given configuration to new or existing WLCs. To do so, you select Configuration ➢ Auto Provisioning, but first you need to set up a filter that determines which controllers will be monitored or auto-provisioned. Create this filter by selecting Auto Provisioning filters from the Auto Provisioning page. The New Filter drop-down box allows you to choose if the device(s) will be only monitored or auto-provisioned, how the device(s) will be identified, which group configuration you want to apply, and so on.

Once the filter has been created, you can set how the controller will be detected on the network—by its MAC address, serial number, or IP address. As soon as the device is detected, the configuration defined by the filter will be applied to it.

Configuring Maps

I know we've accomplished a lot so far, but still, much of the WCS's power and centralized control comes from having a configured campus map and by being able to place and track your APs and clients on that map. The basis for your map can be an existing site plan drawing—even an aerial or satellite photograph. With that image in place and dimensioned for the WCS, you can orient the APs to their physical location and configure the specific type of antenna they have. And once you've got your APs in place, the map displays their coverage and allows you to see possible interference issues, which is really helpful. In fact, you can wizard a ton of marvelous things with the Maps section!

Setting Up Campus Maps

Let's go through the process of adding a map to this WCS:

1. Select Monitor ➢ Maps, which will bring up the Maps page, as shown in Figure 11.40.

FIGURE 11.40   Maps page

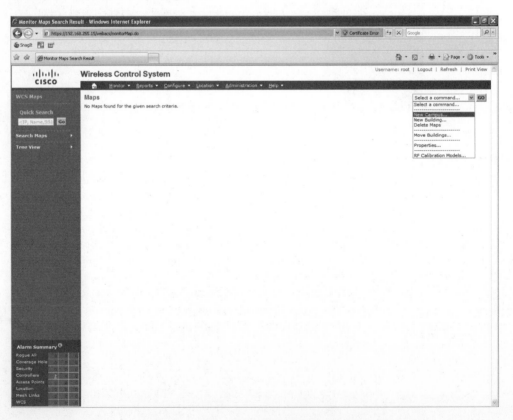

2. Select New Campus from the Action drop-down list box and click Go.

3. When the New Campus page opens, you can configure a campus name and the contact for the campus. Enter a descriptive name for the campus and the name of the contact person who can provide information about that campus.

4. Browse to an image of the campus and select the file you want included in the configuration. Then, click Next when you're done. You can see my configuration in Figure 11.41.

5. Now, dimension your campus map. When you see the image you added to the campus map on the New Campus page, enter the dimensions of the area shown in the image and make sure it's accurate. These distances will be used for showing scale and how far the RF in the network is reaching. When done, click OK to create the map. For an example, check out my map in Figure 11.42.

FIGURE 11.41 Adding a map file

Adding an Image to Your Configuration

But wait... How do you add an image to your configuration? Well, first choose an existing plan or picture. The image file can be a JPEG, GIF, BMP, or PNG file. As I mentioned, site plans or satellite photos work really well. I've even found that online mapping services offering satellite pictures of your area are good sources for appropriate campus images—in fact, the photo you'll see in Figure 11.42 in just a moment happens to be a satellite photo of my office complex. Be sure that the Maintain Aspect Ratio check box on the New Campus page is checked because you want the image to reflect accurate dimensions for your campus. By default, campus maps are dimensioned in feet, but you can modify the WCS to accept metric measurements as well.

FIGURE 11.42   Configuring a map

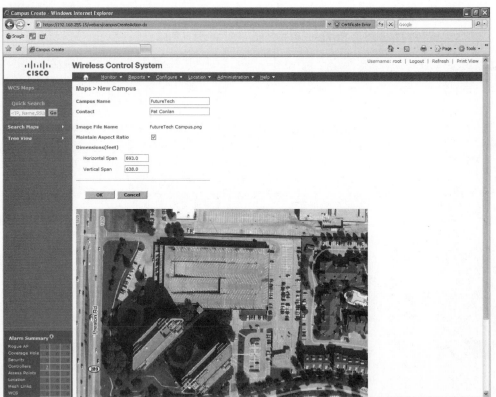

Setting Up Building Maps

As long as no outdoor areas are included or planned to be part of your campus map, buildings can be used as stand-alone entries. To create a building map, choose Monitor ➢ Maps and select the campus map where the building is located. Then complete these two steps:

1. When the MAP page opens, select New Building from the Action drop-down list box and then click Go.

2. Choose a building to be placed in the campus map by dragging the blue rectangular box over to the building of choice. If the box is the wrong size, just press Ctrl and left-click to resize it. Then enter the building's name, its contact for your network, its dimensions, and its characteristics.

   Choosing a building creates a link for a new building map, which is basically a floor plan of the building you've selected. You can then use that floor plan to place your APs more realistically.

   Configuring buildings in this way creates a hierarchy with the maps. Once all the maps are loaded, you can select one of them from the campus map and drill down for details about each building. Figure 11.43 shows a snapshot of the building placement page.

FIGURE 11.43   New Building page

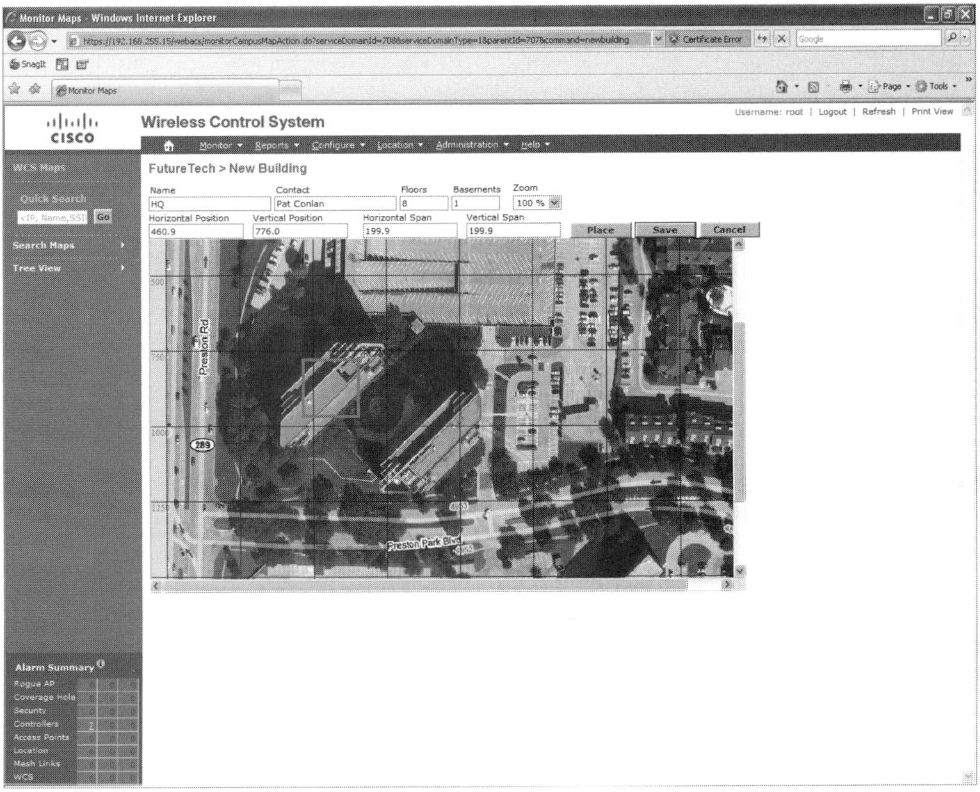

Oh, one last thing—clicking that little house icon on the upper-left corner of any page brings you back to the WCS Home page (see Figure 11.44). If you click it now, you can see that you've added one controller to the interface. Of course, if that controller has any APs associated with it, you'll also see those on the Home page. Here's what my Home page looks like now:

FIGURE 11.44 Home page

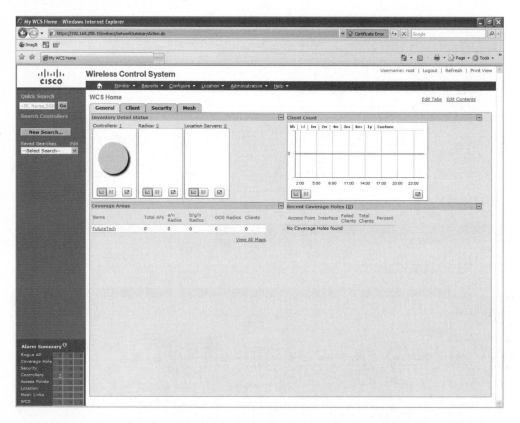

Setting Up Floor Plan Maps

This is all awesome stuff but we're not done yet—once campus maps and building maps are created, you can zero in further by creating floor maps from your building maps. This is where you can get a seriously detailed view of the environment and the location of all devices, which definitely rocks! So let's get to it. To create a floor map, navigate to a building map that you created and select New Floor Area. When the New Floor Area box appears, fill in all relevant information, as demonstrated in Figure 11.45.

FIGURE 11.45 Creating a new floor area

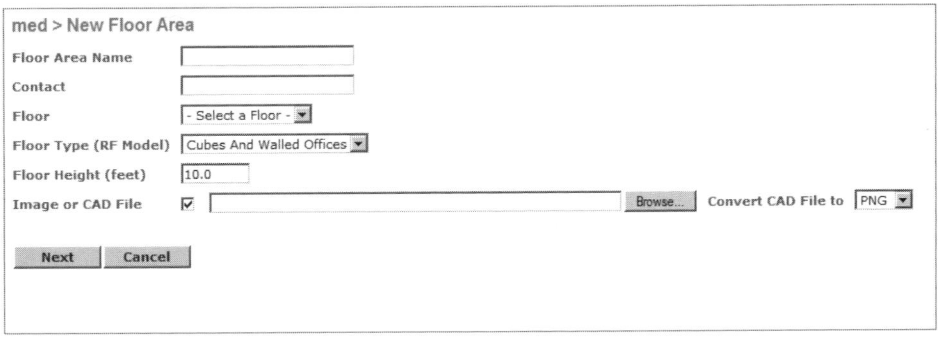

Keep in mind that your map is only as good as the quality of the information that you enter in these various boxes. So make sure everything is totally on target, especially if you plan to use the predictive site survey feature that I'll be showing you soon. You also need to select the check box to launch the Map Editor so you can rescale floors and draw walls. In Figure 11.45, the image file of the floor has been added by browsing to the floor plan's location.

Setting Up APs on Maps

Okay, now it's time to add the APs to your map. To do this, just go to the floor area map you created previously and select Add Access Points from the drop-down box, as shown in Figure 11.46.

When the Add Access Points dialog box appears, check the boxes next to APs you want added, as shown in Figure 11.47.

FIGURE 11.46 Adding APs

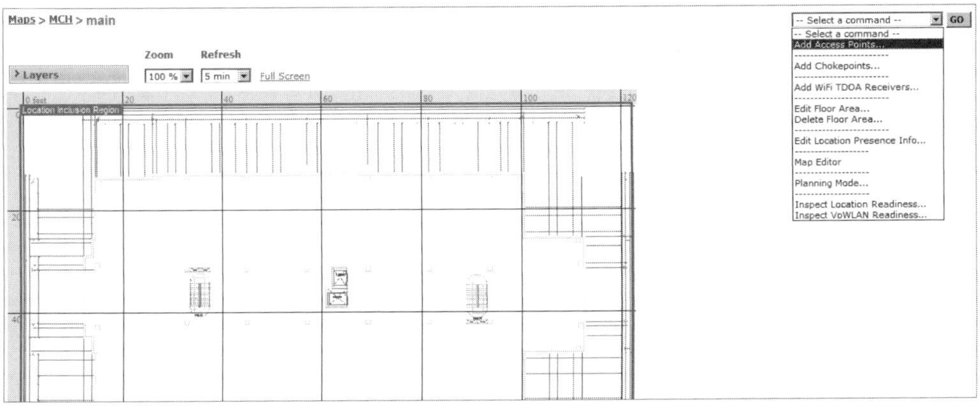

FIGURE 11.47   Select the check boxes next to APs you want to add.

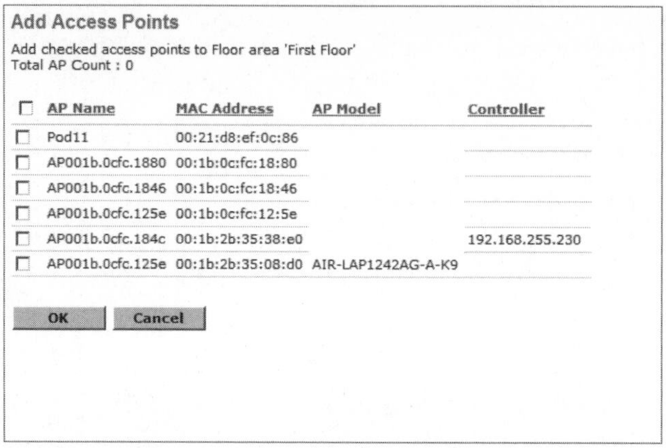

Add Access Points

Add checked access points to Floor area 'First Floor'
Total AP Count : 0

☐	AP Name	MAC Address	AP Model	Controller
☐	Pod11	00:21:d8:ef:0c:86		
☐	AP001b.0cfc.1880	00:1b:0c:fc:18:80		
☐	AP001b.0cfc.1846	00:1b:0c:fc:18:46		
☐	AP001b.0cfc.125e	00:1b:0c:fc:12:5e		
☐	AP001b.0cfc.184c	00:1b:2b:35:38:e0		192.168.255.230
☐	AP001b.0cfc.125e	00:1b:2b:35:08:d0	AIR-LAP1242AG-A-K9	

[OK]   [Cancel]

All the APs you select will be lined up in the upper-left corner of the map. You just drag each one to wherever you want it and drop it there. You should also click on each AP and set its characteristics (such as antenna type and orientation and radio type). Once all your APs are placed and defined, you can run an RF prediction to generate a heat map.

 If you do not indicate otherwise, the WCS will automatically orient the antenna at 90 degrees.

Keep in mind that if you need to edit the map, it's important to use the Map Editor tool that reflects all walls as well as their thicknesses and composition.

Planning Tool

This is a really cool tool—to access it, choose Monitor ➢ Maps, select a map, and choose Planning Mode from the drop-down list. Now you can calculate the number of APs required to cover the area as well as their optimal locations. In the Add APs section on the left side of the Add APs screen, you can choose the type of service the APs will provide, determine the type of optimization (coverage or capacity), the protocol (802.11a or 802.11b/g), and other vital characteristics. When you're done, click Calculate. In Figure 11.48, the Planning Mode tool has determined that three APs are needed, as you can see in the lower-left corner.

By clicking Apply, you open another box depicting the suggested location of your APs, as seen in Figure 11.49.

Now you have the information you need to generate an accurate proposal based on your findings, as shown in Figure 11.50. Very nice! The second image is the heat map for the proposal.

FIGURE 11.48   Planning tool

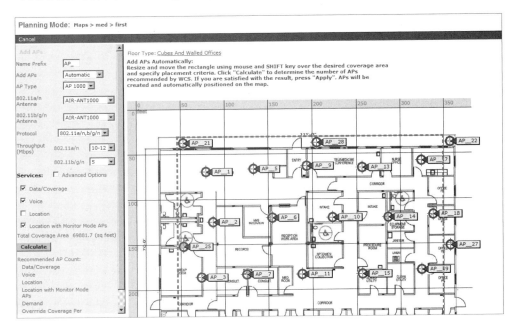

FIGURE 11.49   Suggested location of APs

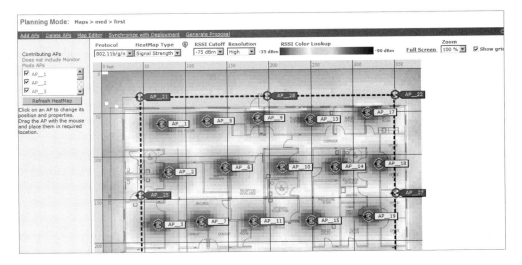

FIGURE 11.50   Generating a proposal

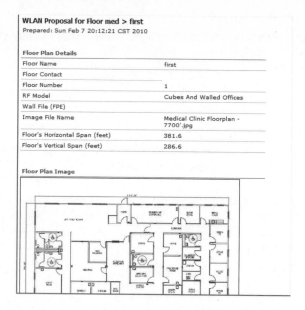

Monitoring the CUWN with WCS

Once your network is deployed, the main thing you'll use the WCS for is to monitor the WLAN. If there will be more than one administrator using the WCS, each user's view of it can be customized to provide them with the events relevant to whatever role they play. We'll cover customization, everything you need to know about the main Monitor page, the Alarms dashboard, and the processes involved in monitoring controllers, APs, and clients. I'll wrap things up by showing you how to locate all devices.

 Real World Scenario

When to Use the WCS in Your CUWN

Well now, here I am once again sitting in my favorite booth, in what *used* to be my favorite coffee shop in Boulder, when my soon-to-be-ex-buddy, who now has pretty much *all* my CUWN gear, approaches with that all too familiar look in his eye... Noooo! We all know by now that this is somehow going to end up with Bean Man keeping more of my wireless gear, right?

Since I am almost done with my book, I'm thinking this guy is totally out of favors. But then, well, I have consumed vast amounts of his inventory. Plus, he already has my complete CUWN network in his corporate office and remote shops anyway, so I might as well just hook up WCS to help me write this chapter and finish it off. Also, turning the situation around by experimenting with Bean Man's network will nicely even the score. After all, his network isn't actually big enough to call for WCS because the network is running fine, and this size network is really easy to administer by just using the web interface of the 2106 controllers instead. But if his network were to grow larger, I'd definitely want to install WCS with Cisco's Spectrum Expert to help manage and troubleshoot that heftier network.

Personalizing the Home Page

After an individual administrative user has logged into the WCS, he or she can customize their own Home page. The Home page is organized by the General, Client, Security, and Mesh tabs, and in the upper-right corner of the page, you'll find an option called Edit Tabs. When the Edit Tabs dialog box opens, you can create new tabs, as seen in Figure 11.51. You can set the order of the tabs and remove any of them—including the default tabs—from view, as shown in Figure 11.51.

FIGURE 11.51 Editing tabs

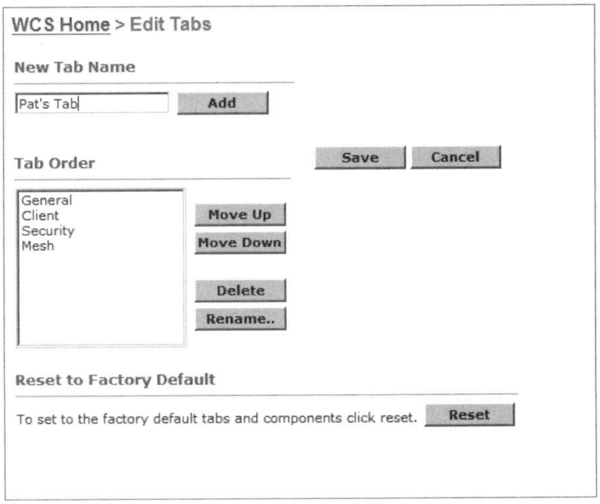

Even better, once the tab has been added, you can populate it with what you would like to see, as shown in Figure 11.52.

FIGURE 11.52   Selecting contents for your tab

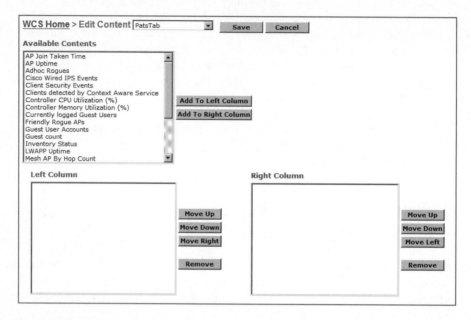

The end result is a personalized tab that shows only the items required by the user, as shown in Figure 11.53.

FIGURE 11.53   Personalized tab

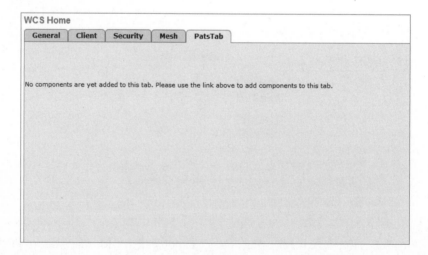

Using the Monitor Tab

I want to make something clear—you don't use tabs to monitor the WLAN; you use the Monitor menu feature from the top of the Home page. When you select Monitor, a drop-down menu allows you to pick whatever you want to monitor from a list. So let me introduce you to some of the things you can monitor and take a look at the screens that these sections provide.

Monitoring Controllers

By navigating to Monitor ➢ Controllers and entering an IP address, you can monitor any individual controller in real time. You'll get to check out important factors like client count, link activity, and version, as you can see in Figure 11.54.

FIGURE 11.54   Monitoring controllers

Just so you know, what you're seeing on this particular page is only a small part of everything that can be displayed. By selecting items on the task menu over on the left of the screen, you can also see which clients are connected, the WLANs configured, port status, and information about roaming, as well as current settings.

Monitoring APs

Selecting Monitor ➤APs instead of Monitor ➤ Controllers allows you to select an AP and display real-time information about it (see Figure 11.55).

FIGURE 11.55   Monitoring access points

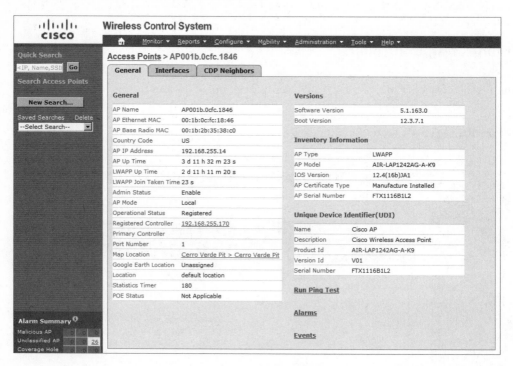

You can also select Alarms or Events on this screen to see if anything like that has been generated by the AP you're checking up on—a great troubleshooting tool!

Monitoring Clients

Arriving at this screen via Monitor ➤ Clients will get you to the same screen as the previous two, which shows you a summary page of clients displayed along with the AP they're associated with, as shown in Figure 11.56. The clients are organized by priority in this order: any APs that happen to be generating notifications, those that are manually disabled, the ones associated with the top five APs in the client count, and those detected by a location device bringing up the rear.

In the lower-right corner of the Clients Summary screen is a graph showing the client count for a specific SSID over time. Below the client count graph is the Client Troubleshooting tool. Entering a client's MAC address will bring up this very handy tool, which we'll cover in detail in Chapter 12.

FIGURE 11.56   Clients Summary screen

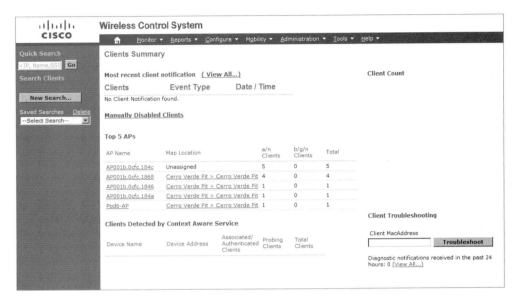

Monitoring Security

Selecting Monitor ➢ Security displays a page offering important security items that are organized like this:

Malicious Rogue APs   APs that have been positively identified as rogues.

Friendly Rouge APs   APs that are non-LWAPP but that have been identified as a legitimate part of the WLAN.

Unclassified Rogue APs   APs that haven't been classified as friendly or malicious yet.

Signature Attacks   Common attacks that are identified by an attack signature.

AP Threats/Attacks   Patterns that indicate a possible attack based on AP impersonation.

Client Security Related   Events that could be caused by replay or encryption-related attacks.

Rogue Ad Hocs   Any ad hoc networks that have been detected.

IPSec Failures   This feature is no longer supported.

So, as you can see in Figure 11.57, there are within each category running totals of each event type by last hour, by last day, and by total active.

FIGURE 11.57   Security Summary page

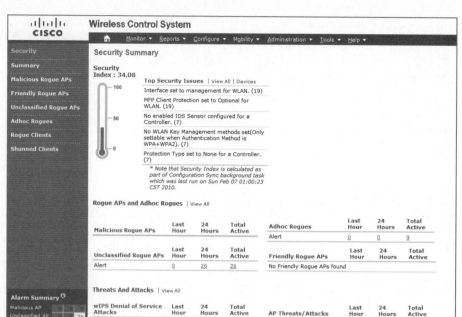

Monitoring Alarms

Selecting Monitor ➢ Alarms will display a list of alarms that have been generated. On the left side of this page are drop-down boxes that enable you to choose the type of event you're interested in and its severity level. Once you've viewed the alarms, you can take an action on them by checking the alarm(s) and then using the Select A Command drop-down box in the upper-left corner. These actions include Assign To Me, Unassign, Delete, Clear, Acknowledged, and Unacknowledged (see Figure 11.58).

FIGURE 11.58   Monitor Alarms page

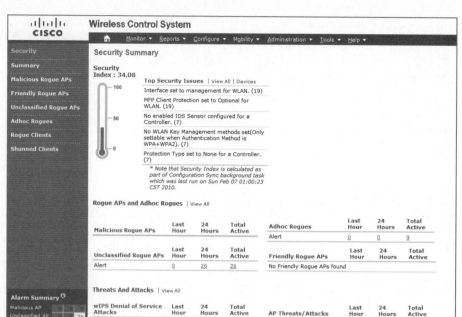

While we're on the subject of alarms, you may have noticed in the main page of the WCS that there's a grid in the lower-left corner comprised of a variety of colors. This is the Alarm dashboard, and it keeps a color-coded count of the alarms generated. As shown in Figure 11.59, the color legend is:

- Clear = no alarm

- Yellow = minor alarm

- Orange = major alarm

- Red = critical alarm

FIGURE 11.59 Alarm Summary page

Monitoring Events

Not all events are considered alarms, so if you want to see all events, just choose Monitor ➢ Events and they'll all be displayed, as shown in Figure 11.60. You'll get to check out each event's date, time, severity level, failure object, and its message. On the left sidebar, events can be filtered by severity and event category, just like on the Monitor Alarms page.

FIGURE 11.60 Monitor Events page

Locating Devices

The WCS offers three types of location tracking that are important for you to understand:

RF Closest AP   This will only identify the signal strength as received by the closest AP and is the least accurate because an individual AP's cell can be thousands of square feet.

RF Triangulation   This uses three points of reference to the signal so it's a lot more accurate, but it doesn't account for building materials.

RF Fingerprinting   This is the most accurate and even uses prediction tools. Fingerprinting includes accounting for loss due to obstructions by comparing the signal received from nearby APs to the expected signal received if no obstructions were present.

When operating without a location device, it can only locate one device at a time, on demand. It is 90 percent accurate to within 10 meters and 50 percent to within 5 meters. But when you add a dedicated location appliance, 2,500 devices can be located!

The Cisco Location appliance queries the controllers and retrieves all MAC addresses seen by all APs. Then it computes the location of each device. The WCS will query the Location device for the data and display it on a map.

The Quick Search feature on the main menu bar can be used to locate a device at any time. These searches can be carried out for a single device or for a category of devices. When the list displays, just click on any single device and the information about it will appear. In the Select A Command drop-down box, choose one of these two items as needed:

Present Map   This will display the device if it's still present.

Recent Map   This will display a device's last known location if it's no longer present.

Summary

In this chapter I covered the most necessary optional component of the CUWN—the amazing Wireless Control System (WCS). I showed you the various types of WCS that you can put on your network, and you learned all about centralized control, maps, configuration with and without templates, monitoring, and location tracking. We covered a lot; congratulations, you made it through!

Exam Essentials

Know how to add a WLS to the WLC and what results from the process.   This process requires the IP address of the management interface of the WLC. When this is completed, the WLC will upload all its information to the database of the WCS.

Be able to navigate the WCS console to view a list of APs or a list of controllers.   This is done for AP through Configure ➢ Access Points and for controllers through Configure ➢ Controllers.

Know the types of images that can be used with the map feature in the WCS.   Four file formats are used when importing a single campus map into the Cisco WCS 5.0: BMP, GIF, JPEG, and PNG.

Understand the importance of downloading the proper version of WCS for your server.   Although the functionality is identical, there is a Windows Server 2003 version and a Red Hat Linux version.

Written Lab

1. True/False: If you leave it to the defaults, any AP placed on a map will have its antenna oriented at 90 degrees.

2. True/False: The only difference between the WCS Base and the WCS Location versions is that the Location version can locate single devices on demand.

3. True/False: The WCS uses RF Triangulation for locating devices.

4. What is the most accurate form of location tracking?

5. How accurate is the WCS in location tracking?

6. How many devices can the WCS with Location Appliance track?

7. What type of license is required to support 500 APs?

8. True/False: Controllers is a tab on the Home page of the WCS.

9. True/False: Noise and inference can be displayed by channel.

10. What device can be added to identify interference in real time?

Hands-On Labs

To complete the labs in this section, you will need a copy of the Cisco WCS software, a computer running Windows Server 2003, and a PC. You will also need a license file for the software using a name that matches the name of the Windows server. The two computers should be connected to the switch.

Here is a list of the labs in this chapter:

Lab 11.1: Installing the WCS

Lab 11.2: Creating an Administrative Account

Lab 11.1: Installing the WCS

For this lab you will need a copy of the Cisco WCS software which can be obtained from Cisco with a valid account. You will also need a license file for the software using a name that matches the name of the Windows Server 2003. Connect the two computers to the switch. You can assign any IP address you like but they should be in the same subnet. In the lab it will be assumed that the address of the server is 192.168.1.1/24 and the PC is 192.168.1.2/24.

1. Copy the WCS software file and the license file to the desktop (or any location) on the Windows server.

2. Double-click the WCS software file to begin the installer program and wait for the initial setup screen to appear. This could take a couple of minutes. When the initial configuration screen appears, read the information and click Next.

3. Read and agree to the software license, and then click Next.

4. When the Check Ports dialog box opens, enter the HTTP and HTTPS ports for your server. The default is HTTP port 80 and HTTPS port 443. Click Next.

5. When the Password Restrictions information appears, read the restrictions, devise a root password that meets all of the requirements, and click Next.

6. Enter the root password and click Next.

7. Verify the root password by reentering it.

8. Devise a new password that meets all the password restrictions. This will be the password that secures the root FTP server. Enter the FTP password in the Enter FTP Password dialog box and click Next.

9. Specify the folder to be used for the FTP server files. Cisco recommends that the folder be located on a path different from that of the WCS installation. This preserves your FTP server files in case you ever uninstall WCS. The default path is C:\. Click Choose and specify a different path, one that is appropriate for your system. When you are finished, click Next.

10. Specify the folder to be used for TFTP server files. Again, Cisco recommends that the folder be located on a path different from that of the WCS installation. This preserves files uploaded from or downloaded to controllers in case you ever uninstall WCS. The default path is C:\. Click Choose and specify a different path, one that is appropriate for your system. When you are finished, click Next. (If your machine is multihoned, you will see an additional screen that lets you choose the interface used to host the WCS.)

11. Specify the installation path for the WCS software. Typically, the default installation path is appropriate for most systems. Click Choose if you need to change the path for your system. When you are finished, click Next.

12. Specify the shortcut folder for the WCS software. Typically, the default new program group is appropriate for most systems, but you have other options. You can drop the shortcut into:

    - An existing program group
    - The Start menu
    - The Quick Launch bar
    - Another location you specify

    You can also choose to create icons for all users or create no icons at all. Click Next when you are finished.

13. When the Pre-Installation Summary screen opens, double-check your settings and make sure that your system has enough disk space for the installation. Click Next to begin the software installation.

14. Wait while the software installs. Installation messages and a progress bar allow you to monitor the installation.

15. Once the installation is complete, a message box opens and allows you to choose whether to begin service immediately. Click Yes.

16. Wait while WCS starts. Once WCS is started, you will be returned to the installer. Review the on-screen information and click Done to exit the installer.

Lab 11.2: Creating an Administrative Account

1. On the PC, launch the browser and enter the address **https:\\192.168.1.1**.

2. When the WCS login box appears, enter the root password you created earlier during the installation.

3. When the License warning box appears, click OK, select the Help menu, and choose Licensing. Select Add A License. Browse to the location of the file and select Upload. Now the WCS is functional.

4. From the menu at the top of the Home page, select Administration. Navigate to AAA, and then click Users on the left side of the page.

5. When the New User dialog box appears, enter a username and password. Confirm the password.

6. At the bottom of this box, select the Admin check box.

7. Click Submit and the account is created.

8. Log out of the WCS and ensure that you can log in as the new user.

Review Questions

1. Which of the following paths will lead to the area used to create a user account?

    A. Administration ➤ AAA

    B. Configure ➤ Users

    C. Administration ➤ Settings

    D. Configure ➤ Accounts

2. What permission must be assigned to the account used to connect to the Navigator from the WCS?

    A. Admin

    B. Config Managers

    C. North Bound API

    D. Superuser

3. Which of the following paths will lead to the area used to configure an email server for the WCS?

    A. Administration ➤ SMTP

    B. Administration ➤ Mail Server

    C. Configure ➤ Administration

    D. Configure ➤ SMTP ➤ Mail Server

4. Which of the following fields is not found in the list of controllers on the Controllers page?

    A. IP Address

    B. Controller Name

    C. AP Count

    D. Type

5. How many Cisco Spectrum Experts can send information to the WCS?

    A. 20

    B. 10

    C. 15

    D. 30

6. Which of the following statements are true of the Cisco Navigator?

    A. The WCS and the Navigator must be on independent machines.

    B. The Navigator requires IE 5.0.

    C. Windows Vista and XP can be used for the Navigator.

    D. Up to 30 WCS instances are supported by the Navigator.

7. What is the total number of APs that the Navigator can support?

    A. 10,000

    B. 15,000

    C. 20,000

    D. 30,000

8. Which of the following is supported to install WCS?

    A. Windows Server 2000

    B. Windows NT Server

    C. Windows Server 2003

    D. Red Hat Linux AS 2

9. Which port numbers must be open on the server running WCS? (Choose two.)

    A. 88

    B. 80

    C. 444

    D. 443

10. Which version of WCS installation software can detect a prior installation and offer an upgrade option?

    A. Later than 4.2.55

    B. Later than 4.2.62

    C. Later than 4.1.20

    D. Later than 4.0.33

11. With respect to the license file for the WCS, what must match between the license file and the server on which it will be installed?

    A. The IP address

    B. The MAC address

    C. The port number used for WCS service

    D. The server name

12. What type of menu is *not* present on the Home page of the WCS?

    A. Horizontal menus

    B. Vertical menus

    C. Status options

    D. Icon-based toolbars

13. In which area of the WCS interface would you schedule regular configuration backups?

   A. Background Tasks

   B. Logging

   C. Settings

   D. AAA

14. When adding a controller, you use the IP address of which interface on the WLC?

   A. Management

   B. Service

   C. Console

   D. Port 1

15. Which function is used to maintain consistency between the WLC configuration and the WCS database configuration?

   A. Synchronize

   B. Replicate

   C. Audit

   D. Transfer

16. Which of the following settings cannot be pushed to the controllers with a template?

   A. Radio settings

   B. Security settings

   C. AP settings

   D. IP addresses

17. What is used when creating a building map from a campus map to define the building?

   A. Blue rectangle

   B. Red pointer

   C. Eyeglass icon

   D. Outline pen

18. After you select the APs to be added to a floor map, where will these APs be located until you place them?

   A. In the center of the map

   B. In the lower-left corner

   C. In the upper-left corner

   D. In the lower-right corner

19. Which information can the prediction tool *not* suggest after running the tool? (Choose all that apply.)

    A. Number of APs

    B. Location of APs

    C. Type of APs

    D. Type of service

20. What color indicates a major alarm in the Alarm dashboard?

    A. Clear

    B. Red

    C. Orange

    D. Yellow

Answers to Review Questions

1. A. The complete path to the New User dialog box is Administration ➢ AAA ➢ Users.

2. C. The username required to contact the WCS must be given North Bound API rights. This API is used for integration with third-party utilities. Since WCS and the Navigator are on different hardware platforms, rights to this API must be granted when adding the WCS to the Navigator.

3. B. The path that leads to the area used to configure an email server for the WCS is Administration ➢ Mail Server.

4. C. The following fields are found in the list of controllers on the Controllers page: IP Address, Controller Name, Type, Location, and Mobility Group.

5. B. Ten Cisco Spectrum Experts can send information to the WCS.

6. A. The WCS and the Navigator must be on independent machines; the Navigator requires IE 6.0 or higher, the Navigator must be installed on a server operating system, and 20 instances of WCS are supported.

7. D. A total of 30,000 APs can be supported by the Navigator.

8. C. Only Windows Server 2003 and Red Hat Linux AS 4 are supported to install WCS.

9. B, D. The port numbers that must be open are 2000, 1315, 21, 8456, 8457, 80, 443, 1299, 69, 162, and 8009.

10. B. WCS installation software later than 4.2.62 can detect a prior installation and offer an upgrade option.

11. D. The server name in the file must match the name of the server.

12. D. There are no icon-based toolbars on the Home page of the WCS.

13. A. Regular configuration backups are scheduled in Background Tasks.

14. A. When adding a controller, you use the IP address of the management interface on the WLC.

15. C. The Audit function is used to maintain consistency between the WLC configuration and the configuration in the WCS database.

16. D. Settings that must be unique such as IP addresses cannot be pushed to the controllers with a template.

17. A. An expandable blue rectangle is used to define the building when creating a building map from a campus map.

18. C. After you select the APs to be added to a floor map, the APs will be located in the upper-left corner.

19. C, D. The type of APs and the type of service are provided before running the tool.

20. C. The color codes in the Alarm dashboard are Red: critical, Orange: major, Yellow: minor, and Clear: no alarm.

Answers to Written Lab

1. True

2. False

3. False

4. RF fingerprinting

5. 90 percent within 10 meters and 50 percent within 5 meters

6. 2,500

7. Enterprise

8. False

9. True

10. Cisco Spectrum Expert

Chapter
12

WLAN Maintenance and Troubleshooting

THE CCNA WIRELESS EXAM TOPICS COVERED IN THIS CHAPTER ARE:

✓ **Conduct basic WLAN maintenance and troubleshooting**

- Identify basic WLAN troubleshooting methods for controllers, access points, and clients methodologies

- Describe basic RF deployment considerations related to site survey design of data or VoWLAN applications, Common RF interference sources such as devices, building material, AP location Basic RF site survey design related to channel reuse, signal strength, cell overlap

- Describe the use of WLC show, debug, and logging

- Describe the use of the WCS client troubleshooting tool

- Transfer WLC config and O/S using maintenance tools and commands

- Describe and differentiate WLC WLAN management access methods (console port, CLI, telnet, ssh, http, https, wired versus wireless management)

Okay, so now that you've got a grasp on how to administrate controllers and APs via the Cisco WCS, plus how to use maps and monitor the network with it too, you're ready to dive into learning about some other very cool ways to access and manage WLAN devices. This is also a great time to fill you in about ongoing WLAN maintenance and some nice strategies for troubleshooting the problems that crop up in WLANs. I'll also cover some key deployment issues related to the environment in which the WLAN is operating, tell you how to manage configurations and back them up as well. It's going to be a pretty long chapter, but chock full of vital information, so get ready!

To find dynamic updates to this chapter, please go to www.lammle.com or www.sybex.com/go/ccnawireless.

Basic Troubleshooting Methods

Troubleshooting a wired network problem can range from an easy tweak to a major exercise in frustration. I'm not trying to scare anyone here, but to be straight with you, even though wired network troubleshooting can drive you to drink, troubleshooting a WLAN can drive you insane!

Wireless users can simply shuffle over a mere three feet and go from excellent reception to none at all stat if the network design happens to be a sloppy one. Plus, there are so many devices that can be involved—is it the client card, the AP, the controller, the RADIUS server, the DHCP server, or interference issues that's your glitch? And that's the short list! Basically, it just usually takes a lot more work and expertise to discover and fix the problem, or ugly mix of problems, when you're dealing with wireless network issues than when you're faced with those that typically come up in a more straightforward wired one.

As we move through this chapter, you'll probably notice a pattern emerging. That's because it's always best to start with the physical elements and work your way up the OSI model when diagnosing WLAN ills. I'm going to introduce you to an organized approach using some simple rules that can make the process as efficient as possible—I didn't say painless! But no worries, I'll also show you some handy tools that can give you some really nice clues to help speed up the process and get you to the root cause of a wireless problem much faster.

WLCs

By now, you know that WLCs are the hub of communication between the main players in a WLAN: the client, AP, RADIUS server, and DHCP server. Figuring out the kind of problem clients are having, like if they can't connect, can't authenticate, they're dropping out, etc. plus the scope of the problem, if it's only one SSID, all SSIDs, a single client, etc. can usually lead you to where things are falling apart. So let's start by exploring some common scenarios and how these problems can involve the WLC.

Your WLAN has been humming along with no problems for weeks and suddenly nothing works. It almost like you never set up the controller to begin with!   The first question to answer here is if there's been a power outage recently. When you make a change to the controller and click Apply, it only saves the change to RAM, not to NVRAM. So if you haven't clicked Save Configuration or typed `save config` from the command-line interface, the change will totally disappear when you reboot the WLC. And if this happens, all APs that are managed by the controller will be affected, along with all their clients. A good way to prepare is to always back up the configuration, which I'll show you how to do later in this chapter.

You've completed configuring the WLC with authentication that requires certificates on the controller, the AP, or the clients, and you were careful to save the configuration in NVRAM this time. But still, none of the clients using authentication methods that rely on certificates can authenticate—why?   In this case, check the time settings on the WLC. They should be in sync with all the other devices in the infrastructure. When certificates are in use, if this setting isn't in sync, the WLC may interpret the certificate as expired or invalid. Another more remote possibility is that the dates in the certificates were improperly configured. A flag that certificates are your problem is that they will probably only affect those specific clients using that form of authentication.

You've just finished configuring a new WLAN on an AP through the WLC and you verified that you saved the configuration, but clients still can't see the WLAN.   Okay, this sounds like a dumb question, but did you actually enable the WLAN? It must be associated with an interface on the controller, which is a VLAN. While you are at it, make sure the configuration of the VLAN is correct as well. If the cause is a VLAN problem, it will only affect the new WLAN and any other VLANs should all still be working just fine.

You find that roaming only works between certain members of a specific mobility group, but not all of them.   Well, does the virtual gateway address agree upon all members of the group? If not, this can clearly affect roaming. If the address matches but it's already in use or unreachable, it will affect all roaming capability on the network.

Clients are associating with the AP at Layer 2 but can't connect to anything else.   Find out if they're getting an IP address from the DHCP server. If these are Windows clients running Windows 2000 or later and you execute `ipconfig` on them, they'll have an IP address that starts with 169—something Microsoft calls APIPA (Automatic Private IP Addressing). So make sure that the controller is set with the address of the DHCP server or the DHCP relay, and that you can ping the DHCP server from the controller. If this all checks out, make sure the DHCP server has a scope for the VLAN to which the WLAN (SSID) is associated, and that enough addresses are configured. If it's a Windows DHCP server, the scope will have a blue exclamation point next to it if it's out of addresses. If the problem is due to a lack of connectivity from the controller to the DHCP server, all APs managed by the WLC and all of their clients will be affected. But if it's a scope problem on the DHCP server, only one WLAN (SSID) will be affected.

You made a change to either the WLC or the RADIUS server and now 802.1X authentication is not working.   This typically indicates one of three disorders: the RADIUS server address is incorrect in the WLC configuration, the port numbers do not match (use RADIUS ports 1812 and 1813), or the shared secret doesn't match on the two devices. Which one, though? For a clue to the culprit, find out if all the controllers are unable to perform 802.1x authentications or if it's just one. If they're all freaking out, it's probably the RADIUS server, but if only one WLC is having issues, it's probably just that one controller.

This list definitely doesn't include all possible nightmares, but it's a good place to start because it really does cover the most common ones.

APs

It's really hard to talk about AP issues and leave out their relationship to the WLC, and we covered most of that stuff above. Still, each AP does have some indicator lights that can tell you much about certain hang-ups. APs usually have one status LED, an Ethernet LED, and an LED for each radio. Each particular combination of colors and behaviors of these three LEDS indicates a different problem. To cover all possibilities for all models of APs would equal a full book in itself, but to give you an example, when the status LED is green and the others are off on an Aironet 1250, it means that everything is normal but that no devices are associated. If the same situation exists with the status LED being blue, at least one client is associated.

Another couple of scenarios appropriate for this book is if the status LED is alternating green, amber, and red. This means the AP is in the process of connecting to the controller. If the LEDs stay this way for an inordinate amount of time, you've probably got a problem between the AP and the controller. And if the status LED is blinking blue while the others are green, it means that it's loading the AP image file. You really need to refer to the documentation for each specific AP to properly interpret the LEDs for the particular model in question.

Another thing to keep in mind is that the AP is connected to a switch. As you probably know, switches also use LEDS to scream for help, so it could be a very good idea to check that connection out as well. Oh, and don't forget that the monitor page of the WLC can be used to determine if the AP is associated with its WLC as well. When an AP and its controller are having a problem connecting, the AP will not work at all.

Clients

If you've been able to narrow down the problem to a particular client, there are two areas to focus on. The first category includes physical problems, and the second, logical or configuration issues. Let's look at the physical issues first.

Physical Issues

Physical issues can and do affect clients even if the configuration of both the client and the AP are correct. Sometimes it's not so bad and you can simply tweak adjustments to either device and save the day. I've got to say, most of the situations I'm going to talk about can totally be avoided by doing a really solid site survey prior to deployment and testing everything well to verify the network once it's been installed!

Distance

The first factor is distance—clearly, the client must be within range of an AP. Sounds way too simple, I know, but sometimes users just don't get that. This is why it's good to clue in your users regarding the range of the wireless network they're on so they can pretty much resolve this issue themselves. But if all your users are complaining, well then, not so much. When this happens, you've got to check the LEDs on the AP and make sure that activity is showing up on the pertinent frequency spectrum (2.4GHz, 5GHz). If you find no activity, you may need to enable the radio, either through the controller or by directly connecting to the relevant AP's web interface.

Hidden Node

Next up is something referred to as a hidden node. This phenomenon occurs when two stations keep sending at the same time, causing collisions and retransmissions. Normally, when one station is sending, all other stations know how long to stay silent by reading a field in the frames called Duration. However, if there's some kind of obstruction between two stations, both may be able to hear the AP but not each other. This scenario is illustrated in Figure 12.1, where two nodes are close enough to hear each other but there's a wall between them that is blocking their ability to hear each other.

FIGURE 12.1   Hidden node

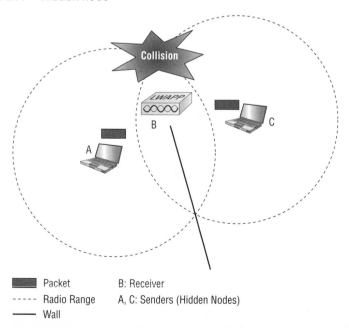

You can approach the hidden node problem in several ways. First, you can reduce the maximum size of the frames, which will reduce the impact of the collisions. However, doing this won't fix the problem.

A better way to deal with this issue is to enable Request to Send/Clear to Send (RTS/CTS) on the stations. It will add an additional step to the transmit process whereby the station will send an RTS frame to the AP and the AP will respond with a CTS. The purpose of the CTS is to ensure that all stations, including those behind walls, will be able to read the Duration field and remain silent. Any station that's associated with the AP should be able to hear this frame because the AP is sending it.

The problem with RTS/CTS is that it adds that extra step to communication even where it's not needed, even when there's no hidden node, which will slow down the WLAN's overall throughput. Of course, the best solution is to just remove the obstacle, but if that obstacle happens to be a load-bearing wall or some other kind of support, that's obviously not possible! This brings me back to nagging you about the importance of doing a thorough initial site survey in the first place, because if you do that, you can take steps to mitigate it (such as adding more APs or different antenna types).

Exposed Node

There's another nasty phenomenon that occurs known as an exposed node. In this case, two stations are close enough to be in range of each other and are operating on the same channel, but they're associated with different APs. Since they're each listening to frames from different BSSIDs about the Duration field, they'll frequently send at the same time, which can cause collisions, force retransmissions, and lower the throughput of both WLANs. This ugly problem can start with only two stations, as shown in Figure 12.2, and will grow worse as more stations enter the game.

Here again, this problem is a design issue that should have been avoided during the site survey and deployment. The APs are just too close to one another to be on the same channel and will cause a particular type of interference called co-channel interference. I'll talk more about this later, but for now, just keep in mind that when two APs have overlapping cells, they should be on channels that are at least five apart in the 2.4GHz range. In the 5.0GHz frequency, the channels technically do not overlap because there is a 20MHz space between them—for example, from channel 36 to 40—but to be safe you should put at least one channel between the two APs and use 36 and 44 instead. Here are three possible solutions:

- Move the APs farther apart, which isn't such a great idea of you want users to be able to roam between them without losing their connection. But, if configured correctly, most deployments would benefit from having APs that are farther apart when there are excessive collisions.

- Reduce the transmit power on each AP, which has the same effect as moving the APs farther apart.

- Change the channel on one of the APs so that the co-channel interference is eliminated. APs do not need to be on the same channel for seamless roaming because the stations follow the SSID, not the channel, and will switch channels in an instant if necessary.

FIGURE 12.2   Exposed node

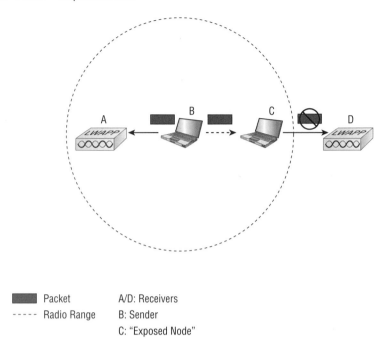

▬▬ Packet	A/D: Receivers
- - - - - Radio Range	B: Sender
	C: "Exposed Node"

Near-Far

Near-Far is really just what it says: this is a problem that can happen when multiple wireless users have wireless devices that are very near an access point and they find themselves much closer than a user who is right on the edge of the radio signal boundary.

Consider that five users can associate with an AP and they each have a laptop, an HP iPAQ, and a wireless phone. There goes all the AP's bandwidth! The user who is farthest away simply cannot be heard over the traffic from the devices closer to the access point. The users who are closest are hogging all the bandwidth.

Be careful with this one, because it can look just like a hidden node issue. The only difference is that a hidden node has collision errors and a near-far error does not. Both hosts will have poor bandwidth/response, which is why they appear similar.

So yes, always remember that the transmit power relationship between the AP and the stations is an important thing. Check out the top part of Figure 12.3.

FIGURE 12.3   Near-Far

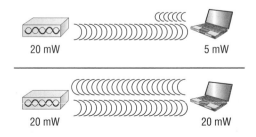

When a transmit power mismatch (which actually should be the name of this problem) is your suspected culprit, look at how the AP receives the signal—not just at what the RSSI or SNR is on the station. If the difference in power isn't all that much and the station is Cisco-Compatible Extensions (CCX) version 2 or later, the AP can instruct the station to adjust its power, as shown in the bottom part of Figure 12.3. But without these extensions, you'll probably have to make manual adjustments by either moving the client, decreasing the power of the clients closest to the AP, or adding a stronger WLAN card to the remote client(s).

Before we move on to configuration issues, I'd like to talk a bit about the Cisco Spectrum Expert. This cool (but somewhat expensive) tool is used to detect non-802.11 interference from things that could be causing physical layer problems, like microwave ovens, jammers, and Bluetooth. This Cisco-proprietary PC card plugs right into a laptop to identify and locate the guilty devices—sources not seen by many standard spectrum analyzers. This information can be sent to a WCS where data from multiple "Expert Stations" can be viewed on a single station. The Cisco Spectrum Expert is pretty awesome, and every high-availability WLAN should have one. It covers 2.4GHz and 5GHz (besides others) and does device identification, which most spectrum analyzers don't support.

Configuration Issues

With everything we just covered, you're ready to investigate issues that occur because of improper configuration. First, I'll cover some common Layer 2 configuration problems that can cause the station to be unable to associate with the AP. Here's a list of questions you need to find the answers to when troubleshooting snags in this category:

- Is the AP enabled for the proper frequency?
- Are the status lights on the AP showing activity?
- Is the client set with the correct SSID?
- Is there a MAC address list on the AP that's preventing the station from associating?
- If you're using open or shared-key authentication with WEP, do the keys and the key length match on the AP and the station?

Layer 3 configuration issues can cause the station to be unable to get beyond the AP to the network. Here are a few things to investigate involving Layer 3:

- Is the client receiving an IP address, or if it's static, is it in the WLAN's subnet?
- Are there any ACLs applied anywhere that may be preventing access to the network?
- Does the client have a local firewall enabled?

One of the benefits of using a WCS is that there are several pages in the interface that can be extremely helpful when you're troubleshooting the above issues as well as authentication issues. In the Troubleshooting Client page (see the next section, "Troubleshooting Tools"), we can see where the process of connecting is breaking down. It shows us that the DHCP process is failing and even provides suggestions on what to do about it.

Performance Issues

Sometimes everything is working but just not very well. Your network's throughput begins to suffer and data starts traveling at the pace of a drunken slug. Let's look at some things that cause degraded performance.

If your users all suddenly start complaining that they feel like they're back in the dial-up days, it could be due to the presence of a legacy station that just can't perform up to par. Some examples are 802.11b in an 802.11g network, or non-802.11n in an 802.11n network. It only takes one of these devices on your network to force all the other stations to slow their transmission rates down to its level. Why is this so? Well, remember earlier when I talked about data rates and mentioned that the higher data rates are achieved using different modulations (DSSS, OFMM, etc.)? When a legacy client that's unable to read information using these advanced techniques comes into the network, the AP will force all the other clients to use the old (read: slow) legacy techniques to match its legacy capacity.

Believe it or not, this can happen even if the station is merely present and not sending data. And worse, like an infection, this disease can even spread beyond the original cell to other cells, slowing them down too, as shown in Figure 12.4.

FIGURE 12.4   Cell spread

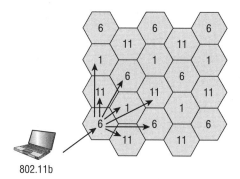

Another thing to note in Figure 12.4 is the proper use of channels when co-locating APs. The cure is to set the APs so that they only allow stations that are capable of the faster speeds by disabling all data rates supported by those older stations.

Troubleshooting Tools

There are a bunch of GUI tools to arm yourself with that really help when troubleshooting and most of them are operated from the WLC but not all. Let me introduce you to what's available in the arsenal.

Troubleshooting a Client Association with a WLAN Analyzer

When troubleshooting a client association, a WLAN analyzer can enable you to check out the raw frames and actually see what's going on between the AP and station. It also clearly helps to understand the association process and how things should be going, so even though I've covered this more than once in this book again, it's worth repeating here:

1. If the station is set with a profile containing the SSID and the AP is not broadcasting beacons, the client will begin by sending probe request frames.

2. The AP (or APs) will respond with probe response frames if probed by a client, but typically this step is provided by a beacon from the AP. These may come from APs on the same channel (or not).

3. If WEP is in use, the station will send an authentication request. Otherwise, it's simply open authentication, and the authentication will be successful every time.

4. The AP sends challenge text to the station and the stations encrypts the challenge using the WEP key before returning the encrypted challenge to the AP. This only happens with shared-key WEP, not with open system WEP, WPA, or WPA2.

5. The station requests association with an association request.

6. The AP sends an association response.

Sniffer in hand, you should be able to see this series of frames. If any step is failing, you should be able to open the frame details and determine the kind of error that's occurring.

This series of frames can be sorted and isolated from all the other frames you capture with a wireless sniffer—but be warned, there will be thousands!

GUI Tools on the WLC

Let's start by looking at some client details. If you navigate through Monitor ➢ Clients and then click the client MAC address in the web interface of the WLC, you can gather information about the AP and the client, which is why I mentioned the sniffer.

You can see the screen in Figure 12.5. Make special note of the Link Test button in the upper-right corner.

Further down on the same screen, as shown in Figure 12.6, you can check the received signal strength from the station as seen from the AP displayed nicely. Make note that CCX is required on the client to obtain this statistic, and non-CCX clients will not report all these displayed fields.

FIGURE 12.5   Note the Link Test button

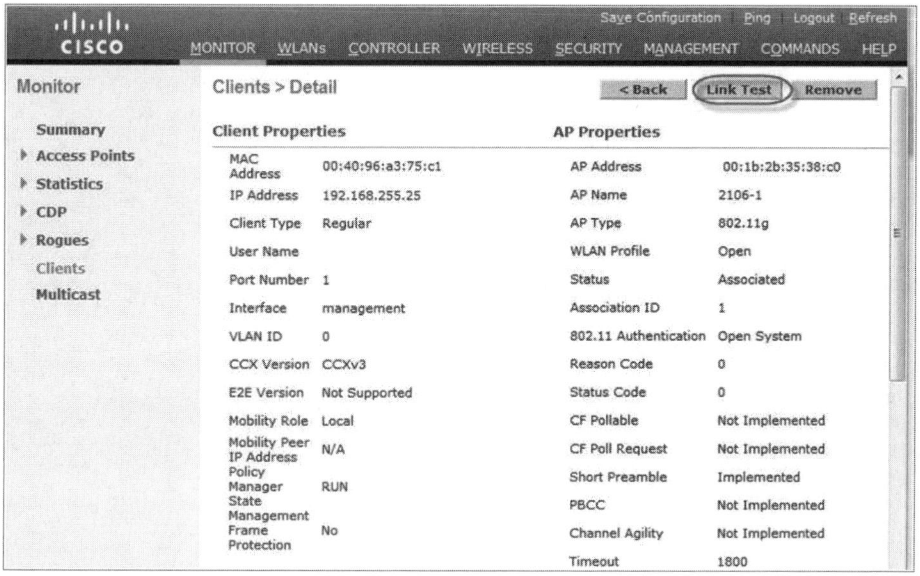

FIGURE 12.6   Checking the received signal strength

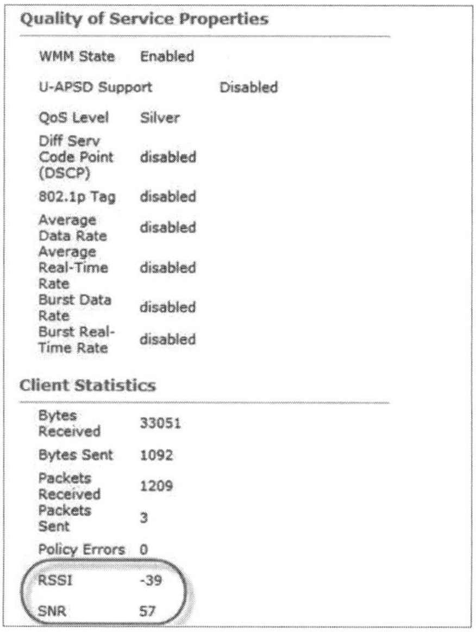

GUI Tools on the WCS

If you're lucky enough to have the Wireless Control System (WCS), it equips you with a trouble-shooting tool that can provide detailed and summary information spanning multiple APs and controllers—nice! Remember from Chapter 11, WCS is management software that you install on a Linux or Windows server, and it will give you a summary page showing a list of defined problems and suggested actions to take regarding them (see Figure 12.7).

FIGURE 12.7 WCS's main page

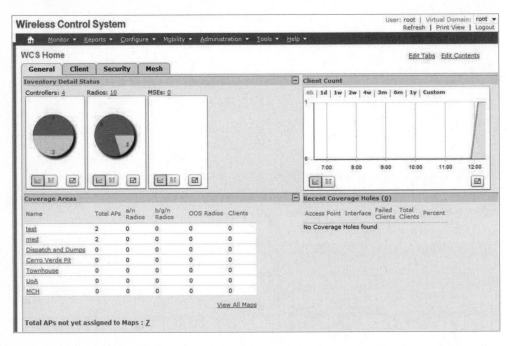

Now click Monitor ➢ Clients and in the resulting screen, enter the client MAC address, as shown in Figure 12.8.

After you type the MAC address, click Troubleshoot and you get two screens. The first is shown in Figure 12.9.

A pop-up screen (you may have to enable pop-up messages to see this screen) will provide more troubleshooting options for the client, as shown in Figure 12.10.

A nice approach here is to track the log messages generated by the process and sort them by message type. Select the Log Analysis tab on the Troubleshooting Client page and click Start, and then have the client attempt to associate. When the messages are generated they'll be displayed in the window at the bottom of this page. You can also sort them by type when you determine which phase the process is breaking down in to get to the bottom of the connection problem.

FIGURE 12.8 WCS client info

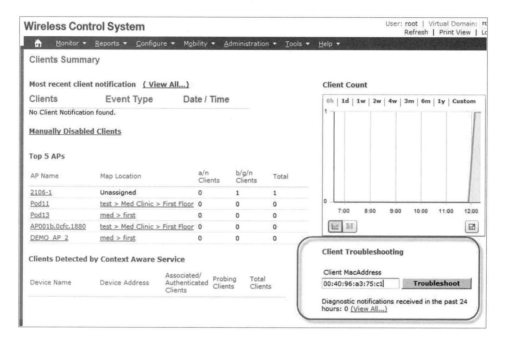

FIGURE 12.9 WCS client troubleshooting

Client 'unknown' - Cisco:a3:75:c1			-- Select a command

General | **Statistics** | **Location** | **Association History**

Client Properties

Client User Name	
Client IP Address	192.168.255.25
Client MAC Address	00:40:96:a3:75:c1
Client Vendor	Cisco
Controller	192.168.255.230
Port	1
Interface	management
VLAN ID	0
802.11 State	Associated
Mobility Role	Local
Policy Manager State	RUN
Mobility Peer IP Address	N/A

RF Properties

AP Name	2106-1
AP Type	Cisco AP
AP Base Radio MAC	00:1b:2b:35:38:c0
Protocol	802.11g
AP Mode	local
Profile Name	Open
SSID	Open
Association Id	1
Reason Code	None
802.11 Authentication	OPENSYSTEM

Security

Authenticated	Yes
Policy Type	N/A
Encryption Cipher	NONE
EAP Type	Unknown
NAC State	Access

FIGURE 12.10   WCS client troubleshooting pop-up

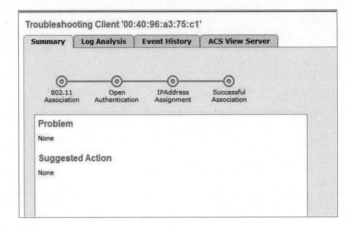

WLC CLI Troubleshooting

The WLC also has a command-line interface (CLI) that can give you some important information, especially if you're good at working from the command line. So let's take at a look at some handy commands that can get you this kind of detail.

debug Commands

If you execute the debug command on the controller with the question mark (?) parameter, you'll be presented with a list of the type of debug commands you can issue. The following is output from a controller:

```
(Cisco Controller) >debug ?
```

```
aaa              Configures the AAA debug options.
airewave-director Configures the Airewave Director debug options.
ap               Configures debug of Cisco AP.
arp              Configures debug of ARP.
bcast            Configures debug of broadcast.
cac              Configures the call admission control (CAC) debug options.
cckm             Configures the CCKM debug options.
ccxdiag          Configures the CCX Diagnostic debug options.
ccxrm            Configures the CCX_RM debug options.
ccxs69           Configures the CCX S69 debug options.
```

```
cdp             Configures debug of cdp.
client          Enables debugs for common client problems.
dhcp            Configures the DHCP debug options.
disable-all     Disables all debug messages.
dot1x           Configures the 802.1X debug options.
dot11           Configures the 802.11 events debug options.
emweb           Configures the WEB debug options.
ft              Configures the 802.11r debug options.
hreap           Configures debug of HREAP.
iapp            Configures the IAPP debug options.
fmchs           Configures the FMCHS debug options.
--More-- or (q)uit
```

You probably already know debug commands demand a lot of processor power, so you shouldn't just leave them running. To disable any debugging that you have running on the controller, just use this command:

```
(Cisco Controller)>debug disable-all
```

Running debug commands to a specific client can give you lots of insight and is a lot less processor intensive than running them against the entire system.

You do this in two steps. First, put the controller in client troubleshooting mode for the specific client you want to check out, and then specify the category of events you're interested in. Here's how that would look for a client with the MAC address 00:40:96:a3:75:c1:

```
(Cisco Controller>debug mac addr 00:40:96:a3:75:c1
(Cisco Controller>debug client 00:40:96:a3:75:c1
```

debug dot11

The debug dot11 command with its various parameters is great for troubleshooting a wide range of snags, including mobility, rogue detection, and load-balancing events. This command will show you each step of the association process, making it a lot easier to figure out exactly where your failure is. At the end of each step, it will indicate if a state transition occurred or not. Here is an example and output from the command:

```
(Cisco Controller) >debug dot11 ?
```

```
all             Configures debug of all 802.11 messages.
load-balancing Configures debug of 802.11 load balancing events.
locp            Configures debug of LOCP interface events.
management      Configures debug of 802.11 MAC management messages.
mobile          Configures debug of 802.11 mobile events.
rldp            Configures debug of 802.11 Rogue Location Discovery.
```

rogue   Configures debug of 802.11 rogue events.

state   Configures debug of 802.11 mobile state transitions.

(Cisco Controller) >**debug dot11 all enable**

(Cisco Controller) >*Jan 28 13:43:25.100: Rogue Classify: rssi=-86, client=0, duration=3060, wep=1, ssid=todds home network

*Jan 28 13:43:25.100: Rogue Classify: Rogue AP: 00:25:3c:26:00:b9 Classification:unclassified, RuleName:

*Jan 28 13:43:25.100: 00:40:96:a3:75:c1 APF update Rogue client: 00:40:96:a3:75:c1

*Jan 28 13:43:25.101: Rogue Classify: rssi=-81, client=0, duration=3060, wep=1, ssid=2WIRE983

*Jan 28 13:43:25.101: Rogue Classify: Rogue AP: 00:1f:b3:ef:f2:c1 Classification:unclassified, RuleName:

*Jan 28 13:43:25.101: Rogue Classify: rssi=-90, client=0, duration=2880, wep=1, ssid=FLIPMODE

*Jan 28 13:43:25.101: Rogue Classify: Rogue AP: 00:1b:2f:de:4b:ce Classification:unclassified, RuleName:

*Jan 28 13:43:25.102: Rogue Classify: rssi=-92, client=0, duration=3060, wep=1, ssid=2WIRE896

*Jan 28 13:43:25.102: Rogue Classify: Rogue AP: 00:14:95:16:57:41 Classification:unclassified, RuleName:

*Jan 28 13:43:25.102: Rogue Classify: rssi=-90, client=0, duration=2340, wep=1, ssid=Jumeh

*Jan 28 13:43:25.102: Rogue Classify: Rogue AP: 00:24:2b:7c:6c:2b Classification:unclassified, RuleName:

*Jan 28 13:43:25.102: 00:40:96:a3:75:c1 APF processing Rogue Client: 00:40:96:a3:75:c1 on slot 0

*Jan 28 13:43:25.102: 00:40:96:a3:75:c1 BSSID 00:1b:2b:35:38:c1 is in a valid APlist - Ignore client entry 00:40:96:a3:75:c1

debug dhcp

Another helpful debug command is debug dhcp, which gives you the skinny on all four steps in the DHCP process: Discover, Offer, Request, and Acknowledgment frames. If you happen to have a DHCP relay agent, it will show you those relay frames too. Here's an example of the debug dhcp command:

(Cisco Controller) >**debug dhcp packet enable**

Jan 28 10:46:08.019: 00:1e:35:ed:f9:d2 DHCP received op BOOTREQUEST (1) (len 308, port 1, encap 0xec00)

*Jan 28 10:46:08.020: 00:1e:35:ed:f9:d2 DHCP dropping packet (no mscb) found - (giaddr 0.0.0.0, pktInfo->srcPort 68, op: 'BOOTREQUEST')

*Jan 28 10:46:08.020: 00:1e:35:ed:f9:d2 DHCP received op BOOTREPLY (2) (len 309, port 1, encap 0xec00)

```
*Jan 28 10:46:08.020: 00:1e:35:ed:f9:d2 DHCP dropping packet (no mscb) found -
(giaddr 0.0.0.0, pktInfo->srcPort 67, op: 'BOOTREPLY')
```

debug dot1x and debug aaa

If you've deployed 802.1X Layer 2 authentication, the debug dot1x and debug aaa commands can show you the authentication and authorization processes:

```
(Cisco Controller) >debug dot1x ?
aaa             Configures debug of 802.1X AAA interactions.
all             Configures debug of all  802.1X messages.
events          Configures debug of 802.1X events.
packet          Configures debug of 802.1X packets.
states          Configures debug of 802.1X state transitions.
(Cisco Controller) >debug aaa ?
all             Configures debug of all AAA messages.
detail          Configures debug of AAA detailed events.
events          Configures debug of AAA events.
packet          Configures debug of AAA packets.
ldap            Configures debug of AAA LDAP events.
local-auth      Configures debug of AAA Local Authentication.
tacacs          Configures debug of AAA TACACS+ eve.
```

After you've got all the intel you need, don't forget to cancel the command by issuing the debug disable-all command to turn off all debugging operations. You can also disable a specific debug command, for example, debug client disable. If you don't turn the debug off, it will stop automatically when the CLI times out.

debug lwapp events enable

Let's say you want to troubleshoot why an AP is failing to successfully associate with the controller. A good approach is to use the debug lwapp events enable command to monitor the process and see where it's breaking down. Here is an example of the debugging output:

```
*Jan 28 12:49:31.658: 00:1e:7a:28:38:b0 Received LWAPP PRIMARY_DISCOVERY_REQ
from AP 00:1e:7a:28:38:b0

*Jan 28 12:49:31.658: 00:1d:a1:ef:31:d8 Successful transmission of LWAPP Primary
Discovery Response to AP 00:1d:a1:ef:31:d8

*Jan 28 12:49:33.553: 00:1b:2b:35:38:c0 Successful transmission of LWAPP Add-
Mobile to AP 00:1b:2b:35:38:c0

*Jan 28 12:49:33.554: 00:1b:2b:35:38:c0 Received LWAPP CONFIGURE COMMAND RES
from AP 00:1b:2b:35:38:c0

*Jan 28 12:49:54.249: 00:1b:2b:35:38:c0 Received LWAPP ECHO_REQUEST from AP
00:1b:2b:35:38:c0
```

```
*Jan 28 12:49:54.249: 00:1b:2b:35:38:c0 Successful transmission of LWAPP Echo-
Response to AP 00:1b:2b:35:38:c0
*Jan 28 12:50:01.647: 00:1e:7a:28:38:b0 Received LWAPP PRIMARY_DISCOVERY_REQ
from AP 00:1e:7a:28:38:b0
*Jan 28 12:50:01.647: 00:1d:a1:ef:31:d8 Successful transmission of LWAPP Primary
Discovery Response to AP 00:1d:a1:ef:31:d8
*Jan 28 12:50:04.511: 00:1b:2b:35:38:c0 Received LWAPP STATISTICS_INFO from AP
00:1b:2b:35:38:c0
*Jan 28 12:50:04.512: 00:1b:2b:35:38:c0 Successful transmission of LWAPP
Statistics Info Response to AP 00:1b:2b:35:38:c0
(Cisco Controller) >*Jan 28 12:50:24.247: 00:1b:2b:35:38:c0 Received LWAPP ECHO_
REQUEST from AP 00:1b:2b:35:38:c0
*Jan 28 12:50:24.247: 00:1b:2b:35:38:c0 Successful transmission of LWAPP Echo-
Response to AP 00:1b:2b:35:38:c0
```

show Commands

While it's true that you can see a lot of this information from the web interface of the WLC, there's an entire buffet of show commands to dig into when you need a wider array of tools to kill your particular beast. The powerful debug commands I just went over with you require live interaction with the controller, so they're only available in the CLI. However, you can see that same information using the show client summary command as you can in the web interface by clicking Monitor ➤ Clients. Here are the two identical outputs:

```
(Cisco Controller) >show client summary


Number of Clients................................. 2


MAC Address       AP Name           Status        WLAN/Guest-Lan Auth Protocol Port Wired
----------------- ----------------- ------------- -------------- ---- -------- ---- -----


00:40:96:a3:75:c1 2106-1            Associated    2              Yes  802.11g  1    No
00:40:96:a3:94:d3 2106-1            Probing       N/A            No   802.11b  1    No
```

Headed back to the CLI, we can use the show client detail *mac-address* command, which will arm you with the same information about a client that you see in Figure 12.11 (which came from the client details page in the web interface). It can score some really handy intel on RF parameters like RSSI and SNR that you'll find helpful when trouble-shooting the physical issues that we discussed earlier.

```
(Cisco Controller) >show client detail 00:40:96:a3:75:c1
Client MAC Address............................... 00:40:96:a3:75:c1
```

```
Client Username .............................. N/A
AP MAC Address................................ 00:1b:2b:35:38:c0
Client State.................................. Associated
Client NAC OOB State.......................... Access
Wireless LAN Id............................... 2
BSSID......................................... 00:1b:2b:35:38:c1
Connected For ................................ 276 secs
Channel....................................... 1
IP Address.................................... 192.168.255.25
Association Id................................ 1
Authentication Algorithm...................... Open System
Reason Code................................... 0
Status Code................................... 0
Session Timeout............................... 1800
Client CCX version............................ 3
QoS Level..................................... Silver
Diff Serv Code Point (DSCP)................... disabled
802.1P Priority Tag........................... disabled
WMM Support................................... Enabled
U-APSD Support................................ Disabled
Supported Rates............................... 1.0,2.0,5.5,11.0,6.0,9.0,
--More-- or (q)uit
```

FIGURE 12.11   Client Summary

Clients				Entries 1 - 2 of 2
Current Filter	None	[Change Filter] [Show All]		
Client MAC Addr	AP Name		WLAN Profile	Protocol
00:40:96:a3:75:c1	2106-1		Open	802.11g
00:40:96:a3:94:d3	2106-1		Unknown	802.11b

Logging

Like all Cisco devices, the controller has message logs. They can be viewed locally on the controller or they can be sent to a syslog server. On the left side of the Management page of the controller, you can view two logs: the Config log and the Message log on the task list. These logs can contain up to 256 entries and operate in a first-in, first-out order. If more than 256 entries need to be maintained, the logs must be sent to a syslog server. In Figure 12.12, you can see what the message log on a controller looks like.

FIGURE 12.12   Message logs

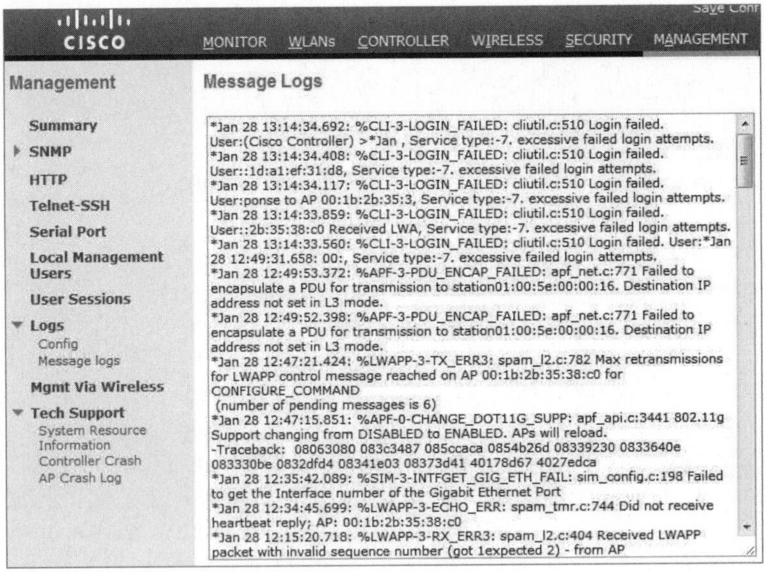

Take another look at Figure 12.12 and find Tech Support in the task list. Within this task are four subtasks; one of them is the AP Crash Log found in the details pane. It contains logs generated by the AP that you can download to the controller and read from there.

The other task I want you to focus on here is called Controller Crash. These logs are created whenever the controller suffers a crash requiring a memory dump. This information is useful for tech support at Cisco but won't be much help to a customer.

Using a Syslog Server

If you need lots of capacity for holding message logs or want a centralized solution for housing them, you need a syslog server. When opting for this, the controller(s) must be configured with the IP address of the syslog server plus other information that controls exactly what log levels will be sent. You can see the Syslog Configuration page in Figure 12.13.

When you set log levels, you're basically telling the controller about the severity levels you're interested in maintaining. There are eight levels of severity, 0 through 7, and they're inclusive, meaning that if you choose, say, level 4, levels 0–4 will be collected and sent. Table 12.1 shows each level and gives you a brief description.

FIGURE 12.13   Syslog Configuration

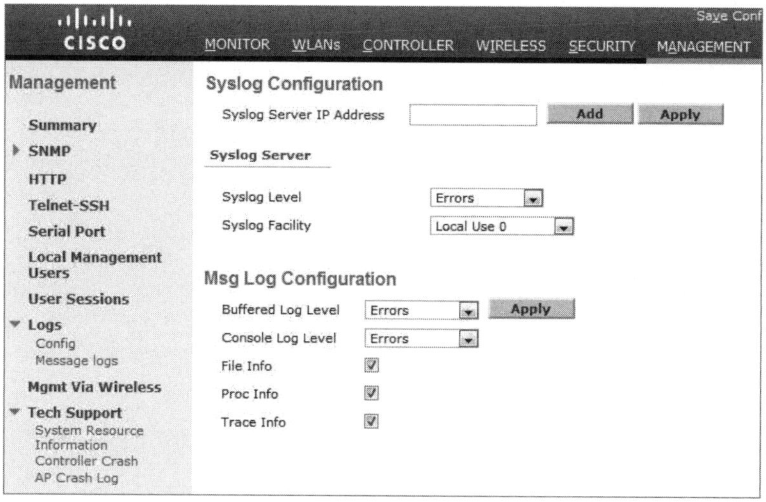

TABLE 12.1   Log Levels

Severity Number	Level Name	Description
0	Emergencies	Panic condition
1	Critical	Failure in primary system
2	Alerts	Should be corrected immediately
3	Errors	Non-urgent failure
4	Warnings	Condition that will lead to failure
5	Notifications	Unusual occurrence
6	Informational	Normal event
7	Debugging	Debugging information for developers

You can also add information fields to the syslog messages in the form of things known as facilities, which are fields used to filter and organize the messages. You get to define which facility you want associated to the message log and what level of event should trigger sending a log message. The available facilities are shown in Table 12.2.

TABLE 12.2   Facilities

Facility Level	Name
0	Kernel
1	User process
2	Mail
3	System daemon
4	Authorization
5	Syslog
6	Line printer
7	USENET
8	Unix-to-Unix copy
9	Cron (clock)
10	Security/authorization messages
11	FTP daemon
12	System use 1
13	System use 2
14	System use 3
15	System use 4
16	Local use 0
17	Local use 1
18	Local use 2
19	Local use 3
20	Local use 4
21	Local use 5
22	Local use 6
23	Local use 7

You set the local log level behavior in the Msg Log Configuration section, where you're essentially choosing the types of messages that will be kept in the buffer and those that will be sent to the console. The last three check boxes determine if you want source file, process information, and trace-back information included in the message logs.

SNMP

Simple Network Management Protocol (SNMP) can be used to manage the controller from a remote management station or from a WCS. You configure this from the controller.

On the SNMP System Summary page in the web interface (Management ➤ SNMP ➤ General), the basic settings are deployed, as shown in Figure 12.14.

FIGURE 12.14   SNMP General

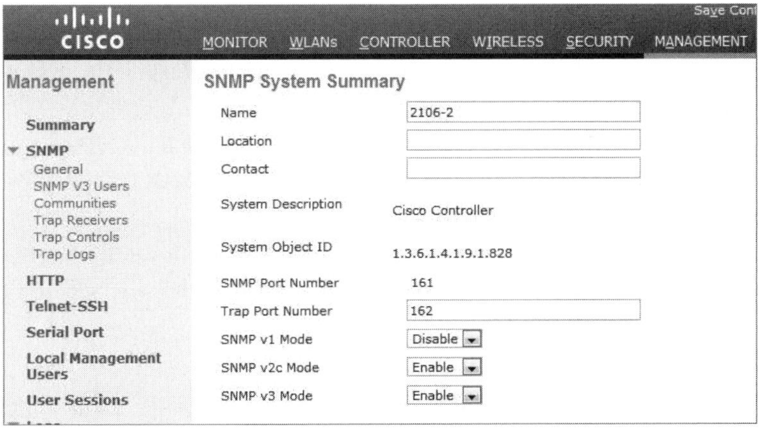

Some of these settings are customer-definable but some are read only and will be supplied by the system:

Name   The name of the controller

Location   The location of the controller

Contact   Contact details

System Description   Read only (device description)

SNMP Port Number   Read only port 161

Trap Port Number   Definable but will default to port 162

SNMP v1 Mode   Enabled or disabled; default is disabled

SNMP v2 Mode   Enabled or disabled; default is disabled

SNMP v3 Mode   Enabled or disabled; default is disabled

At least one of the three modes must be enabled for remote management to take place.

SNMP works by using defined communities, each of which can be used to read information from the controller, write information to it, or both. There are two famous default communities called Public and Private and because they're so well-known, you should definitely change their names. Public is used for read access and Private is used to write to the controller.

You can choose to just use the (renamed) default communities or you can create additional ones. No matter what you decide, you've got to tell the controller where to send the information and what information to send, just as you do when using syslog.

Information is sent through the use of messages, sometimes called traps. WCS and other devices can be defined as trap receivers. When this happens, all devices will be accessing the controller within a security context. With the WCS, the username will be *default*. If you want to change that, you can only do so on the WCS.

One of the benefits of utilizing SNMP version 3—the version used between the WCS and the controller—is that the information is protected in transit.

Regardless of whether you're using the default communities or creating new ones, there's information that must be entered for each one, including:

Community Name   Should be changed from the default names if using the default communities and should be created for new communities as well.

IP Address   The address from which this device accepts packets. It's ANDed with the mask before being compared to the IP address of the controller. If it's set to 0.0.0.0 with a mask 0.0.0.0, all addresses will be accepted. The default is 0.0.0.0.

IP Mask   This address is ANDed with the address of the requesting entity before comparison with the controller IP address. If you set the correct mask, either a single or a range of addresses can be allowed. The default is 0.0.0.0.

Access Mode   Can be either Read Only or Read/Write.

Status   Can be enabled or disabled. If enabled but the name isn't unique, set requests (writing) will be rejected. If set to disabled, no requests will be accepted.

I really need to point something important out to you regarding the address and mask settings. If you leave both of these at their defaults of 0.0.0.0, you're saying that you want to allow access from all addresses—clearly, that must be changed!

Information receivers are usually defined as trap receivers. The WCS is a trap receiver, and other management stations can also be defined with traps. A trap log is displayed in Figure 12.15.

Trap logs are also useful when you're investigating failures. They're also first-in, first-out with a maximum of 256 entries allowed, so again, if you need more space, you need a syslog server. When checking out the logs for AP issues, know that the controller will indicate why the AP is no longer associated or why it couldn't associate in the first place. If you are interested in client failures, each association failure will generate a message (trap) along with a reason code. Table 12.3 defines the reason codes.

   Cisco recommends not to use the default SNMP names as they can be used in an OTAP hack on an enterprise WLC.

FIGURE 12.15   Trap Logs

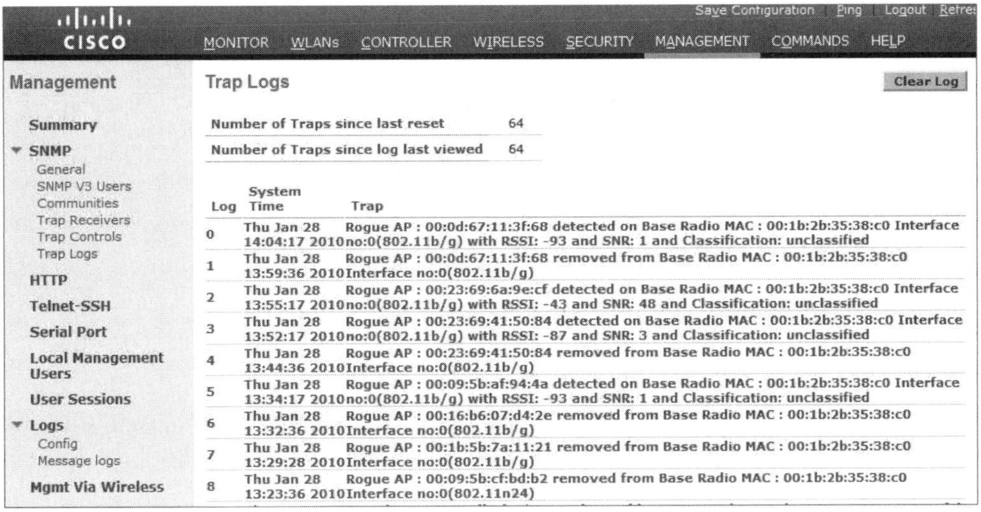

TABLE 12.3   Client Association Failure Codes

Client Reason Code	Field Name	Description
0	noReasonCode	Normal operation
1	unspecifiedreason	Client associated, no longer associated
2	previousAuthnotvalid	Client associated but not authorized
3	deauthenticationLeaving	The AP went offline, deauthenticating the client
4	disassociationDueToinactivity	Client session timeout exceeded
5	disassociationAPBusy	The AP is busy: for example, performing load balancing
6	class2FramefromNonauthstation	Client attempted transfer of data before authentication
7	class2FramefromNonAssSation	Client attempted transfer of data before association

TABLE 12.3 Client Association Failure Codes (continued)

Client Reason Code	Field Name	Description
8	disassociationStaHasLeft	The operating system moved the station to another AP using nonaggressive load balancing, meaning it has reassociated
9	staReqAssociationWithoutAuth	Client not yet authorized, yet is attempting to associate
99	missingReasoncode	Client momentarily in an unknown state

A set of status codes becomes applicable once the station is associated. These codes can also help you learn why a station is cycling back and forth between connected and disconnected. These codes are listed in Table 12.4.

TABLE 12.4 Client Status Codes

Client Status Code	Field Name	Description
0	idle	Normal operation, no rejections of association1 requests
1	aaaPending	Completing an AAA transaction
2	authenticated	802.11 authentication completed
3	associated	802.11 association completed
4	powersave	Client in power save mode
5	disassociated	802.11 disassociation completed
6	tobedeleted	To be deleted after disassociation
7	probing	Client not associated or authorized yet
8	disabled	Automatically disabled by the operating system for an operator-defined period of time

The type of traps or messages can also be defined by navigating to Management ➤ SNMP ➤ Trap Controls. The selections that you make here will apply to all trap receivers and the check boxes you choose will determine the type of messages sent, as shown in Figure 12.16.

FIGURE 12.16   SNMP Trap Controls

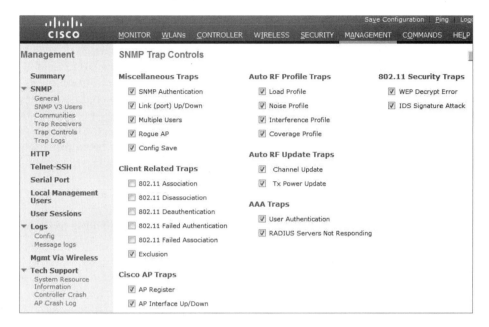

RF Deployment Considerations

Earlier, you learned about some problems that give you grief because a WLAN was designed miserably in the first place. A big reason that this isn't as uncommon as you would think is that the RF environment is always in a state of flux so it's a huge challenge to anticipate every possible scenario during the design phase, even with the most sophisticated predictive site survey tools. Still, difficulty isn't an excuse for bad design and starting with a solid one, and then following up with thorough testing once the WLAN is deployed, will repay you tenfold by mitigating and avoiding the worst design tangles! This is why it's time to cover some common design practices and introduce you to the tools available to help you design well. I'll also get into some of the more common sources of interference.

Interference Sources

Interference in the RF environment can come from active and passive sources. Active sources are those creating RF signals, and passive ones are those creating obstacles that impair the propagation of RF signals.

Passive Sources

Passive sources of interference can be anything from building materials to décor. You can get around interference caused from building materials and features by choosing the location of APs carefully. Predictive site survey tools are available that you can use to determine a good starting point for their placement. There is, of course, a catch—site survey software tools depend on the accuracy of information entered about each wall or ceiling's makeup and thickness because it uses known principles and values based on those factors to determine how to place the APs. Basically, to come up with an accurate way to mitigate interference, the type and amount of interference must be identified correctly. Just as with any software, the quality of the results directly depends on the quality of the information entered by humans. In this case, those humans are you and your team while performing that all-important site survey.

With that in mind, take a look at Figure 12.17, which depicts the heat map from a WCS (you can't see the color in this book so you can only see the AP placement at this point). This map shows the coverage as it should be based on the information provided, as well as on the current location of the APs.

FIGURE 12.17 WCS heat map

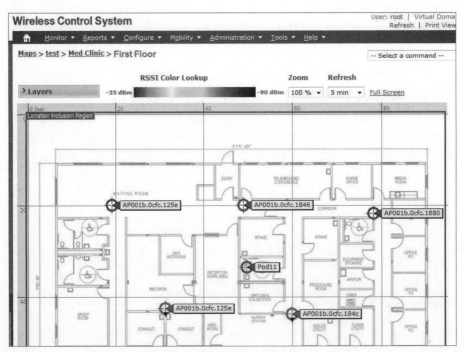

Believe it or not, most of the time you'll need to tweak the placement of devices after testing the initial design even with this type of high-quality information.

So let's say someone nicked your super cool, predictive software gadgets and now you're stuck doing a manual survey. In this case, it's still basically a process of taking a map, locating all the expected sources of interference, locating the APs in your "best guess" spot, and then walking around the area and testing the signal quality and throughput while paying special attention to any nefarious dead spots you discover along the way. See? That's not so bad, right? Now after you've done this, you simply adjust the APs and repeat the whole process. When locating probable and potential sources of wireless grief, pay attention to things like:

- Metal file cabinets
- Elevator shafts
- Stairwells
- Break rooms (especially because of the presence of microwave ovens—remember those?)

Okay—sweet—all done! Well, not quite ... we need a post survey.

What the post survey will tell us is that objects like furniture and filing cabinets are more problematic than the actual building's structure, which is awesome. It's clearly much easier just to move problem stuff out and either move it back in to a different place or get new stuff that doesn't cause interference later, after deployment.

But there's one variable that can be hard to anticipate—the effect of people in the area. Remember, we're made up of 70 percent water, which makes us potential sources of interference especially when gathered together in large numbers or condensed into close quarters. Plus, we wear stuff made out of conductive materials and some of us even have metal parts, like prosthetics and pacemakers, so yes, humans can certainly be sources of interference and must be planned for. The "people premium" happens to be a big reason why testing and adjustment is usually required after deployment.

 NOTE   Always remember that 5GHz equipment will not radiate through walls as well as 2.4GHz.

But let's go back a bit and revisit building materials because once you've nailed down the various sources of passive interference, it's good to have some idea of the effects certain objects and materials have on things. Predictive software will probably already be configured with these values, but it's always good to be able to still do the math without a calculator. Table 12.5 lists the attenuation effects of some common objects and materials.

TABLE 12.5 Signal Attenuation

Object	Attenuation Introduced
Plasterboard wall	3dB
Glass wall with metal frame	6dB
Cinderblock wall	4dB
Office window	3dB
Metal door	6dB
Medal door in brick wall	12dB
Wireless device position	3–6dB

The good news is that combining lightweight APs with controllers and a WCS is an adaptive solution that lets you change channels and power settings to respond to coverage holes, interference, and overlapping issues.

Active Sources

Some sources of interference actually transmit signals into the RF environment. Possible culprits even include other WLANs. Sometimes it's non-WLAN equipment, but either way the Cisco Spectrum Expert I talked about earlier can be used to locate these sources that are seen as noise by the WLAN infrastructure.

How much a given interference source affects the environment depends on two factors: its power, or how strong the signal is, and the duty cycle, which refers to how long the device is on. You measure the duty cycle to find a device's RF utilization value, but both are important factors because if the signal is loud enough, no other devices can transmit within the band the screaming device is transmitting on until the cycle is over. Let's look into the characteristics of some common sources of active inference now.

Microwave Ovens

The ubiquitous microwave oven, found just about everywhere there are or will be people gathered for any length of time, can be a nasty source of active interference because even though the interference it produces is fairly short-lived, it often completely hogs the channel or even the entire band it's transmitting within. Older ones are worse than newer ones because they create a wider band of inference, but even one you took out of the box yesterday can wreak havoc if the door is damaged or the seal gets broken. Let me really bring this home to you— if an oven is leaking a measly .1 percent of its power, it will be radiating 100 watts, which is about 100 times the power of the nearest AP—no contest!

Make a mental note of what you'll see in the spectrum analyzer when a microwave oven is present:

- There will be a loud (strong) moving signal seen in the upper-left corner panel that shows the max peak just to the left of channel 11.
- There will be somewhat of a drift in the signal as seen in the lower-left corner panel— the spectrograph.
- The duty cycle displayed in the two panels on the above right will be higher in part of the band.

Bluetooth Devices

Worse than microwave ovens, which when fairly new and undamaged only create narrow-band interference, are Bluetooth devices that have a nasty habit called frequency hopping. What this means is that these devices use a range of channels and hop very quickly from one to another. The good news is that the interference will only affect a particular channel momentarily. The bad news is that it will eventually affect all channels. Version 1.2 has the ability to sense channels that are crowded, like a WLAN, and can avoid these channels; version 2.0 made changes that resulted in a lowered duty cycle.

Remember that there are three types of Bluetooth devices: Class 1, 2, and 3. Consumer devices are usually Class 2 or 3, which means they're low power, and don't really interfere a whole bunch. Class 1, however, is rated at 100mW/20dBm, which can cover 33 meters. One of these devices (usually stereo headsets or retail barcode readers) or lots of consumer devices in an area can bring you to tears.

The Cisco Spectrum Expert will show a Bluetooth device's pattern. The analyzer will show you how Bluetooth hops across the frequency range in the upper-left panel. You'll also notice a speckled pattern in the spectrograph. Finally, you'll observe that the duty cycle will be spread across the entire band. So, it can identify that the interference source is a Bluetooth device and help you locate it by tracking signal strength.

Wireless Phones

Cordless phones, or digitally enhanced cordless telecommunications (DECT) phones, can also upset a WLAN. Sometimes they use frequency hopping, sometimes they don't, but they can be really loud—deafening, up to the legal limit of 4 watts for some types—but you can't find a radio that transmits at 4 watts—that's illegal, but an EIRP can be up to 4 watts.

Analog Cameras

Analog cameras use the 2.4GHz spectrum and are more problematic than digital phones. In this case the signal will have a heavy impact on one channel. If it's on channel 1, 6, or 11, it will leave only two nonoverlapping channels available for use. If it's on an intermediate channel like 8, it could affect two of the nonoverlapping channels and leave you with only one nonoverlapping channel. This can create a very ugly problem when an area needs multiple APs to operate at capacity.

Another problem with cameras seen is that the duty cycle is typically 100 percent!

Conducting the All-Important Site Survey

By now and beyond a doubt, you know where I stand on this—site survey is positively, vitally imperative to bringing a premium-quality—even just a reasonably viable—WLAN into this world. You should carry out a predeployment survey and a postdeployment survey, but your predeployment survey isn't the first step to this important process. Let's take a look at the three major steps and issues within each step along the way:

Information Gathering   This is your actual first step and in it, you've got to determine:

- The scope of the network, including all applications that will be used, data types that will be present, and the sensitivity of the data types to delay

- The areas that need to be covered and the expected capacity at each location

- The types of wireless devices that will need to be supported: laptops, PDAs, IP phones, barcode readers, etc.

I like to create a coverage model that refers to all areas that need coverage and those that don't, and have my client sign off in agreement to this document before I do anything else. I'd recommend that you do this too—just trust me!

Predeployment Site Survey   In the second step, I use live APs to verify the optimal distance between their prospective locations. I base this placement on the expected speed at the edge of the cell, the anticipated number of devices, and other information gathered in step 1. Usually after I get one AP positioned, I'll place the next one based on the distance from the first, as well as any sources of interference I've found.

Postdeployment Site Survey   Step 3 is the postdeployment survey used to confirm and verify the original design and placement is happily humming along problem-free when all stations are using the network. Since this pretty much never happens at this point, it's common that some significant changes are required and made to optimize the performance of a WLAN operating under full capacity.

Providing Capacity

This is a big issue and one that frequently rears its ugly head: providing enough capacity in areas where many wireless stations will be competing for the airwaves. Remember that stations share access to the RF environment with all other stations in the BSS as well as with the AP, so really, the only way to increase capacity is by increasing the number of APs in the area requiring density.

This can get complicated, but basically, it comes down to placing APs on nonoverlapping channels while still sharing the same SSID. Take a look at Figure 12.18.

In Figure 12.18, nine APs have been configured in the same area using the three non-overlapping channels in the 2.4GHz frequency (1, 6, and 11). Each color represents a different channel (if you could see this in color). Even though the APs that are on the same channel have been positioned far enough away from one another that they don't overlap or interfere, it's actually better if there is overlap. However, the channels must be used in a way that no APs that are on the same channel overlap. Another thing that's not so ideal about this arrangement is that all the APs would have to run at full power, which doesn't do much for your fault tolerance.

FIGURE 12.18   Basic coverage

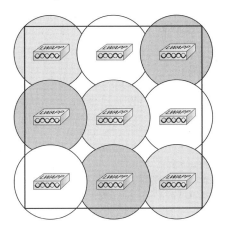

Okay—so we've got two problems with our design: lack of overlap and lack of fault tolerance. To address both issues, you need more APs using 802.11a, b, and g, which would get you more channels and provide better throughput, as shown in Figure 12.19.

FIGURE 12.19   Enterprise design

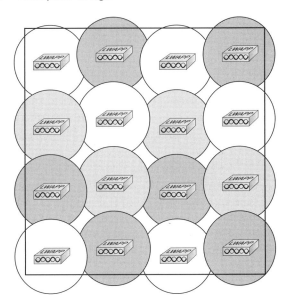

Importantly, this design would also gain the critical ability to run the APs at less than full power, allowing the controller to boost the power of specific APs in the event of an AP outage in one area.

When you know exactly the type of applications and activity a WLAN will need to support, you can then determine the data rate that must be attained in a particular area. Since RSSI, SNR, and data rate are correlated, the required data rate will tell you what the required RSSI or SNR should be as seen at the AP from the stations. Keep in mind that stations that are at the edge of the cell will automatically drop the data rate but will increase the data rate as the station moves toward the AP. Also, the required Rx should be padded by 10dB.

Overlap Issues

So yes, I said that having a fairly good amount of overlap between the APs is good, striking a good balance is really what you're after because when you've got too much, performance grinds to a crawl. Too little overlap, and you'll have coverage holes all over the place between your APs. Controllers can be set to address this issue, but I can't stress enough that beginning with a solid design is going to make you much more able to deal with any issues that crop up. Remember, when the APs are operating at full power, the controller just can't boost any AP to compensate. If there is too much overlap, the APs will interfere with one another and the stations will switch back and forth between APs, resulting in an inconsistent connection.

VoWLAN

Running voice over IP on a WLAN (VoWLAN) really raises some challenges. This type of traffic is extremely sensitive to delay drops and jitter. Jitter occurs when delay is inconsistent in the network. When running VoIP, your requirements for a good signal rise dramatically. Some factors to keep in mind are:

- The signal strength at the edge of each cell should be –67dBm.
- The cells should overlap by 15–20 percent.
- There should be at least 19dBm of separation between the cells operating on the same channel.

When you're planning capacity for VoIP phones in the 2.4GHz band, the density shouldn't exceed seven concurrent calls per AP with a default G.711 codec. Using a different codec will alter this. When using 802.11g only, this can be increased to 15 to 20 calls, and with 802.11a only up to 25 concurrent calls can be supported.

Multiple Floors

Another special challenge is a multistory building where WLANs are located on all floors. In these conditions, you've got to think about channel usage in a three-dimensional way. And you may need to play well with the other WLANs' administrators to make this work as well. Channel spacing should be deployed as shown in Figure 12.20.

To prevent bleed from one floor to another, semidirectional or patch antennas should be used to control radiation patterns.

FIGURE 12.20   A multifloor installation

Location-Based WLAN

When using a location device such as the Cisco 2710, your restrictions get even tighter. The additional requirements for the location device to operate properly are:

- APs should be placed at the edge even when they're not needed there for normal coverage purposes so that devices at the edge can be located.

- The density of APs must be higher. Each AP should be 50 to 70 feet apart—much closer than is normally required.

- Some APs will need to be set in monitor or scanner mode only so that they won't transmit and interfere with other APs.

The final placement will be denser and a bit more symmetrical than usual.

Site Survey Tools

As I touched on at the beginning of the site survey section, there are some highly specialized, very cool site survey tools that can greatly aid you in achieving all this. The AirMagnet Survey and Ekahau Site Survey tools make it possible to do a client walk with the unit running and click each location on the map. It will gather RSSI and SNR from each AP in the range, and at the end of your tour, a global coverage map will be magically displayed. AirMagnet is shown in Figure 12.21.

Since the Cisco Aironet Desktop Utility will read real-time values of RSSI and SNR while moving through a facility, it can help you do a basic site survey and assist you with troubleshooting too.

FIGURE 12.21   AirMagnet

WLC and WCS Configuration and OS Files

Nothing is really maintenance free, and so it should come as no surprise that WLCs as well as WCSs require maintenance. The tasks I'll cover in this section are Code upgrades and WLC Configuration Backups. Let's take a look.

Code Upgrades

I am going to start by covering both controller and WCS Code upgrades.

Controller Code Upgrades

You can tackle controller code upgrades from the GUI or from the CLI. But more often than not you won't know the code version that's running on a specific WLC, and clearly, you need to find that out. To do so, consult the main Monitor page of the controller in the web interface, as shown in Figure 12.22.

Navigating to Controller ➢ Inventory will gain you additional information, including the options installed and number of APs supported, as shown as in Figure 12.23.

Although you can accomplish code upgrades from the command line, I recommend going the GUI route. The code you'll get from Cisco will be in the form of a single, compressed AES file that contains:

RTOS   The real-time operating system of the controller

CODE (Airwave Director)   The part of the code that handles RRM, the CLI, and the switch web interface

ppcboot.bin   The bootloader of the controller

FIGURE 12.22   Checking the code version on the Monitor page

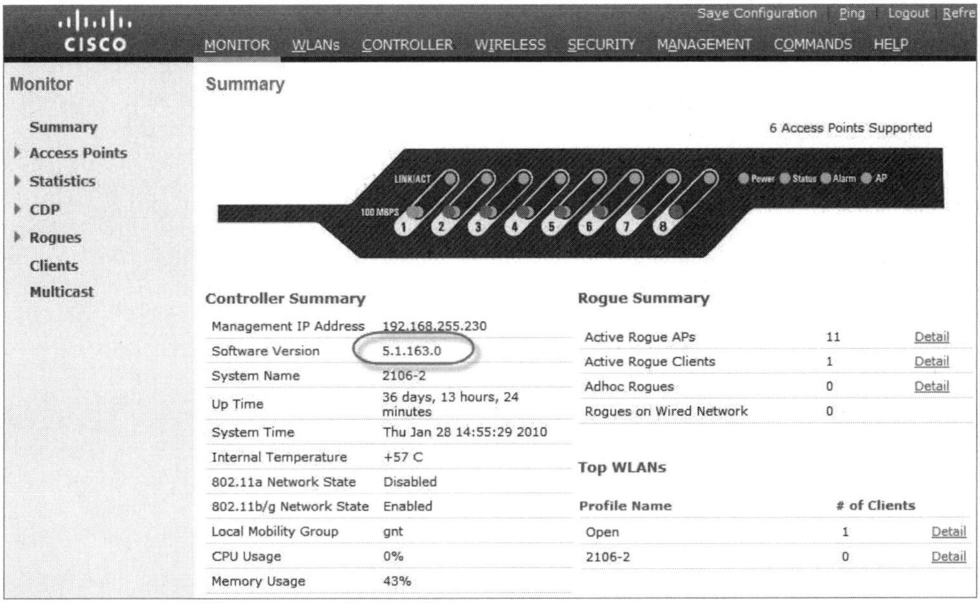

FIGURE 12.23   The Controller page

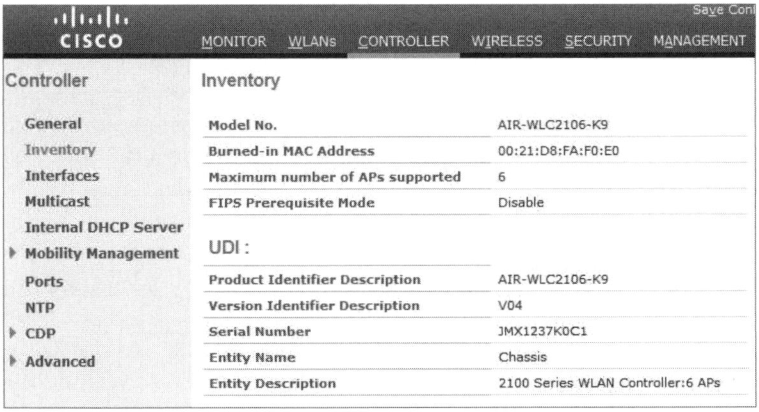

You should place the code on a TFTP server, navigate to Commands ➢ Download File, enter the information about the name of the file and the location, and then click Apply to start the download, as shown in Figure 12.24.

FIGURE 12.24 Code download

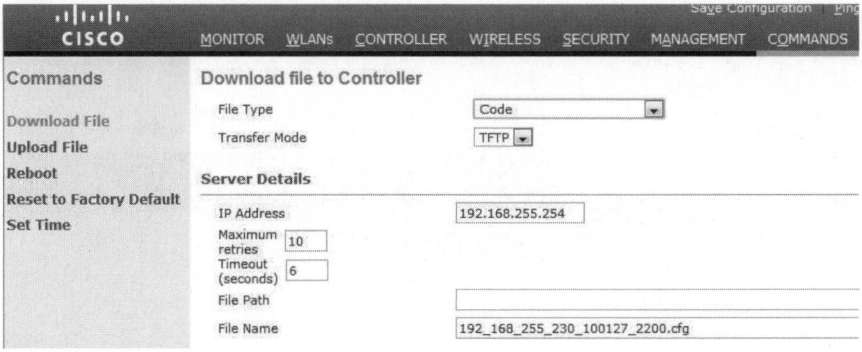

The page shown in Figure 12.24 is used for downloading a lot of different types of files. The File Type drop-down box can be set for file types other than Code, as shown in Figure 12.25.

FIGURE 12.25 File type

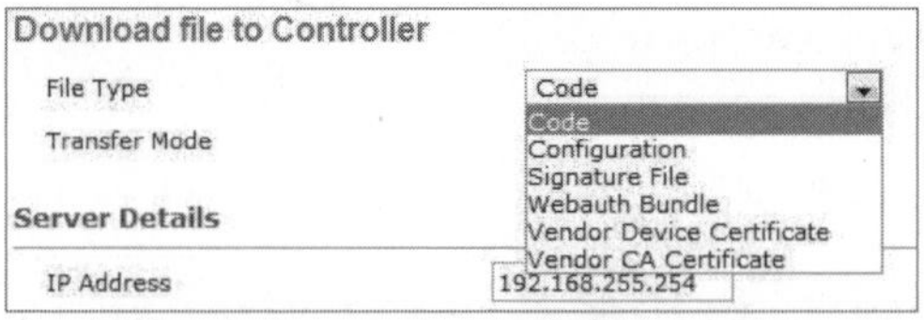

When the download starts, it will first load into memory and then into flash. The new image will become the primary image, and the old image will become a backup to allow for recovery from a failed upgrade. For instance, if the transfer is interrupted while writing to flash, corruption will occur and it's that backup image that gives you the ability to recover.

Good to know that when the controller is upgraded, the APs will follow suit and be upgraded to the same code version. This only takes about two minutes. The reverse is also true—if you've got to downgrade a controller so it matches the others, your APs will be downgraded along with it. The actual time for upgrade and downgrade is solely dependent on the WLC model and code version.

The process from the CLI requires a series of commands that define the mode of transfer, the TFTP server address, the path to the software on the TFTP server, and the name of the file. Here's a list of these commands in order:

```
Transfer download mode ftp
Transfer download serverip
Transfer download path
Transfer download filename
```

Let's take a look at the transfer download command and the available options that go along with this command.

```
(Cisco Controller) >transfer download ?
certpassword    Set a Certificate's private key password.
datatype        Set File Type.
filename        Set Filename on Server.
mode            Set transfer mode.
path            Set File Path on Server.
serverip        Set Server IP Address.
start           Initiate download.
username        Set Server Login Username.
password        Set Server Login Password.
port            Change Default Server Port.
tftpPktTimeout Enter the tftp Packet Timeout in secs between 1 and 254.
tftpMaxRetries Enter the tftp Packet Max Retries allowed between 1 and 254.


(Cisco Controller) >transfer download mode ?
tftp            Enter mode: tftp.
ftp             Enter mode: ftp.


(Cisco Controller) >transfer download serverip ?
<IP addr>       Enter server IP addr.


(Cisco Controller) >transfer download path ?
 [path]          Enter directory path.


(Cisco Controller) >transfer download filename ?
<filename>      Enter filename up to 16 alphanumeric characters.
```

Here is an example on how to start the download:

```
(Cisco Controller) >transfer download start


Mode........................................... TFTP
Data Type...................................... Config
TFTP Server IP................................. 192.168.255.254
TFTP Packet Timeout............................ 6
TFTP Max Retries............................... 10
TFTP Path......................................
TFTP Filename.................................. 192_168_255_220_100127_2200.cfg
Encrypt/Decrypt Flag........................... Disabled


Warning: Downloading configuration will cause the switch to reset...


This may take some time.
```

```
Are you sure you want to start? (y/N)
Are you sure you want to start? (y/N) y

TFTP Config transfer starting.

TFTP receive complete... updating configuration.

TFTP receive complete... storing in flash.

System being reset.


Resetting system ...
```

WCS Code Upgrade

How complicated upgrading the code in a WCS is depends on the version it's currently run-ning. If it's version 4.2 or earlier, it will not retain the directories, root password, or license information in the upgrade process. So if this is your situation, you'll need to stop the WCS server, back up the database, uninstall the old WCS version, install the new version, restore the database, and finally, restart the WCS. You're in luck if you're dealing with OS version 4.2 or later because in that case, all these processes are automated—nice!

WLC Configuration Backups

Now, before you back up the configuration, make sure that you've saved the configuration on the controller. When you select Apply after making changes, it copies the configuration into RAM, but as you know that will disappear if the controller reboots. To save it in NVRAM and be assured it will be there after a reboot, you must select Save Configuration at the top of the main page, as shown in Figure 12.26.

FIGURE 12.26   Select Save Configuration.

The WLC can be returned to the factory defaults when required as well. Navigate to Commands ➢ Reset To Factory Defaults. Click Reset and then click OK to confirm. When this happens, only the file in NVRAM is deleted—not the file in RAM. To delete that as well, just reboot the controller and answer No when it asks if you want to save the configu-ration. You can reboot the controller via Commands ➢ Reboot System.

Viewing the Configuration and Controller State

Two very handy commands can be used to view the current WLC configuration file and the controller state. The show running-config command will give you the configuration file, which displays information a lot like how it's shown on a Cisco router:

```
(Cisco Controller) >show run?
run-config      running-config
 (Cisco Controller) >show running-config
 802.11a cac voice tspec-inactivity-timeout ignore

 802.11a cac video tspec-inactivity-timeout ignore

 802.11a cac voice stream-size 84000 max-streams 2

 802.11b 11g Support disable

 802.11b cac voice tspec-inactivity-timeout ignore

 802.11b cac video tspec-inactivity-timeout ignore

 802.11b cac voice stream-size 84000 max-streams 2

 aaa auth mgmt   local radius


 Location Summary

 Algorithm used:              Average
 Client
        RSSI expiry timeout:  5 sec
--More-- or (q)uit
        Half life:            0 sec
        Notify Threshold:     0 db
 Calibrating Client
        RSSI expiry timeout:  5 sec
        Half life:            0 sec
 Rogue AP
        RSSI expiry timeout:  5 sec
        Half life:            0 sec
        Notify Threshold:     0 db
 RFID Tag
```

```
          RSSI expiry timeout:     5 sec
          Half life:               0 sec
          Notify Threshold:        0 db

 location rssi-half-life tags 0

 location rssi-half-life client 0

 location rssi-half-life rogue-aps 0

 location expiry tags 5

 location expiry client 5
--More-- or (q)uit
```

The show run-config command gives you information about the controller itself, as shown here:

```
(Cisco Controller) >show run-config

Press Enter to continue...

System Inventory
NAME: "Chassis"    , DESCR: "2100 Series WLAN Controller:6 APs"
PID: AIR-WLC2106-K9,  VID: V03,  SN: JMX1146K0D7


Burned-in MAC Address........................... 00:1E:13:50:5F:80


Press Enter to continue Or <Ctl Z> to abort

System Information
Manufacturer's Name............................. Cisco Systems Inc.
Product Name.................................... Cisco Controller
Product Version................................. 5.1.163.0
RTOS Version.................................... 5.1.163.0
Bootloader Version............................. 4.0.191.0
Build Type...................................... DATA + WPS


System Name..................................... 2106-1
System Location.................................
System Contact..................................
```

```
System ObjectID............................... 1.3.6.1.4.1.9.1.828
IP Address.................................... 192.168.255.220
System Up Time................................ 36 days 9 hrs 47 mins 38 secs
System Timezone Location......................
Current Boot License Level....................
Next Boot License Level.......................

Configured Country............................ US  - United States
Operating Environment......................... Commercial (0 to 40 C)
Internal Temp Alarm Limits.................... 0 to 65 C
Internal Temperature.......................... +56 C
--More-- or (q)uit

Switch Configuration
802.3x Flow Control Mode...................... Disable
FIPS prerequisite features.................... Disabled
secret obfuscation............................ Enabled

Press Enter to continue Or <Ctl Z> to abort
```

Collecting Information on the APs

There will definitely be times when you need to collect information about your APs. One example would be to determine the code level, which you can do right on the controller by navigating to Wireless ➢ All APs ➢ Details and clicking the Inventory tab. You'll see information about the code version, which should be the same as that of the WLC that it's associated with, as shown in Figure 12.27.

FIGURE 12.27 The Inventory tab of the Details page for All APs

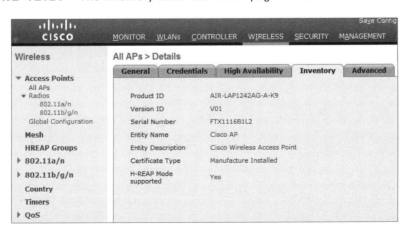

Configuring the APs

The APs will get their code upgrade and their configuration from the WLC. You manage this on the General tab (Figure 12.28) of the Details page of All APs.

On the General tab, you set the name, location, status, and mode of the AP. At the bottom part of the page you can set a global username and password that will be inherited by all APs associated to this controller. At the very bottom of this page is the button Clear All Config, which you click to delete any settings that may have been present on the AP. The Clear Config Except Static IP button will clear everything except for the IP address. Finally, the Reset AP Now button power-cycles the AP without clearing any items at all.

FIGURE 12.28   The General tab of the Details page for All APs

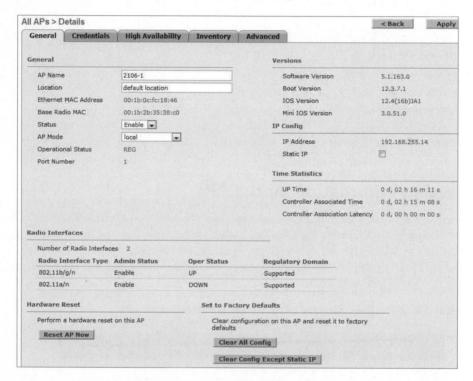

WLC Access Methods

As you've probably guessed by now, you can manage the WLC via a variety of connection methods, including the GUI (web interface) CLI, HTTP, HTTPS, and SSH. You also can specify settings through the WCS if one is being used to manage the controllers. You can even connect and manage the WLC wirelessly, but you won't be allowed to upload any files to the controller this way.

GUI

A web browser is built into each controller and up to five users can browse into the controller. When using the web browser, the session can either be established as an HTTP or an HTTPS session. I recommend disabling the HTTP connection and enabling the HTTPS connection. By entering the IP address of the controller in the browser and authenticating, you'll be presented with a web interface like the one you see in Figure 12.29.

FIGURE 12.29   HTTPS web interface

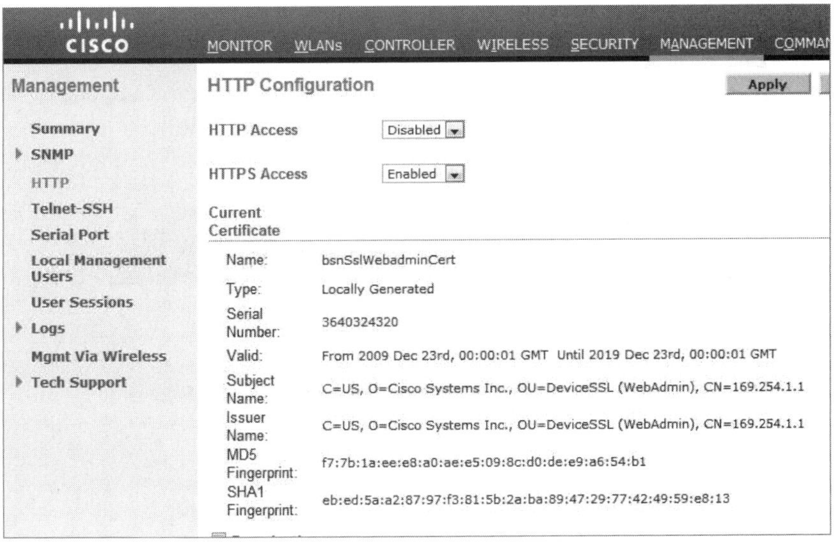

CLI

If you need to enable web mode from the CLI, do this with the command `config network webmode enable` for HTTP, and use `config network secureweb` for HTTPS. The CLI can be used to do anything that you can do through the GUI. But going through the CLI will require either a connection to the controller console port or a remote console session through the preconfigured service port or the distribution system ports.

Telnet

As I described in the section on remote console sessions, a telnet session can be established remotely using a DOS session or a terminal emulation program. Once the session is established, all operations work just as though you were connected directly with the console cable at the CLI.

SSH

Since telnet sessions are insecure, it's a much better idea to use SSH for any remote connections. This must be configured in the controller and can be done at the command line or in the GUI.

Enabling Telnet and SSH Sessions

Both of these functions can be enabled either at the CLI or in the GUI. To enable these at the command line, use the following commands:

(Cisco Controller) >**config network telnet enable**

(Cisco Controller) >**config network ssh enable**

In the web interface, you can enable telnet and SSH sessions from the Management page with the Telnet-SSH task on the left side of the page (see Figure 12.30).

FIGURE 12.30   Enabling Telnet and SSH

I want to mention just one last tiny but important thing before I summarize this chapter. Look at the left hand side of Figure 12.29 or 12.30 and notice the "Mgmt Via Wireless" section. Click this and enable the controller to be managed by wireless clients. Although you cannot upload or download files, you can enter HTTP or HTTPS into the controller to manage it. This is not enabled by default.

Summary

In this chapter you learned about all kinds of ways to access and manage WLAN devices. You also found out about the ongoing maintenance of the WLAN as well as a legion of approaches for troubleshooting problems with WLANs. You discovered the importance of making sure you've done a thorough and accurate site survey, plus how to perform one, step by step. As a part of that discussion, we covered deployment issues related to the environment in which the WLAN is operating. Finally, we wrapped the chapter up with a detailed talk about the management of configurations, including how to ensure you've backed them up properly. Essentially, if you've learned this material well, you now know quite a bit and should be well prepared for the exam—congratulations!

Exam Essentials

Know what type of show and debug commands are available for troubleshooting and how to use them.   These commands include:

- debug dot11
- show running-config
- show client detailed
- show client summary
- debug lwapp events enable
- debug mac address
- debug dhcp packet enable
- debug 802.1x
- debug aaa

Understand the methods used to upgrade the code version on a WLC.   These include using the web-based method (recommended) and using the CLI. Both methods involve placing the code file on a TFTP server.

Know the difference between saving a configuration on the controller and applying the configuration.   Saving the configuration only saves the configuration to RAM whereas applying it saves it to NVRAM, where it will still be if you reboot the controller.

Know what background tasks are and how to configure them in the WCS.   These are maintenance tasks that can be scheduled to occur automatically. They include configuration backups and WCS server backups.

Written Lab

1. True/False: The WSC database can only be backed up by scheduling it as a background task in the GUI.

2. With which versions of the Cisco WCS code does the upgrade script automatically save directories, root password, and license information?

3. What would be the expected attenuation introduced by a plasterboard wall?

4. True/False: Microwave ovens only affect 802.11a devices.

5. What type of spread spectrum technology is Bluetooth?

6. True/False: When a radio is transmitting, the signal strength can be as much as 4 watts.

7. True/False: The predeployment site survey is the first step in a wireless project.

8. How is additional wireless capacity provided in a small area?

9. True/False: For proper roaming, wireless cells should overlap at least 30 percent.

10. True/False: When location services are used, the restrictions for coverage are tighter than normal.

Hands-On Labs

To complete the labs in this section, you will need an installed version of Cisco Wireless Control System (WCS) version 4.2 or later and a later version than what is installed in CD form. You will also need a Cisco WLAN controller (WLC) and a newer version of the code than what is installed. These items can be downloaded from the Cisco site with a technical support agreement. For the WLC code update, you will need a TFTP server. The TFTP server and the WLS should be reachable through the network or connected to the same switch or hub.

Here is a list of the labs in this chapter:

Lab 12.1: Upgrading the Code Version on the WCS

Lab 12.2: Performing a Manual Backup of the WCS Database

Lab 12.3: Performing a Controller Code Update

Lab 12.1: Upgrading the Code Version on the WCS

1. Insert the Windows Cisco WCS CD into the CD-ROM drive and double-click the WCS-Standard-K9-*6.0.x.y.*exe file where *6.0.x.y* is the number of the software build.

2. After the Install Anywhere window appears (long enough to prepare the system for installation), the Introduction window appears followed by the license agreement. Accept the agreement and click Continue.

3. The wizard will now detect whether your system is a version that can be upgraded automatically (later than version 4.2).

4. Select Upgrade.

5. Select a location to store the Cisco WCS. It must be different than the location of the current installation.

6. Follow the remaining prompts. The process will update you as it proceeds through:
   - Checking for disk space
   - Uninstalling previous version
   - Backing up files
   - Installing new version
   - Restoring files

7. The upgrade is complete when you are asked if you would like to start the WCS service. Select Yes. The code is now upgraded.

Lab 12.2: Performing a Manual Backup of the WCS Database

1. Log into the server hosting WCS as administrator and create a directory to hold the backup. Name it **WCS6.99.0_backup** or whatever is intuitive to you, but do *not* include spaces. This will generate errors.

2. Navigate to Start ➤ Programs ➤ Wireless Control System ➤ Backup. When the Enter Information dialog box appears, browse to the location of the directory that you created earlier.

3. Click OK.

4. The DBAdmin window will appear and will display the status of the backup. When the Close button becomes available, click it.

Lab 12.3: Performing a Controller Code Update

Before beginning this lab, ensure that the controller and the TFTP server are reachable through the network. If the controller is connected with the service port, the two devices must be in the same subnet. If the controller is connected with the distribution network service port, that step is not required. You also must obtain the upgrade file from the Cisco website, which can be done with a technical support agreement. You also must place the file (which will have a name that will be similar to AIR-WLC440-K9-5-2-178-0.aes) in a directory on the TFTP server and make note of the filename and path (you will need them in step 3). To make your life easier, if you place this file in root of the TFTP server, you can simply enter a period (.) in the file path in step 3.

1. Connect to the web interface of the WLC and log in.

2. When the Monitor window appears, you will be able to review the current version of the software to ensure that the new version is in fact an upgrade. Click Commands at the top of the page.

3. When the Download File To Controller window appears, enter the following values:
   - TFTP Server Address
   - File Path
   - Maximum Retries
   - Timeout
   - File Name

4. Click Download to start the upgrade.

5. Reboot the controller so that the code takes effect. You can be redirected to the reboot page by clicking the Click Here link at the bottom of this page.

6. In the System Reboot window, click Save And Reboot.

7. After the reboot and login, the Monitor page will appear. Note that the version of the code has been updated.

Review Questions

1. Which of the following is *not* one of the three files that are a part of a WLC code upgrade?

   A. RTOS

   B. AIR.aes

   C. CODE

   D. ppcboot.ini

2. Which of the following commands is used on the WLC to troubleshoot issues with rogue detection?

   A. debug lwapp details

   B. debug lwapp

   C. debug dot11

   D. debug aaa

3. What value is used to derive the RF utilization of an inference source when using a spectrum analyzer?

   A. Duty cycle

   B. Maximum hold

   C. RSSI

   D. SNR

4. Which command is used to view the configuration file on the controller?

   A. show run-config

   B. show running-config

   C. show config

   D. show rconfig

5. What is required for using the show client detailed command to view information about a client?

   A. The client must have an IP address.

   B. The client must be associated with an AP.

   C. The client must be authenticated.

   D. The client must use a certificate.

6. How could you approach troubleshooting an AP that cannot associate with the WLC? (Choose all that apply.)

   A. Telnet to the AP.

   B. SSH to the WLC.

   C. Execute debug lwapp events enable on the WLC

   D. Execute debug lwapp events enable on the AP.

7. When using the client troubleshooter in the WCS, what is required to identify the client?

   A. IP address

   B. Hostname of the client

   C. MAC address

   D. Mobility group

8. Which of the following tools are installed on a computer? (Choose all that apply.)

   A. WLC

   B. Cisco Spectrum Expert

   C. WCS

   D. WLSE

9. How many messages will the message log on the WLC hold?

   A. 128

   B. 200

   C. 230

   D. 256

10. What is the default SNMPv3 username for the WLC?

   A. Cisco

   B. Tsunami

   C. Default

   D. Admin

11. Which of the following commands would be useful when a client can associate with the AP but cannot access network resources?

   A. debug aaa

   B. debug dhcp

   C. debug dot11

   D. debug ip dot1x

12. What will be the result when an 802.11b client associates with an AP in an 802.11g network?

   A. Only the 802.11g clients can transmit.

   B. Performance will be poor for all clients.

   C. Performance will be poor only for the 802.11b client.

   D. Performance will not be affected.

13. When cells are too close and the APs are using the same channel, which behavior can occur?

   A. Hidden node

   B. Exposed node

   C. Near/Far

   D. Multipath

14. What behavior can occur when two clients associated with the same AP are blocked from hearing each other by an obstruction?

    A. Hidden node

    B. Exposed node

    C. Near/Far

    D. Multipath

15. Which of the following will *not* prevent a client from associating with an AP?

    A. MAC address filter

    B. Wrong SSID

    C. Different channel

    D. Different key length

16. How close should the APs be for good location fidelity?

    A. 30 to 50 feet

    B. 50 to 70 feet

    C. 70 to 90 feet

    D. 90 to 110 feet

17. Which of the following represents three nonoverlapping channels?

    A. 1, 3, 5

    B. 1, 4, 7

    C. 1, 6, 11

    D. 3, 5, 9

18. Which of the following is *not* a source of interference in an 802.11b/g network?

    A. Microwave oven

    B. Wireless phone

    C. 802.11a AP

    D. Bluetooth device

19. Which obstruction will cause the most attenuation of the wireless signal?

    A. Cinderblock wall

    B. Office window

    C. Metal door in a brick wall

    D. Plasterboard wall

20. What does the `show run-config` command display when executed on a WLC?

    A. The configuration of the WLC

    B. The complete state of the system

    C. Only the name, IP address, and code version of the WLC

    D. The message log on the WLC

Answers to Review Questions

1. B. The three files that are contained in the compressed AES file are the Real-Time Operating System (RTOS), the CODE (Airwave Director, CLI, and switch web interface), and the bootloader or `ppcboot.ini`.

2. C. The `debug dot11` command is used to troubleshoot mobility, rogue detection, and load-balancing events.

3. A. RF utilization of an interference source is derived from measuring the RF duty cycle.

4. B. The `show running-config` command shows the controller configuration in a way that is similar to the way that it is displayed on Cisco IOS routers.

5. B. To gather information about a client using the `show client detailed` command, the client must be associated with an AP.

6. B, C. To troubleshoot an AP that cannot associate with the WLC, you could connect the SSH to the WLC and use the GUI to observe the message logs, or you could execute `debug lwapp events enable` on the WLC.

7. C. Only the MAC address of the client is required to identify the client.

8. B, C. The Wireless Controller System and the Cisco Spectrum Expert are installed on computers. The Cisco Spectrum Expert will also include a PC card to be inserted and an external antenna.

9. D. The WLC will hold 256 messages in the message log.

10. C. Default is the default SNMPv3 username for the WLC is default.

11. B. An inability to access network resources usually indicates an IP address problem so the `debug dhcp` command can be used to see if the client is receiving an address.

12. B. When an 802.11b client associates with an AP in an 802.11g network, performance will be poor for all clients.

13. B. When cells are too close and the APs are using the same channel, transmissions will collide, causing retransmissions. This is called an exposed node.

14. A. When two clients associated to the same AP are blocked from hearing each other by an obstruction, they could transmit at the same time. This is called a hidden node.

15. C. If the channel of the AP is different than that of the AP, the client will change to that channel if the SSID matches.

16. B. For good location fidelity, the APs should be within 50 to 70 feet of one another.

17. C. Channels must be at least five channels apart to be nonoverlapping.

18. C. An 802.11a AP is transmitting in a different frequency than the 802.11b./g network.

19. C. The metal door in a brick wall will cause the most attenuation, about 12dB.

20. B. The `show run-config` command displays the complete state of the system when executed on a WLC.

Answers to Written Lab

1. False

2. Version 4.2 or later

3. 3dB

4. False

5. Frequency hopping

6. False. The EIRP can be up to 4 watts, but a radio transmitting at 4 watts is illegal.

7. False

8. With multiple access points using the same SSID but on nonoverlapping channels.

9. False

10. True

Appendix

About the Companion CD

IN THIS APPENDIX:

✓ What you'll find on the CD

✓ System requirements

✓ Using the CD

✓ Troubleshooting

What You'll Find on the CD

The following sections are arranged by category and summarize the software and other goodies you'll find on the CD. If you need help with installing the items provided on the CD, refer to the installation instructions in the "Using the CD" section of this appendix.

Some programs on the CD might fall into one of these categories:

Shareware programs are fully functional, free, trial versions of copyrighted programs. If you like particular programs, register with their authors for a nominal fee and receive licenses, enhanced versions, and technical support.

Freeware programs are free, copyrighted games, applications, and utilities. You can copy them to as many computers as you like—for free—but they offer no technical support.

GNU software is governed by its own license, which is included inside the folder of the GNU software. There are no restrictions on distribution of GNU software. See the GNU license at the root of the CD for more details.

Trial, *demo*, or *evaluation* versions of software are usually limited either by time or by functionality (such as not letting you save a project after you create it).

Sybex Test Engine

The CD contains the Sybex test engine, which includes all of the assessment test and chapter review questions in electronic format, as well as two bonus exams located only on the CD.

Electronic Flashcards

These handy electronic flashcards are just what they sound like. One side contains a question or fill-in-the-blank question, and the other side shows the answer.

PDF of the Book

We have included an electronic version of the text in .pdf format. You can view the electronic version of the book with Adobe Reader.

Adobe Reader

We've also included a copy of Adobe Reader so you can view PDF files that accompany the book's content. For more information on Adobe Reader or to check for a newer version, visit Adobe's website at www.adobe.com/products/reader/.

System Requirements

Make sure your computer meets the minimum system requirements shown in the following list. If your computer doesn't match up to most of these requirements, you may have problems using the software and files on the companion CD. For the latest and greatest information, please refer to the ReadMe file located at the root of the CD-ROM.

- A PC running Microsoft Windows 98, Windows 2000, Windows NT4 (with SP4 or later), Windows Me, Windows XP, or Windows Vista
- An Internet connection
- A CD-ROM drive

Using the CD

To install the items from the CD to your hard drive, follow these steps:

1. Insert the CD into your computer's CD-ROM drive. The license agreement appears.

Windows users: The interface won't launch if you have Autorun disabled. In that case, click Start ➤ Run (for Windows Vista or Windows 7, Start ➤ All Programs ➤ Accessories ➤ Run). In the dialog box that appears, type **D:\Start.exe**. (Replace *D* with the proper letter if your CD drive uses a different letter. If you don't know the letter, see how your CD drive is listed under My Computer.) Click OK.

2. Read the license agreement, and then click the Accept button if you want to use the CD.

The CD interface appears. The interface allows you to access the content with just one or two clicks.

Troubleshooting

Wiley has attempted to provide programs that work on most computers with the minimum system requirements. Alas, your computer may differ, and some programs may not work properly for some reason.

The two likeliest problems are that you don't have enough memory (RAM) for the programs you want to use or you have other programs running that are affecting the installation or running of a program. If you get an error message such as "Not enough memory" or "Setup cannot continue," try one or more of the following suggestions and then try using the software again:

Turn off any antivirus software running on your computer. Installation programs sometimes mimic virus activity and may make your computer incorrectly believe that it's being infected by a virus.

Close all running programs. The more programs you have running, the less memory is available to other programs. Installation programs typically update files and programs; so if you keep other programs running, installation may not work properly.

Have your local computer store add more RAM to your computer. This is, admittedly, a drastic and somewhat expensive step. However, adding more memory can really help the speed of your computer and allow more programs to run at the same time.

Customer Care

If you have trouble with the book's companion CD-ROM, please call the Wiley Product Technical Support phone number at (800) 762-2974. Outside the United States, call +1(317) 572-3994. You can also contact Wiley Product Technical Support at http://sybex.custhelp.com. John Wiley & Sons will provide technical support only for installation and other general quality-control items. For technical support on the applications themselves, consult the program's vendor or author.

To place additional orders or to request information about other Wiley products, please call (877) 762-2974.

Glossary

A

access point (AP)   Wireless connection point for wireless devices operating in Infrastructure mode.

AirPort Extreme   Tool included in the Mac operating systems to manage wireless connections.

AP mode   The mode than an AP operates in when it is simply transferring data for wireless clients.

AP priming   The process of connecting the AP and its controller together before the AP is deployed so the AP can learn the address of the WLC.

association   Process by which an AP becomes connected to its controller or by which a client device becomes connected to its AP at Layer 2.

asymmetric roaming   Roaming in which the client device uses a router to determine the path to the destination computer but uses the tunnel that is created between the anchor and the foreign controller for the return trip.

B

Bridge mode   AP mode in which the AP can be a bridge in a point-to-point or point-to-multipoint link.

C

Cisco Aironet Desktop Utility (ADU)   Cisco utility that can be used to manage Cisco wireless adapters only.

Cisco-Compatible Extensions (CCX)   Program that allows for partners to take advantage of and implement Cisco proprietary features implemented through additional functionality called extensions.

Cisco Mobility Express (CME)   Part of a complete system of voice, data, video, and wireless networking products offered for small businesses called the Cisco Smart Business Communication System.

Cisco Secure Services Client (SSC)   Cisco utility that can be used to manage wired or wireless adapters, including non-Cisco adaptors.

Cisco Unified Wireless Network (CUWN)   Wireless networking model that allows for centralized control of devices using LWAPP. The CUWN is composed of five elements that work together to provide a unified enterprise solution. The elements are client devices, APs, network unification, network management, and mobility service.

client adapter   Network interface card that provides devices with wireless connectivity.

complementary code keying (CCK)   Coding technique used by IEEE 802.11–compliant wireless LANs for transmission at 5.5 and 11Mbps.

D

dB   Decibel; a unit for measuring relative power ratios in terms of gain or loss. Units are expressed in terms of the logarithm to base 10 of a ratio, and are typically based on a comparison of power level expressed in watts. A decibel is not an absolute value; rather, it is the measure of power loss or gain between two devices.

dBd   A ratio, measured in decibels, of the effective gain of an antenna compared to a dipole antenna (*see* dipole). The greater the dBd value, the higher the gain and, as such, the more acute the angle of coverage.

dBi   A ratio, measured in decibels, of the effective gain of an antenna compared to an isotropic radiator. The greater the dBi value, the higher the gain and, as such, the more acute the angle of coverage.

DHCP vendor option mode   Discovery option whereby the AP receives the addresses of the WLCs when they receive their configuration from DHCP.

Differential Binary Phase Shift Keying (DBPSK)   Modulation technique used by IEEE 802.11–compliant wireless LANs for transmission at 1Mbps.

Differential Quadrature Phase Shift Keying (DQPSK)   Modulation technique used by IEEE 802.11–compliant wireless LANs for transmission at 2Mbps, 5.5Mbps, and 11Mbps.

dipole   A type of low-gain (typically 2.2dBi) antenna consisting of two (often internal) elements.

Direct Sequence Spread Spectrum (DSSS)   A type of spread-spectrum radio transmission that spreads its signal continuously over a wide frequency band in order to improve the likelihood of a successful transmission.

directional antenna   An antenna that concentrates transmission power into a direction such that coverage distance increases at the expense of coverage angle. Directional antenna types include yagi, patch, and parabolic dish.

discovery   Process by which an AP locates its controller or the process by which a station identifies available APs.

diversity antenna systems   A system using two antennas and an intelligent radio that continually senses incoming radio signals, or a transmitted signal's success rate, and automatically selects the antenna best positioned to receive or transmit.

DNS vendor option mode   Discovery mode option whereby the AP obtains the Cisco WLC IP address from a DNS server.

Dynamic Host Configuration Protocol (DHCP)   A protocol available with many operating systems that automatically issues IP addresses within a specified range to devices on a network. The device retains the assigned address for a specific administrator-defined period.

F

Frequency Hopping Spread Spectrum (FHSS)   A type of spread-spectrum radio transmission in which the transmitter and receiver hop in synchronization from one frequency to another according to a prearranged pattern.

Fresnel zone   An area surrounding the direct line of sight between two antennas where the transmitted radio signal may be degraded by physical objects.

G

gain   The ratio of the output amplitude of a signal to the input amplitude of a signal. This ratio is typically expressed in decibels (dB).

gateway   A network point that acts as an entrance to another network.

global parameter   Any parameter set on the controller that is shared by all WLANs.

H

hertz (Hz)   The international unit for measuring frequency, equivalent to cycles per second. One megahertz (MHz) is one million hertz. One gigahertz (GHz) is one billion hertz. The standard U.S. electrical power frequency is 60Hz, the AM broadcast radio frequency band is 0.55–1.6MHz, the FM broadcast radio frequency band is 88–108MHz, and wireless 802.11 LANs operate at 2.4GHz and 5GHz.

hidden node   A station on a wireless LAN that attempts to transmit data to another station but, because of its location relative to the others, cannot sense that there is a third station simultaneously communicating with the intended recipient. Lost messages and multiple retries are the result. A packet retry at the radio protocol level may occur.

H-REAP mode   AP mode in which the AP is in a remote location via a WAN link and the location does not warrant an onsite WLC. In this mode, unlike the normal mode, the AP can lose contact with its WLC and still function and the AP terminates data locally rather than forwarding it to the WLC for termination.

I

IEEE 802.X   A set of specifications for local area networks (LANs) from the IEEE. Most wired networks conform to 802.3, the specification for CSMA/CD-based Ethernet networks. The 802.11 committee completed a standard for 1 and 2Mbps wireless LANs in 1997 that has a single Media Access Control (MAC) layer for the following physical-layer technologies: Frequency Hopping Spread Spectrum, Direct Sequence Spread Spectrum, and Infrared. IEEE 802.11b, an 11Mbps version of the standard, and IEEE 802.11a, a 5GHz, 54Mbps version of the standard, were both ratified in 1999.

Image Data state   Phase of the connection process between the AP and the WLC where the AP will synchronize its code version with the WLC.

Independent Basic Service Set (IBSS)   A network that provides (usually temporarily) peer-to-peer connectivity without relying on a complete network infrastructure.

Infrastructure mode   A client setting that provides connectivity to an AP. As compared to Ad Hoc mode, where PCs or other client devices communicate directly with each other, clients set in Infrastructure mode all pass data through a central AP. The AP not only mediates wireless network traffic in the immediate neighborhood, but also provides communication with the wired network. *See* access point.

infrastructure network   A wireless network centered about an access point. In this environment, the access point not only provides communication with the wired network but also mediates wireless network traffic in the immediate neighborhood.

integrated services router (ISR)   A router that has additional capabilities built in or provided by feature cards or modules.

isotropic radiator   A theoretical construct of an antenna that radiates its signal 360 degrees both vertically and horizontally—a perfect sphere.

iwconfig   Command-line utility that can be used in Linux to manage wireless connections.

J

Join phase   Phase where the AP connects to the WLC after discovering it.

L

Lightweight Access Point Protocol (LWAPP)   A new encapsulation type used to carry and encapsulate control information between the APs and the WLC over an encrypted tunnel.

Lightweight model   Model of the Cisco Unified Wireless Network solution that allows centralized control. The central control is provided with the Cisco WLAN Controllers (WLCs).

line of sight   An unobstructed straight line between two transmitting devices. Line of sight is typically required for long-range directional radio transmission. Because of the curvature of the earth, the line of sight for devices not mounted on towers is limited to 6 miles (9.65 km).With certain wireless bridging technologies, there must be a clear, unobstructed path between the transmitters and the receivers.

Local mode   AP mode in which the AP will perform data transfer for the clients and will also monitor all channels.

M

management information base (MIB)   A collection of network operational information residing in a virtual store that may be accessed, typically through a Simple Network Management Protocol (SNMP)-compliant system, for analysis.

master controller   Each mobility group can have a master controller designated. If one is designated, it will be the WLC that unprimed APs will be looking for in their discovery attempts.

maximum transmission unit (MTU)   The largest frame size allowed on a particular Ethernet segment.

Media Access Control (MAC)   In a wireless LAN (WLAN) network card, the MAC is a radio controller protocol. It corresponds to the OSI Network Model Layer 2 Data Link layer. The IEEE 802.11 standard specifies the MAC protocol for medium sharing, packet formats and addressing, and error detection.

microcell   A bounded physical space in which numerous wireless devices can communicate. Because it is possible to have overlapping cells as well as isolated cells, the boundaries of the cell are established by a predefined rule or convention.

mobility group   A set of WLCs that have been grouped together to enhance roaming.

modulation   Any of several techniques for changing the properties of radio waves in order to transmit data over a radio signal.

Monitor mode   AP mode that allows channel monitoring but no regular client servicing.

multipath   The reception of a signal that takes multiple paths to the receiving antenna due to the echoes created as a radio signal bounces off physical objects.

N

N+1 solution   Redundancy solution where one WLC is used as a backup for multiple other WLCs.

N+N solution   Redundancy solution where live WLCs are set to back each other up in the event of a failure.

N+N+1 solution   Redundancy solution where the WLCs will be set to back each other up as in N+1 but will have a third WLC (this one is not active as the tertiary).

netsh wlan   Command-line tool used to manage wireless network connections in Windows Vista and Windows 7.

Network Address Translation (NAT)   The translation of an Internet Protocol address (IP address) used within one network to a different IP address known within another network. One network is designated the internal network and it appears as one entity to the outside world. In the case of wireless LANs with an outside Internet connection, the NAT capability of Internet-sharing software allows the sharing of one Internet connection among all the wireless PCs connected.

Network And Sharing Center   Control panel option in Windows Vista and Windows 7 where all network connections of all types can be created and managed.

NetworkManager   GUI utility used to manage wireless network connections in Linux.

NetworkManagerDispatcher   Supplemental tool in Linux that allows scripting or automation of actions when the computer boots up or when a particular SSID is encountered.

O

omnidirectional antenna   An antenna that provides 360-degree transmission coverage along a horizontal plane.

orthogonal frequency-division multiplexing (OFDM)   A radio modulation technique that involves using multiple subchannels to transmit large amounts of data over one wider wireless channel. It is used for 802.11a/g/n WLANs, and provides 54Mbps in the 5GHz.

over-the-air provisioning (OTAP) mode   Discovery mode whereby the AP listens for Radio Resource Management (RRM) packets to discover the controller.

P

parabolic   A concave or dish-shaped object; often refers to dish antennas. Parabolic dish antennas tend to provide the greatest gain and the narrowest beamwidth, making them ideal for point-to-point transmission over the longest distances.

patch antenna   A type of flat antenna designed for flush wall mounting that radiates a hemispherical coverage area.

peer-to-peer network   A network design in which each computer shares and uses devices on an equal basis. In WLANs, this typically refers to an IBSS or ad hoc network.

Physical layer (PHY)   Provides for the transmission of data through a communications channel by defining the electrical, mechanical, and procedural specifications for IEEE 802 local area networks. The PHY is the lowest layer within the OSI reference model. It deals primarily with transmission of the raw bit stream over the physical transport medium. In the case of wireless LANs, the transport medium is free space. The PHY defines parameters such as data rates, modulation method, signaling parameters, transmitter/receiver synchronization, and so on. Within an actual radio implementation, the PHY corresponds to the radio front-end and baseband signal-processing sections. In WLANs, this term defines the modulation and coding method.

preferred networks   A list of SSIDs that the client will attempt to connect to, in order from top to bottom.

profile   A saved set of configuration parameters that can be used to connect to a specific wireless network.

R

radio frequency (RF) terms: GHz, MHz, and Hz   The international unit for measuring frequency is hertz (Hz), which is equivalent to cycles per second. One megahertz (MHz) is one million hertz. One gigahertz (GHz) is one billion hertz. For reference: the standard U.S. electrical power frequency is 60Hz, the AM broadcast radio frequency band is 0.55–1.6MHz, the FM broadcast radio frequency band is 88–108MHz, and microwave ovens typically operate at 2.45GHz.

Radio Resource Management (RRM)   The Radio Resource Management (RRM) engine is the component of the WLC that creates an environment that is completely self-configuring, self-optimizing, and self-healing. By receiving information constantly from the APs under its control, the WLC maintains a broad and comprehensive view of the RF environment.

range   A linear measure of the distance that a transmitter can send a signal.

receiver sensitivity   A measurement of the weakest signal a receiver can receive and still correctly translate it into data.

redundancy   Any process that provides backup to a connection or device.

Reverse Polarity Threaded Naval Connector (RP-TNC)   Unique connector for Cisco Aironet radios and antennas. Part 15.203 of the FCC rules covering spread-spectrum devices limits the types of antennas that may be used with transmission equipment. In compliance with this rule and like all other wireless LAN providers, Cisco equips its radios and antennas with unique connectors to prevent attachment of nonapproved antennas to radios.

roaming   Movement of a wireless node between two basic service sets. Roaming usually occurs in infrastructure networks built around multiple access points.

Rogue Detection mode   AP mode in which the AP operates on the wired side without the radio. The AP in this mode listens on the wire for ARP packets. When it sees one of the MAC addresses of a rogue AP or client, it will generate an alarm that not only is there a rogue but that it has also been seen on the wired side.

S

service set identifier (SSID)   Name given to a wireless LAN.

Simple Network Management Protocol (SNMP)   The network management protocol that defines the transfer of LAN operational data between management information bases (MIBs).

Sniffer mode   AP mode in which the AP captures all frames on a specific channel and sends the frames to a station running an analyzer such as OmniPeek, AirMagnet, or Wireshark.

split MAC   The splitting of 802.11 data link layer functions between the AP and the WLC. The AP handles real-time portions of the communication and the Cisco WLC handles the items aren't time-sensitive.

spread spectrum   A radio transmission technology that "spreads" the user information over a much wider bandwidth than otherwise required in order to gain benefits such as improved interference tolerance and unlicensed operation.

Stand-alone mode   APs operating in the stand-alone mode are called autonomous APs. They operate independently of any wireless controllers. Autonomous APs have their own internetwork operating systems and are configured individually.

symmetric roaming   Roaming in which the client uses the tunnel that is created between the anchor and the foreign controller in both directions (to the destination computer and back).

subnetwork broadcast mode   Discovery process whereby the AP sends a subnet broadcast discovery request on the local subnet.

V

virtual LAN (VLAN)   Used to logically segment either wired or wireless network segments.

W

wide area network (WAN)   A wide area network connects local area networks together. Typical WAN interfaces include plain old telephone service (POTS) lines, digital subscriber lines (DSL), cable, T1/T3, and ISDN.

Windows Wireless Zero Configuration(WZC)   Utility included in Windows XP that can be used to manage your wireless adapter card.

Wired Equivalent Privacy (WEP)   Optional security mechanism defined within the 802.11 standard designed to make the link integrity of the wireless medium equal to that of a cable. The encryption is based on RC4.

Wireless Access Protocol   A language used for writing web pages that uses far less overhead than other mobile protocols, and is a full protocol stack, not just a single protocol, making it preferable for wireless access to the Internet by personal digital assistants (PDAs) and web-enabled cell phones.

wireless control system (WCS)   Software installed on a server that is used to manage multiple WLCs via a web interface.

Wireless Domain Services (WDS)   A feature on an AP or Cisco switch that allows wireless clients to authenticate locally to an AP rather than having to access a centralized RADIUS server for each authentication.

Wireless Services Module (WiSM)   A blade that is installed into the Catalyst 6500 Series chassis to provide the features and functionality of the 4400 Series controllers.

wireless node   A user computer with a wireless network interface card (adapter).

Wireless Solution Engine (WLSE)   A device that can provide some central control and monitoring of autonomous APs.

WLAN Auto Configuration   Tool included in Windows Vista that provides the same functionality as the Windows Wireless Zero Configuration in Windows XP.

WLAN controllers (WLCs)   Device by which the APs are controlled and monitored in CUWN. All of the clients and APs transmit information back to the WLC, unless the APs are using H-REAP.

Y

yagi   A type of midrange-gain, directional antenna.

Index

Note to the reader: Throughout this index **boldfaced** page numbers indicate primary discussions of a topic. *Italicized* page numbers indicate illustrations.

Wiley Publishing, Inc.
End-User License Agreement

The Best CCNA Wireless Book/CD Package on the Market!

Get ready for your CCNA Wireless certification with the most comprehensive and challenging sample tests anywhere!

The Sybex Test Engine features:

- All the review questions, as covered in each chapter of the book.

- Challenging questions representative of those you'll find on the real exam.

- Two full-length bonus exams available only on the CD.

- An Assessment Test to narrow your focus to certain objective groups.

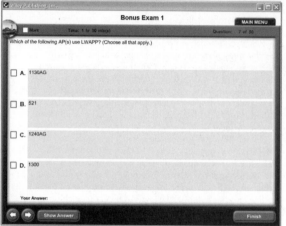

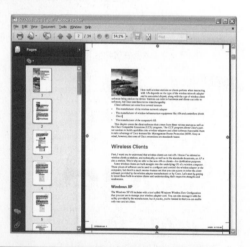

Use the Electronic Flashcards to jog your memory and prep last-minute for the exam!

- Reinforce your understanding of key concepts with these hardcore flashcard-style questions.

- Now you can study for the CCNA Wireless exam (IUWNE 640-721) anytime, anywhere.

Search through the complete book in PDF!

- Access the entire *CCNA Wireless Study Guide* complete with figures and tables, in electronic format.

- Search the *CCNA Wireless Study Guide* chapters to find information on any topic in seconds.

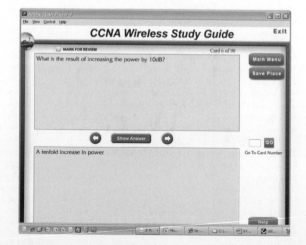